A Mandarin Paperback
MARILYN: THE LAST TAKE

First published in Great Britain 1992
by William Heinemann Ltd
This edition published 1993
by Mandarin Paperbacks
an imprint of Reed Consumer Books Ltd
Michelin House, 81 Fulham Road, London SW3 6RB
and Auckland, Melbourne, Singapore and Toronto

Copyright © Patte B. Barham and Peter Harry Brown, 1992

A CIP catalogue record for this title
is available from the British Library
ISBN 0 7493 1110 X

Printed and bound in Great Britain by
BPCC Hazell Books Ltd
Member of BPCC Ltd

Marilyn:
– The Last Take –

Peter Brown is a freelance journalist and author of several books on Hollywood and its stars, including *Oscar Dearest: Sixty Years of Scandal Behind the Academy Awards.*

Patte Barham, also an experienced Hollywood journalist and award-winning non-fiction author, was one of the last people to interview Marilyn Monroe. Both live in Los Angeles.

D1331528

Also by Peter Harry Brown

Oscar Dearest: Sixty Years of
Scandal Behind the Academy Awards
The Real Oscar

Also by Patte B. Barham
Rasputin: The Man Behind the Myth

PETER HARRY BROWN
PATTE B. BARHAM

MARILYN
- *The Last Take* -

For my wife, Pamela Twedell Brown
— Peter Harry Brown

For my husband, Capt. Harris Boyne
— Patte B. Barham

– Contents –

– *Acknowledgements* –

Crafting an investigative book is a complicated task. We were fortunate in having the assistance of numerous valuable experts and advisors.

Our editor, Michaela Hamilton, guided us step-by-step in fashioning the dramatic framework for this tale of greed, studio tyranny, and the destruction of a great film star. She was behind us from the beginning, and her suggestions strengthened the story. And she was fun to work with besides.

Many thanks also to her assistant, Rena Korb, for handling the intricate details of the editorial process.

Our agent, Mitch Douglas of International Creative Management, worked with us selflessly as we crafted the book proposal. His enthusiasm was contagious and provided a foundation for *The Last Take.*

Dutton's associate publisher, Arnold Dolin, believed in this book from the start. His impact added a sophisticated sheen to the story.

Working with us every step of the way was Pamela Twedell Brown, who unearthed previously unpublished photos, coordinated the research, and helped us with particularly difficult sections of the exposé.

We also owe a great debt to the journalists of Fox Entertainment News, and investigative branch of the Fox Broadcasting Network. Their remarkable television documentary, *Something's Got to Give,* provided a three-dimensional glimpse of the politics of Twentieth Century-Fox and the ego clashes that doomed Monroe's final film. It was Fox Entertainment News that originally hired author Peter Harry Brown as a creative consultant and researcher on *Something's Got to Give* in May 1990. Henry Schipper, formerly an entertainment journalist for *Daily Variety* and now a producer-director at Fox Entertainment News, encouraged Brown to delve deeper into this story. Schipper, who was director, producer, and narrator of *Something's Got to Give*, found time to give interviews (initially for *TV Guide*) about his long but finally fruitful search for Marilyn Monroe's 'lost film'.

Thanks also to Fox Entertainment News executive director William K. Knoedelseder, who hired Brown and who provided a wealth of details in his interview. Shawn Griggs, associate producer of the *Something's Got to Give* documentary, was an outstanding researcher who located many eyewitnesses who had been out of the Hollywood limelight for decades.

At Twentieth Century-Fox, Ben Begun, chief counsel for the studio, provided several telephone interviews on the lost footage from the film *Something's Got to Give*. Likewise, Mindy Herman of legal affairs located actors and *Something's Got to Give* crew members who had scattered to cities and towns all over America.

During our research into *Cleopatra*, film scholar-author Brad Geagley accomplished what could have easily been two years of research in just a few months. And he provided a fresh body of facts and behind-the-scenes details from the making of the $42 million disaster.

Also particularly adept in roping in difficult facts and interviews was Cathy Griffen, a private investigator who specialises in probing the Hollywood scene.

Among the 340 interviews conducted during a nine-month period, some sources were paramount:

Peter G. Levathes, the renowned Manhattan and Washington, D.C., attorney, who was production chief at Fox during Marilyn's last weeks, granted us more than eleven hours of interviews.

Fox executive secretary Lee Hanna, who was production secretary on both *Something's Got to Give* and *Cleopatra* (during the

Egyptian epic's postproduction period), helped us understand the inner workings of Fox at the time.

One of our sources – with contacts high up in the Twentieth Century-Fox hierarchy – must remain nameless, but he provided facsimiles of 'hundreds' of documents.

Also crucial to the success of *The Last Take* were television producer Ted Landreth, formerly of the CBS Evening News, who produced the breakthrough documentary, *Say Goodbye to the President – Marilyn Monroe and the Kennedys*, a BBC project. He provided us with a rich background for our story.

And, finally, Robert Slatzer, Monroe's friend, confidant, and lover over a sixteen-year period, submitted to more than thirty interviews and telephone conversations as we recreated the last fourteen months in the life of Marilyn Monroe. Additionally, he gave us copies of almost a hundred documents that he has collected during his thirty-year search for the actress's murderer.

We would also like to thank the following players in this thirty-year-old mystery who submitted to interviews – most of them multiple sessions.

Hal Kanter, Theodore Strauss, Rupert Allan, Michael Selsman, Patricia Newcomb, Natalie Jacobs, Walter Bernstein, Jean Louis, Teresa Brocheta, William Travilla, Sheree North, Ray Strait, John Miner, Louis Nizer, Milton Rudin, Milton Gould, Henry Weinstein, Buck Hall, Lee Remick, Dorothy Manners, Dorothy Treloar, Hazel Washington, Charles Lang, David Bretherton, John Springer, Whitey Snyder, Marjorie Plecher, Hildi Greenson, Joan Greenson Aibe, Dr. Daniel Greenson, Dr. Robert Litman, Dr. Michael Gurdin, Richard Meryman, James Bacon, Dick DeSick, Pat H. Broeske, Irv Letofsky, Dr. Thomas Noguchi, Edwin Guthman, former L.A. mayor Sam Yorty, former police chief Tom Reddin, Gene Allen, Laurence Schiller, Deputy Los Angeles District Attorney Mike Carroll, Richard Zanuck, Darrilyn Zanuck, Nico Minardos, Christopher Morley, Alexandra Heilweil, Eva Wolas Heilweil, Jim Pinkston, Nora Johnson, Mrs. Dorris Johnson, George Zeno, Sabin Grey, David Brown, Richard Adler, Tom Mankiewicz, Chris Mankiewicz, Cesare Danova, Mrs. Sybil Brand, Patrick Miller, Lucy Freeman, Fred Laurence Guiles, Stephen Papich,

– *Acknowledgements* –

Maurice Zolotow, Thomas Tryon, Bebe Goddard, Steve Allen, Cyd Charisse, Jet Fore, Terry Moore, Harriet Parsons, Ralph Roberts, Greg Schreiner, Susan Strasberg, Chuck Panama, Patti Morris, Evelyn Moriarity, Philip Dunne, Henry Ephron, Betty Hulihan, Eleanor Griffin, Margaret Burk, Terry Trahan, Jack Clemmons, Maggie Banks, George Light, May Munn, Julian Myers, Frank Green, William K. Knoedelseder, and Mickey Song.

Our special gratitude goes to Barbrah Messing for help with chapter titles; for help in organising the book and for reading the manuscript day-by-day, policing continuity and clarity; to the team who put this book on the computer, corrected the grammar, and correlated the 10,000 pages of interview transcripts: Jennifer Boller and David Valliere; and finally, to Douglas Domeier, who offered invaluable advice on style and on how to deal with the mass of transcripts.

– Cast of Characters –

Marilyn Monroe's Circle

RUPERT ALLAN: Assigned by Arthur Jacobs to work with Monroe as a publicist. Allan spent most of 1962 with Princess Grace of Monaco.

DR. RALPH GREENSON: Monroe's psychoanalyst during 1961 and 1962. Greenson was a Freudian analyst who had been trained in Europe.

ARTHUR JACOBS: Founder of the Arthur Jacobs Public Relations Agency and director of Monroe's publicity worldwide.

EUNICE MURRAY: Monroe's housekeeper, who was also a psychiatric nurse working for Greenson.

PATRICIA NEWCOMB: Assigned by Jacobs as Monroe's personal publicity handler. Newcomb became the star's close friend as well.

STEPHEN PAPICH: Fox choreographer who developed an on-the-lot camaraderie with Monroe during the filming of *Something's Got to Give* and *Let's Make Love*.

RALPH ROBERTS: Hollywood and New York character actor who became Monroe's personal masseur as well as her friend.

MILTON RUDIN: Harvard-educated attorney who guided Monroe's career in 1962. Frank Sinatra and Elizabeth Taylor were among the other stars Rudin represented.

ROBERT SLATZER: Monroe's close friend from 1947 through 1962.

WHITEY SNYDER: Monroe's makeup man for sixteen years and a confidant.

LEE STRASBERG: Founder and director of New York's Actors Studio, where Method actors were trained. Monroe began lessons at the studio in 1955.

PAULA STRASBERG: Strasberg's wife, who served as Monroe's drama coach for all of her films beginning with *Bus Stop*.

WILLIAM TRAVILLA: Costume designer for Fox on *Gentleman Prefer Blondes* and other films. Travilla became Monroe's confidant during *Something's Got to Give*.

HAZEL WASHINGTON: Assigned by Fox to serve as the star's studio maid. Washington also worked for Monroe in her Brentwood house.

Something's Got to Give: The Principals

GENE ALLEN: Former Los Angeles police officer who served as art director and associate producer of the film.

WALTER BERNSTEIN: New York writer who was brought in, despite Monroe's objection, to rewrite Nunnally Johnson's original script.

DAVID BRETHERTON: Veteran Fox film editor who produced a rough cut of scenes from *Something's Got to Give*.

GEORGE CUKOR: The film's director, who had also directed Monroe in 1960's *Let's Make Love*.

AGNES FLANAGHAN: Hairstylist on most of Monroe's Fox films.

SYDNEY GUILAROFF: Designer of the trendy hairstyles for the film's actors and actresses.

BUCK HALL: Assistant director of the film and a longtime enemy of Monroe.

NUNNALLY JOHNSON: Principal author of the film's screenplay. Johnson was also a longtime friend of Monroe.

JEAN LOUIS: Former Parisian couturier who designed the costumes worn in the film.

EVELYN MORIARITY: Monroe's stand-in for *Let's Make Love, The Misfits* and *Something's Got to Give*. Moriarity became a close observer of Monroe's last days.

MARJORIE PLECHER: Monroe's dresser, who later married Whitey Snyder.

LAWRENCE SCHILLER: Photographer for *Paris Match, Life* and other publications. Schiller shot the nude swimming sequence for *Something's Got to Give*.

DR LEE SIEGEL: Studio doctor who verified Monroe's illnesses during the making of the film.

THOMAS TRYON: Handsome young actor who had campaigned hard to play a starring role opposite Monroe.

Cleopatra: The Principals

RICHARD BURTON: Welsh actor and Shakespearean performer who became Elizabeth Taylor's lover, both on and off the screen.

CESARE DANOVA: Romantic lead of the fifties and sixties who costarred in the Egyptian epic.

CHRIS and TOM MANKIEWICZ: Joseph Mankiewicz's sons, who worked in various capacities on the set of *Cleopatra*.

JOSEPH L. MANKIEWICZ: Writer and director of *Cleopatra*. A director from Hollywood's golden era, Mankiewicz was revered for his work on films such as *All About Eve* and *A Letter to Three Wives*.

ELIZABETH TAYLOR: Star of the film, she was paid a record $2.1 million for the role of Cleopatra. Taylor had a public rivalry with Monroe.

Twentieth Century-Fox

In New York:

MILTON S. GOULD: Wall Street lawyer who ran Fox for ten months in 1961 and 1962.

SPYROS SKOURAS: Fox President and a giant of the industry. During the making of *Something's Got to Give* Skouras functioned only as a figurehead.

In Century City:

PHIL FELDMAN: Adjutant to Peter Levathes, who presided over the failing film studio.

FRANK FERGUSON: Fox's top lawyer on the West Coast and, technically, the man who fired Monroe.

PETER G. LEVATHES: Fox's chief of production. Levathes was a lawyer who had begun his film career as an assistant to Skouras.

DARRYL F. ZANUCK: Former production chief at Fox. Zanuck was working on a series of films for the studio from his office in Paris.

The Studio Publicists

HARRY BRAND: Chief of Hollywood publicity since 1935. Brand had helped guide Monroe to stardom.

JACK BRODSKY and NATHAN WEISS: Unit publicists on *Cleopatra* and authors of the best-seller *The Cleopatra Papers*.

JOHN CAMPBELL: Former journalist who worked as union publicist for *Something's Got to Give*.

E. CHARLES EINFELD: Director of marketing and public relations in New York. Einfeld was Brand's boss.

PERRY LIEBER: Brand's adjutant. Lieber became Monroe's enemy when he tipped off the press about her 1952 nude calendar shot.

FRANK NEILL: Former police reporter who helped clean up the death scene at Monroe's house.

The Kennedy Circle

ED GUTHMAN: Robert Kennedy's press aide and his companion on one trip to Monroe's Brentwood house.

JOHN F. KENNEDY: President of the United States from 1961 to

1963. JFK was Monroe's lover during the early weeks of *Something's Got to Give.*

ROBERT F. KENNEDY: JFK's brother and Attorney General of the United States. RFK became intimate with Monroe in 1962.

PAT KENNEDY LAWFORD: Sister of JFK and RFK, as well as the wife of Peter Lawford. She was also Monroe's close friend.

PETER LAWFORD: Monroe's friend since the early fifties. Lawford helped arrange and, later, cover up her affairs with the Kennedy brothers.

– *Prologue* –

On an August evening in 1988, five master videotapes of supposedly 'lost' Marilyn Monroe film footage were smuggled out of the Twentieth Century-Fox archives and driven off the studio lot in the trunk of a studio employee's automobile.

They were immediately ferried across town to a Hollywood office building, where an enormous video monitor and a handpicked audience – mostly officers of the Marilyn Remembered Fan Club – waited.

'There was no fanfare,' recalled publicist Rupert Allan, who wangled an invitation to the private screening. 'They interrupted a speaker in midsentence, locked the doors, dimmed the lights and showed a series of absolutely spellbinding sequences.'

The scenes, unedited and unscored, were preceded by a close-up of a film clapper that bore the legend: 'Reel 17, *Something's Got to Give*, May 14, 1962.'

A surge of excitement spread through the crowd. Except for a few brief flashes in Fox documentaries, all of the film from *Something's Got to Give*, Monroe's final, unfinished motion picture, had been locked out of sight for twenty-six years.

The crowd fell silent as a radiant Monroe strolled into view. 'We were packed together – about a hundred and seventy of us,' recalled Monroe's foster sister, Bebe Goddard. 'Still, nobody moved as the years dropped away and we saw this film – film the studio told us had been destroyed back in the sixties.'

'We didn't know what to expect,' said columnist May Mann, who had also been one of Monroe's closest confidantes in the Hollywood press corps. 'All of us had heard the studio's version – that Marilyn's work on that film was terrible; that she was on drugs and that it showed.'

The film was foggy, badly faded in places, but the contents were stunning. Monroe looked radiant – in her prime.

The man who had assembled the clips had a deft touch. Outtakes and snatches of dialogue had been spliced together with some of the finest comedic turns of the star's career: Monroe collapsing onto the floor of a shoe store and onto the lap of a flustered Wally Cox; Monroe carrying Dean Martin's luggage and complaining about it with a Greta Garbo accent; Monroe wooing Martin from the bed of his bride – on their wedding night.

One scene was particularly impressive. 'Marilyn had to work with a dog – a very uncooperative animal,' said Mann. 'And she never missed a beat nor a word. Not once in an incredible eleven takes. Marilyn never fluffed her lines. I was shocked – after all I had heard. After all I had heard about this film, I was surprised.'

Towards the end of the screening, there was an eleven-minute sequence of Monroe, obviously nude, swimming in an azure pool. With her eyes wide open and her nipples just beneath the water line, she dog-paddled back and forth. Then, with a wink at the camera, she pulled herself out of the water and slid into a terry-cloth robe.

There was a burst of applause just as the tape ran out and the monitor filled with video static.

Without waiting for a rewind, the studio employee collected the master tapes and rushed them back to the studio archives – where they promptly disappeared.

'Everything we heard about *Something's Got to Give* was obviously wrong,' said May Mann. 'It took a few days for the implications to sink in.'

With whetted appetites, the members of the Marilyn Remembered Fan Club began lobbying Fox for a public screening of the film. 'We wanted to know how much there was and what else it showed,' said Greg Schreiner, president of the loose network of

Monroe fanatics. 'We hoped to persuade Fox to restore the film and to release it publicly.'

'In my eyes, the film vindicated Marilyn,' said Goddard, the foster sister who had shared her bedroom with the actress when both were teenagers. 'It proved what we *always* believed; that her work at the end was as good as her work at the beginning of her career.'

But the studio still stubbornly denied that the film existed. Those who inquired were told that 'there is only about ten minutes of footage' and that all of it had been released in the studio's 1963 documentary *Marilyn*.

When the fans tried to use their contacts within Twentieth Century-Fox, they learned that the film and the tapes made from it had vanished.

Then, in the spring of 1990, the tapes suddenly reappeared. Henry Schipper, a young Fox News producer in Los Angeles, was browsing through the archives for a Monroe birthday tribute when he picked up clues to the whereabouts of *Something's Got to Give*. Schipper was luckier than previous sleuths; he was armed with Fox's new master computer. Sitting at the keyboard at Fox Entertainment News, he could prowl endlessly through one of the largest film graveyards in the world. And he discovered a treasure trove of Marilyn Monroe film.

It seemed as if Fox cameras had followed their favourite star everywhere, from supermarket openings to her bridal suites, from her first screen test to the doors of the Los Angeles County Morgue.

Schipper's fingers raced across the keys, entering code after code in his search for the rarest gem in this tomb of images. Finally it appeared at the end of a long list. The computer had transported Schipper effortlessly to the depths of a salt mine in the middle of Kansas. There, in a vault 360 feet beneath the plains, he found the reels from *Something's Got to Give*. Like most film studios, Fox stores its prints in a massive Hutchinson, Kansas, salt mine. The salt absorbs moisture and prevents deterioration of both negatives and prints. A detailed roster rolled up on the screen. Science had finally caught up with the inefficiency of half a century, the computer listed every piece of film in the vast network – a billion-dollar inventory.

Schipper knew instantly that he had found one of the key pieces to the puzzle of Marilyn Monroe's life. To a Hollywood historian, it was the equivalent of discovering the mummy of a long-lost pharaoh.*

The value of the find to Fox Entertainment News was incalculable – a news bombshell. Schipper had to find a way to see the film and, perhaps, to rescue it.

The security surrounding the company's stock of Monroe film is legendary. Anything related to Monroe's last days at Fox is shrouded in a cloak-and-dagger aura. Records have been purged; files have been embargoed and questions meet with a stony silence. As the single most valuable resource in the Fox library, the Monroe collection always weighed heavily in the purchase price of the corporation. Access is severely limited.

Even so, there have been unnerving breaches. Fox lawyers had most recently gone on alert in May 1990 when the tabloid TV show *A Current Affair* broadcast an entire scene from *Something's Got to Give*.

It showed a comedic confrontation among Monroe, Dean Martin and Wally Cox. Since the scene had never been shown publicly, and since it was fully edited, it could only have come from within Fox. But the print was so bad that the trio of actors was barely visible through a Technicolor fog. Extensive computer enhancement was used to clarify the images.

Alarmed at this second security breach, studio lawyers served the producers of *A Current Affair* with a restraining order barring any future showing of the controversial film. Although the tapes were turned over to Fox that same afternoon, it took another restraining order to prevent a second tabloid show, CBS's *Hard Copy*, from showing the same scenes.

So Schipper was prepared for trouble. But getting the film was

*As rumours spread through Hollywood after the fan club screening, the Fox corporate lawyers declared the *Something's Got to Give* film 'hands off'. It was even purged from the corporate inventory. But when the studio archives were converted to a new computer system in 1989, all eight hours were coded and put back into the current catalogue of Fox film holdings.

deceptively easy. It took only one phone call. The clerks at the salt mine must have considered Fox Entertainment News worthy of their trust. 'Where do you want it?' one of them said breezily. 'We'll Fed Ex it.' At 9 A.M. the next day, Schipper found six massive crates of film on the Fox Broadcasting loading docks.

He rushed it off to the screening room – where he remained for two days.

He too was spellbound by the raw, unedited film, and was even more excited to find that almost every frame was intact, including impromptu sessions showing director George Cukor in action. And there was take after take of Monroe doing the same scenes, sometimes twenty times, never missing a cue and rarely flubbing a line. 'The studio had said that she drifted through her scenes in a drug-induced haze,' said Schipper. 'And it has been accepted ever since that her work on *Something's Got to Give* was a sad finale to an otherwise spectacular career. This film proves *the studio* wrong. In fact, Monroe never looked better. Her work there is on a par with the rest of her career – funny, touching and, at times, superb. She was lighting up the screen as only she could.'

Schipper concluded, 'For their own reasons, the studio heads at the time lied.' It went unsaid that they had hurriedly buried the evidence, fully aware that film, as Louis B. Mayer once said, never lies.

The implications of the film were far-reaching. From the minute he screened it, Schipper realised that all accounts of Monroe's last days would have to be drastically revised: 'Everyone apparently believed the studio version.'

Hollywood history, and forty-two biographers, have depicted Marilyn Monroe as a stumbling, pill-ridden wreck on the set of *Something's Got to Give*. When Fox fired her after eight tumultuous weeks of shooting, the fearsome studio publicity machine quickly put out the word that her film was unusable and whispered nasty little rumours to the gossip columnists of the day.

Schipper expected to see a badly faltering Monroe, lost to Twentieth Century-Fox and to herself. Instead he found an actress remarkably in control despite take after difficult take.

When he showed an hour of the film to his boss, William

K. Knoedelseder, executive producer of Fox Entertainment News, Knoedelseder, a veteran Hollywood journalist, commented, 'This film is part of a quintessential Hollywood story. Fox forced Marilyn to make this movie. And it killed her!'

Shortly after Schipper's private screening, a cassette of the film found its way to the Manhattan offices of gossip columnist Liz Smith. After watching it in silence, Smith declared, 'This is so wonderful, it's like a religious experience. It makes me wonder, now, how much we really know about the last weeks in Marilyn's life. It really makes me wonder.'

Schipper later used some of this priceless footage in his documentary *Something's Got to Give*, for which Brown served as creative consultant. When it was aired in December 1990, it became the most highly rated entertainment-news programme in the history of the Fox Broadcasting Network. The Associated Press called it 'a breakthrough event which is sure to change the perception of Monroe's final film'. *Time* magazine also singled it out for special mention.

But Schipper was constrained by time (just forty-seven minutes) and format. The details of Monroe's final months deserve a much closer examination.

This book is the true and full story of those fourteen weeks . . . the story of superstar lovers (both lucky and unlucky); of duelling moguls on both coasts; of hidden suicide attempts and of corporate double-dealing. It encompasses the fall of the studio system, the last power grabs of Darryl Zanuck and Spyros Skouras (both founding fathers of the studio); the debacle of *Cleopatra* and the wandering, promiscuous ways of the Kennedy family.

It goes behind the Fox corporate curtain to show why and how Monroe lost her fight with the studio and why Elizabeth Taylor won hers; why Fox finished *Cleopatra* and sacrificed *Something's Got to Give*; and why studio operatives destroyed crucial evidence during a mop-up operation at Monroe's death scene.

It will show how the misguided leaders of a huge studio deliberately plotted against the most important and commercial star in the studio's long history.

It's a story which has never been told.

Peter Harry Brown
Patte Barham
Hollywood, January 1992

– PART ONE –
April

Chapter 1

Into the Fox Lair

It was only 4 A.M., but light already blazed from the windows of the house on Fifth Helena Drive. Shadows fell across the glazed tiles of the Mexican walkway as the housekeeper, a small bird of a woman named Eunice Murray, bustled about the kitchen. She had already brewed strong Italian coffee and poached two eggs and was running a tepid bath in the dressing-room suite.

As the water swirled near the top of the marble tub, Murray poured in a capful of Johnson's Baby Oil and a full ounce of Chanel No. 5.

A Frank Sinatra ballad was barely audible through the locked doors of the master bedroom – a sure sign that Marilyn Monroe was awake and her nightly battle for sleep was over once again.

Outside, a royal-blue limousine straddled the driveway, its engine idling softly and its heater warming the deep velvet seats inside. The driver stood nearby, smartly turned out in a black uniform. Almost invisible on the left side of the car was a small shield in real gold. Beneath it, in swirling gold leaf, were the words 'Twentieth Century-Fox'.

The luxurious studio car seemed out of place. More than

a few of the neighbours, mostly middle-class lawyers and junior executives, would remark on its incongruity during the coming weeks. By then the address would be famous across the globe and forever linked with duplicity, tragedy and death. But on this day, April 10, 1962, it was just another mock-adobe hacienda at the end of a cul-de-sac in a green forest of cul-de-sacs. Nothing distinguished the house on Fifth Helena from the others in this tangle of avenues, drives and boulevards stretching inland from the Pacific Ocean.

It wasn't listed as yet on the garish movie-star maps which out-of-work actors hawked on Hollywood Boulevard and from stands in fabled Bel Air. The tour buses hadn't found it yet, nor, for that matter, had the private detectives and locust-like paparazzi who made their livings by haunting the famous. The house hadn't been featured in the saccharine 'at home' layouts so prevalent in the voracious fan magazines of the era. It was such a well-kept secret that not even Hedda Hopper, the blackest witch in the Hollywood press corps, knew that the world's most famous film star had fled to the comforting obscurity of a middle-class suburb.

The house itself was reachable only by traversing a tangled little lane that, at that time, didn't even bear a street sign. It was shielded from view by a high wall and a stand of eucalyptus trees which had been planted at the turn of the century when Brentwood was still a rolling quilt of ranches and farms.

Marilyn Monroe had always longed for this sort of obscurity. She told one realtor that she didn't want 'one of those big movie-star houses'. Beverly Hills and Bel Air were out, as were the Trousdale estates and the newly fashionable Colony at Malibu. 'I want a hideaway, a place where I can go and live a completely private life.'

Since early February, the house in Brentwood had been that hideaway. It had also been a refuge from her own fame. Who would have suspected that the gold-laméd, platinum-blonde screen goddess would retreat to a house built by a studio accountant? The ruse worked beautifully. Attorney General Robert Kennedy visited her there. And nobody noticed. Other visitors included Monroe's former husband Joe DiMaggio and friends Frank Sinatra and Carl Sandburg.

Monroe was to confide to Sinatra that she 'finally felt safe, finally at home'.

Since her days as a starlet, Monroe had lived in forty different rented apartments, homes and hotel rooms on a slowly ascending scale of luxury. She had lived in the Hollywood YWCA and the Beverly Hills Hotel; in a railroad flat in Van Nuys, California, and a luxury suite in Manhattan. She had slept in renovated garages and presidential suites – but never once in her own home.

She had never really seen a house she wanted until she had turned onto Fifth Helena on a crisp January morning four months earlier. 'This is it,' she cried to Eunice Murray. 'It's perfect.'

All four of her physicians noticed that she blossomed here, safe in the suburban shadows. The cabinet jammed with plastic vials – her hoard of Seconal, Demerol and Nembutal – went virtually untouched for several charmed months. Now she took only chloral hydrate, the mildest of sedatives, to fend off her lifelong enemy – insomnia.

But suddenly on this gorgeous April morning, the nightmare was beginning again. At 9 A.M. she would walk onto a film set for the first time in sixteen months. She had collapsed on the set of her last film, *The Misfits*, and had had to be rescued from a sea of barbiturates and amphetamines.

It took twice-daily sessions with Dr. Ralph Greenson, a high-profile Beverly Hills psychiatrist, and ten days in a psychiatric hospital to erase the traumas of this single film – her first real dramatic part in eleven years. And it was beginning to appear that her crippling bouts of stage fright had kept pace with her growth as an actress. The closer she came to being considered a serious talent, the more she was engulfed by panic.

It was a bitter irony that the most photogenic woman of all time was deathly afraid of the device that launched her – the movie camera.

Drawn to the power and magic of movies since childhood, Monroe had always been fearful – of the camera, of the front office, of her acting coaches and of her directors. When John Huston noticed her trembling violently before a simple scene in *The Asphalt Jungle*, he wondered aloud 'if it was worth it'.

As she prepared for this new film, her panic had become almost life-threatening. The film's director, George Cukor, told reporters that she 'is so fraught with nerves she can't even match one take with the other'. When a columnist tried to question Cukor further, he snapped, 'How should I know the reason? I'm not a psychiatrist.'

But even the psychiatrists were confused. Greenson, who forced Monroe back before the cameras, considered it a phobia, 'a passing thing'. When director Billy Wilder hired an analyst to cure her nerves during *Some Like it Hot*, the psychiatrist remarked, 'It's fairly simple, actually. She doesn't want to be a movie star any more. She's tired of being Marilyn Monroe.'

Privately, even Greenson was afraid that Norma Jean Baker was fully prepared to 'murder Marilyn Monroe' – that rarefied creature invented by the actress herself – with the connivance of Twentieth Century-Fox.

Opinions varied. But one thing was certain that morning thirty years ago: Monroe no longer wanted to be a movie star at Twentieth Century-Fox.

Monroe had signed her first Fox contract in 1946 when she was twenty years old. The six-month deal paid $75 per week – the lowest salary allowed by the Screen Actors Guild and $75 a week less than she had been making as a model. She joined the ranks of two hundred other unknown actors and actresses with similar deals. The studio renewed for six more months and she was dropped at the end of her first year.

She made films at Columbia (*Ladies of the Chorus*) and MGM (*The Asphalt Jungle*), but failed to win a contract at either. While she was still free-lancing, Fox hired her for a sexy cameo in *All About Eve*. After seeing the rushes for that film, Darryl F. Zanuck, the studio's production chief, signed her for another six-month pact. Only after she made a publicity coup out of bit parts in lightweight comedies did the studio offer a full seven-year contract – starting at $500 per week with yearly raises to $1,500.

In 1954, when Monroe was the top box-office attraction in the world, Zanuck kept her bound by the original, shortsighted deal and froze her salary at $1,500 per week.

To retaliate, the star fled Hollywood for New York and let her career lie dormant. Under pressure from the Twentieth Century-Fox board of directors, Zanuck reluctantly renegotiated a contract that paid her $10,000 for each of four films. By 1962, when Fox was paying Elizabeth Taylor $1 million (for *Cleopatra*), James Stewart $700,000 a picture and Dean Martin $500,000 (for *Something's Got to Give*), the terms of Monroe's contracts were woefully out of date.

She hungered for the multimillion-dollar deals that awaited her at other studios. In addition, the film was such a trifle for a star of her calibre that she refused it twice. When she balked a third time, in the winter of 1961, Fox sent her a three-page telegram. It was full of fancy legal jargon and littered with condescending rhetoric. However, the message was quite clear: Make *Something's Got to Give* or we'll tie you up in court for a decade. Litigation could stop her career in its tracks.

The studio that had made her was now in a position to break her.

In December 1961, she gave in and signed to make *Something's Got to Give*. But she had come to despise the studio and what it represented. Even the Fox logo, glimpsed on a letterhead or billboard, caused waves of nausea to rush over her.

7

To gird herself for battle with her old enemy, Monroe immersed herself in the tedious rituals of beauty. She clung to the vain hope that polishing the surface might assuage the fears she held inside.

Like drones around a queen bee, the hangers-on of fashion trekked to Fifth Helena to practise their Tinseltown voodoo. Hairdresser Pearl Porterfield, who had invented 'hot platinum' for Jean Harlow, used sparkling peroxide and plain laundry blueing to produce for Monroe an ever-whiter shade of pale. Later a crew from Elizabeth Arden buried Monroe in mudpack and hot wax while slick Beverly Hills physicians delivered soothing tranquillisers and megavitamins.

Monroe paid friend and masseur Ralph Roberts to reserve all of his time for her. He worked on her for hours as she stretched out on the table, film script in hand. Roberts would feed her cues as he pounded her mercilessly.

She had a similar arrangement with Greenson, and some sessions with the analyst lasted all afternoon. Sitting on a couch in the den of his Santa Monica home, the actress complained endlessly about the physical and psychological rigours it took for her to become Marilyn Monroe.

Housekeeper Eunice Murray noted that she 'seemed to need all this, the perfumed baths, the makeup, the background music, to woo that sensual persona into existence'.

The preparation was unbelievably time-consuming. On April 10, Monroe had already been up for three hours before climbing into the limousine to drive through the deserted Los Angeles streets towards the gates of Twentieth Century-Fox.

Her old studio was floundering. Top-heavy with pricey writers who weren't writing, with name directors who weren't directing and with executives who weren't doing much of anything, the studio was only a hair's breadth from bankruptcy. As Monroe's limousine dropped down from the foothills of Brentwood, enormous clouds of dust were visible over what would soon become Century City. To pay the escalating costs of Elizabeth Taylor's *Cleopatra*, then filming in Rome, Fox had sold its lot to a conglomerate that planned to erect a canyon of boxy condominiums and sterile office towers. Throughout the short history of *Something's Got to Give*, the bulldozers moved closer and closer to the soundstages.

They would destroy a complete small town, a decaying Southern mansion, an artificial lake, a river and a medieval German village. Tyrone Power's sprawling hacienda from *The Mark of Zorro* would make way for a film theatre; the Argentinian pampas ranch where Betty Grable and Don Ameche had cavorted in *Down Argentine Way* would become a gourmet supermarket; and Lana Turner's quaint town square from *Peyton Place* would disappear so that the gleaming Century Plaza Hotel could rise in its stead.

As Monroe rode through the gates erected when Tom Mix rode horses on the back lot and when the studio was still called 'Movietone City', she was painfully aware that hers was the only project on the lot. Almost one hundred and fifty well-paying jobs depended on her whims, her health and her flagging energy. It cost almost $1 million a week to run the Fox lot, and *Something's Got to Give* was the only game in town. Times were so tough that the world-famous commissary had been closed and the studio's police force reduced to a handful.

Two days after the start of filming, studio executives even shut off the water for the studio's forest of ten thousand trees and shrubs and for its twenty-five acres of lawns and rolling valleys. A stand of royal palms, an acre of ferns and a tropical arboretum would slowly wither and die – like the studio itself.

'It was old Hollywood at Sunset,' recalled Walter Bernstein, who was to rewrite the Nunnally Johnson screenplay for *Something's Got to Give*.* 'It was like being on hand for the fall of the

---

*Irving Shulman and Gene Allen had both written outlines for the screenplay before Nunnally Johnson wrote his draft in the winter of 1961–62.

Roman Empire. The streets had once overflowed with pirates and dancing girls, with cowboys and Indians. The air vibrated with excitement.'

Now the streets were silent and deserted, resembling, as Bernstein said, 'a small tropical town during a siesta'.

This miasma of financial collapse, corporate ineptitude and fear had turned Fox into a ghost town – in which Marilyn Monroe was the last remaining saloon girl in the last remaining tavern.

When Monroe had arrived at Fox in 1946, it had been the largest, most successful studio in Hollywood. Not even the venerable Metro-Goldwyn-Mayer measured up to it. Fox's films that year grossed $185 million, $25 million more than those of its nearest rival, Paramount. In 1946, seventy-five films were at various stages of production, and the fabulous stable of contract stars ranged from Betty Grable to Gene Tierney; from Tyrone Power to Clifton Webb (and all four were among the top twenty box-office attractions). It was an empire that stretched across nearly three hundred acres and encompassed sixteen soundstages. In this postwar glow, four thousand Fox employees thought the gravy train would never run out.

Once she gained entrance to that fabled world, Monroe hung back in the shadows of the soundstages and watched Grable sing and dance through crowds of extras – the brilliant focus of an army of technicians. 'It was magical to watch,' she confided to her lover at the time, Robert Slatzer. 'And that's where I'm going to be.'

Now she returned as queen of a humbled and defeated empire. In 1962, the nine hundred remaining employees were adrift on less than fifty acres – and even that space was leased back from the Aluminum Corporation of America for $1.5 million a year. The corporation was much closer to complete collapse than anyone on the West Coast realised. Fox had lost $61 million between 1959 and 1962 – $21 million in 1961 alone.

Even more frightening, at least for the stockholders, the price of the corporation's stock had fallen from $39 to $20 per share during the first ninety days of 1962. By April, prices were falling *six cents per day*.

Common shareholders and their lawyers were pounding on the doors of the company's New York headquarters, threatening to overthrow the board and depose Fox president Spyros P. Skouras.

The studio had been sped on its way to bankruptcy by the great haemorrhage of cash known as *Cleopatra*. Initially pegged to cost $5 million, the Egyptian epic had already cost $25 million and would eventually consume more than $40 million. The entire lot was sold to keep it afloat, and when that wasn't enough, Skouras and company borrowed to the hilt on every asset remaining – including the studio's golden library of films.

As the cameras turned on *Something's Got to Give*, *Cleopatra* was devouring $150,000 per day.

By August 5, Twentieth Century-Fox, barring a miracle, would no longer be able to meet its payroll, pay its utility bills or keep its New York skyscraper open for business. Sworn to secrecy, every employee earning $20,000 or more had taken a 50 percent pay cut.

Given this bleak backdrop, it was no wonder that greedy executive eyes were trained on Monroe, the studio's last remaining star. Her films had grossed more than $40 million for the studio since 1950 – more even than Betty Grable or Shirley Temple.* 'They were desperate, as desperate as a big studio would ever be,' recalled producer David Brown. 'If Marilyn Monroe was lucky enough to survive the film, she could literally rescue the company.'

---

*Worldwide grosses for *Niagara*, *Gentlemen Prefer Blondes* and *How to Marry a Millionaire* were $25 million, causing film writer Maurice Zolotow to estimate Monroe's annual worth to Fox at $10 million.

A confidential report for Spyros Skouras indicated that the studio planned to have *Something's Got to Give* edited and in the theatres by October, just in time to pay the postproduction bills for *Cleopatra*.

Had Monroe been aware of these plans, she might have been even more ambivalent about this final film. To her, Fox was the dark attic of her career, full of murky places and concealed humiliations. She would have had no desire to salvage it.

To reach her new bungalow for *Something's Got to Give*, the limousine had to run the gauntlet of executive buildings looming over the lot like prison guard towers. The corporate headquarters was perched atop a building of gunmetal grey which boasted thick carpeting, luxurious furnishings and cavernous antechambers. This was a calculated effect on the part of the moguls who had once ruled there. It never failed to humble the lowly actors summoned before them. Snappy young adjutants and tight-lipped secretaries completed the effect.

From strategically located windows, Fox executives could easily monitor the comings and goings of its stars. Always sensitive to this attention, Monroe now became obsessed by it. 'I can feel them watching me, and then writing their nasty memos,' she told chauffeur Rudy Kautsky. 'I hate it. Why don't they do their job and let me do mine?'

If Twentieth Century-Fox had once been a shabby surrogate family for Monroe, it was now the hated authority figure, resented by the rebellious child within her. Just days into this film, she learned that the security guards – many of them old pals – were carefully recording her entrance and exit times in confidential reports. These documents, she learned, even contained notes on her appearance.

This knowledge sent her into a tailspin. Some mornings she would scamper out of the car at an old rear entrance, sending the limousine through the front gate empty. The perverse game worsened as the troubled film continued. Even on days when Monroe failed to appear, the empty car arrived to sit conspicuously outside her dressing room.

Soon, Monroe's entrances were monitored and catalogued as if she were a queen entering a royal enclosure. The minute Kautsky drove her through the main gate, the guard grabbed the phone and dialled the executive suite. The words 'Marilyn's here' echoed from desk to desk and office to office. Soon there was a nervous buzz on the set as crew members huddled over the latest bit of 'Marilyn intelligence'.

Phrases such as 'She seemed drugged up' or 'It must have been a bad night' were passed about frequently and appeared in the confidential reports that flew back and forth between executives on both coasts. In some perverse way, Fox's middle management seemed to blame Monroe for their troubles. Most still considered her a traitor for deserting them in the mid-fifties.

In early 1955, Monroe had disappeared from sight, turning her back on Fox, which she said was determined to cast her in 'tasteless projects with amoral heroines, and ruin her Hollywood career'. After a month of media speculation over her vanishing act, the star turned up in Manhattan, where she announced the formation of Marilyn Monroe Productions. She also declared that she would return to Fox only when the studio offered her more money, her choice of directors and 'Class A' productions.

'Truthfully, I've made my last film for Twentieth Century-Fox,' she told Louella Parsons.

At Fox, where sentiment ran against the recalcitrant star, Zanuck reacted angrily. 'This will be her last film for *anyone but* Fox for three years and four months. She is under contract and she will fulfil all of its terms.'

The coast-to-coast battle of words between Zanuck and Monroe lasted for six months. By August, however, after Monroe's film *The Seven Year Itch* soared to the top of the box-office lists, Fox capitulated to all of her demands.

'But nobody ever felt the same about her; she was a traitor,' said Lee Hanna, one of Zanuck's executive secretaries. 'She deserted us.'*

No one at Fox, from the executive suite to the studio garage, understood Monroe's burning desire to be a respected actress. To them, she was still the busty blonde ripe for the casting couch. 'The guys who ran Fox all wanted to get her into bed,' said her makeup artist, Whitey Snyder. 'They couldn't see her any other way.'

Something's Got to Give producer Henry Weinstein remembered calling her into his office and urging her to lie down during a story conference. 'She was exhausted, and we had a long afternoon ahead.' Monroe looked up at Weinstein with a glint in her eye. 'You know, Henry, you're the first producer to tell me to lie down for a rest and really mean it.'

When Fox hired her for the first time in the forties, it was as a sex object – literally. She was paid $75 a week to serve drinks and provide cigarettes (with a light) at gin rummy sessions held by Zanuck and former Fox president Joe Schenck. In fishnet stockings and a black satin costume (not unlike *Playboy* Bunny attire), the 'Gin Rummy Girls' became the butt of filthy corporate jokes. 'They always thought of her that way – as a saloon girl,' said director John Huston.

'They would never allow her to have *any* dignity,' said producer David Brown.

Still, Monroe sought out Fox again and again as she kept knocking on Hollywood's door in the boom years after World War II. Zanuck's zeal to make films of quality dazzled

*Monroe had already been forced to make two artistically bankrupt films, *River of No Return* and *There's No Business Like Show Business*, and was to have made a third, *How to Be Very, Very Popular*, in the year before she left Hollywood. *How to Be Very, Very Popular* was made using the studio's Monroe replacement, Sheree North. It was not a success.

her. She sat through *Laura*, the film-noir classic with Gene Tierney, seven times – until she knew the dialogue by heart. And Betty Grable's work in the stark wartime drama *I Wake Up Screaming* so impressed her that she used the script again and again in acting workshops.

To her, Zanuck represented the best of Hollywood, and she admired him intensely. 'Later, I had nightmares about Mr. Zanuck,' she told Eunice Murray. 'I would wake up in the morning thinking I would make him appreciate me. But I never got in to see him – not even when I was a big star.'

She couldn't have known then that the nightmare would come true.

Monroe had been fighting with Twentieth Century-Fox all her adult life. In the mid-forties, she struggled to be noticed, to be picked from the endless line of blondes at the studio's casting calls. She was on the run from an unhappy first marriage (to merchant seaman James Dougherty) when she walked onto the lot for the first time in July 1946. Wearing a come-hither white sundress, her mousy brown hair rinsed golden blonde for the first time, she was answering a summons from Fox casting director Ben Lyon.

Lyon, a onetime Lothario of the silent screen, 'discovered her' while he was browsing through the magazine racks at the Hollywood Boulevard Newsstand. He couldn't fail to notice that one very wholesome young woman monopolised the July covers of four cutie magazines (*Click*, *Pic*, *Laff* and *Sir*). After tracking her down through her agency, Blue Book Models, Lyon took her to lunch on July 28 and scheduled a screen test for the following morning at 5:30 A.M.

The talent scout was so certain of Monroe's potential that he ordered an expensive Technicolor test – using the set for a Betty Grable film, *Mother Wore Tights*, and a red sequinned gown designed for departed musical star Alice Faye.

'I could see right away that she would eventually be a major star,' said cinematographer Leon Shamroy, who shot the six-minute test. 'She had "flesh appeal", something I hadn't seen since I tested Gloria Swanson in the twenties. Flesh impact is very, very rare. Harlow had it. And Clara Bow. And Monroe.'

Lyon sneaked the Monroe test into a series of daily film clips to be screened by Zanuck that same evening. Though the mogul had already refused to sign her on the basis of the magazine photographs, he liked the test well enough to offer her a standard starlet contract.

'At first, Marilyn had no idea what it meant to be a starlet in a town full of starlets,' said author Maurice Zolotow. 'She didn't know that the odds were against her or that most starlets usually got married or became carhops.'

But Monroe was hungrier for fame than the average starlet. The girl with no real identity of her own decided almost instantly that she would be the next Betty Grable, the song-and-dance star who still ruled the Fox lot. After watching Grable in action, portraying a 'dancing kitten' in *Mother Wore Tights*, she had a hunch that she could do anything that Grable could do – perhaps with more verve and certainly with more sex appeal.

The trouble was that in 1946 Fox was already awash with blonde stars. In addition to Grable, who was at the peak of her box-office power, June Haver and Vivian Blaine were being groomed for stardom.

As the studio's 'extra blonde', Monroe did everything but appear in the movies. She rode on floats. She stood in parades. She opened supermarkets. But mostly she posed for still photographs – in swimsuits and strapless evening gowns.

After checking the casting lists day after day and in vain, Monroe grew increasingly despondent. One day, after haunting a Grable set for hours, she grabbed Ben Lyon's arm and whispered fiercely, 'What do I do to become a star? Tell me how to become a star.'

Lyon was stunned by the tone of desperation in her voice.

'She had her heart set on becoming queen of the lot,' he later told Maurice Zolotow. 'Fox had become home to her, a replacement for the family she never had.'

Although Lyon had no surefire plan to make her a star, he did introduce her to former Fox president Joe Schenck – who still wielded some influence and who was to become the first in a series of father figures who guided her ascent. 'Let's put it this way,' said Zolotow, 'she indulged in sexual adventures to keep her dream alive.'

Schenck not only saw to it that Monroe's contract was renewed in February 1947, he convinced Zanuck to create a cameo role for her in a quickie musical titled *Scudda Hoo! Scudda Hay!* (But Schenck couldn't stop Zanuck from cutting her speaking part to a single word, 'Hello.')

Zanuck, who now referred to Monroe as 'Schenck's girl', abruptly cancelled her contract on August 25, 1947 – thirteen months after Lyon had been dazzled by the magazine covers.

'In many ways, this was her ultimate rejection,' recalled Monroe's former lover Robert Slatzer. 'She vowed to return to Fox and decided, no matter what, she had to become their biggest star.'

At first this seemed unlikely. A few quick bit parts in forgettable films at Columbia, United Artists and MGM failed to win her contracts, and Warner Brothers and Paramount returned her stills with no comment.

Then she met a second father figure – the dapper 'dean of Hollywood agents', Johnny Hyde. A chance meeting at a cocktail party led to an affair which, in turn, led to a big buildup. Hyde, one of the top men at the William Morris Agency, convinced an old pal, John Huston, to cast Monroe in a pivotal role in *The Asphalt Jungle*.

When the Huston film was previewed, Monroe's portrayal

---

*[see page 18] During Monroe's freelance years (1947 to 1950), she made *Dangerous Years*, *The Fireball* and *A Ticket to Tomahawk* for Fox; *Ladies of the Chorus* for Columbia; *Love Happy* for United Artists; and *The Asphalt Jungle* and *Right Cross* for MGM.

of smouldering girl on the make Angela Phinlay caused ripples of excitement in the audiences. But, again, MGM passed.*

Obsessed with Monroe and with her career, Hyde called in a favour from Darryl Zanuck – a big favour. The coveted contract was offered. It was the barest, most minimal contract, but a contract nonetheless.

Now Monroe fought Fox anew – for roles. At first no part was too small or too demeaning: the dumb blonde secretary; the amoral streetwalker; the single-syllable Miss America contestant. Step by step, in movies of ascending importance, Monroe made seven films for Fox between 1950 and 1953. She seemed to be perpetually on the verge of making it big, yet never broke through.

Zanuck was stubborn. Though Betty Grable's star was setting, he refused to promote Monroe. 'I just didn't see the potential,' he told his son Richard. 'I was wrong perhaps, but I didn't see it.'

'To Zanuck, she remained "Schenck's girl",' said Zanuck's onetime executive secretary Lee Hanna.

By 1951, it was obvious to everyone at Fox, but most of all to Monroe, that Zanuck had no intention of giving her really important roles, nor did he plan to tailor vehicles for her unique talents. 'In her mind, Zanuck became the *bête noir*, her nemesis,' recalled Zolotow. 'He just wasn't interested, and she soon decided there was little she could do about it.'

So Monroe pulled a series of artfully staged publicity stunts. She plunged into the nightclub circuit on the arms of such up-and-comers as Robert Wagner; she courted gossip queen Louella Parsons and plied her with juicy and exclusive tales of her impoverished past; she posed for Max Factor commercials; and she gleefully modelled diaphanous gowns from Frederick's of Hollywood. Not surprisingly, her fan mail soon outstripped that of any other star on the lot – despite the fact that she had only played minor roles in minor productions.

Yet Zanuck, unaware that powerful winds of change were

wafting through Hollywood, remained unconvinced that the industry was ready for a new Harlow.

Monroe decided to go over his head and, to this end, approached the studio's leading costume designer William Travilla, in late March 1951. 'You know, Billy, Skouras is going to be out here for that big exhibitors' luncheon . . . I need a special dress.'

'She was already smart enough to realise that, as powerful as Zanuck was, Skouras was even more powerful,' Travilla recalled. 'He was the money man, and money is the absolute bottom line in Hollywood. But Skouras [usually] remained in New York – out of reach.'

She had only a couple of minutes to attract his attention. It turned out to be enough.

While Travilla whipped up a luncheon gown of chiffon and thick satin, Monroe began reading up on Skouras – the Greek immigrant who had worked his way up from bellboy to theatre magnate to president of Twentieth Century-Fox. She learned that he had long envied MGM for its carefully nurtured stable of sex goddesses such as Lana Turner and Ava Gardner – stars who could turn a B picture into a bonanza just by their presence.

Monroe decided to demonstrate publicly that Skouras already had just such a star under contract – and that she wasn't being used. When the exhibitors' luncheon had been underway for ninety minutes, and when the theatre owners had had their fill of Anne Baxter, Jeanne Crain and Clifton Webb, there was a commotion at the door of the Fox commissary as Monroe, sewn into the Travilla gown, sauntered down the stairs.

With the still photographers gathered around her, Monroe took an empty chair at a huge table of theatre men from the Midwest. 'They leaned forward eagerly and asked again and again, "And what pictures are you going to be in, Miss Monroe?"' Zolotow said. 'Marilyn just fluttered her eyelashes and said, "You'll have to ask Mr. Skouras."'

Watching the furore, Skouras asked the same question of a West Coast executive. When he was told that she was not in *any* forthcoming productions, the studio president glowered in the general direction of Zanuck.

'If the exhibitors like her, the public likes her,' Skouras commented before plunging through the crowd, bowing to Monroe and deftly guiding her to the head table.

The Zanuck contingent watched helplessly as Monroe drew Skouras into a whispered conversation – a meeting which sparked a blazing affair between the twenty-five-year-old starlet and the fifty-three-year-old magnate. He was soon to become the most important of her Hollywood benefactors. 'The affair didn't last long,' recalled actor Nico Minardos, who was Monroe's sometime lover and a Skouras protégé. 'But it helped make Marilyn a star.'

Several days after the exhibitors' luncheon, the obviously dazzled Skouras ordered Zanuck to 'put her in any film which has a role for a beautiful blonde.'

Zanuck continued to argue. 'I think her talent is very limited.'

Skouras flew into a rage. 'This is my choice; my order. Put her in anything, but use her *now*!'

This started a five-year battle between Skouras and the all-powerful Zanuck and his henchmen – most of whom considered Monroe beneath notice. Zanuck's best friend, screenwriter Nunnally Johnson, summed up the prevailing attitude. 'She is a phenomenon of nature, like Niagara Falls or the Grand Canyon. You can't talk to it. It can't talk to you. All you can do is sit back and be awed by it.'

'Because she slept with Skouras and because she accepted his protection, she had made her choice,' recalled Minardos. 'Zanuck had been spurned.'

Nevertheless, Monroe became an international superstar who almost single-handedly saved Fox from financial ruin when television exploded onto the scene. Her value was already obvious from the public reaction to an unpretentious little comedy called *Monkey Business*, the first film after the start of her affair with Skouras. This B-grade film, which cost only $250,000 to make, earned almost $3 million – a surprising take for a film designed for the lower half of a double feature.

Niagara, Monroe's first starring role, launched her as a full-fledged star less than a week after it opened in 1953. And it was quickly followed by *Gentlemen Prefer Blondes* and *How to Marry a Millionaire*. *Photoplay* magazine named Monroe 'the fastest rising star of 1953'. A year later, the same publication selected her for its Best Actress award for *Gentlemen Prefer Blondes* and *How to Marry a Millionaire*.

But the burst of success only led to more serious troubles between Monroe and Fox.

The new star fought desperately to escape the twilight world of the casting couch and to erase her image as the 'sleep-around blonde who made it on her back'. 'Of course, Marilyn never really deserved that reputation,' said Robert Slatzer. 'What she had done was nothing more than dozens of actresses had done.'

Feminist Gloria Steinem, who studied the star's years at Fox, agreed. 'Today, they would call what happened to Marilyn "sexual harassment"; then they just called it "life".'

Monroe was an amazingly good sport about it; she negotiated the traps and mazes with remarkable agility. She played appallingly crude roles in appallingly bad films, such as *Niagara* and *River of No Return*. She wore garish costumes and tartish makeup. She participated in tawdry production numbers, such as 'Heat Wave' in *There's No Business Like Show Business*, and cheap publicity stunts that traded on her breasts.

Already a full-fledged star and box-office champion, she accepted the penurious salary of $1,500 per week (most other stars of her calibre earned $10,000 per week) and made do with the 'extra girls' dressing room'. The William Morris Agency convinced her to suffer in silence.

'The studio played parent and master,' said Steinem, 'while Marilyn desperately wanted to be taken seriously, to have dignity, not to be made fun of, not to be seen as a dumb blonde.'

Finally, in 1955, Monroe was assigned to make one bad movie too many. When ordered to appear as a brash song-and-dance girl in *How to Be Very, Very Popular*, she fled to New York and disappeared from sight. The paparazzi chased her, and leg-men for the columnists searched in vain. When she surfaced, it was on the arm of photographer and soon-to-be-producer Milton Greene.

She invited the television cameras of Edward R. Murrow's *Person to Person* into the Greenes' living room and publicly pleaded her case against Fox. She wanted good roles in good films, she said. She wanted director approval and a bigger salary – a salary such as her international stardom should command.

An avalanche of angry letters crashed down on the studio, and even the exhibitors complained. With public opinion strongly in her favour and most of the film industry behind her, Twentieth Century-Fox grudgingly capitulated. A four-picture deal was hammered out: $100,000 per film; director approval; a real dressing room; and some marginal say in the roles she was to play.*

Something's Got to Give was to be the final film under that pact, the terms of which had become hopelessly outdated. Monroe, now the biggest box-office draw in the world, received $300,000 and 10 percent of the profits for *Some Like It Hot*, and $300,000 and expenses for *The Misfits*.

By 1962, $100,000 was a bargain-basement price.

---

*Monroe's residual bitterness towards Fox was expressed by Clause 11 in the 1956 contract. It read: 'Marilyn Monroe's services are of a special, unique, unusual, extraordinary and intellectual character. They are of great and particular value to Fox. The artist's talent and services cannot be replaced.'

This financial slight was just another of the emotional burdens Monroe dragged along with her to the set of *Something's Got to Give*.

However, a more benevolent despot was now in charge of production at the studio – a fair-minded lawyer named Peter Levathes.*

Monroe had reason to believe that this would be her most trouble-free film. There were no dramatic scenes, no song-and-dance extravaganzas, and no philosophical monologues of the sort which had plagued her last few films.

Something's Got to Give was the simplest and slightest of domestic comedies. The plot was an old Hollywood standby: Wife is shipwrecked on tropical island with sexy man and declared dead; husband remarries; wife is miraculously rescued and returns to reclaim her husband.

It had taken less than a month for Irene Dunne, Cary Grant and director Garson Kanin to complete the original version – a 1939 RKO film titled *My Favourite Wife*. Considered one of the classic screwball comedies of the thirties (it was actually the last of them), *My Favourite Wife* received a nomination for Best Original Screenplay by the Academy of Motion Picture Arts and Sciences.

'At first, we had a healthy star and a script which Marilyn adored,' recalled producer Henry Weinstein. (Earlier versions that displeased her had been tailored for Monroe by ace screenwriter Nunnally Johnson.) 'Who could blame us for missing the storm clouds which were on the horizon?'

---

*When Zanuck resigned in 1956 to produce Fox films in Europe, he was succeeded by producer Buddy Adler (*From Here to Eternity*). When Adler died of cancer in 1959, he was succeeded by Robert Goldstein, who had headed the studio's foreign operations. Goldstein resigned in 1961 and was quickly replaced by Levathes, who was then director of Twentieth Century-Fox Television. Levathes was a protégé of Skouras and had come to work in the studio's New York office at the age of twenty-six – fresh out of law school.

Chapter 2

Lights, Camera . . .

By 9 A.M. on that first day, a small army of technicians was jammed into Monroe's studio bungalow. Holding cups of coffee in one hand and combs, brushes, and makeup jars in the other, they buzzed about, creating the dozens of small touches that went into 'the Marilyn Monroe look'.

The star was reclining on an upholstered slant board wearing only a transparent flesh-tone bikini – the undergarment for a silk swimsuit that would soon become world-famous.

Whitey Snyder, the veteran makeup man who had been with Monroe since her Fox screen test in 1946, was using small watercolour brushes to highlight the star's cheekbones – the final step in a gruelling two-hour ritual.

Nearby, Bunny Gardel was standing at a counter directly in front of the slant board, mixing body makeup for the bikini test. To a quart of Max Factor's 'sun tan base', she added a half cup of 'ivory' colouring and an eyedropper of 'clown white' in a formula that perfectly matched the star's natural flesh tone.

In the bungalow's anteroom, Monroe's dresser, Marjorie Plecher, was organising and lightly pressing the six costumes to be tested for cut and texture before the Technicolor camera. The daring lime-green swimsuit, with bows at the side, had already been steamed and treated with a waterproof chemical.

Many of the artisans would later remember that they felt an undercurrent of tension that morning. Most of them had already heard the rumour that the film's director, George Cukor, a major figure in Hollywood's golden era, had stubbornly refused to supervise the first round of tests – tests that would determine a thousand details when filming actually began.

'But we didn't know for sure,' said Hazel Washington, Monroe's studio maid. 'At the start of any film, you hear all kinds of wild stories and rumours. All the same, I kept my ears open.'

Then, just before Monroe went under the hair dryer, she received an urgent phone call from the production office. The gossip was correct. In a terse memorandum dictated to his secretary the night before, Cukor politely and regretfully bowed out of the tests, citing 'pressing production business'.*

The star merely shrugged, as if the news didn't faze her in the least. But this was a woman who never wore her troubles on her sleeve.

The lot was buzzing with rumours as to why Cukor had spurned his star this early in the game. Some said he had to screen-test the child actors who were so crucial to the plot of *Something's Got to Give*; others said he was working on the script. Those closer to Cukor, including secretary Hanna, saw it as a sign of Cukor's simmering hatred of Marilyn Monroe. 'He had come to despise her,' said Hanna.

Tom Tryon, who became a friend of Cukor's when signed to play Monroe's fellow shipwreck victim, believed that the

---

*This memorandum, which Cukor's secretary Lee Hanna, who had also been Zanuck's secretary, remembers typing, has disappeared from the Twentieth Century-Fox files. Nor is there a copy among Cukor's papers at the Academy of Motion Picture Arts and Sciences. Several weeks later, the director did direct a second round of tests.

director 'considered it an exercise in vanity which could have been accomplished by shooting colour stills. He told me that Marilyn's insistence on such elaborate tests was only a self-indulgent ego trip which he didn't intend to become a part of.'

Whatever the cause, Monroe was obviously hiding her dismay. These tests were always a major event for her – almost an obsession.

Like Marlene Dietrich, Greta Garbo and Joan Crawford, like all the great stars who owed their initial success to fairness of face and form, she knew these tests were like divining rods that could indicate how the final film would turn out.

Betty Grable had told Monroe early in the fifties that 'the big screen doesn't lie. If it looks good up there, honey, it really looks good.' An example of this very personal concern for such tests had occurred when Monroe saw the disastrous tests for her previous film, *The Misfits*. She had run from the screening room and locked herself in the dressing room for five hours. Not even director John Huston or her husband at the time, Arthur Miller (who had written *The Misfits* for her), could adequately console her.

To the Fox management, Cukor's refusal was like a red light – a warning sign of trouble ahead. The executives were justifiably nervous about these tests. By design, the studio was about to unveil a new Marilyn Monroe.

For twelve years (and fourteen hit films) she had been sold to the public as the sexy blonde from the wrong side of the tracks. She had portrayed hookers, cabaret singers and an entire gallery of amiable gold diggers. She had never played a suburban housewife and mother.

Her gowns had always been flashy and obvious – most of them satin and sequin affairs created by Fox's resident designer, William Travilla. Her makeup and hairstyles had followed suit, trading on thick red lips, heavy pancake and variations on the lacquered pageboy.

Something's Got to Give was designed to change all that.

'We were taking a risk by casting her as an upper-middle-class wife and mother,' Levathes recalled. 'We didn't know how the public would react to a Monroe who looked and dressed so differently.'

For months, designer Jean Louis, hairstylist Sidney Guilaroff and Whitey Snyder had been working on the various components of this classier image.

Jean Louis, the former Parisian couturier who had created the sleek Rita Hayworth look in the overdressed forties, had used muted Chinese silk (in six different colours and prints), cashmere and mink to fashion Monroe's 'department store' dresses as dictated by the Nunnally Johnson screenplay.

To complement the clothes, Guilaroff, who had been discovered by Joan Crawford in the twenties and had once worked exclusively for Greta Garbo, had sculpted seven rather conventional hairstyles.

In the preliminary watercolour sketches by Jean Louis and Guilaroff (from which the costumes and the hairstyles were designed), the woman in the mockups looked more like Grace Kelly than Marilyn Monroe – a soignée creature with trailing scarves and understated afternoon wear.

'The change in her was breathtaking,' admitted Jean Louis. 'It was made even more startling because Marilyn had just lost twenty-five pounds. She had never been so slim and glowing. And, because she was to wear a bikini in several scenes, she had been working out – and walking a great deal. She was thrilled that she could wear high-fashion clothes for the first time in her career.'

'Giving up all these things – the lush makeup and sexy clothes – had to have been terrifying for her; they had been part of the foundation for her success,' recalled Monroe's fellow Fox star, Sheree North, a blazing platinum blonde who had originally been signed as a threat to Monroe. 'It would have been safer to retain the old image.'

Both Monroe and Fox were anxious to see how the new

look came across on the Cinemascope screen. And this made Cukor's decision not to attend the tests even more baffling.

'It was a terrible breach of studio etiquette,' said Travilla. 'When Marilyn told me about it, I was shocked. Most other stars would have walked off the lot at such a slight. If this had happened to Elizabeth Taylor, they would have been looking for another star. Liz would have walked.'

Something's Got to Give producer Henry Weinstein, a twenty-seven-year-old theatre whiz from New York City, was forced to direct the tests himself. 'I was never able to determine why George didn't want to do them. It was just another of those inexplicable decisions which plagued this film.'

To many veteran members of the production team, the incident marked the revival of a bitter grudge match between Monroe and Cukor which had begun in early 1960 during the filming of the musical *Let's Make Love*.

'That film was a disaster to make. It turned into an artistic bloodbath involving both Marilyn and George,' recalled Evelyn Moriarity, who was hired by the director to serve as Marilyn's stand-in during *Let's Make Love*. (Moriarity continued in the job on the sets of *The Misfits* and *Something's Got to Give*.)

The problems started early – when Fox forced Monroe to make what would arguably become her worst film as a major star. It was late summer in 1959, and the star was the undisputed queen of the box office thanks to the enormous success of *Some Like It Hot*. That scintillating comedy, which costarred Jack Lemmon and Tony Curtis, had been number one for three months running and would eventually earn $12.5 million in first release.

Hoping to ride that film's coat-tails, Fox executives ordered producer Jerry Wald to rush ahead with a project known as *The Billionaire*. Although it had been in the works for more than a year, the studio had found it impossible to pin Monroe down to a starting date.

At best, she considered the story lame and tired – a throwback to the passé musical comedies she had left behind in the early fifties. She was to portray a cabaret singer who gets the rush from a buttoned-down industrialist. Gregory Peck had already been signed for the part.

To force her hand, Fox warned that it would use legal means to stop her from making further independent films until *Let's Make Love*, the renamed *Billionaire*, was completed.

Monroe reluctantly agreed, provided certain demands were met. From the Connecticut home she shared with her playwright husband, Arthur Miller, she rejected the first draft of the screenplay (written by Oscar winner Norman Krasna). 'She began scheming from the outset – to fatten her part,' said film scholar Patrick McGilligan. 'So, Peck bowed out,' leaving *Let's Make Love* without a leading man.

While Krasna was rewriting the script, Monroe, exercising the powers granted in her 1956 contract, insisted that Cukor be hired to direct. She cited his 'special sensitivity to this sort of project'. Still, Fox had to threaten legal action to get her onto the set for rehearsals.

Let's Make Love was still without a leading man. Fearful of being upstaged, Yul Brynner, Cary Grant, Rock Hudson and Charlton Heston had all turned it down. It was Cukor who came up with the replacement for the departing Gregory Peck – Yves Montand, a French actor virtually unknown in America. The director had seen Montand's song-and-dance routine on *The Ed Sullivan Show* and was dazzled. 'This man is going to be a very big star,' Cukor told Monroe. 'He's the man for *Let's Make Love*.' Having just seen Montand in his New York cabaret debut, she agreed instantly.

Monroe and Cukor had been chummy at first, teasing each other during rehearsals and taking time out for tea. Then Montand arrived. Accompanied by his celebrated wife, Simone Signoret, he seemed to cast a pall over the production. Lean, handsome and intense, the Frenchman soon drove a wedge between star and director. Within days they were competing for his attention. Both wined and dined him, and Monroe insisted that Fox install the Montands in a bungalow adjacent to hers in the garden compound of the fabled Beverly Hills Hotel.

Montand apparently came to the set with an ambitious agenda. He had been jousting for international stardom since the late forties, when chanteuse Edith Piaf discovered him in a Paris music hall. He had made fifteen French films between 1946 and 1959, but was little known outside France.

Norman Mailer wrote of Montand that 'Marilyn Monroe was his ticket to notoriety; she had been famously faithful to Miller for three and a half years and was vulnerable.'

Soon Montand was ardently courting Monroe on and off the set – even under the nose of Signoret, who was in town to collect the Academy Award for Best Actress in *Room at the Top*.

'It was shameful,' said Monroe's publicist Rupert Allan, who temporarily took on Montand as a favour to Monroe. 'He not only seduced her, he told Hedda Hopper about it to purposely kick up a scandal.'

Privately, Montand bragged to his friends, 'She will be anywhere I say. And she will be there on time.' To others he confided, 'Marilyn has gotten so that she will do whatever I ask her to on the set. She's constantly looking to me for approval.'

But Montand wooed Cukor as well.

'This may not be the nicest thing to say,' said Cukor's friend William Travilla. 'But Cukor was smitten with the French star. It was latent, of course, but you could see it in the way he was treated – often at Marilyn's expense.'

Cukor, the only admitted homosexual among major Hollywood directors, was not invulnerable to such attention. Montand acted the part of willing protégé, malleable in the hands of the veteran director.

To Monroe, Montand was the ultimate conquest. He had

even been on an ideal list of 'future lovers' which she and friend Shelley Winters had drawn up in the fifties. 'The real animosity between Marilyn and Cukor began there; he was incensed when the affair became public.'

'Montand used both director and star to gain a foothold in Hollywood,' Allan concluded.

However, some of the ill will that blighted the set of *Let's Make Love* was Monroe's fault. She had returned to Fox thirty pounds overweight and addicted to massive doses of alcohol and sleeping pills. She had also adopted the airs and temperament of a prima donna.

One of her first official acts was to install Arthur Miller in an office near the set, where he worked furiously on additional dialogue for his wife – and occasionally for his rival, Montand. According to Mailer, 'Once again, the playwright tried to add funny dialogue [to] a film that was not funny.' (Miller had performed a similar chore for *The Prince and the Showgirl* in 1957.)

The star also persuaded producer Jerry Wald to allow her (and sometimes Miller) into the editing sessions for *Let's Make Love*, where she often barraged Cukor with suggestions and demands. *New York Times* reporter Murray Schumach attended one such screening, during which Monroe provided a running commentary of things Cukor needed to do to improve the film. These suggestions sounded like commands and were usually prefaced with the statement: 'You know, George, Arthur and I believe it would be better if you . . .'

Schumach was also on hand one afternoon when Monroe burst in and gave Cukor curt instructions on the editing of the film. The *New York Times* journalist remembered it as a very ugly situation. Cukor just sat in his armchair and listened politely to the star's tirade. But Schumach could tell that the director was barely controlling his rage.

Cukor retaliated by scheduling his own screenings during the noon hour – in a secret projection room.

By early February 1960, Monroe and Cukor were no longer speaking to each other. The director relayed all his requests through choreographer Jack Cole – who also returned with Monroe's answers.

'I'm sorry to say that she was out of control on that film,' recalled editor David Bretherton. 'She often appeared on the set drinking gin from a teacup – a ruse which fooled no one.'

One afternoon, the film editor saw Monroe 'standing at the edge of the set looking totally lost'. Another time, she ran up to an extra player and grabbed him by the arm, pleading, 'Help. Help. What do I do next?'

Still refusing to talk to Cukor, Monroe assaulted Cole with a similar request for help. Eventually her behaviour brought the dance director, who normally treated her superstar antics with a 'let's just humour the poor dear' attitude, to his breaking point. One day in March, Cole barked back, 'You want me to tell you what to do? Okay, Marilyn. I'll tell you. Why don't you go stick your finger up your ass?'

Some days it took hours to rouse Monroe from her sleeping-pill hangovers and ready her for the elaborate production numbers. After it took eleven days to film a six-minute song and dance, 'My Heart Belongs to Daddy', Cukor threw up his hands and entrusted the remaining production numbers to Cole.

'When production ended, Cukor refused to throw the usual wrap party,' said stand-in Evelyn Moriarity. 'We all just crept away.'

Cukor would exact a bitter retribution on the set of *Something's Got to Give*.

The director's first act was to boycott the costume tests. Surprisingly, Monroe shrugged it off and became lost in the makeup rituals.

As the artisans worked on her, the *Something's Got to Give* set was finally coming to life on the other side of the lot.

High up on the catwalk, cinematographer Franz Planer was checking the precise positioning of the fifty spotlights strung like huge Christmas lights above the set. There were banks of amber (for softness), groupings of pink (to subtract age), and dozens of small beams to highlight the shoulders, the bridge of the nose and the arms and hands.

Weinstein was justifiably nervous. The cinematographer soothed him. 'We'll get her through it together,' said Planer, who had photographed the tests on three previous Monroe films. 'It's going to be fine.' Soon Planer was behind the camera and Weinstein was pacing as the minutes slipped by.

Coquettishly, Monroe lingered in the dressing room. She made her usual excuses: 'Look, Whitey, right under my chin, it looks a little dark there.'

'No, no, no, Marilyn. It's fine.'

'Whitey, I really think the eyelids are too prominent.'

'No, no, Marilyn, it's fine.' Whitey later remembered that Monroe 'would call me in and close the door. She would tell me there's something wrong here, there's something wrong there. This eyebrow is different. Of course, nothing was wrong. Nothing was different. It was just a crutch, a delaying tactic that Marilyn and many other big stars used again and again.'

When Weinstein made his second trip to the bungalow, Monroe looked at him and snapped, 'Mr. Weinstein, what do you have to do when you get up in the morning? Do you have to put on makeup? Or eye shadow?' Evelyn Moriarity watched Marilyn walk closer and closer to the producer, finally shaking her finger at him. 'And what about hair? Does it take fifty minutes to style your hair?' Weinstein retreated in haste.

Eventually, at 11 A.M., Snyder took Monroe by the shoulders and propelled her out the door, as he frequently had to do. 'That first little step was the hardest. She could stop a clock with her beauty. But she wanted to be the most perfect Marilyn Monroe she could be.'

Wearing the lime-green bikini and matching beach wrap, teetering on high-heeled sandals, she slid into a limousine for the short trip to the soundstage.

A red light was flashing above the door and two impressive security guards stood beside the entrance. A sign with big orange letters read: 'This is a closed set. Only cast and crew members are to be admitted. Henry Weinstein is solely responsible for those admitted to and from this set.' The guards remained at the door throughout the production of *Something's Got to Give*.

The give-and-take camaraderie and the wandering journalists that had been features of earlier Monroe sets were banished from this one. Monroe didn't request this prohibition. It was ordered by executives in the New York office, as though they already knew that torment and tragedy would stalk this production. Or was it deliberately designed to exile Monroe's natural allies – the ladies and gentlemen of the Hollywood press corps?

The effect was the same. With no one to argue, Twentieth Century-Fox was free to present its own version of what occurred behind the locked doors on soundstage fourteen. Its version was to have a remarkable tenacity.

Monroe's entrance in the bikini recalled the day years earlier when she had undulated onto the set of *Niagara* wearing a tight red dress, tossing her head back in what would become an immortal trademark. Because of censorship standards that insisted that her navel be covered, Jean Louis had fashioned a two-piece swimsuit from triangles of cloth which were full in the middle and narrow at the sides. 'It was *the* most daring swimsuit yet onscreen,' the designer recalled. 'And Monroe, with her new svelte figure, looked sensational in it.'

As on the 1952 set of *Niagara*, wolf whistles rang from the rafters and applause sounded from the sides of the set. The gaffers stood and bowed to Monroe. Planer, an old friend, leaned around his camera and beamed, 'Welcome back, Marilyn.'

'Those whistles made Marilyn's day,' Henry Weinstein remembered. 'She was so insecure about her sex appeal that whenever it was reinforced by one whistle, two whistles, a bunch of whistles, it changed her attitude completely. It reinforced all the work she put into the glamorous image.'

Buoyed by the attention, Monroe postured for the Cinemascope cameras in a rigorous six-hour session. There were six costume changes and seven new hairstyles. Observers noted that the star hadn't displayed so much concentration and poise since *Gentlemen Prefer Blondes* ten years earlier.

Much later, the studio executives claimed she had stumbled through the tests in a drug-induced haze. They also said she had missed her cues and had been unsteady on her feet. Looking at these scenes today, a viewer can plainly see that her performance is flawless. Her eyes look clear, her movements are secure. She was at her best.

Weinstein remembers that he was flushed with triumph when he screened the tests that night. Never had Monroe shown such delicacy. 'In many ways, Marilyn had leaned toward the more obvious kind of sex goddess,' he said. 'I saw she was doing something new here.' Watching Monroe move in the Jean Louis costumes, Weinstein realised that she could now hold her own against Audrey Hepburn, Grace Kelly or Deborah Kerr.

Sheree North looked at the costume tests and was surprised to see that Monroe had finally banished the image of the blonde nymphet. 'The over-sexy tricks of the fifties had been retired,' North said. 'There was a more natural style, but it must have scared the hell out of her to take this step. You could see the beginnings of this transformation in *Bus Stop* but you could also see then that she wasn't comfortable with it yet. Her confidence had increased immeasurably. I couldn't help thinking then and now that this was a very scary thing for Marilyn Monroe to do. Her career had been launched and maintained by that breathless voice and Betty

Boop style. Now it was gone. I was lost in admiration for her bravery.'

Weinstein wasn't aware of the deliberate self-control that had resulted in this incredible change. He only knew that the film was some of the best ever shot of Marilyn Monroe.

'I thought we had it made. I really did,' he recalled. 'We had every reason to feel optimistic.'

Oddly for such an experienced film company, no one at the time gave a thought to the effects of Cukor's refusal to direct these tests. But the first shots of what would be a bitter cinema war had been fired. And not by Marilyn Monroe.

– Chapter 3 –

Warning Signs

Something's Got to Give producer Henry Weinstein was flushed with victory on the morning of April 10.

Overnight, the costume tests had been processed and rushed to the executive screening room, where Philip Feldman, Fox's executive vice-president for studio operations, and Stanley Hough, vice-president and director of production operations, had viewed them enthusiastically.

Feldman described the tests as 'radiant'. And Hough replied, 'We're on our way; keep it up.' Prints of the tests were already on their way to New York, where Fox president Spyros Skouras had scheduled a screening for later that day.

Weinstein could hardly wait to give Monroe the news. She was due at the studio for a luncheon meeting with the producer – who planned to turn it into a celebration.

Since the film had gone into preproduction in January, Weinstein and his star had developed a warm and light-hearted relationship. He was her new 'corporate hero', and the actress liked to tease him about his new status. 'Before you, Henry, it was just me against them,' she would say, referring to the Fox brass.

For a while, they were allies against the impersonal giant

Twentieth Century-Fox.

Monroe would breeze into Weinstein's office in the pro-ducers' building, wearing a cloud of Chanel No. 5 and with her signature black mink slung over one shoulder. She would chat for a few minutes and then dash off. She and Weinstein also shared frequent and soulful telephone conversations, usu-ally late at night.

For reasons that no one really understood, this latest of all Hollywood ladies had never kept Weinstein waiting – at least not for long. She had never bestowed such a sign of respect on anyone, not even Frank Sinatra or Marlon Brando (who were romancing her at the time).

But this morning proved to be different. The studio lim-ousine sent to fetch her returned empty, its driver reporting that the house was dark and that no one responded to repeated knocks at the door.

By early afternoon, Weinstein began to panic. The producer was the only studio executive allowed to call Monroe at her Brentwood house. He waited another hour and then tele-phoned. The private line rang 20 times, but no one answered – not even housekeeper Eunice Murray.

Weinstein's mind raced. The studio had been rife with stories of Monroe's supposed suicide attempts – tales of mid-night ambulance rides and forced hospital stays.

He tried again, this time using an emergency number known to only a handful of people. He felt a rush of relief when Monroe answered on the eleventh ring.

But her voice was foggy and distant. It took several long seconds for her to say 'Hello'.

'Then she began to fade away,' Weinstein recalled. 'I knew immediately that something was wrong, but I didn't know what. I certainly didn't think it was drugs. You have to remember that I was a rather naive kid then and unschooled in the ways of Hollywood.'

Monroe tried to break the connection twice, but Weinstein

soothed and nursed her along. 'Don't worry, I'm coming right over,' he said.

'Uhmmm,' Monroe whispered, 'but there's only one bedroom. If you're going to spend the night, where will you sleep?' Her voice was sounding even more distant.

Weinstein knew he was in trouble. It was broad daylight.

'I'm coming over anyway, Marilyn,' he said.

'Be careful. Be careful,' she said. 'Don't race, Henry, it's raining outside. Promise me you won't get in an accident on the way over here.'

'That really touched me,' Weinstein said, 'because it *was* raining outside. That combination of absolute reality within unreality was very, very touching.'

Weinstein called psychiatrist Ralph Greenson for help and then drove out to the house. 'It seemed to me she was in a drug coma when I got there,' he said.

Weinstein and Greenson found Monroe lying across the bed. Her hair was in disarray and one hand clutched a white satin comforter. Statements about this incident made by one of the psychiatrists who investigated Monroe's death indicated that the star had gulped a combination of Nembutal, Demerol, chloryl hydrate and Librium in a frantic search for sleep. The dose, however, wasn't life-threatening. Monroe had mixed these drugs dozens of times before – usually terrifying those who weren't aware of her exact knowledge of pharmacology. 'She had a clinical awareness of her own tolerance,' said Robert Slatzer.

Monroe's insomnia was usually fuelled by rejection of any kind, and George Cukor's inexplicable refusal to direct the costume tests had undoubtedly reawakened the near-paranoia that always lay just beneath the surface of her psyche. Agonising bouts of sleeplessness usually followed. And Cukor's was a rejection of the worst kind – from a director she had once called the 'best comedy director in the history of Hollywood'.

Greenson had more trouble calming Weinstein than Monroe.

A low-key physician with a soft Viennese accent acquired during years of studying in the Austrian capital, he patted the producer on the shoulder and offered a string of remarks like 'Don't worry' and 'She'll be okay tomorrow.'

Nonetheless, a badly shaken Henry Weinstein drove back to Twentieth Century-Fox. Although the whole episode had taken less than ninety minutes, Weinstein never forgot it. Twenty-nine years later, Fox Entertainment News producer/director Henry Schipper found that Weinstein was still haunted by the experience. 'He was particularly upset about the incident because it followed those exquisite costume and makeup tests,' said Schipper.

Back in his office at the studio, Weinstein saw what was ahead for *Something's Got to Give* and was shattered by it. Monroe wasn't ready for this film. So why force her into it?

He sat down at his typewriter and pounded out the strongest plea for a postponement that he could muster.

'This whole thing frightened me very badly, of course,' he remembered. 'I believed that Monroe was even more unstable than I had been led to believe. I just didn't see how we could go ahead with the picture – that spring. She needed and deserved much more time to rest.' (The actress had filmed two gruelling movies almost back to back: *Let's Make Love* in the winter and part of the spring of 1960, and the stark drama *The Misfits* in Nevada in late 1960 and early 1961.)

Though he knew it wouldn't endear him to the studio, Weinstein filed a series of pleading memos and phone calls with the executive office, seeking a postponement of several months.

To convince Weinstein to plunge ahead with *Something's Got to Give*, Phil Feidman, the operations vice-president who was second-in-command to studio head Levathes, scheduled an emergency meeting of the highest-ranking executives on the West Coast. (Levathes was in Rome working out problems on the set of *Cleopatra*.)

They assembled in the grey-panelled board room just outside Darryl F. Zanuck's former suite. Besides Feldman, the small group included Frank J. Ferguson, the studio's resident counsel and corporation secretary, and Stanley Hough, vice-president and director of production operations. At the last minute, the studio's worldwide director of marketing, E. Charles Einfeld, agreed to sit in.

Feldman ran the show and indicated his bias from the first. 'Miss Monroe has had minor psychological problems since *Gentlemen Prefer Blondes*,' he explained. 'If we had shut down for every minor crisis, none of her films would have been completed.'

Weinstein was passionate, pointing out that he was the one who had discovered Monroe in a 'semicomatose' state. 'All I'm seeking is a postponement, at least until late summer or perhaps early fall.'

Weinstein recalled later, 'They were very condescending. They all told me that I was being very melodramatic.'

One of the executives reiterated, 'No, Henry. Absolutely not. We'll go on.'

Weinstein questioned whether Fox's considerable production insurance (and life insurance on Monroe) would apply, considering the overdose. *Something's Got to Give* had $10 million in production insurance from the Continental Casualty Company of New York, and bodily injury coverage on Marilyn Monroe from Lloyd's of London.

'After a close call like this, could we still collect?' he asked. 'After all, if she had had a heart attack, we would cancel the film immediately. What's the difference?'

Feldman, a Harvard-schooled lawyer, looked Weinstein in the eye. 'Ah, but if Marilyn Monroe had suffered a heart attack, we'd never get the insurance. But, despite this or any other overdose, she's perfectly fit medically.'

Weinstein remembered the behaviour of the executives at the meeting as cold and heartless, particularly in the light of later events. 'If this happened today, I would probably put up a much stronger argument, going to the New York office if I had to. I would also resign. But I was just a kid then, and I thought they had all been through it before. Who was I to argue?' Because he was a greenhorn, the Fox executives paid Weinstein scant attention. He wasn't one of them.

When Henry Weinstein was dispatched to the studio front lines for the Monroe film, he was an earnest and artistic young man who had been transplanted from the New York theatrical world. He had been an intimate of Monroe's husband, Arthur Miller, and had produced Miller's *A View from the Bridge* in one of his own theatres.

He was (and is) a courtly figure with immaculate grooming, impeccable manners and finely tailored suits, which he wore even on the warmest day. When he spoke or wrote, his words had a literary flavour. In a town where the major power brokers wore tight Sy Devore suits and alligator shoes and talked in coarse single-syllable jargon, this introspective producer stood out.

Weinstein had produced only one other film, the Cinemascope version of the F. Scott Fitzgerald novel *Tender Is the Night*. His star in that production was the uncomplicated Jennifer Jones. Industry insiders had shaken their heads when his appointment to *Something's Got to Give* was announced. Most agreed that with the mercurial Marilyn Monroe as star and the temperamental George Cukor as director, the film needed one of the strongest producers on the lot.

In fact, *Something's Got to Give* had started off with just such a man – David Brown, a former magazine editor who had risen under Darryl Zanuck to head the scenario department. An old acquaintance of Monroe's, Brown was the Henry Kissinger of Twentieth Century-Fox. As the Zanuck years wound down and the studio faced stiff competition from television, Brown became adept at matching stars with projects important enough to bring business back to the box offices of Middle America. In the early Cinemascope era, he had unearthed stories for a string of box-office hits including *How to Marry a Millionaire*, *Beneath the Twelve Mile Reef*, *Prince Valiant* and *River of No Return*.

When Zanuck resigned as production chief, citing 'artistic and professional burnout', and moved his production company to Paris, Brown's career waned.

Brown originated *Something's Got to Give* shortly after Levathes took over as production chief in 1961. From the minute he suggested that Monroe remake *My Favourite Wife* as a star vehicle, Brown expected eventually to be removed from the picture. 'They would never have turned a Monroe project, especially a big one, over to one of the old crew,' he said.

Just before the start of production, the axe fell. Richard Zanuck called Brown on the telephone and said, 'Watch out, David. I just saw your script for *Something's Got to Give* in the hands of Henry Weinstein.' The younger Zanuck had stepped into an executive elevator with Weinstein and edged close enough to read the title page of the script he was holding. 'It doesn't look good for you, buddy,' he warned Brown.

Though he expected to be replaced, Brown was amazed that it happened so quickly – and that he was replaced by such a novice. He was determined to find out why. Using his background as a New York journalist, he unearthed the story of this strange selection.

It seemed that Weinstein was appointed on orders from the New York office. The powers there had formed an uneasy alliance with Monroe's psychiatrist, Ralph Greenson, one of the most enigmatic figures in superstar medicine.

Weinstein was just part of a much larger deal that originated on the psychiatrist's couch. Did Monroe authorise this extraordinary deal? It seems unlikely. Later, when her relationship with the studio deteriorated further, she seemed completely mystified about the source of Weinstein's power.

In tracing the history and collapse of *Something's Got to Give* through thousands of documents in the Fox archives, the Spyros Skouras papers, and papers at the British Film Institute in London, the authors have found Greenson's name everywhere. Phone transcriptions detail numerous late-night discussions between the analyst and key studio officials.

Testimony contained in the studio archives and later presented before the Suicide Investigation Team points to Greenson as one of the main architects of the disaster that followed. Throughout the history of the film and even beyond, the analyst remained in contact with studio lawyers, with Weinstein, and even with Theodore Strauss, story editor on the project.

It's now clear that Monroe wouldn't even have started the film if Greenson hadn't persuaded her to make *Something's Got to Give* 'for the sake of her emotional health'.

Her return to Fox, Weinstein's appointment and the timing of the film were all part of a bizarre prescription Greenson had devised for Monroe. 'Greenson told me that, psychologically, Marilyn had to go back to work,' said Strauss. 'He was very serious about it.'

Joan Greenson, the analyst's daughter, believed that her father's real concern 'was to get Marilyn through this one last commitment to Fox so that she could get on with her life and career. This thing was hanging over her head.'

The studio executives didn't really care about Greenson's motives. They intended to get one last film out of Monroe, and if Greenson could help, so much the better.

To Fox, Ralph Greenson was little more than a voice on the telephone. They had no face-to-face meetings. But the psychiatrist's voice was a powerful one.

Greenson was fifty and at the zenith of a brilliant career when Marilyn Monroe stumbled into his life in 1960. He first treated her during the turbulent filming of *Let's Make Love*, when the actress was involved in the incendiary love affair with her French co-star, Yves Montand. Distraught over the course of that brief liaison and feeling guilty over her faithlessness to Arthur Miller, she collapsed in a flood of alcohol and sedatives. Greenson made a rare house call to Bungalow 2 at the Beverly Hills Hotel.

He found her 'dangerously addicted' to barbiturates and to 'immense quantities of scotch whisky and champagne'. Reportedly as a favour to Frank Sinatra, a onetime patient, Greenson sat with Monroe for two hours, holding her hand and coaxing her out of her hysterical state. But his assistance was just an emotional bandage. He urged her to find a permanent psychotherapist as soon as possible. Shaken by what he saw and heard, Greenson later told Fox executives that Monroe was headed for major trouble. And secretly he heaved a sigh of relief that she wasn't his permanent patient. But Monroe was very impressed with the doctor.

Through her fog of pills and alcohol, she felt an instant rapport with Greenson. Although he initially turned her down, she courted him as her primary analyst. His name and private phone number were added to her personal guide of New York and Beverly Hills physicians. Always in search of quick prescriptions, she had compiled a five-page list of willing doctors. The analyst, however, turned down all requests for pills, winning enormous respect from Monroe.

When Sinatra added his recommendation, the actress laid siege to Greenson's office. Finally, and with many misgivings, he took her as a patient.

It was to be a disastrous decision for both.

Trained in Switzerland as well as Vienna, Greenson had impressive credentials. Besides being recommended by Sinatra, his numerous treatises and textbooks had established him as one of the world's foremost experts on psychoanalysis. (He would later write the landmark *Explorations in Psychoanalysis*.)

A year later, the rigours of *The Misfits* delivered Monroe into Greenson's hands again. *The Misfits* offered the star her first dramatic role since *Don't Bother to Knock* eleven years earlier. In twenty-two films she had played variations of Lorelei Lee, the blonde preferred by all gentlemen in *Gentlemen Prefer Blondes*. True, the roles varied from myopic gold digger in *How to Marry a Millionaire* to misguided chanteuse in *Bus Stop*, but all were sex symbols.

In *The Misfits* she was playing the most daunting role of all: herself. Miller had written it for her using lines she herself had spoken. Never before had her peculiar brand of stage fright engulfed her so completely as on *The Misfits*. She sought reassurance in pills. Her acting coach, Paula Strasberg, once found dozens of Seconals crammed into Monroe's mouth in various states of dissolution. Strasberg pulled them out, a fingerful at a time, and immediately recommended a hospital stay. Still later, Monroe overdosed and was revived in a Las Vegas emergency room.

Soon filming on the set couldn't begin before 10 A.M., as Monroe tried to shake off the aftereffects of the drugs. Before long, she never appeared earlier than 1 P.M., and then 4 P.M. Even the studio physicians were powerless to coax her onto the set. 'But the physicians in the *Misfits* company were partly to blame,' said publicist Rupert Allan. 'To help her sleep, they prescribed enormous doses of Seconal, Demerol and Nembutal.' Finally director John Huston realised that barbiturates *were* the problem. He telephoned Greenson and put Monroe on a plane to Los Angeles. The psychiatrist checked her into a suite at the chic Westside Hospital and quickly withdrew her from the barbiturate regimen.

It only took a week. 'Although Marilyn resembled a hard-core addict, she was not the usual addict,' Greenson said later. 'She could stop cold with no physical symptoms of withdrawal.'

She was Greenson's responsibility from then on.

'She called him the miracle worker,' said George Cukor in a 1979 interview. 'He was the only physician I know of who didn't harm her in one way or another. She really listened to him.'

In a letter to Paula Strasberg, Monroe referred to Greenson as 'my saviour; my ally against the whole world.'

By the spring of 1962, Greenson's word was law to Monroe. He told her New York was bad for her. So she fled Manhattan, where she had been reasonably content, and moved to Los Angeles, where she had always been unhappy.

He told her she needed roots – a house, a bit of land. She was busy house-hunting the next morning, eventually purchasing the small Brentwood hacienda that, though much smaller, was very like the Greenson home. (What isn't generally known is that her hideaway became more and more like the home of her mentor during the remodelling process that consumed her in March and April.)

The final ingredient of the Greenson prescription was a housekeeper who would have been at home in a Gothic novel. Eunice Murray's background was as a psychiatric nurse, but in this case, the psychiatrist used her as a spy – one who was to provide regular reports to her real boss, Ralph Greenson. 'Marilyn never knew that Murray was a psychiatric assistant planted in the Brentwood house to watch for warning signs,' said Dr. Robert Litman, who later investigated Monroe's death for the Los Angeles County Coroner.

The psychoanalyst's requests, orders and prescriptions soon extended into every area of Monroe's life, from the men she dated (he advised against any more involvement with Frank Sinatra and former husband Joe DiMaggio) to the movies she made. Greenson even became her de facto agent. In the late winter of 1961, the actress ended her long association with the huge talent agency MCA at the most perilous point in her career; after two resounding box office failures, *Let's Make Love* and *The Misfits*, Marilyn Monroe was without an agent. Greenson and his brother-in-law, attorney Milton Rudin, stepped into the breach.

Perhaps Greenson believed he could ensure better treatment for Monroe by simply providing a physical and emotional buffer between the star and the studio she mistrusted so violently.

When Greenson recommended Henry Weinstein to studio executives as producer of *Something's Got to Give*, he also offered a surprising guarantee. If Brown were replaced by the new young man from New York, Greenson and Weinstein would guarantee that Marilyn Monroe would be punctual and that the shooting would be completed on schedule.

Word of this remarkable deal provided great amusement for the old-timers at Fox. No one had ever been later than Marilyn Monroe. This was a woman who was late to her own first screen test, late to the premiere of *Gentlemen Prefer Blondes*, and so late for her appearance on Jack Benny's television show that she had to be shoved through an opening in the curtain. Marilyn herself told friends that she was 'psychologically incapable of being on time'. So everyone on the lot had a hearty laugh.

Director George Cukor, however, didn't find the situation funny. 'Cukor was furious that Brown was fired,' recalled screenwriter Walter Bernstein. 'He needed the most experienced, most talented producer for that film. And Brown was a good choice. It wasn't going to make any difference whether or not Henry Weinstein, the producer, knew Marilyn's psychiatrist.'

When the director was informed of Weinstein's appointment, he raged at the executive chosen to break the news. 'So you think you can get Marilyn to the set on time? Let me tell you something. If you placed Marilyn's bed on the set and the set were fully lighted, she wouldn't be on time for the first shot!'

Cukor's bungalow was the scene of a stormy session just

seconds after the director had met with Weinstein for the first time. The producer was reportedly going over some minor details when Cukor regally ended the interview. Then, just after Weinstein had closed the door, Cukor picked up a crystal Queen Anne inkwell and hurled it at the door. As the crystal shattered, Cukor cursed. The antique, a gift from Greta Garbo, was irreplaceable.

To this day, Weinstein refuses to believe that his connection with Greenson had anything to do with his appointment. 'I think it had more to do with the fact that I knew Marilyn slightly from New York,' he said.

Cukor's adjutant, associate producer Gene Allen, disagreed. 'We were told that Weinstein's primary job was to get Marilyn Monroe to the set and to get her there on time. We also heard that he was appointed because of his direct connection with Marilyn's psychiatrist.'

Documents in the Fox archives support the idea that Henry Weinstein was appointed on Greenson's orders. Weinstein had been a personal friend of the Greenson family for more than a decade. Greenson and the producer shared a love of chamber music and attended concerts together as often as once a week. The two had met when Weinstein was a Broadway theatre producer.

Weinstein's appointment ruined Monroe's shaky relationship with George Cukor. Cukor became convinced that Monroe had succeeded in having David Brown fired and replaced by Henry Weinstein. His appointment was just another wedge in the cracking foundation of *Something's Got to Give*.

Chapter 4

The Director

When the huge outer doors on Fox's soundstage 14 opened to the sun, the cavernous interior was bathed in a ghastly shade of pink. Inside was a set that would have filled a football stadium – one of the most elaborate indoor sets ever constructed at Twentieth Century-Fox.

It was also one of the most expensive. Built at a cost of $200,000 (by artists working overtime), it was a bizarre monument to the fussy egotism of director George Cukor.

Since Cukor had complained that he simply couldn't get the feel of *Something's Got to Give*, art director and associate producer Gene Allen rebuilt the director's own Mediterranean villa within the walls of the soundstage.

As the bilious pink walls began to rise in February, the set became a private 'must-see' on VIP tours of the lot. As soon as the plasterers were through, the glaziers began, attempting lovingly to duplicate the 17th-century-style casements in Cukor's Sunset Strip hideaway.

Then came the landscapers with rare bushes and succulents of the kinds that grew on the walled grounds of Cukor's mansion. Even the swimming pool, an odd angular affair, had been reproduced, down to the baby-pink beach balls given to Cukor by Vivien Leigh.

Filling every corner of the soundstage, the house reminded screenwriter Walter Bernstein 'of a Barbie-doll mansion grown to proper size'. Fully lit, it was a vision of salmon stone interrupted by slathers of stucco, a decorative trait popular during the Roaring Twenties, when Cukor had emigrated from Broadway to Hollywood.

All around the edges of the set were pockets of darkness. Far above stretched a spiderweb of catwalks and lighting platforms. This tableau was tailor-made for the executive espionage and runaway gossip that would dog *Something's Got to Give*. Unseen onlookers could easily hide in the darkened nooks and caves; a coterie of secretaries and publicists would witness the many struggles and temper tantrums.

The fanciful set was a sure sign that, first and foremost, *Something's Got to Give* was a *George Cukor production*. 'We'll just have to make do with it, honey,' Paula Strasberg told Monroe. 'But just think of the ego behind it.'

'I was confronted with an exact replica, and I mean an exact replica, of George Cukor's house above Sunset Boulevard when I first came to the set of *Something's Got to Give*,' said Walter Bernstein. 'I have always been awed by the miracles that film technicians can achieve. But this was astounding. The first day I arrived, they were painting the trees and the bushes to colour them the precise shade of green [to match] the foliage around the Cukor mansion.'

Fox executives were at a loss to explain this lapse of taste – this set that was ungainly and almost impossible to photograph. To compensate, cinematographers captured the action through a series of vignettes in tight close-up.

But Cukor was an enigma to the executives in any case, as he was to much of the Hollywood establishment. He lived his life according to European standards of opulence.

The morning when Cukor was allegedly too busy to direct Monroe's costume tests, he was actually lying between French silk sheets in a British Regency bed drinking bitter Parisian coffee and reading the *New York Times*. Fluttering about him was a covey of domestics who catered to his every whim. 'Never had I seen a man live in such luxury,' said Bernstein. 'There was an old-world flavour about it.'

The director's sumptuous over decorated estate sprawled across six acres at the top of a narrow, twisting roadway – one of a series of fanciful villas erected during the first flush of the silent era. Jonquils, hyacinths and pink camellias blossomed in a perfumed, terraced garden on the steep hillside. The centrepiece was a turquoise swimming pool surrounded by Italian and Greek statues, potted gardenia bushes and strange, rococo lawn furniture. Garbo swam there, in the nude, as did Tallulah Bankhead and Katharine Hepburn.

The garden would become legendary (notorious might be a better word) for a series of high-toned gay parties to which the director imported stalwart sailors from Long Beach and handsome unattached actors, all attracted by the luxurious hospitality and the chance to snag bit parts in Cukor's films.

The interior of the villa was a jumbled jewel box filled with exotic antiques – dripping with velvet, crystal and mother-of-pearl. A stark contrast to Monroe's homespun bungalow, it symbolised the chasm of screenland social status that separated star and director.

On the morning of the screen test, Cukor's valet stood near the bed with a pad as Cukor dictated his preferences for lunch. Minutes later, the kitchen was abuzz as the cook prepared finger sandwiches, one small slice of pâté and tiny silver bowls of niçoise salad. Soon the meal would be packed in a wicker hamper and deposited in the backseat of a Rolls-Royce.

Cukor's valet was equally busy, setting out a linen shirt, a pair of Savile Row slacks and Italian leather shoes. Finally Cukor roused himself from his regal boudoir, ordered the Rolls and began the hated trip to Fox.

Exhausted and manic from the rigours of starvation dieting* (and with most of his cinematic successes behind him), Cukor, like Monroe, had been forced to make *Something's Got to Give*. Fox had signed him to a two-picture deal when he agreed to direct the lamentable *Let's Make Love*. For two years, the director had tried to duck his responsibilities to the troubled studio.

Then Richard Zanuck offered him *The Chapman Report*, a racy film about sexual researchers and their subjects. Halfway through that project, Spyros Skouras shut it down, claiming that it was 'too suggestive to bear the Twentieth Century-Fox trademark'. After the film was transferred to Warner Brothers, Skouras curtly informed Cukor that he still owed Fox a second film. Shortly after *The Chapman Report* wrapped in 1961, Cukor received a telegram from Skouras informing him that he was to report for *Something's Got to Give* in February 1962. Cukor chose to fight against making another film with Marilyn Monroe, and had his lawyers file letters of protest.

Skouras was furious. After studying the iron-clad contract between the director and Fox, the corporation president wrote to Philip Feldman, executive vice-president for studio operations, 'Cukor will report whenever we want him to, or we can keep him in court for years.'

The director capitulated, but not without expressing his utter contempt for Marilyn Monroe. He even appealed to Darryl F. Zanuck in Paris, hoping the mogul could use his clout with Skouras to free him from *Something's Got to Give*. During *Let's Make Love*, Cukor and Zanuck had corresponded weekly through a series of transcontinental cables in which Zanuck sympathised with the director. 'Marilyn is the

---

*Cukor would lose ten pounds during *Something's Got to Give*, thanks to a terrible regimen that included diet pills, harsh laxatives and debilitating exercises. The side effects included hyperactivity, depression and temper tantrums. The victim of Cukor's mood swings would be Marilyn Monroe.

least professional performer I have ever worked with,' Cukor wrote in one cable to Zanuck. And Zanuck replied, 'Agreed. If I could, I would launch a torpedo from here – aimed directly at her dressing room.'

Cukor's contempt for Monroe was confirmed by screen-writer Nunnally Johnson, who quoted the director as saying, 'I have come to loathe Marilyn Monroe. She is a spoiled, pampered superstar and represents all that is bad about Hollywood today.' Johnson later recalled that he could hear the raw hatred in the director's voice.

Monroe also confided in Johnson, 'Nunnally, I am scared to death of working with him again. You have no idea what he did to me on the set of *Let's Make Love*. He treated me in the worst way.' Johnson's widow, Dorris, said, 'She was so terrified that she once burst into tears when talking to Nunnally about him. My husband was convinced that all the bad things which were to happen resulted from this animosity generated by Cukor.'

Both star and director were trapped in the movie neither wanted to make.

This effeminate man from Hollywood's golden era, whose setside manner could frequently become shrill and dictatorial, was a disastrous choice to direct Monroe at this juncture. On the Hollywood scene since 1929, Cukor had made his mark as a 'woman's director' by piloting a series of hit films for Greta Garbo, Katharine Hepburn and Norma Shearer. His leading ladies coddled and lionised him, attending his teas and bringing him bibelots for the curio closets that filled his house. And he repaid them in kind on the set. He paid no end of attention to costumes and makeup, and was always indulgent of 'girl talk'.

His best work was done with these strong women. As a young man excited by the advent of talking pictures, Cukor had made some of the finest movies of the thirties: *A Bill of Divorcement* and *Little Women* for RKO, and *Camille*, *Dinner at Eight* and *Romeo and Juliet* for MGM.

The only thing that held back Cukor's career was his homosexuality. It prevented him from directing macho stars such as Gable, Gary Cooper and Errol Flynn. He was the only openly gay director during Hollywood's golden age. When rumours of his alleged affairs with Somerset Maugham and Christopher Isherwood surfaced, the homophobic Louis B. Mayer, Cukor's boss at MGM, called him on the carpet.

'Are you queer?' Mayer asked.

'Yes,' answered Cukor, matching the mogul stare for stare. 'But that never interferes with my work. Ask Barrymore. Or Leslie Howard. Ask any of the men who've worked for me. I'm completely fair.'

For once Mayer backed down. He had almost universally weeded out all the homosexuals on his lot. Many had been forced to date glamorous female stars for the sake of image. Some, like matinee idol Billy Haines, quit rather than indulge in such pretence.

On one shadowy weekend in the late thirties, Cukor himself was arrested during an incident involving a brawl with sailors. 'It was crucial that the arrest be squelched at the highest possible executive level,' said Cukor's biographer, Patrick McGilligan. According to Cukor's friend Joseph Mankiewicz, he was called before the brass at MGM (possibly for a second grilling by Mayer) and ordered to be more discreet in his private life.

Monroe was fascinated with the rumours which swirled around the director's private life and even angled for invitations to his fabled pool parties – the soirées that had so intrigued Greta Garbo and Vivien Leigh. But Cukor made a point of excluding her.

'She couldn't understand it. He even invited Yves Montand when they were filming *Let's Make Love*,' remembered publicist Rupert Allan. But he didn't invite her. 'She considered it an affront. But I think he was the worst possible director for her at this time – with his artsy, fancified approach to film-making. But Fox forced him on her nonetheless.'

Cukor's avowed sexual preference affected his career only once. But that one time was enough for a lifetime. Chosen by his friend David O. Selznick to direct *Gone With the Wind*, Cukor lasted only ten days. Annoyed with the constant chatter among Cukor, Vivien Leigh and Olivia de Havilland, MGM publicity director Howard Stricking remembered, Clark Gable stalked off the set in a rage claiming that 'George is giving all the scenes to his little girlfriends, Vivien and Olivia. He goes or I go.'

It's possible that Gable used much stronger words. Screenwriter Frances Marion said that Gable stalked into the office of Louis B. Mayer, confronted Mayer and Selznick and said, 'The little fag goes or I go.' In any event, Cukor was replaced the next day by Victor Fleming, one of Gable's hunting and fishing buddies.

In the long run, Cukor's loss of *Gone With the Wind* was only a dropped stitch in an illustrious tapestry that would weave in *The Philadelphia Story*; Judy Garland's *A Star Is Born*; *Adam's Rib* and *The Marrying Kind*.

After the difficult *A Star Is Born*, Cukor suffered a prolonged career drought in which each succeeding film was worse than the last until the worst of all, *Let's Make Love*. In that same year Cukor and his friend, screenwriter Walter Bernstein, shared the disaster of *Heller in Pink Tights*, a Sophia Loren costume vehicle that was grounded at the box office.

As *Something's Got to Give* was getting underway, rumour had it that Cukor had already been secretly offered *My Fair Lady*, then the most successful Broadway musical in history. But before he could take it, he had to satisfy his obligation to Fox.

Humbled by Fox, Cukor was a vengeful man when he reported to the lot a month later.

Adding insult to injury, he was technically an employee of Marilyn Monroe Productions. His position left him very little room in which to manoeuvre. He fought back by demanding all the perquisites of an old-time star director. With a wave of his hand, studio art directors were bidden to turn his office into a symphony of rich fabrics, thick carpets, antique furniture and specially carved panelling.

'He was assigned to a decaying bungalow, so he ranted and raved until the place was completely restored,' said David Brown, who was amazed at all the commotion. 'George,' Brown asked the director, 'why are you worried about draperies with all the trouble that's likely to come in regard to *Something's Got to Give*?'

Cukor smiled. 'If there's one thing I've learned in this business, it is that you ask for everything in the first five minutes. Because later, nobody will answer your telephone calls.'

Brown noted that Cukor got everything he wanted and 'quite a bit more'.

Many of Cukor's colleagues were amazed that the director would accept this assignment for any reason. 'George had pretty well had it with Marilyn by that time,' recalled actor Tom Tryon, whom the director would coax into appearing in *Something's Got to Give*. 'I'm surprised that he didn't just take the suspension, that he agreed to do this film under *any* condition.'

But Cukor fought back in a most subtle way. Quickly and quietly, he began rewriting almost every scene of *Something's Got to Give*.

Despite the project's inconsequence (even Monroe could see that it wouldn't be one of her 'great' films), she at least had the satisfaction of having been intimately involved in its creation. And she believed Johnson had done the best possible job of jazzing up a tired plot line.

But several days after the costume tests, Cukor began carving up the Nunnally Johnson script.

Associate producer and art director Gene Allen was on hand when the director slammed the script down on his desk.

'Marilyn has been screwing around with this,' Cukor said furiously. 'You know what I think? I think Marilyn and Nunnally Johnson had secret meetings and *this* script is the result. There are scenes here that Nunnally and I never discussed. This is dishonest – those two sneaking around behind my back.' Cukor raged through his bungalow.

Despite the fact that Nunnally Johnson was one of the most respected screenwriters in Hollywood history, Cukor was convinced that the writer had fallen under Monroe's spell and had carefully tailored the script according to her dictates. 'This script might be good for Marilyn – but it is bad for the movie as a whole. I will not film this,' he roared.

Pressed as he was for time, Cukor halted production on *Something's Got to Give* four days after the tests and ordered a complete rewrite.

Henry Weinstein was summoned into the director's presence and told that a new writer, a New York intellectual named Walter Bernstein, had been given instructions to produce a revised script.

Weinstein panicked. Production was ready to go. Both Monroe and Dean Martin had cleared their schedules to start principal photography on April 14.

'Marilyn loves this script,' the producer protested. 'And I like it as well.'

Cukor looked him in the eye. 'But you don't have to direct it; I do. And parts of it simply don't work.'

Weinstein had to concede. Cukor's contract gave him full control over the final screenplay. So began a war of words between Monroe and Cukor, a battle over syllables, phrases and endearments that would eventually doom the production and taint the studio. It would be fought in the living room of Monroe's Brentwood home; it would be fought through the night in Cukor's office; and it would be fought on soundstage 14 – in full view of the cast and crew. Before it was over the actress would have learned three complete versions of the script, and the story costs alone would have reached $400,000.

Monroe would fight using whispers to production chief Peter G. Levathes and messages borne by acting coach Paula Strasberg. Cukor would fight using the voice of thirty years' experience and the adroit phrases of his imported wordsmith, Walter Bernstein.

Monroe would be the principal loser. She hadn't the fire-power to win. When Cukor announced cavalierly on the eve of filming that he was going to pillage the Johnson script, Monroe and her lawyers girded for battle. But they soon discovered a flaw in her contract: she didn't have 'script approval'. In writing all the artfully worded guarantees of casting and costumes, of hairdressers and dressing rooms, some of the best legal minds in Hollywood had forgotten about those words. The verdict was clear: Monroe would say what Cukor wanted her to say.

Thus ended the first collaboration of sorts between a screenwriter and Marilyn Monroe. She hadn't even had a voice in *The Misfits*. For reasons he never explained, Nunnally Johnson, who had written *The Three Faces of Eve* and *The Keys of the Kingdom*, had decided to give the actress a voice in the creation of *Something's Got to Give*. Perhaps he meant it as a gesture of chivalry toward a lady in distress. When Monroe met with him early in 1962, she grasped his hand and said, 'Oh no, I see they have trapped you into this as well.'

The screenwriter was genuinely touched. 'No, I haven't been trapped in the least. I think this was a good story when it was made before. I was offered fully half a dozen other things to do and I selected this, Marilyn.'

Monroe's eyes widened. Johnson had stirred her interest. 'But tell me,' she said, burrowing farther into the folds of her black mink, 'why do you like it? Why should I do it?'

Softly, with his cultured Southern drawl, Johnson began selling her on his vision for *Something's Got to Give*. They sat at a centre table in the fabled Polo Lounge in the Beverly

Hills Hotel, which was, as usual, a swirl of celebrities. As Tony Curtis, Charlton Heston and Zsa Zsa Gabor ordered lunch at their own tables, Monroe and Johnson drifted through three bottles of Dom Pérignon, lost in the story of Ellen Arden and her return from a south sea island.

'Nunnally told her she'd be wonderful in it,' remembered his widow, Dorris. 'After they had worked together a few weeks and they were comfortable and stimulating to each other, she would make suggestions and he would usually approve of them. She soon became as excited as he.'

Johnson's daughter Nora recalled that her father 'was particularly impressed with Marilyn's suggestions about character. Dad told me they showed a growing self-confidence Marilyn had never displayed before.'

Towards the end of the brief collaboration, Monroe delivered a preliminary draft of the script to Dean Martin. When he told her it was 'first-rate', there was a look of triumph on her face.

'When Dean said it was great, Marilyn was really soaring,' Johnson said later. 'When I had first met with her she had been so wary and suspicious of everybody. When I left she was really soaring, happier than I'd ever seen her.'

Monroe was so happy, in fact, that she provided Johnson with a spectacular sendoff. 'What time are you leaving?' she asked on the eve of his return to London.

'Eight-thirty A.M.,' he answered, 'too early for you.'

'You'd be surprised,' said Marilyn, smiling.

And at 8:25 the next morning, the actress offered Johnson a rare gift – punctuality.

The desk clerk, however, interfered. 'They won't let me up,' Marilyn whispered on the house phone at a Beverly Hills hotel.

Johnson chuckled. 'Tell them you're a hooker and that you're here because I sent for you.'

A moment later she returned to the phone. 'It worked. I'll be right up.'

'Nunnally opened the door and found her standing there with no makeup at all on her face,' said Dorris Johnson. 'He told me that she looked like a beautiful child. It had taken ten years off her age.'

The drive to Los Angeles International Airport passed quickly, with Marilyn chattering gaily about the completed script. 'I have rarely spent a happier time with any woman,' Johnson wrote to an understanding Dorris. 'She was quick. She was gay. She probed certain aspects of the story with the sharpest of perceptions. But,' he added, 'she confessed she was terrified of the director.'

When the limousine reached the British Airways gate, both Monroe and Johnson realised that they hadn't touched the champagne – so lost had they been in conversation. As the screenwriter kissed the actress good-bye, he decided not to tell her the bad news. The day before, producer Henry Weinstein had called Johnson to say, 'George wants a writer on the set. You know, just for the little things.'

Johnson issued a warning. 'You can do what you want, Mr. Weinstein,' he said. 'But if you give a director a writer on the set, no matter what he tells you, you've lost your picture.' Johnson noticed that Weinstein looked frightened, but helpless.

'The minute the wheels of my plane left the ground, George had another writer changing my stuff,' Johnson said. 'Henry just didn't have the strength. When the new pages started coming in, it was like hitting Marilyn over the head with a hammer. To her it was the ultimate betrayal.'

'Actresses like Marilyn think the director is God,' Johnson told his daughter. 'These changes shook Marilyn up so badly she couldn't even get out of bed. She was terrified.'

Allen, a protégé and confidant of the director, explained that Cukor had become obsessed with the secret meetings between Johnson and Monroe. 'Cukor felt Johnson was betraying him.'

'He had a sense that this was a big star getting her way,'

said Bernstein. 'Cukor liked the original script for *My Favourite Wife*. I was brought in to restore that flavour.'

By any yardstick, Bernstein seemed an odd choice to produce witticisms for Monroe's effervescent style of comedy. An over-serious, frenetic man, he had written four cinematic failures in a row before he was imported by George Cukor for this project. These disappointments, *That Kind of Woman*, *Heller in Pink Tights*, *A Breath of Scandal*, and *Paris Blues*, were also his four main screen credits. Blackballed by the industry in the wake of the House Un-American Activities Committee hearings, Bernstein had been unable to work from 1948 through 1958. During the banishment, he had written a series of dramas for live television shows such as *Danger*, *Philco Playhouse* and *Studio One*.

The day Bernstein arrived, Weinstein called a meeting with Cukor, Allen and the new screenwriter. 'Weinstein's face shone with a kind of eager worry,' Bernstein recalled. 'He was very, very anxious that I not make too many changes in the script.' Pacing nervously about Cukor's bungalow, Weinstein announced, 'The script doesn't need much work. Just a bit of polishing here and there, don't you agree?' Neither Cukor nor Bernstein said a word.

After Weinstein rushed out for an executive meeting, Cukor leaned toward Bernstein. 'Nonsense. This script needs to be taken apart, line by line. I would like to restore as much of the *My Favourite Wife* script as possible. We don't have time for a detailed rewrite, but we can do the best we can.'

Unknown to Fox, Cukor had quite an emotional stake in the *My Favourite Wife* script. It had been partially written by the director's closest friend in the industry, Garson Kanin – who had also directed the Cary Grant–Irene Dunne version. (The other writers on the earlier film were Sam and Bella Spewack and Leo McCarey.)

So, Bernstein was dispatched to the film library to screen the earlier film and then to restore as much of the 1939 flavour as possible. 'I was charmed by the original film,' he admitted.

Word reached Monroe the next day, and she was gripped by panic. She felt with some justification that Cukor was out to sabotage her. She also felt that the restoration of the *My Favourite Wife* script was dangerous. Since that project had been written specifically for Irene Dunne (a Cukor favourite), comparisons were inevitable. Monroe wanted to avoid them at all costs. To do so, she would have to fight word by word with Cukor and Bernstein in the coming weeks.

Bernstein had been rewriting for several days when studio production manager Peter Levathes, who was also a lawyer, learned of the drastic revisions. When he demanded to see the pages, he was amazed at the extent of the rewrite. Weinstein was immediately called on the carpet. 'Quit hacking up the screenplay,' Levathes said, 'and tell Mr. Bernstein he was hired to polish, not to disembowel!'

With that warning, Levathes became the man in the middle – trapped in a bitter duel between George Cukor and Marilyn Monroe.

Peter G. Levathes, fifty and fresh from a stellar career as founder and president of Fox Television, had the ill luck to inherit *Something's Got to Give*, *Cleopatra*, Elizabeth Taylor and Marilyn Monroe when he was promoted to production chief six months earlier. Neither his law degree nor his six years as Spyros Skouras's assistant had prepared him for the combat already underway on the set of *Something's Got to Give*.

When he took over from departing studio chief Robert Goldstein, Levathes met Marilyn and her attorney, Milton Rudin, for lunch at the Polo Lounge and came away with stars in his eyes. 'I admit I saw her as that glamorous character from *The Seven Year Itch*,' he said. 'I didn't see beyond the surface.' That was the general idea. The actress had trotted out her glamour treatment, complete with black mink, clinging Pucci dress and breathless voice.

Bernstein remembered that 'Levathes sometimes carried

Monroe's orders to Cukor. Levathes, who had the studio's face to save, offered them as suggestions of his own.'

Cukor erupted in fury. 'I would not care if they said the only way to make this picture was to lie down and let Marilyn Monroe walk all over us. At least that would be honest. But this way! The lying! The indecency!'

His accusations may merely have been another sign of Cukor's growing paranoia. Levathes today remembers passing along only his own recommendations, never Monroe's. 'As far as I know, she passed along her own requests through Henry Weinstein.'

Evidence that Monroe fought her own battles with some skill also comes from Bernstein, who had at least two face-to-face meetings with the actress, including a rare one at her house. Not long after Cukor ordered the rewrite, probably around April 19, the New York screenwriter was asked to the house on Fifth Helena Drive. The invitation came by phone and intimated that the actress was willing to work as closely with Bernstein as she had with Nunnally Johnson.

Having written three films for Sophia Loren, Bernstein wasn't shy of stars. But he was more than a little curious about Monroe. And he was shocked when she greeted him at the door completely devoid of movie-star trappings. 'She wasn't trying to put on any airs for me,' he said. 'I was just a screenwriter. She wasn't going to dress up for just a writer.'

Monroe greeted Bernstein at the door in dark slacks and a simple white cotton blouse. 'Without makeup, she looked refreshingly young,' he recalled. The actress blushed slightly as Bernstein surveyed the empty living room. 'I've ordered truckloads of furniture from Mexico,' she explained. 'But much of it is still being manufactured.'

Bernstein noted that 'there was only one chair, and she insisted that I take it, while she sat on the floor, her script before her on a low, makeshift coffee table.'

Sitting cross-legged on the white carpet with a bright light in her face, Monroe looked fresh and rested. 'She looked like a small-town girl,' Bernstein said, 'or I should say like many small-town girls. There was no attempt to make herself pretty or to use her wiles.' As the discussion of the content of the script began, Bernstein soon encountered the movie star. 'Many of her ideas were very good for her, but not good for the story,' he said. 'But if I hinted at this, her face would go blank for a second, and then she would continue as though I had said nothing at all.'

Monroe showed no shyness as she acted out her part for the screenwriter. She was particularly intent when she tried out her Swedish accent for a peculiar scene in *Something's Got to Give*. Bernstein remarked that she 'sounded like Garbo' and applauded spontaneously.

She actively courted the man who was ruining Nunnally Johnson's script. She served him tea, conducted the Cook's tour of the small hacienda and, later in the evening, brought out Mexican beer and appetisers.

'She was nice to me,' Bernstein said. 'She was perfectly pleasant and darling when I introduced my infant son to her – oohing and aahing.'

But Monroe had been wasting her time. Walter Bernstein came to the house on Fifth Helena Drive a doubter and left unimpressed. 'We discussed nothing that could not have been handled easier at the studio,' he said somewhat bitterly. 'The meeting was pointless, except as a way for Marilyn to reinforce her authority and her star power.'

He recalled that he was 'very conscious of the split between the extremely pleasant, attractive woman and some other entity called Marilyn Monroe. I would suggest something and she would talk about herself in the third person,' Bernstein said. 'She would say, "Oh no, no, no. Marilyn couldn't do that," or "Yes, Marilyn Monroe would do that."'

Thirty years later, Bernstein retained his dark view of the star. 'Her talent was very slight. By that I mean she wasn't an actress like Bette Davis. And power, that was paramount to her. She stood there before the camera knowing that she had all the power of the biggest movie star in the world. I mean, you would kill for something like that!'

Monroe did come to Cukor and Bernstein – once. On Friday, April 13, the star announced, through Weinstein, that she would be at the studio for a script conference originally requested by Cukor. 'Miss Monroe will be here at ten,' announced Weinstein. 'I think we should all try and make it.'

Bernstein and Cukor clocked in at ten, Weinstein at ten-forty-five and Gene Allen at ten-fifty. Monroe sailed in at noon. 'She was breathless and apologetic,' Bernstein remembers. The actress was in disguise – black slacks, flowered shirt, bandanna completely covering her platinum hair and oversized sunglasses. The ruse must have worked to a point, because Bernstein noticed that 'she wasn't at all glamorous, she wasn't even pretty.'

Pacing the room in high-heeled sandals, Monroe read from a list of specific suggestions for the script. Many of them were identical to those she had supplied earlier for Johnson.

Then she made an announcement that alarmed Weinstein. Rolling up the new pages of script Bernstein had just handed her, she said absently, 'I'm on my way to New York to discuss the screenplay with Lee Strasberg.' (The founder and director of the Actors Studio had become a counsellor to Monroe.)

She leaned over and kissed Weinstein on the cheek. 'I've got to oil the pipes, Henry. You know, to tune up my technique.'

Weinstein nodded. But he kept to himself his strong reservations about Strasberg and his school of Method acting, which forced a performer to look within himself or herself for help in understanding the character he or she was playing. Cukor had already warned the producer of the influence (he called it 'the infernal meddling') of the Strasbergs on the set of *Let's Make Love* and, before that, on the location shoot for Billy Wilder's *Some Like It Hot*.

Monroe's insistence on turning to Strasberg was even less welcome to Cukor than to Weinstein, who had worked with the Strasbergs during his theatrical days in New York. 'I don't know if I can handle them on this set,' he raged to Lee Hanna who was now *Something's Got to Give* production secretary. But he noted that he was particularly wary of Paula Strasberg, who had been Monroe's setside coach since *Bus Stop* in 1956. 'She creates a working hell wherever she appears,' he muttered.

Ever since Monroe had been lured to the Actors Studio by Shelley Winters in 1955, the star had been spellbound by Lee Strasberg, the high priest of Method acting, who was also guru to Marlon Brando, James Dean, Eva Marie Saint, Maureen Stapleton and Eli Wallach.

Sitting next to Winters in a scarf, no makeup, and a Navy surplus coat, Monroe watched a student production of a one-act play featuring Eva Marie Saint – with Lee Strasberg portraying the other characters. 'She was enthralled,' Winters remembered. 'She didn't know that acting could be approached in such a scholarly manner – or that you could *learn* to be a good actor.'

Cheered on by Winters, Monroe timidly asked if she might take lessons. Strasberg whirled around and was taken aback by the movie star before him. At first he was reticent, fearing, he said, that movie acting might have suffocated her natural talents. Nevertheless, he agreed to meet with her for an exploratory session.

What he saw was astounding. 'She was just waiting to be awakened,' he later told producer David L. Wolper. 'After this one session, this movie star realised that she could perfect her craft, and recognised that films might actually be restraining her real talent.'

The Prophet of Method acting, a diminutive figure who had begun as an actor in the twenties, got Monroe started by hosting a series of one-on-one chats before the fireplace in his rambling New York apartment. With the roaring fire lighting Monroe's face, and Strasberg in an easy chair, he asked her to discuss her hopes and dreams for her future.

'Then I told her what I saw inside of her – which was a limitless talent,' Strasberg told columnist Cindy Adams. 'It was almost as if she had been waiting for someone to push a button. And, when it was, a door to her soul opened, and I saw a treasure of gold and jewels inside her.'

Strasberg and Monroe met daily for three months of private sessions. (Later, she would enact scenes from *Anna Christie*, *Golden Boy* and *A Streetcar Named Desire* before packed and enthusiastic audiences at the Actors Studio.)

Monroe embraced the Strasberg school of acting with religious fervour. Soon she was deeply involved with character motivation – even when she was playing such brainless creatures as Sugar Kane in *Some Like It Hot*. 'People said it didn't matter, that all this work didn't show,' said John Huston. 'But look how many levels Marilyn brought to *Some Like It Hot*.'

'Monroe's use of the Method was controversial, and crews on her sets [from *Bus Stop* forward] were deeply divided about its usefulness,' said Dr. Carl Rollyson of the City University of New York, who studied Monroe's career and acting style. 'Some believed that the Method fractured her ego by having her recall past experiences.'

At first, Monroe paid nominal fees for the coaching by Strasberg, but the financial stakes soon rose. Monroe pleaded with him for 'on-set help – someone who can be there when I really need help. It would revolutionise my effectiveness . . . You do it.'

But he suggested that his wife, Paula, a former actress herself, take on the assignment. When he was tied to the Actors Studio, his wife could be there – scene by scene, hour by hour – to nurse Monroe through her most crippling bouts of stage fright.

The actress agreed, and began to form an artistic, emotional and financial bond with the Strasbergs that lasted until her death. At a starting salary of $1,500 per week (for *Bus Stop*), which rose to $3,000 (for *Something's Got to Give*), Paula Strasberg became a fixture on every Monroe set.

'Without Paula, she soon felt she was lost,' Arthur Miller later wrote. 'In effect, Paula was Marilyn's mad mother all over again . . . a fantasy mother who would confirm everything Marilyn wished to hear.'

Monroe blossomed for the camera with a fiery intensity she had never shown before. 'The result of my mother's work is up there on the screen,' said Susan Strasberg. 'Just look at the change in her on *Bus Stop*, *The Prince and the Showgirl*, *Some Like It Hot*, *The Misfits* and *Something's Got to Give*.'

But the improvements came at a price. Paula Strasberg soon usurped the power of Monroe's directors. 'Marilyn quit paying attention to the director on whatever film,' said the actress's lover Robert Slatzer. 'She relied only upon Paula.' (John Huston admitted that he had to deal with Paula Strasberg for most of the scenes in *The Misfits*.)

'Marilyn paid no mind to Cukor during *Let's Make Love*,' said associate producer Gene Allen. 'Marilyn would complete a scene, and then look past George to Paula, who was standing on the sidelines. If Paula shook her head "no", Monroe would insist upon repeating the scene – often again and again until Paula shook her head "yes".'

Soon, 'everybody dreaded her', said makeup artist Whitey Snyder.

When Monroe reported for the costume tests minus Paula Strasberg, a feeling of relief swept through the studio – from the executive offices to the editing rooms. 'People were jubilant,' recalled Thomas Tryon. 'We all thought, "If we can keep the black witch away, this movie might even be great fun."'

Then Cukor began rewriting the script and ordered a postponement. 'It just took an extra ten thousand words and three weeks to doom that film.'

'Monroe was there, ready to film,' said stand-in Evelyn Moriarity. 'Despite her overdose, she was healthy, she was happy with the Nunnally Johnson rewrite. If the camera had turned on time, the disaster might have been avoided.'

Weinstein had a premonition of disaster and pleaded with Monroe to remain in town. 'Stay here,' he said. 'And we'll move as quickly as possible.'

'But Henry,' Monroe chided, 'you don't have a finished script, you haven't cast the children yet, and I've got things to do in New York.'

Weinstein knew that such sudden trips had resulted in illness and disaster on four previous Monroe sets, costing the studios involved hundreds of thousands of dollars. But he couldn't forbid her to go. Her presence wasn't required. And even though Bernstein was working twelve hours a day, not even the opening scene was completed. The first day of filming had to be pushed back to April 23.

'I knew that the slightest change in climate could wreak havoc on her delicate respiratory system,' Weinstein recalled. 'I had a very bad feeling.'

'Don't worry, Henry,' Monroe said as she kissed him on the cheek and dashed out to the limousine.

But Weinstein was correct. When Monroe returned on April 19, she was desperately ill with a viral cold and had Paula Strasberg at her side – a double whammy.

However, even if *Something's Got to Give* had been filming as scheduled, Monroe would have made this weekend trip. The visit to the Actors Studio was merely a cover for a romantic liaison which would drastically affect the future of the film – and of Fox.

– Chapter 5 –

The Prez

Monroe arrived at Los Angeles International Airport just in time to board her direct flight to New York City. Disguised in a tweed car coat, dark glasses, and a babushka designed by William Travilla, she raced onto the plane and settled into a first-class seat. Behind her came Hazel Washington, Monroe's studio maid, carrying a glittering Jean Louis gown over one arm and a ranch-mink evening cape over the other.

Though she fully intended to consult with Lee Strasberg about what Cukor and Bernstein were doing to 'a perfectly fine script', she was actually rushing to Manhattan to attend a command performance for the President of the United States.

Monroe was already a year into her blazing yet remarkably secret love affair with John Fitzgerald Kennedy, and her infatuation was in danger of overwhelming all other personal and professional areas of her life.

'She went east for one of those super-private fund-raisers for the rich and beautiful of Manhattan; a ten-thousand-dollar-a-plate affair,' said her publicity consultant, Rupert Allan, who dined with Monroe in New York on April 14. 'The President had promised his well-heeled supporters that Monroe would attend, and he complied. But she would have jumped at the chance anyway.'

One of Monroe's biographers Fred Lawrence Guiles concurred: 'At this time in her life, when the President beckoned, Marilyn responded.'

But Monroe's appearance at this private political soirée marked a new boldness in her clandestine adventures with JFK. Such close advisers as Dave Powers, a Kennedy aide, Kennedy's brother-in-law Peter Lawford, and Lawford's agent, Milt Ebbins, were charged with making sure Cinderella made it to the ball. Secretly Lawford also arranged for Monroe to share the President's bed at his New York hideaway that same night. 'She slept with him off and on – whenever there was a scrap of time,' recalled Hazel Washington.

Preparation for the black-tie gala required all afternoon and necessitated a parade of cosmeticians in and out of Monroe's 57th Street apartment. First came the masters of facials and rouge (courtesy of Elizabeth Arden), followed by an expert in body makeup (loaned by Marlene Dietrich) and, finally, Kenneth, the town's preeminent hairstylist.

But at 7:30 P.M., when Milt Ebbins arrived to collect her, Monroe was still closeted with her maid. Lawford phoned at 8 P.M. – in a rage. 'She must be here by eight-thirty,' he yelled. 'Dinner is already late because of her.'

Washington served Ebbins a drink and told him, 'It shouldn't be long.'

Lawford called again at nine. 'Where the hell are you?' he thundered. 'The President is furious.'

Ebbins paced about Monroe's white-on-white living room for several more minutes before invading the bedroom.

He found Monroe, still naked, gazing in the mirror while she languidly tried on several pairs of aquamarine earrings.

'Miss Monroe, please! We've got to get out of here.'

Ebbins and Washington, working in tandem, got the star into her beaded gown, into the fur wrap and into the elevator.

'It took fifteen minutes to get it zipped, fastened and straightened,' Ebbins told James Spada, Peter Lawford's biographer. 'But at last we were underway.'

As the limousine approached the gates of the Park Avenue skyscraper that was the scene of the party, Ebbins groaned. More than fifty photographers were milling about the lobby, having been tipped off that Monroe would be one of the celebrity guests. 'What are we going to do?' he asked. Monroe smiled as she put on a pair of sunglasses and carefully positioned a red wig over Kenneth's elaborate hairstyle. Then, taking Ebbins by the arm, she sailed past the unsuspecting newsmen.

Upstairs, Monroe's entrance brought the party to a halt as well-heeled socialites gathered around. 'Dinner was forgotten, and nobody paid any attention to the musical quartet; every eye was on Marilyn,' said Rupert Allan, who was in Manhattan vacationing from his duties as publicist for Princess Grace of Monaco. 'When Marilyn finally moved close to the President and they exchanged a few words, I suddenly realised that she had fallen in love with him. It frightened me, because I knew Marilyn never did anything by halves.'

After the fund-raiser wound down at 4 A.M., a presidential limousine carried Monroe back to the 57th Street apartment, where the chauffeur bid her a courtly goodnight, seeing her to the elevator before departing.

Upstairs, the actress shimmied out of the dress, put on pants and a blouse, and took a cab to the Carlyle Hotel, where JFK had a bachelor pad perched among the trees and shrubs of a roof garden. 'Marilyn soon became intimately familiar with his suite,' recalled Monroe's friend and masseur, Ralph Roberts.

Rupert Allan, anxious to hear about Monroe's growing relationship with President Kennedy, called her apartment repeatedly until about 7 A.M. Later, when he called from the royal palace in Monaco, Monroe filled him in on the rapidly accelerating affair.

The dalliance between the world's most famous film star and the President of the United States, which began with a series of seaside flirtations at the Santa Monica mansion of Peter and Patricia Kennedy Lawford, would soon progress to assignations at the Beverly Hilton Hotel and meetings aboard Air Force One.

After April 15, and perhaps because of her success with the political high rollers at the Park Avenue fund-raiser, Monroe conducted the affair with a new boldness. Where she had once telephoned JFK from the privacy of her bedroom, she now openly called the Oval Office from her crowded bungalow on the Fox lot.

One of the star's most trusted confidants, Fox choreographer Stephen Papich, was at her side one afternoon in late April when she called the President to discuss his upcoming birthday gala at Madison Square Garden. She had dialled the Oval Office and was chatting with JFK's personal secretary, Evelyn Lincoln, when Papich noticed a pout on her face. Monroe laughed and looked at Papich. 'He said he was too busy to talk about it right now. Said he was involved in crucial business.' She winked. 'But, Stephen, as you know, he's never too busy for "you know what".'

When the announcement of Monroe's appearance at the gala was finally splashed across the pages of Hollywood trade papers, many insiders perceived the danger. 'This was deliberately bringing the rumours out into the public,' said screenwriter Nunnally Johnson. 'Many of us felt that her appearance at Madison Square Garden would be like Marilyn making love to the President publicly after doing it privately all these months.'

There were other small indiscretions as well, sedate whispers here and there which could eventually unleash a national scandal and ruin JFK's chances for a second term in 1964. Papich was amazed at the openness of Marilyn's phone calls to the White House from the *Something's Got to Give* dressing room.

'She said quite flatly, "This is Marilyn Monroe, could I please speak to Jack?"' Furthermore, she made these long-distance calls through the Fox switchboard.

Operators who worked there in the summer of 1962 know that there were 'dozens of calls between Marilyn's dressing-room extension and the White House.' The operator who verified this asked for anonymity. According to the same source, Monroe made $66 worth of long-distance calls to the White House and the Justice Department in Washington during the filming of *Something's Got to Give*, an enormous sum at that time.

The telephone, which had always provided a connection between Monroe and the wider world, was now her link with her lover, John F. Kennedy.

'She told me she had a private number to Jack in the Oval Office,' said her friend, actress Terry Moore. 'She was proud and that was a very, very exciting thing for her.'

This line also rang through to John and Jackie Kennedy's private apartments after office hours. 'Frequently, Jackie would answer the phone when Marilyn called the President,' remembered Patricia Seaton Lawford, Peter Lawford's third wife. 'And she was able to talk to Jack – in the presence of Jackie. This shows that Marilyn was more than just a casual sex partner.'

Though Monroe and President Kennedy had allowed themselves open flirtations at the beach house of Kennedy's brother-in-law Peter Lawford, their truly intense relationship began after a breathtakingly beautiful Christmas party hosted in December 1961 by Patricia Kennedy Lawford.

With the First Lady on the East Coast, Monroe and the President eventually slipped away from the living room, with its lighted tree and forest of poinsettias, to the privacy of the largest of the Lawford mansion's fourteen bedroom suites.

After a bubble bath, during which Monroe poured champagne over the President's shoulders, they shared a languid hour in a bed that had once belonged to film magnate Louis B. Mayer, who had originally built the mansion. Later, private detective Fred Otash claimed that his bugs in the Lawford mansion picked up the steamy love scene between politician and movie star during the posh Christmas party. Otash even hinted that 'state secrets were discussed'.

Hollywood was soon humming with 'rare sightings' of 'the President and the showgirl'. Early in 1962, they spent a night at the Beverly Hilton, where they dined on room-service lobster thermidor; they had an after-midnight assignation in a penthouse at the Beverly Hills Hotel; and they trysted on the sands of Santa Monica Beach.

But their most brazen night of love took place during a state visit to Palm Springs two weeks before the *Something's Got to Give* costume tests. After Air Force One dropped the presidential entourage in the desert, it diverted to Los Angeles to pick up brother-in-law Lawford and an amazingly disguised Monroe.

Wearing a brunette wig (a cheap one at that), sunglasses and a severe grey suit from Sears, Roebuck, Monroe even carried a stenographer's pad and a handful of sharpened pencils. 'She called me a day later,' said her friend Ralph Roberts, 'and we joked about it. She said Lawford even made her take dictation just as if she was a real secretary. That particular act burned her up.'

With the Secret Service and several young political aides watching, the disguise was an absolute necessity. But Monroe let Lawford have it when they were safe in the presidential limousine. Although the President was quartered in the sprawling Bing Crosby mansion (which was carefully guarded), he slipped away several times for interludes with Monroe. Several reporters saw them walking arm in arm in the desert sunsets. Another journalist noticed Secret Service agents in the shadows of a nearby bungalow and caught a glimpse of a platinum-blonde woman who occasionally parted the bedroom curtains.

Later, after the formal doings in Crosby's baronial dining room, the President hosted a more exclusive bash in the secluded guest house, hidden from the main house by trees and shrubs. JFK had changed from dinner clothes to khaki pants, a blue turtleneck and penny loafers without socks.

An up-an-coming young Democrat named Philip Watson was one of those favoured, and he sensed immediately that Monroe was the unofficial hostess, though she was seriously underdressed in a white silk robe and Coco Chanel evening pyjamas.

Watson later commented that 'it was obvious that the President and Marilyn Monroe were intimate and that she was there for the night.' This didn't shock him; he had already seen the lovers in the back room of a political affair at the Beverly Hilton. (Watson later was elected Los Angeles County Coroner.)

Still in Palm Springs and still ensconced in bed with the most powerful man in America, Monroe made a quick telephone call to Roberts. 'Ralph,' she said, 'I've got a friend here I want you to talk with. We have been discussing the way I developed my walk. You know, "the Marilyn walk." Anyway, he wants to know the name of the muscles I had to develop in order to achieve this.'

Roberts thought he knew what to expect, but he was a bit tongue-tied when the inimitable Boston voice boomed out, 'Hello, Mr. Roberts. What can you tell me?'

Roberts explained, in great detail, how Monroe had exercised for years to develop muscles in her pelvic region as the foundation for the flowing, undulating walk that so many other starlets had tried to imitate. Roberts was amazed when JFK prolonged the conversation, asking about massage techniques that might alleviate the back pain he had suffered almost constantly since World War II.

'Thank you very much, Mr. Roberts,' said the President of the United States before turning back to Monroe.

After whispering, 'I'll tell you all about it later,' Monroe said goodbye.

Later she kidded Kennedy. 'You know, don't you, that Ralph could give you a far better massage than I can – he's a pro.'

The President grinned. 'Now, that wouldn't be the same, would it?'

'As I understand it,' said Roberts, 'they spent the weekend together.' Several days later, Monroe regaled Roberts with descriptions of the increasing difficulties she and the President had as they tried to elude Secret Service agents. 'It's getting harder and harder every week,' she said.

As the affair continued, the actress conceived a vain hope that President Kennedy would divorce Jackie and somehow make her First Lady of the land. She confided that dream to her friends Robert Slatzer, Stephen Papich, Terry Moore and Ralph Roberts.

'You have to remember that Marilyn worked and lived in a dream world,' said Roberts. 'She began to live her dreams, and her newest dream was to marry Jack Kennedy – and supplant Jackie.'

'Why is President Kennedy married to the statue?' Monroe asked Roberts. 'I bet he doesn't put his hand up her dress like he does mine. In fact I bet no one does. Boy, is she ever stiff.' She also confided later, 'I'm sure their families made them get married. And imagine that, locked into a marriage neither one of them likes. I can tell from being with him myself that he's not in love with her.'

And costume designer William Travilla noticed that Monroe 'became gleeful when she heard that old Joe Kennedy had to pay Jackie a million dollars so that she would continue to live with JFK in the White House'.

As Hollywood dreams go, Monroe's might not have been that farfetched. *Something's Got to Give* associate producer Gene Allen remarked, 'After all, what were the odds of this little girl from nowhere marrying the world's greatest athlete, Joe DiMaggio? But she did it. And what were the chances of her marrying the world's greatest playwright, Arthur Miller? But she did it. Given those successes, maybe she could have become First Lady – if it had all worked out perfectly.'

But first Monroe had to separate herself from the pack of women who continually encircled the President – the beautiful and the famous who threw themselves across his path.

John F. Kennedy's presidency had launched a somewhat pitiful parade of sex, indiscriminate partying and an obsession with alcohol and drugs unparalleled in White House history. As the President amorously courted a starry-eyed Monroe, he was simultaneously intimate in one way or another with dozens of women – known and unknown, plain and beautiful, young and old. His infamous affair with mobster Sam Giancana's girl-friend Judith Campbell Exner was crowded into a hectic 1962, as was an intense relationship with actress Angie Dickinson.

'Her liaison with the President would become the most brutal, destructive relationship she would ever endure,' said Patricia Seaton Lawford of Monroe's affair. 'Marilyn didn't realise that JFK wasn't interested in having sex with Marilyn Monroe, he wanted to have sex with the greatest movie star of the day. She was just a symbol to him. Nothing more.'

'The Kennedys were important to the actress because they represented a stage on which to perform which was even greater than that offered by Hollywood,' said Carl Rollyson. 'The Kennedys added to the high gloss in which she immersed her life.'

The reflected glory from America's First Family was never brighter than during Monroe's week in New York – a respite she owed to Cukor's involvement with the *Something's Got to Give* screenplay.

Before she reluctantly returned to Hollywood on April 19, the actress had several sessions with Lee Strasberg. With his help, she dissected *Something's Got to Give* scene by scene and character by character. By the time these private meetings ended, Monroe's copy of the Nunnally Johnson script was crammed with notes in the margins and at the beginning of each scene. Basically, Strasberg told her which scenes she should fight to retain and which were negligible.

All through the visit, Monroe had been getting reports concerning the new dialogue that was flying out of Walter Bernstein's typewriter. Eunice Murray had made a point of organising all the new pages as they were sent by messenger to the Brentwood house.

What Murray told her convinced Monroe that she needed an ally to fight this skirmish. Over dinner on April 18, she convinced Paula Strasberg to return to Hollywood and, for the fifth time, resume her duties as the star's private coach and director.

Monroe returned to the coast with another gift from Lee Strasberg – a viral cold that would spread to her lungs and sinuses. In spite of Strasberg's warnings that he was sick and his plea that they confer via telephone, Monroe had virtually lived in his New York apartment.

On the way to the airport Monroe told Paula, 'I think I'm coming down with Lee's cold.'

Back in Hollywood, Twentieth Century-Fox was also suffering – from financial ineptitude. Studio executives Stanley Hough and Philip Feldman informed their bosses that there might not be enough ready cash to complete *Something's Got to Give*, *Cleopatra* and Darryl F. Zanuck's epic about the Normandy landings of World War II, *The Longest Day*. Now the studio's future hinged on the actress's fragile health.

– Chapter 6 –

A Very Sick Girl

Monroe shivered beneath her white satin comforter for hours before she finally stopped fighting the pain – and the insomnia. When she reached across the coverlet to switch on a lamp, she realised that her bed was soaked with perspiration. 'Dripping wet', as Eunice Murray would later describe it.

Monroe had been racked alternately with chills and fever since 11 P.M. – about the same time that her Nembutal sleeping capsule wore off. Because a storm had swept across the coastal foothills, the Brentwood house was damp and draughty.

Although Murray was in the house, Monroe lacked the strength to cross the long hall which led to the housekeeper's bedroom.

It was 3:30 A.M. on Saturday, April 20, a day after the star returned from New York and fifty hours before *Something's Got to Give* was finally to begin filming.

'At first, she refused to accept the fact that she was really sick,' Murray later told Hedda Hopper. 'She wanted that film to get over with so badly that she felt she could ward off the cold.'

But now, virtually unable to leave her bed, Monroe reached for the phone and called Henry Weinstein – who would soon bear the responsibility of convincing studio executives that she was not merely feigning illness, as she had done several times in the past.

Now sound asleep in his comfortable duplex in Beverly Hills, seven miles from Brentwood, Weinstein had been looking forward to his first free weekend since he took over as producer of the already troubled motion picture.

He knew it was Monroe before he picked up the phone, remarking later that 'it was one of those calls which you know will come. The only question was when.'

Monroe offered no apology for calling at such an early hour, but instead launched into a catalogue of symptoms: a rasping cough, violent headaches which caused blurred vision, and laryngitis. 'I wanted to tell you as early as possible,' she whispered. 'I'm not going to be on the set this Monday.'

As she rambled on about her exhaustion, Weinstein was reminded of her recent overdose; she sounded no better that morning.

The producer felt both sympathy and panic – sympathy because she sounded truly ill, and panic because of the consequences of shutting down a film on its first day. The huge studio had just awakened from slumber to pour its life blood into *Something's Got to Give*. After four months of little activity on the lot, the cameras of Twentieth Century-Fox were ready to roll again. And now the film's star – who was in almost every scene – was all but guaranteeing that she would be a no-show.

For days, crews had been working overtime to finish the replica of Cukor's house for the Monday start. On the previous Wednesday, a seam in the swimming pool had burst, flooding the soundstage. Workmen had barely enough time to drain the fibreglass tank, patch it and refill it with the special blue-tinted water Cukor had demanded.

High above on the web of scaffolding, electricians were installing seven amber spotlights and nine blue ones. Technicolor tests had shown the set to be inadequately lit. Though the house and all its grounds would be shot *inside* the vast soundstage, the lighting technicians had to create an illusion of bright sunlight.

Four miles away, in the Beverly Hills workshop of designer Jean Louis, seamstresses were altering the floral print gown that Monroe would wear in the first scenes. Fitter Elizabeth Courtney· had even pitched in to hem, worried that the dress and matching coat wouldn't be finished by Monday morning.

Late Friday, when Paula Strasberg had flown in from New York, the entire cast and crew had been primed to go.

As with any Marilyn Monroe film, the film crew felt a vague uneasiness. 'We were waiting for that second shoe to drop. It always did,' said Monroe stand-in, Evelyn Moriarity. 'There was the usual tension and jitters.'

Now, with that telephone call in the predawn darkness, the shoe had dropped. After Monroe had flown to New York ten days earlier, the studio executives had held their breaths. Her respiratory system was notoriously frail – as frail as Elizabeth Taylor's, and Taylor's illness had already cost a seven-month delay on *Cleopatra*. The price tag for Taylor's bouts of pneumonia and bronchitis was to reach $8 million – the cost of the aborted London version of *Cleopatra*.

In Monroe's case, colds and throat problems had caused costly delays on *Some Like It Hot*, *Let's Make Love* and *The Misfits*. So Weinstein listened with growing alarm as Monroe talked of her cold and of how it had aggravated her already pronounced insomnia. He consoled her as best he could and suggested they talk again later that day.

Hanging up the phone, Weinstein knew that Monroe had better be pretty damned ill if she was going to convince Fox executives to delay the start of this film. He talked to her again at 4 P.M. and she sounded much worse. Two more predawn phone calls followed on Sunday morning.

Finally, Eunice Murray called Weinstein on Sunday afternoon to explain, 'Marilyn cannot make it tomorrow.'

'In your opinion, how ill is she?' Weinstein asked.

'Ill enough to stay out all week.' Murray further described her charge as 'too weak to get out of bed, and troubled by severe headaches and a high fever'.

On Sunday at 2 P.M., Monroe's temperature was 101 degrees and a bed was reserved at Cedars of Lebanon Hospital.

Her internist called Weinstein as well. The producer unhappily accepted the diagnosis. As he made the required calls – to Cukor, Levathes and Dean Martin – he had the uneasy feeling that *Something's Got to Give*, already crippled by the bitter dispute between director and star, might be finished off by a virus.

At the Brentwood house, a parade of doctors was well underway. After her return from New York three days earlier, Monroe had complained of 'unbearable pain behind my eyes'. The chills had begun by Friday night. As Murray piled blanket after blanket on top of her, Hyman Engleberg, her primary doctor, rendered a preliminary diagnosis of 'sinusitis'.

Tests at Cedars of Lebanon Hospital the next day confirmed that opinion. An acute viral cold had developed into a massive sinus infection as a residue of streptococcus bacteria invaded Monroe's sinus passages. She suffered high fevers and dizziness, unbearable headaches and lethargy. The tests also showed that she had contracted the most severe form of the disease, 'chronic sinusitis', which usually required a month of massive antibiotic treatment to cure.

On Sunday afternoon, studio doctor Lee Siegel arrived to formulate his own opinion. New York executives were always sceptical of rulings by the private medical community. Until the studio medic examined her, Monroe's illness simply didn't exist. Siegel, a tall, handsome man with a suave bedside manner, had been treating the actress since 1951.

It was Siegel who recorded her temperature at 101, described the condition of her respiratory tract as 'badly occluded' and noted that she had a 'nasty secondary infection in her throat'.

'It will take weeks to cure this infection,' he wrote in an official memorandum. Along with a corporate physician, he drafted a confidential telegram to the head office in New York, recommending that *Something's Got to Give* be postponed for at least a month. 'If this doesn't happen,' Siegel said, 'the film could eventually collapse under the weight of Marilyn's illness.'

Eunice Murray told Siegel of headaches that 'were so severe that they were disabling'. Murray recalled that 'Marilyn woke up each morning at 3 A.M. with the headache and a bad fever. Each day she tried to go in, but wasn't able to make it.' Studio logs would show that Monroe called for the Fox limousine four times during the first seven days of her illness. On one of those days, chauffeur Rudy Kautsky was told that she had passed out in the bathtub. 'She knew she was sick, but was still guilty about not going in,' said masseur Ralph Roberts.

At Fox, the mood was grim. On soundstage 14, where 104 crew members were ready to roll, there was a doomsday atmosphere. Screenwriter Bernstein noted a mixture of anger, panic and concern. 'Henry Weinstein was pacing around the pool, looking ready to jump in,' he said. 'There was no joking. Now that the production had actually begun, jokes were dangerous.'

'Marilyn's going to be out all damned week,' predicted Buck Hall, the assistant director and an avowed enemy of Monroe. 'Then she might try to come in next week. But she'll go right home and be out all that week. Then maybe, just maybe, she'll come to work on the third week.'

When Hall's story got around, nobody listened as intently as the studio executives. A mood of panic pervaded the Darryl F. Zanuck Building. 'Everyone knew that unless Marilyn felt in perfect condition, she wouldn't shoot,' said Weinstein. 'We were now at the mercy of all these doctors.'

As it happened, Buck Hall was right. Monroe remained in

her sickbed for two full weeks. She tried to come in the second week, but fainted under a hair dryer and was summarily packed off to bed.

The accuracy of Hall's prediction only fuelled the belief that Monroe was malingering. A flurry of memos between the teams of studio doctors and the sceptical executives speculated on the precise nature of the star's ailment. They included catalogues of her temperatures, detailed analyses of symptoms and a careful medical description of chronic sinusitis as 'the most severe of all respiratory ailments'. Fox president Spyros Skouras preserved a series of plaintive messages from Dr. Siegel as he tried valiantly to convince the board of directors that Monroe was really ill.

'My husband was crushed that they didn't believe him,' said Noreen Nash Siegel, the studio doctor's widow. 'He would never have made up a diagnosis for anyone, not even Marilyn Monroe. He felt that she was very, very ill. And in hindsight, it's unfortunate that they didn't believe him.'

As 'Marilyn memos' flew, the body temperature of Marilyn Monroe became more important to the corporation than the price of its stock. Interestingly, stock prices actually shot up and down as medical bulletins from Hollywood reached the media.

'I called three of Marilyn's doctors at 7 A.M. each morning,' said Weinstein. 'I took down all the symptoms and the various opinions and then reported on this to Fox. There was the nose and throat man, the internist and even the ophthalmologist, since Marilyn also suffered from a major eye infection.'

For the first time in his career, studio doctor Lee Siegel became an integral part of the production staff of a major motion picture, a key player in many of the decisions made involving Monroe. He was invited to attend staff meetings and to consult daily with Fox vice-president Philip Feldman. Siegel was also a major link to Monroe's physicians, Greenson and Hyman Engleberg.

A studio physician since the forties, Siegel enjoyed his new status for about a day or so, until he realised that the Fox leadership intended to force Monroe onto the set – healthy or not. 'They were only interested in finishing that film, and in finishing it quickly,' Siegel recalled for writer Maurice Zolotow. 'Their attitude seemed to be: "Let Marilyn collapse after we finish." They were aware it was her last film for them, in any case.'

As the only member of the executive corps to understand the seriousness of the star's sinus infection, Siegel found few allies.

Just as Weinstein had done three weeks earlier, the studio physician pleaded for a postponement. 'If we give Marilyn a few weeks to lick this sinus infection, then the movie can proceed without a hitch,' he told Feldman. Noreen, who had known Monroe since her starlet days, recalled 'He also tried to convince Fox to allow Monroe to shoot later in the day – from noon until eight P.M., as they do in Europe.' In a memo to Feldman, Siegel pointed out that 'they film in the afternoon in France and Italy with no problems at all. Most workers are glad to honour this system.'

Noreen Siegel noted that the studio angrily refused to even consider the plan. 'Somebody told him, "This is America; Monroe will work a normal workday."' Ironically, the studio was allowing Elizabeth Taylor to work from 11 A.M. to 7 P.M. on the set of *Cleopatra* in Rome.

Instead, executives (many believe it was Philip Feldman) pressed Siegel and a subordinate to treat Monroe with a course of drugs – mostly pep pills – so that she could work despite her illness. This treatment, which began on April 23, would ravage the star's resistance, exacerbate her insomnia and camouflage the symptoms of her worsening sinus infection.

Siegel was told to begin a twice-daily regimen of injections – referred to in studio jargon as 'hot shots' – while Monroe was still recuperating at home. He also made daily visits to gauge her temperature for insurance purposes.

The tradition of providing drugs to stars and directors stretched back to the early silent era, when stars such as Mary Pickford, Clara Bow and Rudolph Valentino worked as many as eighteen hours a day. Studio doctors handed out pills for all occasions: hypnotic drugs for sleep, barbiturates to ease nervous tension, morphine derivatives for pain and amphetamines for exhaustion and weight problems.

The administration of 'hot shots' to Monroe would be counterproductive in the end – by increasing the severity of her insomnia and reducing her ability to fight the massive sinus infection – ironically Cukor received these injections as well.

There is no record as to the strength of the injections given to Monroe or their precise chemical composition. But those who were present on the *Something's Got to Give* set described the jolts of energy that occurred shortly after they were administered.

'Marilyn would be standing at the edge of the set, listless and lifeless,' recalled editor David Bretherton. 'Not long afterward, Monroe would be ready to go – visibly energised.'

The effect of those injections on Cukor was almost manic. 'You could see the energy level increase before your eyes,' recalled costume designer Travilla. But he was dieting too strenuously to work without them.

Publicist Rupert Allan, who had seen Monroe receiving similar injections on the set of *The Misfits*, asked the doctor about the composition of the drugs. 'He said they contained methamphetamines, a few vitamins, glucose to give an immediate lift, and a small amount of Librium to smooth out the effect of the uppers.'

Naturally, these chemical administrations fascinated the cast and crew of *Something's Got to Give*. One afternoon, when

Evelyn Moriarity was feeling tired, she asked Siegel for one of the shots he had just administered to Cukor. 'He answered, "Honey, you don't need any of this dope,"' she recalled.

Most Fox executives were probably unaware of the dangers inherent in such regular use of speed. Their physicians had been pumping drugs into studio stars for decades. In the thirties, Tyrone Power took amphetamines by the handful so that he could fit into his tight cavalry uniform for *The Mark of Zorro*. For days, his diet consisted of two eight-ounce steaks, a green salad, four Benzedrine spansules and two phenobarbital tablets for sleep – all supplied by the studio doctor.

Several years later, when Betty Grable was too heavy for the hourglass gowns in *The Shocking Miss Pilgrim*, studio doctors handed her two envelopes of pills. In the morning she took the green ones, and at night the dark red ones. 'God only knows what they were,' said William Travilla, a friend of Grable's.

During the golden era, studio contract stars were *expected* to take drugs. By the time Monroe had become a major star, pill-taking was the vogue. The entire Hollywood studio system was awash with drugs. In those days before stringent government control, cast members wafted through eighteen-hour days on waves of methamphetamines, codeine and morphine – often laced with vitamins and glucose.

The important drug was methamphetamine, the man-made chemical that kept everyone working far beyond normal tolerance. It gave a rush just at the right time. It pepped up musical numbers and, if mixed properly, lasted through endless retakes.

Everyone in a key position on a set could get a 'Fox hot shot' – sometimes without even asking. 'Marilyn took these shots, I took them, we all did,' recalled Sheree North. 'When you came to the set in the morning, the doctor would ask, "How do you feel?" If you said, "Groggy", he gave you a shot. It was an upper. And, wow, you'd be real wide awake in just a matter of minutes.'

On the 1956 musical *How to Be Very, Very Popular*, North took the shots and received bottles of Benzedrine for the afternoons and Nembutal capsules for sleep. 'In those days we didn't know sleeping pills were bad for you,' she said. 'We only knew that the studio doctor gave them to you. I became addicted. As did Marilyn. You never questioned it. The words "side effects" didn't exist.'

Monroe's studio drug habit had begun on the set of *River of No Return* in 1954, when she suffered from mild exposure and exhaustion during location filming in Montana. The company doctor prescribed Nembutal for sleep, Demerol for pain and the so-called 'vitamin shots' for energy.

Once introduced to barbiturates, stimulants and hypnotics, Monroe outfitted herself with a portable medicine chest. She collected prescriptions and hoarded pills. When journalist Maurice Zolotow came to the set of *There's No Business Like Show Business*, he found fourteen bottles of codeine, morphine, Percodan and sleeping pills on Marilyn's makeup table. 'Many of these drugs were provided by studio doctors to relieve the excruciating cramps she suffered during her menstrual cycle,' Zolotow said in an interview. 'She also showed me another complete stash hidden inside her purse.'

Studio doctor Siegel himself wrote that Monroe 'suffered episodes of unbearable pain during her period. The technical term for her condition was endometriosis, in which womb-lining tissue forms in places other than the womb, such as the ovaries or fallopian tubes. She was often in agony.' If Siegel wanted to keep Monroe working, he had to provide painkillers, amphetamines and sleeping pills. 'You've got to remember that this was routine in those days,' he said. 'It was the same at Metro-Goldwyn-Mayer and at Paramount. This had been true for decades.

'In those days, pills were seen just as another tool to keep stars working,' he said. 'We doctors were caught in the middle. If one physician wouldn't prescribe them, another would. When I first began treating Marilyn in the fifties, everyone was using the pills.'

Monroe's fascination with drugs soon grew into an obsession. She spent hours poring over *The Physician's Desk Reference*, the reference book used by all doctors and pharmacists. 'She had an immense knowledge of every barbiturate and painkiller on the market,' said Robert Slatzer. Monroe often astounded friends with her knowledge of pharmacology. Early in 1962, Peter Lawford eavesdropped on a serious discussion between the actress and President Kennedy about prescription drugs. At the time, both were receiving amphetamine shots, Monroe from Fox and the President from New York's 'Dr. Feelgood', Max Jacobson. Lawford was amused to hear Marilyn cataloguing side effects and dosage information for the President.

Later that spring, she astounded Peter Levathes by showing him the ingredients for what she called her 'bedtime cocktail'. She poured half a tumbler of champagne, opened a Nembutal capsule, dropped it in, followed it with a tablet of chloral hydrate, and took it all in a single gulp. She explained to Levathes how many minutes would elapse before all the chemicals took effect. He came away fascinated, but frightened. 'She took all this so lightly,' he recalled.

The amount of chemicals Monroe ingested, provided by the studio physicians, her own doctors (who didn't consult with the corporation doctors) and her private hoard of pills, badly aggravated her sinus infection, causing her system to grow weaker and weaker. She missed the first week of filming (when Siegel's reports noted that her fever never fell below 100 degrees), and Cukor was forced to shoot scenes involving Cyd Charisse and Dean Martin.

On April 30, against Siegel's advice, Monroe filmed for about ninety minutes before collapsing in her dressing room and being rushed home. She was confined to her bed again from May 5 through 11, although she had to be ordered by Siegel to stay at home on several of those days.

As the three weeks sped by, alarm spread through the executive offices, and Cukor began muttering that 'she's malingering – just as she did during *Let's Make Love*.'

'Nobody believed that she was sick,' said Lee Hanna, who, as production secretary, processed most of the *Something's Got to Give* documents.

'Despite the fact that Monroe ran a high fever for all of that time and that she couldn't talk most days, they thought she was just being wilful and using all that free time to party,' recalled Joan Greenson. 'But she wasn't out doing anything; she was home feeling miserable and regretting that she couldn't be on the set.'

While Monroe tried to regain her health and Cukor rooted around for sequences to film without her, the studio executives all but forgot their panic about *Something's Got to Give* and became riveted instead on the troubles of another film – a film which now threatened to bankrupt Twentieth Century-Fox.

Chapter 7

Cleopatra I

On the morning of April 20, Milton Gould, the New York financier who was now chairman of the Twentieth Century-Fox executive committee, was told that *Cleopatra*, filming in Rome with Elizabeth Taylor, was eventually going to cost the studio $42 million.

Gould, a Wall Street lawyer who was famous for rescuing sick corporations – like Fox – was stunned by the auditor's report, which showed that the film's daily costs now ranged from $50,000, on a very good day, to $150,000, on days when thousands of extras were required.

Because Gould had been put onto the Fox board of directors by stockholders who were afraid the studio was going bankrupt, this news had special impact for him. The dismal facts and figures meant that this one film might indeed break the studio before Taylor, as the doomed Egyptian queen, was finally killed by that famous asp in a basket of figs.

'By the time I got on board, the film was out of control and most of the money had already been spent,' said Gould. 'We had only one choice – to finish the film as sensibly as possible.'

From that day on, the shadow of *Cleopatra* hung over

the set of *Something's Got to Give*, causing each member of the company – from script girl Teresa Brocheta to Marilyn Monroe – to resent the bloated production underway in Rome, the costliest film yet made in Hollywood at that time.

As the bulk of Fox's revenues flowed to the Holy City, Monroe took it personally. 'She felt it was a slap in the face,' said Robert Slatzer. 'Here she was, Fox's last great contract star, and Liz was making ten times her salary.' *Cleopatra* even stole Monroe's favourite cinematographer, Leon Shamroy, and the handpicked lighting technicians who had illuminated her films as far back as *Gentlemen Prefer Blondes* in 1953.

The inefficiency, waste and eventual scandal that swirled around the *Cleopatra* set in Rome would soon result in parsimonious controls on the set of *Something's Got to Give*. For instance, an enchanting desert island scene between Monroe and Thomas Tryon was cancelled, and a fanciful dream sequence that was to have involved fog and considerable pyrotechnics was nixed at the last minute. 'They sliced away at the *Something's Got to Give* budget bit by bit,' recalled William Travilla. 'The cash for Marilyn's seaside idyll went to pay for more elephants or something.'

But it wasn't only the money itself that angered Monroe. She was furious and deeply resentful that Fox had ignored her own passionate desire to play *Cleopatra*, a desire which stretched back to the origins of the project. It was early 1959 when Monroe first learned, via the gossip mill, that Spyros Skouras was planning to remake *Cleopatra*, which Fox's parent company, William Fox Films, had made with screen vamp Theda Bara in 1917. Monroe launched a vigorous campaign to obtain the part, which included a telephone plea to Skouras in New York.

'Darling,' he said. 'This will be a very low-budget affair – using old costumes and even older sets. We're even casting a starlet – Joan Collins. Believe me, you don't want this one.'

When informed that the budget was to be $210,000, even

less than the budget of the Theda Bara version, Monroe lost interest. But always wary of executive promises, she told her agent, George Chasin of the powerful MCA Agency, then the largest talent pool in the world, to keep an eye on the project 'just in case'. Chasin recalled that Marilyn had fought for, and lost, the leading female role in *The Egyptian*, the 1954 film that would have placed her opposite Marlon Brando. She had even offered to test in a black wig and period dress. But Gene Tierney got the part. Ultimately, Fox was the loser. When Zanuck refused to cast Monroe, Brando walked off the project, leaving the part to Edmund Purdom. *The Egyptian* bombed at the box office.

Filming of *Cleopatra* began in late 1958 on a plaster and papier-mâché set with a cast that included Collins, Peter Finch as Julius Caesar and Stephen Boyd as Mark Antony.

Then MGM's *Ben-Hur* went into production in Hollywood and abroad. When Skouras was allowed to preview the chariot race with its ten thousand extras, its monumental religious overtones, and its obvious star power, he instantly cancelled his makeshift epic, but politely told Collins she would be 'strongly considered' for the lead in the new, big-budget version.

Skouras secretly hired producer Walter Wanger, a man whose credits stretched back to the silents, and charged him with fashioning a glitzy, monumental *Cleopatra*.

True to his word, Monroe's agent, George Chasin, intercepted a Fox interoffice memo that indicated that the studio was actively courting 'major stars' to play the Queen of Egypt.

In May 1959, when Fox forced her to sign for *Let's Make Love*, Monroe appealed to Buddy Adler, who had succeeded Zanuck as production chief. She flew into town from the Connecticut farm she shared with husband Arthur Miller and wooed Adler in person. She had chosen a form-fitting black dress, added five strands of faux pearls, and pleaded her case for half an hour. 'You've got my vote,' said Adler. 'But this is a Skouras deal from start to finish; he doesn't even consult me about it.'

Monroe turned her attentions to Skouras, her former lover. She sent him a colour portrait of herself costumed as Theda Bara, whose version the mogul had recently shown to the Fox board of directors. The photograph captured Monroe decked out in a black wig, ropes and ropes of pearls, kohl-ringed eyes, and filmy harem clothes. Taken by celebrity photographer Richard Avedon, it was one of a series of photographs that appeared in the December 22, 1958, issue of *Life Magazine*. The layout also featured Monroe costumed as other screen vamps, including Clara Bow, Jean Harlow and Marlene Dietrich.

Skouras made no official comment about Monroe's battle plan. But shortly after she met with Adler, a memorandum from Skouras to Wanger listed the 'five front runners for *Cleopatra* as Joanne Woodward, Elizabeth Taylor, Marilyn Monroe, Brigitte Bardot and Gina Lollobrigida'.

'She desperately wanted to play that role,' said Monroe's stand-in, Evelyn Moriarity. 'And she could use the portrayal to successfully escape from the typecasting prison Hollywood had built around her.'

Documents in the Skouras collection show that the Fox president held a series of 'casting dinners' with Susan Hayward (a last-minute suggestion), Taylor and Lollobrigida. 'Marilyn was never considered for that role,' said William Travilla. 'Everyone involved was afraid that she would be laughed off the screen. But, truthfully, she was the only star on Fox's contract list who *could* do it.'

After he screened Lollobrigida's scenes from *Solomon and Sheba* and Taylor's performance in *Cat on a Hot Tin Roof*, Skouras offered the part to the Italian bombshell, known in Europe as 'La Lolla'. He also increased the film's budget to $5 million – which was considered foolishly extravagant.

Wanger was unhappy. He feared that Lollobrigida might

not have enough name identification to make *Cleopatra* a hit in America. Skouras was worried enough to poll major exhibitors. 'Who will sell the most tickets? Taylor or Lollobrigida?' he asked in 250 telegrams sent to leading executives of distribution companies around the world.

The resounding choice was Taylor. Skouras dispatched Wanger to sign Taylor – no matter the cost.

Super-agent Kurt Frings drafted a history-making contract for Taylor: she was to get $125,000 for the first sixteen weeks, $50,000 a week after that and 10 percent of the gross (meaning she would get her money off the top – whether or not the film ever turned a profit). She was also to receive $3,000 per week living expenses, and would have a secretary, a hairdresser and a physician. (Thanks to the number of weeks it took to shoot *Cleopatra*, Taylor's weekly payroll added up to the famous 'two million-dollar salary'.)

When the Taylor contract was signed, Monroe was toiling in the broiling Nevada desert shooting *The Misfits*. She was angry and bitter. 'They put me in a disaster, *Let's Make Love*, but turn to Elizabeth for the biggest film they have ever made,' she lamented to Rupert Allan.

To Slatzer she said, 'I'm the one who's under contract, and they treat me like hell. Liz isn't the only star who can act.'

Taylor's victory – the talk of show-business circles – reawakened the antagonism Monroe had felt for her since the mid-fifties, when Taylor walked off with a series of roles that Monroe had coveted. Most notably, she regretted losing the leads in two Tennessee Williams films, *Cat on a Hot Tin Roof* and *Suddenly, Last Summer*, both adapted from Broadway plays. After Monroe met Williams at Rupert Allan's Bel Air home, he agreed that she would be the perfect Maggie in *Cat on a Hot Tin Roof*. Both projects, however, were purchased for Taylor.

'There was definitely a feud between the two most famous

actresses in the world,' said Randall Riese, author of *The Unabridged Marilyn*.

Taylor had equally strong feelings. When author Max Lerner wrote in *The New Yorker* that 'Elizabeth Taylor is a legend, but Marilyn Monroe is a myth', Taylor raged at Lerner: 'You have a nerve saying Marilyn is "a myth" and I'm just a lousy "legend". I'm much more beautiful than Marilyn Monroe ever was, and I'm certainly a much better actress.'

Looking back on Taylor's lengthy career and scandalous private life, one can hardly imagine that they ever considered anyone else for *Cleopatra*. By 1959, she was the world's most notorious femme fatale. She had already married and divorced hotel scion Nicky Hilton, had married and divorced British actor Michael Wilding, and had then been tragically widowed by the death of the flamboyant producer Michael Todd. Just the year before, she had snatched away the husband of her best and dearest friend, America's sweetheart, Debbie Reynolds.

Reynolds had dispatched husband Eddie Fisher on a mission of mercy to console 'poor Elizabeth' on the death of her husband. A week later, Fisher was in Taylor's bed. Reynolds appealed to the world press. She even held a front-yard conference, a baby over one shoulder and a diaper over the other. Newspapers and tabloids branded Taylor 'an international homewrecker'. The same press that had deemed her a madonna on the death of Michael Todd now conferred upon her the scarlet 'A'.

Hedda Hopper predicted ruination. MGM checked its morals clauses. But quickly and quietly, Taylor's millions of fans trooped back. When she played vixens, as in *Cat on a Hot Tin Roof* and *Butterfield 8*, she sold even more tickets. She was the Queen of Hollywood when Walter Wanger offered her *Cleopatra*. In a bubble bath, a pink telephone cuddled in one hand, she cooed, 'Well Walter, I'd love to do it – for one million dollars.'

The leadership of Fox gulped. Skouras took another poll,

asking, 'Is she worth it?' The distributors replied, 'Affirmative.' The Fox president soon grew expansive. 'This is going to be the biggest hit ever,' he told journalists.

Buddy Adler, production chief at the time, didn't necessarily agree. The cool, battle-weary producer of *From Here to Eternity* and other major hits had a luncheon meeting with Taylor and was alarmed by her grandiose ideas for the film. 'Watch out,' he warned Skouras. 'Elizabeth's demands may soon become unrealistic. If the studio cannot produce this film without Taylor's interference, there is absolutely no guarantee that it can be made at a profit.'

It was an ominous warning. But no one listened. According to Peter Levathes, Fox executives were already greedily counting on the $60 million *Cleopatra* would earn. The film was suddenly a high-stakes affair with a budget of $10 million. The Roman forum and Cleopatra's palace were rebuilt, this time at Pinewood Studios outside London, a location famed for grey skies and drizzles during most of the year.

Filming began on a typically rainy day – September 28 1960. At the helm was Rouben Mamoulian, a master director who specialised in lush period pieces and high-fashion comedies.

Rain, sleet, and their effect on Taylor's respiratory system caused a postponement of almost five weeks. But Taylor's voice was strong enough to demand a new director, old friend Joseph Mankiewicz, and fresh costars to replace Stephen Boyd and Peter Finch, both holdovers from the Joan Collins attempt. Mamoulian, who had slaved on the project since October 1959, departed a gentleman – praising Taylor for her vibrancy and sensuality.

Taylor suggested Rex Harrison, a friend from her MGM days, for Caesar, and an actor she had just seen in *Camelot* for her leading costar. 'Richard Burton would be perfect,' she told Wanger. 'I don't know much about him, but I think he would make a dashing Mark Antony.'

Just as the production was to have resumed, the icy winds off the North Sea resulted in pneumonia for Taylor – who hovered near death for three days. Eddie Fisher slept in her hospital room, Queen Elizabeth II sent her own physician to help, and the world press latched onto the story with a vengeance. When an emergency tracheotomy saved her life, the press declared Taylor's survival a miracle. It was as though God had forgiven this woman for her transgressions.

But Fox and Skouras faced bad news – Taylor would not be able to work again for five months. The star's physicians also decreed that she could not work in Britain and suggested a sunny climate.

The studio would have to start from scratch a third time. The sets back in Hollywood had long since been demolished, and in London the $3 million of palaces, forums, lakes, and even an artificial forest of palm trees were dismantled and sold.

When the studio took stock, it found that the eight minutes of film from this new *Cleopatra* had cost $8 million. Even worse, Lloyd's of London, which had insured the production, would reimburse Fox for only $1.6 million. Still worse, Lloyd's refused to insure Taylor if and when the film resumed.

The claims committee from the respected firm fired off a letter to Skouras, beseeching him to 'cast Miss Marilyn Monroe as "Cleopatra". This is an arrangement we could fully insure.'

The only bright spot came when Taylor, whose miraculous resurrection attracted a maudlin wave of Hollywood sympathy, won the Academy Award for her performance in *Butterfield 8*.

If there was ever an opportune time to kill *Cleopatra*, this was it. But like a drunken, desperate gambler going for higher and higher stakes, Skouras gambled everything on a fresh start – this time in Rome.

When Elizabeth and Mankiewicz suggested filming in sunny Italy, the idea seemed dandy. What could be better than filming their epic where it had all happened, in Rome, with its clear skies and balmy weather? This seemed an ideal location for Taylor's *Cleopatra* to develop into a blockbuster.

Of course, no one knew then that the winter of 1961–62 would be the coldest, wettest and windiest since ancient times. And no one bothered to tell Fox that the Sicilian Mafia controlled the Italian trade unions or that Roman artisans were notorious spendthrifts.

Even if Skouras had foreseen these problems, he probably wouldn't have reconsidered. Looking at the vouchers, overcharges and frantic memos in the archives thirty years later, an observer could almost conclude that Mankiewicz, Taylor and Wanger were hell-bent on extravagance – as if this costly sex-and-sandals epic was a balm for all the indignities they had suffered under the studio system.

Mankiewicz, normally a cautious, almost frugal filmmaker, made the first toss of the dice. By throwing out the script and starting from scratch, he added an estimated $15 million to the cost of *Cleopatra*. Working by night and spending by day, he ordered sets and costumes on a scale unequalled before or since.

With Taylor as a bewigged, bejewelled cheerleader, Mankiewicz ordered that ancient Alexandria and the Roman forum be reconstructed at Rome's Cinecitta studios. What's more, he had them built on overtime and on a scale 40 percent larger than the originals.

The bill for sets alone topped $5.5 million – an expense made all the more bitter when Fox learned that only 60 per cent of the vast panorama ever made it onto the screen.

Taylor herself added an estimated $10 million to the cost by insisting that the spectacle be filmed in Todd A-O, the wide-screen process created by her late husband, Michael Todd. This meant that the screen had to be filled with thousands more extras, dozens more buildings and larger interior sets. Of course, Taylor pocketed substantial royalties for the costly process. Fox would have preferred to use Cinemascope – which it owned outright.

Long considered the pampered, indulged Queen of Hollywood, Elizabeth Taylor had all the prerogatives of superstardom. A wave of her bejewelled hand brought a dozen obsequious executives to their knees. 'They literally burned incense before her,' said Aldo Novarese, one of the Italian art directors of the film. 'It was as if she were perched atop an altar. After this, how did they expect her to act normally?'

When she asked for living expenses, she also supplied the definition of that term. Fox would eventually pay their modern-day Cleopatra $228,000 in expenses alone – more than double Monroe's entire salary for *Something's Got to Give*.

And Taylor's demands were regal indeed. For transportation around Rome, she requested a Rolls-Royce Silver Cloud. Fox provided several. Then her husband, the slightly passé crooner Eddie Fisher, needed a job. Done! The studio made him an 'assistant' at a salary of $1,500 per week. There were doctors and drugs; imported china and cases of wine; cooks and butlers; secretaries and hairstylists.

Elizabeth Taylor, the girl who literally grew up inside the walls of Metro-Goldwyn-Mayer, brought the make-believe studio world into the broader real world. And the stockholders of Twentieth Century-Fox, and to a lesser extent Marilyn Monroe, paid for her fantasy. The line between the Queen of Egypt on the set and the movie star in the Villa Papa had grown perilously thin.

Installed in her fourteen-room 'home away from home,' Taylor behaved in the grandest of manners. Small trucks from Rome's gourmet grocery stores zipped in and out of the gates, bearing delicacies that cost at least $150 per day. The liquor bill alone ran over $500 per week.

The two Italian butlers, veterans in service to princes and dukes, were often frazzled by the star's imperious ways. She insisted that everything at dinner be colour-coordinated – flowers, napkins, candles and tablecloths – all to match whatever gown she might choose for dinner.

'When you get up in the morning and spend the day pretending you're the Queen of Egypt, the line between fantasy and reality disappears. This is what happened to Elizabeth Taylor,' said Fox production chief Peter Levathes.

Even Spyros Skouras admitted: 'I am the king of a great empire. But its entire destiny depends upon the whims and moods of the queen. And the queen, of course, is Elizabeth Taylor.'

Before too long, Monroe's destiny also depended on the outcome of the Roman scandals on the set of *Cleopatra*. Looking at the desperate telegrams, statements of cost overruns, and production logs in the Fox archives, we can easily see why the executives sold the back lot, mortgaged all their corporate property and borrowed heavily to keep *Cleopatra*'s barge afloat. To a man, they were half in love with this raven-haired star with the violet eyes.

Taylor won every corporate battle in which she engaged. When the money men quibbled over budget details at an early meeting, she cut them short. 'Why fight over dollars and cents when you're about to make one of the greatest films of all time?'

Perhaps the most obvious folly was the royal dressing room constructed for her in the centre of the Cinecitta studio. Early in August 1961, interior decorators, loaded down with swatches of brocade, chips of paint and samples of French wallpaper, invaded a six-room office building. Working around the clock, they converted it into a miniature villa in the Louis XVI style. The suite included two bathrooms, a bedroom, a wig room, a makeup and hairdressing salon and a conference room – all outfitted with expensive antiques.

When Taylor finally arrived in Rome for makeup tests in September 1961, producer Walter Wanger proudly conducted her from room to room, pointing out the Oriental carpets, the Venetian mirrors and the fully equipped kitchen.

Taylor followed regally behind him. Then she winked at Eddie Fisher. 'Walter,' she said, 'isn't this a bit much?'

By the time *Something's Got to Give* began filming in Hollywood, Elizabeth Taylor and *Cleopatra*'s director, Joseph L. Mankiewicz, were spending $575,000 a week in Rome. The money from the sale of the back lot was used up, the proceeds from bank loans were exhausted, and almost all of Fox's weekly income was wired to Italy to meet the payroll.

In May 1962, the star went on overtime at the rate of $10,000 per day. 'Taylor was aware of the financial difficulties facing the studio,' said Brad Geagley, a film historian who spent five years studying *Cleopatra*. 'As the Monroe picture began, Elizabeth Taylor began doubting Fox's ability to pay her, so she insisted on receiving her ten thousand dollars at the beginning of each day or fifty thousand dollars at the beginning of each week. When she had determined that the money was in her bank, she finally reported to the set.'

'It was a river of cash – an avalanche of dollars flowing down the drain,' recalled actor Cesare Danova. 'The money was spent in utter confusion.'

Internal documents from the Fox archives showed that *Cleopatra* and *Something's Got to Give* became symbiotically joined. Extravagance on the *Cleopatra* set led to obsessive frugality on the set of *Something's Got to Give*; tolerated illnesses in Rome led to intolerance in Century City. 'They were like Siamese twins, these two films,' said Brad Geagley, who wrote his doctoral dissertation on the waste and mismanagement of *Cleopatra*.

Many months later, when this waste became public and the corporate executives began to look like imbeciles, some would claim that these millions had been spent almost by accident. Studio production chief Levathes was fond of saying, 'It just grew – like Topsy.' Such assertions are nonsense. Research for this book uncovered a preliminary budget written in pencil by Fox president Spyros Skouras. The cost of the Mankiewicz version was, from the very beginning, pinpointed at $28.75 million. These documents prove conclusively that this celluloid calamity was no accident. Fox executives, at some juncture, knowingly decided to make the most expensive motion picture in Hollywood history. At the time when stockholders were told the film would cost somewhat less than $15 million, Skouras had already decided to dismantle the studio in order to pay the bills of the frivolous gamble in Rome.

'It was like being involved in war games, the huge numbers of people constantly training and riding – not to mention the dancers, the costumes and the construction,' Tom Mankiewicz, the director's son, remembered. The Italians 'stole us blind because of the scope alone. They saw Hollywood coming and ran away with millions.'

'Once you start saying, "All right, I need five hundred Praetorian guard outfits, I need six hundred Nubian slave outfits" – this is like an invitation to larceny,' Mankiewicz said.

And there was stealing, like the disappearance of 1,400 Roman swords and 800 pikes. And junior-grade fraud, like charging executive consultant Darryl F. Zanuck's Paris laundry bills to the *Cleopatra* budget. And there were suspicious transactions, such as Skouras's catering of on-set lunches, then billing Fox for food they'd already bought.

'They charged countless thousands of dollars, all kinds of corporate expenses to *Cleopatra* that had nothing to do with the film itself,' said Levathes. 'When I took over as production head, I looked at this billing and this huge budget and soon found evidences of fraud. I told the leadership in New York that what they were doing was illegal. And they told me it was their company and they could do as they wished.'

Levathes blamed Mankiewicz for adding the $15 million overruns to the cost by rewriting the script and then insisting on shooting it in chronological order. 'Sets were built on over-time and then not used for months,' said Levathes. 'Actors sat around for weeks on full salary without saying a line.'

Richard Burton worked only five times in the first seventeen weeks and only thirty days in the entire first year. Carroll O'Connor was kept in Rome, on salary and expenses, for fourteen months for two close-ups.

Cinematographer Leon Shamroy warned Walter Wanger about the dozens of 'unnecessary sets'. But the producer waved him aside.

Like Cukor on the set of *Something's Got to Give*, Mankiewicz wasn't really listening to anyone. Also like Cukor, he was raging out of control in a similar war of words – working twenty-one hours a day while writing approximately five new pages of script every night.

Tom Mankiewicz watched with alarm as his father slowly lost control. 'What really depressed him was his inability to get a handle on the picture. It had grown into an international event rather than a movie in which he was a player. But as a director, he knew that you always want to be in control of your own movie.'

The younger Mankiewicz said he waited for his father to take control of Taylor, 'to tell her to get to the set on time, to quit staying out at all hours. But it never happened.'

Taylor returned from long wine-soaked lunches 'entirely sloshed', according to Tom Mankiewicz. 'And still my father didn't say anything. I think he was definitely afraid that she would get sick again, so he had to handle her with kid gloves. Remember, this time she was uninsured.'

National and international insurance firms provide secure but costly insurance to film companies which pays off if the film is cancelled by calamity such as flood or fire, or by the death or illness of a star. In addition, they provide life insurance for the leads in any film. Marilyn Monroe was insured for $3 million for *Something's Got to Give*. But no corporation would underwrite *Cleopatra* as long as Elizabeth Taylor played the title role.

The younger Mankiewicz also saw his father lose control publicly for the first and only time in his career.

The day Marilyn Monroe filmed her costume tests in Hollywood, Joseph Mankiewicz was directing the enormous barge scene, in which Cleopatra sails into Mark Antony's arms from Egypt. Three Todd A-O cameras were trained on the 200-foot vessel, which was covered with gilt and built precisely from plans described by the Greek historian Plutarch. As tugboats hauled the barge into view, the curtains parted to reveal Taylor in an elaborate robe. She looked absolutely dazzling.

Then Tom Mankiewicz noticed a look of alarm on his father's face. 'Dad's voice dropped real low, and he said, "Cut it." Dad turned to the production manager and said hysterically, "The sails! Look, the sails aren't up! How is the boat travelling?"' The director grabbed his head and slumped into a chair. A production manager said consolingly, 'Joe, it's not your fault.'

Mankiewicz began screaming, 'This is my fucking picture! Everything in it is mine! You work for me! And this big-titted broad,' he pointed to Taylor, 'works for me! So don't tell me it's not my fault! This fucking thing is a fucking disaster and it is my fucking fault!'

The Fox executives were starting to feel the same way.

'Mankiewicz refuses to cut the script,' Levathes warned Skouras in a memo. 'If we continue at this rate, we will have a six-hour picture.'

Levathes believed the director had lost all touch with reality. 'If he didn't like the curtains in a scene, he would say, "I don't like the colour." Everything stopped while seamstresses made new curtains. Since it took two days to make them, Fox was out two hundred and fifty thousand dollars. And even then, the curtains never showed up on film.'

On April 20, Skouras received a dismal report from the

head of accounting. If the money continued to pour out at the present level, work on all films would have to be halted in early July. Skouras panicked; that gave them barely time to finish both *Cleopatra* and *Something's Got to Give*.

With the report in hand, Skouras called business affairs officer, Stanley Hough, director of production operations and told him, '*Something's Got to Give* must start on Monday, April twenty-third – in accordance with the revised schedule just released by Cukor.'

'I see no problem with that,' Hough said. 'We're ready to go on Monday.' His words were vastly overoptimistic.

– PART TWO –
May

– Chapter 8 –

The Children's Hour

Late on the morning of May 4, Monroe lay propped up in her bed with tears in her eyes.

Hazel Washington, who also worked for Monroe at home, hadn't seen her so upset since her marriage to Arthur Miller had crumbled.

All around her lay piles of newspaper clippings from Hollywood and New York, Paris and Berlin. The evidence was irrefutable; the press had turned on her.

She had been reading gossip columns all morning as she lay huddled in her terry-cloth robe, a heating pad on her chest and an array of nose sprays spread across the bedside table.

She was angry and hurt. She had never been so brutally savaged in the gossip columns – not even when she had deserted Hollywood and her studio seven years earlier. The world's press had been making great fun of her illness.

In the two weeks since she had returned from New York, her sinusitis had become big news. The big-name columnists – Louella Parsons, Walter Winchell and Hedda Hopper – had led their columns with it. But these stories had been full of snide insinuations that Monroe was an imaginary invalid.

'They don't believe I'm sick,' she said to Washington. 'I can't figure it out.'

'It's just news, honey,' Washington replied. 'It wouldn't be as good a story if they just said you were sick. They gotta be nasty about it.'

Monroe made token appearances on the set on April 30 and May 1, but collapsed from exhaustion both times. Only a few minutes of her entrance scene were captured on film.

The headlines spread around her told the story: 'Bosses Sick and Tired of "Sick" Marilyn'; 'All Fox Wants Is a Healthy Glamour Girl' and 'Is Marilyn Ill or just Ill-Advised?'

These columns mirrored the cynicism on the Fox lot. In one memo from Philip Feldman to Spyros Skouras, the two-week absence was described as a 'sick out'.

By the morning of May 5, the pressures – from both the press and the studio – had thrown Monroe into a panic. Particularly stung by the public criticism reflected in the news articles, she was determined to return to the set the next morning.

But her sinusitis worsened during the night. She awakened at 5 A.M. with chills and again found her sheets drenched in perspiration. Medical logs show that she had a fever of 101 early that morning, and that the sinus pain was so intense that she complained of blurred vision. Both Murray and Lee Siegel told her to stay in bed.

Monroe ignored them. 'Wake me again at six A.M.,' she said. 'I'm going in today.'

As the actress sank back onto the pillow, Eunice Murray telephoned chauffeur Rudy Kautsky, Dr. Hyman Engleberg and assistant director Buck Hall, setting in motion the elaborate machinery required to get Monroe to the set and ready for filming.

When Kautsky first saw her, he declined to drive her to Fox. 'You still look too sick,' he said. But Monroe insisted. 'I can't really stay out any longer.' He finally agreed and

Monroe left Brentwood loaded with massive doses of antibiotics, amphetamines and painkillers. Added to the residue of Nembutal, chloral hydrate and phenobarbital from the night before, at least five chemicals, with all their side effects, were fighting for control of her system.

When she was dropped at the door of her bungalow at 7:30 A.M., she was so weak that Whitey Snyder had to help her into the makeup chair. Fifteen minutes later, however, Siegel's 'hot shot' was beginning to work. A warm rush flooded over her, followed by an instant feeling of well-being and immense energy.

Just before Monroe stepped onto the soundstage, her mood soared as the amphetamines raised her blood pressure and released endorphins in her brain. Because the drug revved up the respiratory system, it also masked the symptoms of her sinus infection.

At 8:30, Monroe left her bungalow in the vibrant silk outfit Jean Louis had designed for Ellen Arden's reunion with her children.

On soundstage 14, a sizeable crowd had gathered in the dark pockets at the edges of the set. Anyone with the power to gain entrance was there. It was impossible to resist the spectacle of Monroe portraying a mother for the first time since she had become a star. She would finally get the chance to have children – at least on screen.

Given her history of miscarriages (at least four) and abortions (as many as seven) this make-believe reunion was bound to be incredibly poignant. Monroe had been personally involved in this scene from the beginning. She had roused herself from her sickbed to fight with screenwriter Bernstein over the interpretation of the reunion between the shipwrecked wife and her children. In Bernstein's rewrite of the Johnson script, Monroe would have been forced to engage in silly antics to win back her children's affection.

'It wouldn't happen that way,' Monroe complained to

Henry Weinstein. 'Their own mother would win them over instantly. The old memories would simply be too deep.' Similar notations were made in the margin of her script. Although the producer recognised the fine meddling hand of Paula Strasberg, he agreed with Monroe and passed this verdict on to Bernstein.

The New York writer fumed. 'This doesn't make for good drama. These children haven't seen their mother for seven years.' Bernstein was still rankled over the incident thirty years later. To him, it was simply another sign of a spoiled, out-of-control star getting her own way.

That opinion was reinforced by Cukor when he suggested that 'Marilyn rewrote the script because she can't abide even a hint of rejection – even make-believe rejection. If she has any power at all to affect it, she will change it so that in the scene, even though it's not about her personally, she is not rejected.' Which is exactly what happened.

'We more or less let Marilyn structure those scenes her way,' Weinstein said. 'It made good sense.'

At Fox, this was just one more paper battle. Among Monroe's intimates, the realisation slowly dawned that this cinematic confrontation would pack a devastating emotional wallop. Robert Slatzer noted that his former lover was 'preoccupied with the world of children during the last spring and summer of her life.'

Gossip about Monroe's first encounter with child actors Chris Morley and Alexandra Heilweil this first day of filming was an irresistible lure. Fox executives and their secretaries gravitated to the soundstage as Monroe prepared to make her entrance.

'Marilyn watching' had been great sport since the early fifties. She was the dirty corporate joke, the golden calf who saved the studio and who was resented for it. Now it was the sixties, and she was in a position to rescue the studio again. Even members of the publicity department came and crowded behind the electricians on the catwalks above, adding their whispers to the malevolence down on the soundstage.

'You could feel the hatred,' recalled stand-in Moriarity, who walked onto the set just behind the star. 'It was scary.'

'Marilyn was the brunt of all derision,' said actress Sheree North. 'In the entire studio, in every department, there was the most ugly feeling toward her.'

The powers at Twentieth Century-Fox always saw Monroe as a high-class strumpet. One producer on the set that day watched her with the children and dismissed her performance instantly. 'Why on earth would they cast this woman as a mother when everybody knows she's the greatest whore in the world?'

At the weekly card games held by the publicity department, there was a running joke speculating on the number of blow jobs it had taken Monroe to earn her break in her first big film, *All About Eve*. The card players also kibitzed about Joe Schenck's fondness for her breasts and about Skouras's affair with her in the early fifties.

Monroe understood the crowd's hostility. 'Studio bosses are extremely jealous of their powers,' she said to *Life* in July of 1962. 'They're like political bosses. They want to be able to pick out their own stars. They don't like the public rising up and dumping a girl in their laps and saying, "Make her a star because we want you to make her a star," which is what happened to me.'

'The children in *Something's Got to Give* reminded her of her own barrenness,' Slatzer reflected. He also remembered meeting her often in a children's playground not far from her Brentwood home. She was 'transfixed by the children for hours'. Another friend, Pat Kennedy Lawford, confided to others that 'Marilyn seemed haunted by her childlessness, asking endless questions about my children and about all the Kennedy children.' Peter Lawford sometimes found her in the playground of his beach house 'silently admiring my children's toys and books'.

As a zealot of Method acting, Monroe had to confront all her own juvenile demons as she prepared for the family reunion on soundstage 14. The foster homes, her absent mother and invisible father made for a bitter brew. Her pain was bound to show as she approached the children for the first time. Her detractors counted on that.

But there were friends in the crowd as well. The studio's story editor, Theodore Strauss, slipped onto the soundstage before the cameras turned. He was mesmerised by the transparency of Monroe's emotions. 'It was truly a touching scene,' he said. 'It wasn't forced, it wasn't overdone.'

Strauss noted to himself that it was like cinéma verité. 'I couldn't escape the realisation that Marilyn's own life was coming alive in this scene. She could easily have been one of those motherless children.' Strauss thought back fifteen years to his first meeting with her – when he was a magazine reporter and she was still a hustling starlet.

'We met in a corner booth in the old Romanoff's Restaurant,' he said. 'And she told me one of the various versions of her childhood. The intensity of those emotions had survived all these years, and despite all that success, she hadn't emerged yet from the crisis of her childhood.'

Watching her now, Strauss was lost in admiration. 'Not many stars would have allowed that vulnerability to come to the surface.'

Monroe's dresser, Marjorie Plecher, also noticed that the actress's personal heartbreak was close to the surface. 'She came over to me during a break in the filming and said that if her daughter had lived, she would have been the same age as the youngest girl on the set. Emotionally, that was very tender to her.'

It was 10:30 A.M. before Monroe walked onto the soundstage and into the glare of the white and amber lights. This vibrant lighting was reflected in her shining blonde hair and intensified the brilliant fuchsia and green of the Jean Louis gown. She came through a door, looked about the set and smiled broadly.

Cukor, making sure he remained a gracious and courtly figure before the large audience, bounded over and kissed her hand. A spontaneous round of applause came from the crew. It spread up to the catwalks and eventually to all corners of the set.

'She looked marvellous despite her illness,' remembered Plecher. 'Her beauty had matured and there was a luminosity to it that had never been there before.'

Monroe moved forward to meet the child actors, Heilweil and Morley. 'I remember looking up at her, and it was as if she drifted out of a mist,' recalled Alexandra Heilweil. 'To this day, she is the model of femininity to me. I think it was the way she carried herself and the sweetness of her voice – totally feminine and totally elegant.'

To Chris Morley, Monroe was a 'glamorous mirage of strong perfume and the loveliest face I had seen before or since.'

Monroe knelt down to the children's level and whispered to them, 'We're going to have a lot of fun on this film. I promise you.' And then she hugged them both tightly.

The actress looked over at cinematographer Franz Planer, winked and parodied her famous walk. There was a second burst of applause.

At 11:05 on Monday, May 5, the cameras finally turned on *Something's Got to Give*.

Monroe was positioned just outside the entrance to the courtyard. The child actors were racing around the pool playing tag. Slowly Monroe entered and walked with mincing steps up a small flight of stairs, clutching her purse and looking wonderingly at the house her character had left five years before. As soon as she caught sight of the children tears welled up in her eyes. This was honest emotion and Marilyn's eyes misted through twenty-seven takes of that first scene.

Just out of camera range stood editor David Bretherton, also in tears. 'I cried right there on the set. I couldn't help it. She was so gentle with these kids and she was so "up" for them. There was a tenderness there that is almost impossible to describe. She wanted to be loved so badly.'

Cukor filmed Monroe's entrance for several hours – much of it silent footage of her wide-eyed reaction upon returning home.

'Marilyn was magnificent,' recalled Alexandra's mother, Eva Wolas Heilweil. 'You never really knew how sick she was. And I can tell you, she was sick indeed. At one point, I saw her leaning against the wall between scenes, all the colour having drained out of her face.'

Fox Entertainment News producer Henry Schipper, who reviewed every frame of film and every document from *Something's Got to Give*, believed Monroe made it through the scenes 'because she wanted to explore the maternal feelings that had been thwarted in her own life'.

As they filmed the same scene over and over again, Monroe finally became suspicious. Later that night, as Ralph Roberts massaged away her tension, she confided in him that Cukor 'was filming the same little bits repeatedly. But I knew we had it perfect by the second take. I think he's up to something.'

After the crew took a brief lunch break, a nine-year-old cocker spaniel named Jeff was led onto the set with great fanfare. He was to be the centrepiece of Monroe's reunion with her children.

Coached by famed trainer Rudd Weatherwax, the man behind the four dogs on the *Lassie* television show, Jeff had a fairly simple job. Monroe would enter the house for the first time in five years and whisper the dog's name. He would bound over, bark twice and kiss her on the chin.

While Monroe was still in her bungalow across the lot,

Jeff was introduced to his director, Cukor, and the two child actors.

Cukor seemed distant and preoccupied during the rehearsal. Jittery from the amphetamines and almost starved for food, and for sleep, he paced the set.

'He wasn't himself,' recalled Eva Wolas Heilweil. 'To me, he seemed older than his actual age, and his old vibrancy, a vibrancy I remembered well, had vanished.'

The director seemed almost uninterested when Monroe arrived with Paula Strasberg and Pat Newcomb, Monroe's personal press agent, at 2:10 P.M. When Weatherwax led Jeff up to her, Monroe impulsively leaned down and gathered him up. 'Look, she wants to steal the dog's allegiance,' Cukor told costume designer William Travilla. 'She's making it into a contest between herself and the animal trainer.' Cukor turned away disgustedly.

Within a few minutes, another contest began – an endurance match between Cukor and Monroe that would finally bring their undeclared war out into the open. The scene called for Monroe to walk slowly towards the pool, say hello to the children and then kneel down as Jeff recognised her and ran over, his tail wagging wildly. She breezed through her entrance, through the greeting and up to the dog in just three takes.

Then the trouble started. Jeff ran up to her, wagged his tail and then flopped down comfortably in front of her, missing all of his cues. No greeting, no kiss on the chin. In the unreleased *Something's Got to Give* footage, Weatherwax can be seen hugging Jeff and then leading him through his cues one more time.

Cukor's voice can be heard snapping at the trainer, then ordering the camera to pull back for a second take. According to Robert Slatzer, the director virtually ignored Monroe as he moved the camera in and out and rehearsed Jeff three more times, while she remained crouched down in her heavy silk coat and her spike heels.

Despite the fact that Jeff still didn't get it right, Cukor ordered the cameras to turn again. But Jeff was no closer to perfection in takes three through five, and he was becoming overheated from the huge arc lights. An hour later, he was panting and twirling in circles. Cukor pressed on with Monroe still crouched uncomfortably. Eleven takes were completed in this second attempt – none of them usable.

When the afternoon break came, an exhausted Monroe was helped to her bungalow, where she collapsed on a sofa. She was fortified by coffee and by a second injection from Lee Siegel. For the first time in two weeks, Weinstein thought Monroe seemed strong enough to last through the week, and everyone was determined to keep her that way.

Everyone but George Cukor.

At 3:30 P.M., he ordered a third try at the scene with Jeff. 'There were a number of scenes that could have been shot instead, while they retrained the dog or replaced him,' recalled stand-in Moriarity. 'It seemed to me that they should have gotten another dog.'

In a move that must have been deliberate, Cukor continued to film Monroe and the errant dog for three hours and twenty minutes. In twenty gruelling takes, cinematographer Franz Planer never obtained one usable sequence. (There may have been as many as thirty-two takes, but only twenty survived.)

Because the interior set was lit to simulate a bright summer day, a bank of one hundred lights raised the temperature on the floor to ninety-four degrees by 4 P.M. Looking carefully at the twenty takes of this scene in the studio archives, an observer can see Monroe wilting.

For ten takes she pitched in, trying to coach Jeff on her own. 'Jeff, Jeff,' she whispered. 'Come on, come on, Jeff.' On take ten, the actress looked up pleadingly at the director, wiping her left hand across her forehead. Her head dipped with fatigue.

Cukor was almost screaming at this point. 'Speak, speak,

speak, Jeff! Speak!' Still the director refused to throw in the towel. Instead he switched to silent film, apparently intending to dub the barks later with a more cooperative dog.

By take fifteen, Monroe was laughing, but it was a shrill, forced laugh. At the cut, she glared up at the director with narrowed eyes. 'Why stop?' she said facetiously. 'He's starting to get *good*.'

Despite the star's increasing weakness, both physical and emotional, Cukor pushed ahead. He dropped down into a squat just behind the camera, his dark eyes locked on Monroe's face. Then he proceeded to imitate her every gesture, acting along with her in a bizarre, swishy pantomime of her breathless style.

Grabbing the dog, she said again, 'Tippy, how fat. What have they been feeding you?'

Cukor parroted the lines sotto voce – a mocking singsong challenge.

In Robert Slatzer's still photographs taken the same day, Jeff can be seen knocking Monroe over and, a few seconds later, lunging at the director. Cukor would later maintain that the dog performed beautifully during rehearsals, but was unable to execute his tricks during the actual filming. (All Slatzer's photos were shot during rehearsals.)

A veil of hatred now clouded the production – a spreading distaste that, according to Evelyn Moriarity, 'you could feel in your bones'.

Cukor's innate conceit, his indulgent habit of acting alongside his female stars (it's noteworthy that he never attempted it with the men), originated during his glory days at MGM – where he had been a pampered star. His face would wrinkle up and his eyes roll backward as this mimicry carried him away.

Monroe responded by staring absently over his head – locking eyes instead with Paula Strasberg.

Though Monroe appeared remarkably placid on the set, she later erupted in anger. 'This is getting ridiculous, Ralph,' she said to Ralph Roberts. 'How many takes did we do? Thirty!'

When Roberts came to give her a massage later that day, Monroe was still discouraged. 'If an actress had behaved that way, they would have gotten rid of her on the second or third take. Why the hell didn't they just get another dog?'

Hazel Washington also noted that Monroe's opinion of Cukor was transformed by the needless retakes. 'Marilyn's teeth clenched,' said Washington, as if she was actually seeing the real Cukor for the first time. She now regarded him as an enemy – this director she had once described as 'the finest comedic director in Hollywood'.

The director might even have been cashing in on Monroe's illness, hoping to call forth a burst of incandescence by playing on her vulnerability. But he showed no compassion for the star's delicate psyche.

Cukor had done much the same with the equally troubled Judy Garland during the filming of *A Star Is Born*. Observers watched him remind her of her tortured childhood, of her drug and alcohol addictions, of her terrible career disasters – such as the abortive *Annie Get Your Gun*.

Del Armstrong, makeup artist on the Garland film, told author Patrick McGilligan, 'Cukor knew how to hurt a woman, and he used those tactics to get them in the mood for a crying scene.'

McGilligan, Cukor's biographer, revealed that 'the director almost seemed to enjoy taking Garland to the brink. He would ask her, "Do you understand the unhappiness and desperation of the character you're playing?" – knowing full well that she did. He would work her into a frenzied state.' Then the scene would be done again and again.

Monroe had heard these horror stories from Garland herself.

Over the coming weeks, she watched Cukor more closely, and gradually came to believe that he was sabotaging *Something's Got to Give*. After the shameful sequence with the dog, Paula Strasberg commented drily, 'At least we know what we're up against.'

The same Monday evening brought an intensification of the war of words over Nunnally Johnson's fast-evaporating script. Instead of a page or two every night, the new pages from Bernstein's typewriter were coming by the handful.

'The messengers arrived several times a night,' Eunice Murray recalled. 'Marilyn's copy of the screenplay soon resembled a rainbow as the coloured pages indicating changes were stapled inside' – blue pages of dialogue and yellow pages of technical and wardrobe cues.

Monroe complained to Robert Slatzer, 'They're correcting the corrections. Last night I memorised one scene, only to have it changed again at 8 P.M., then changed again the next morning.'

Because of an understanding between Monroe and Levathes, she regularly reported to him on the verbal reshuffling. On May 15, Phil Feldman delivered a three-word message to the director from Levathes. 'Cut it out!'

But Cukor was obsessed. Night after night he paced back and forth in his bungalow, dictating ideas for scenes, memos and letters. He soon earned the nickname 'the Great Dictator' from the secretarial pool. Some stenographers were required to work until one in the morning to type his new material.

Determined to continue rewriting despite Levathes's dictum, Cukor came up with a ruse. Instead of printing the script revisions on the required blue paper, he started sending them out on plain white. Obviously he hoped to fool Monroe into thinking that these were the original lines.

But the actress caught on instantly. 'Marilyn became hysterical,' Eunice Murray remembered. Nunnally Johnson wrote, 'To her this was the ultimate betrayal. She was much too smart to be fooled by this trick. Only a foolish or egomaniacal director would so shake and shock as nervous a star as he had on his hands. It was very bad business.'

Moriarity got the feeling that George Cukor 'always had to be right. He always thought he knew better than everyone else. That's why he was unable to leave the script alone.'

Susan Strasberg, who was privy to her mother's involvement with *Something's Got to Give*, summed it up. 'Here's a director who finally got his star back! What kind of man would spend the entire day filming a scene with an uncooperative dog and the whole night rewriting the script?'

Cukor's tactics, whatever their cause, placed further demands on Monroe, weakening her physically. After she collapsed into bed that night, her fever returned. Studio doctor Siegel, along with her personal physician, Engleberg, urged her to spend another week in bed. But the brief and incandescent scenes filmed on April 30 worked against her. When Levathes and Feldman saw the film, they agreed that the star had never looked better. 'They didn't know whether her illness was real or imaginary,' said Fox Entertainment News's Henry Schipper.

'The feeling that she wasn't really ill spread through Fox leadership,' said Noreen Siegel. 'Of course, this time she really was ill, but she had cried wolf too many times.'

Monroe's relapse kept her off the set until Monday, May 14.* But when she returned, she seemed not only healthy, but vibrant.

---

*Although much has been made of Monroe's absences from the set, most of them fit the definition of the Screen Actors Guild rule on 'excused absences'. From April 23 through April 27, the actress stayed home on the orders of studio physician Lee Siegel. She then came to the set briefly on April 30 and began filming her entrance. Illness soon forced her to go home again. When she tried to film on May 1, she fainted under the hair dryer and was rushed to her Brentwood house. Studio doctors kept her there until the morning of May 5. On that date, she spent almost nine hours working with the children and the cocker spaniel. She suffered a relapse on May 6. Siegel kept her confined to bed until May 14, when filming resumed and all of Monroe's absences were "excused", a point Dean Martin would later make when the production was shut down.

– Chapter 9 –

Principal Photography

At 7:30 A.M. on Monday, May 14, Monroe caught the studio napping.

The security guard who logged her in immediately telephoned Cukor – who was still at home. 'Monroe just arrived,' the guard said. 'And she's already in makeup.'

For the past five days, Monroe had called in sick – but always at the last moment. Now the company wasn't quite ready for her. Cukor had already planned to film a beach sequence with the hot young star Thomas Tryon and five Fox starlets.

At that minute, Tryon was on his way to Newport Harbor, about fifty miles from the Century City lot. He was crammed into a van with the actresses and a makeup artist. His costume, a Lycra bikini, was in a small handkerchief box.

'When we got to the Balboa Bay Club [in Newport Harbor], we found a message ordering us back to Fox,' Tryon recalled. 'Monroe was back!'

Though Monroe's spirits were up, a sense of hopelessness had settled onto the company of *Something's Got to Give*.

'One hundred and four people had been standing by since May fifth,' recalled Gene Allen. 'Each day we expected her to show up, and each morning at 6 A.M. she cancelled out. Morale was very low.'

Cukor had completed endless retakes with Cyd Charisse, who was playing Martin's new wife, Dean Martin and the children, and was fast running out of scenes that didn't involve Monroe.

'[Cukor] felt he had lost all control; he turned inward and shut himself off,' said Weinstein. 'Because the studio refused to postpone until Monroe was well, as I had recommended, he was caught in the middle.'

In his first Monroe film (*Let's Make Love*), Cukor had compensated for the star's absences by filming at breakneck speed whenever Monroe made it to the set. He made no such attempt this time.

For the next three and a half days, Monroe arrived on time and was fully prepared to film fifteen pages of script. Instead, Cukor squandered most of this time – expending almost twenty-seven hours and more than a hundred takes on two and a half pages of script, just nine lines of dialogue.

To mask his sluggish pace, the director reported to Phil Feldman that Monroe's work was useless. 'She can't match her takes,' he told the operations chief. 'She cannot pick back up where she left off on the previous take.' To compensate for her 'ineptitude', Cukor told Feldman, he was forced to shoot endless retakes.

On the basis of Cukor's production charts, especially when they are matched with the actual film, it seems that the director was engaged in a subtle sabotage of his star – perhaps subconsciously.

The director's explanation to Feldman was accepted for nearly thirty years – until Fox producer/director Schipper rescued the seven hours of film shot for *Something's Got to Give*. Now it's possible to see that at least three-fourths of the 131 takes that have survived are carbon copies of one another. Occasionally, Cukor shot as many as five close-ups in which

Monroe repeated the same few words again and again. And there is virtually no difference among these takes.

The film preserved by Fox contains only four significant errors. In fact, Monroe's precision was amazing. Not even during the ordeal with the spaniel did she so much as alter the tone of her voice. She repeated the line 'Tippy, how fat! What have they been feeding you?' fourteen times, faltering only when the dog leaped into her lap.

'I don't remember a major mistake in the film I edited,' said David Bretherton, who processed a 'rough cut' for George Cukor every night. 'Marilyn Monroe never looked or acted better. Of course, I had seen her in fairly bad shape in *Let's Make Love*, but there was none of that here.'

When Bretherton had edited *Let's Make Love* in the late spring of 1960, he had found it hard to match takes because of Monroe's abuse of alcohol and sleeping pills. Some mornings her face appeared to have aged five years from the previous day – no amount of makeup could disguise the effects. Her weight fluctuated wildly as well – as much as ten pounds from week to week.

As rumours of Monroe's drinking and drug abuse during *Something's Got to Give* circulated in Hollywood, she completed a series of physically gruelling scenes with child actor Chris Morley. The scene called for Morley to make a stinging belly flop into the pool. Alarmed, Monroe had to drop her bag and coat, race around the pool, kneel down and pull him up. The tight silk dress and spike heels made for tricky negotiation. But Cukor shot the scene twenty-six times, and Monroe never missed her mark once.

'The early reports were very good,' admitted Levathes. 'We were swept with a sense of optimism.'

'Cukor took two weeks to shoot Marilyn's entrance,' Moriarity noted. 'And that was less than a page of script.' In all, about an hour of film remains of the reunion scene between Monroe and the children.

Production logs from the archives show that the director began filming the pool scene with Monroe and Chris Morley on April 30 (when Monroe reported in for a few hours) and was still filming parts of the scene on May 21. Even taking into account the star's absences, most of her scenes for *Something's Got to Give* could have been completed if Cukor had proceeded at a normal pace.

'Marilyn slowly came to believe that the director was sabotaging the film in some way,' said Ralph Roberts. 'But she couldn't understand it. It made no sense to her.'

When she heard that Cukor had originally told Evelyn Moriarity he didn't even want to make the film, Monroe said, 'Gee, Evvy, I wish you'd told me that. That might have made all the difference in the world. I would have insisted on a replacement.'

The perplexing incident with Jeff the dog was followed by an outbreak of rudeness on the set. First to suffer were the children, Alexandra and Chris. As they splashed about in the pool, the director seemed to forget that they were amateurs, and his voice became angrier and angrier as the children missed their cues repeatedly. Because Cukor always believed in letting the camera run a few minutes before and after a scene, his nastiness is preserved in the rough cut.

'Marilyn was very upset because Cukor yelled at the children,' said Roberts, who gave her a massage the same night. 'She looked up at me and said, "You know, Ralph, he'd really like to do that to me. But he can't."' A day or so later, communication between director and star broke down completely. 'He would get her in a scene and wouldn't tell her [when she could] leave,' recalled Moriarity. 'He just left her standing there. I've never seen that happen to another major star. It was shameful.'

'The rudeness spread to one of the assistant directors,' said Moriarity. 'Instead of calling Marilyn for a scene, he would stand there and glare at her, tapping his foot for as long as he could. There would eventually be a big blowup, when all the man had to do was say, "Excuse me, Miss Monroe, we're ready for you." She was denied all the prerogatives of a star.'

As Monroe's panic increased, Robert Slatzer appeared more frequently on the set to offer moral support. 'I never saw a director so unsure of himself in my life,' Slatzer said. 'I mean, he allowed thirty and forty takes of some scenes. Marilyn didn't deserve that. Yet, in the end, she got all the blame.'

Mistrustful of Cukor and frustrated by the script changes, Monroe revived the spells of temperament and near-paranoia that had plagued the sets of *Let's Make Love*, *The Misfits* and *Some Like It Hot*. It didn't matter that the illness had isolated her at home or that her on-set appearances were sporadic; she still drove Weinstein insane with her rages and complaints. These fits of temper had seemed to function as safety valves during the earlier films, as they now did on the set of *Something's Got to Give*.

Since filming had begun, Monroe had been obsessed with Cyd Charisse, the classic Hollywood beauty who was playing her rival for Dean Martin's affections. Charisse, whose days as an MGM musical star were behind her, was five years older than Monroe, but looked years younger.

When Monroe had still been a struggling starlet, Charisse had been a popular star, with *Singing in the Rain*, *Ziegfeld Follies* and *Words and Music* to her credit. Possessed of an incredible physical discipline that Monroe lacked, Charisse still danced four hours a day, and her body was flawless.

From her sickbed Monroe had heard about 'sensational footage' of Charisse and Dean Martin. She was so intrigued that she had the film screened for her one evening.

The next morning before dawn, Weinstein was awakened by an angry Monroe. 'Henry, I see that Cyd Charisse is padding her breasts. I always suspected that and now I can see it for sure.'

'What?' said Weinstein. 'What are you talking about?'

'It's no use, Henry. I've seen the film. She's padding her breasts. Anyone can see it.'

Weinstein sighed. 'In the first place, Marilyn, we're showing her in a very sheer negligee. How can she possibly pad her breasts?'

Monroe giggled. 'Oh, Henry, you're so naive. It's done with tape underneath. That's really very effective.'

'That's very interesting, Marilyn, but if you think I'm going to tell Miss Cyd Charisse that her breasts are too big, you're very much mistaken.'

Monroe said, 'Okay, then I'm going to pad mine.'

'Oh, Marilyn,' Henry said. 'Those lovely breasts! You're not going to pad those lovely breasts.'

'Yes, I'm going to pad them. And you will have to redo all of my costumes.'

'Do you realise how ridiculous that sounds?' Weinstein said.

The actress dissolved in laughter. 'I guess so.'

Weinstein considered himself lucky to have weathered such a crisis so easily. But there was another call two days later.

'Henry, I can see that Cyd Charisse is slowly dyeing her hair blonde,' said Monroe. 'Don't try to argue with me, I've seen the daily rushes. I know what's happening.'

'Nonsense,' said Weinstein. 'Her hair colour is the same shade it was when we all did the hair and makeup tests together.'

'No, it isn't,' the actress replied. 'She's slowly streaking it with blonde, and I want it stopped. I want her hair dyed back immediately.'

The producer didn't get off so easily this time – a careful review of the *Something's Got to Give* footage shows that Charisse's hair turns inexplicably darker about halfway through. For good measure, Weinstein also had the hair of the actress who was playing a secretary dyed a darker shade.

'I remember Cukor going bananas about these incidents,' said screenwriter Bernstein. 'Again, it was the self-centred movie-star thing. I think she was conscious of how beautiful Cyd Charisse was, but I don't think there was any deliberate meanness in it.'

Another outburst about hair colour proved to be more serious. This one cost half a day's filming.

The incident warrants some detail here because the studio would later be used to show that Monroe was unbalanced and going mad during the filming of *Something's Got to Give.* It was also the only one of her supposedly paranoid episodes that occurred before a large group of people.

Cukor had assembled a crowd of extras to portray shoppers during a shoe store scene involving Marilyn Monroe and her friend, character actor Wally Cox. The trouble started when Whitey Snyder pushed his way through the crowd on the way to the makeup trailer. 'I noticed this platinum blonde, a real knockout and dressed up beautifully,' said Snyder. 'And this gal's hair was identical to Marilyn's, a real white platinum blonde.'

Snyder decided it was better to prevent an on-set blowup by informing Monroe ahead of time. 'I guess you could say the incident was my fault,' said Snyder. 'But I knew what would happen if Marilyn was surprised by her.'

Two dressers were helping Monroe into a wool suit with mink and silk trimmings when Snyder approached her. 'Marilyn, there's an extra in this scene, a platinum-blonde extra, and I don't like it one bit.'

Monroe whirled about. 'I don't like it, either.'

Assistant director Hall was summoned from the set. He found Monroe fully made up and in costume. 'Mr. Hall, I don't want to make too big an issue out of this,' she said, 'but there's a girl out there who looks too much like me. You'll have to get her off the set.'

'As with most stars, Marilyn was very sensitive about any other actress who looked like her,' recalled Synder. 'In those days, a lot of young actresses tried to look precisely like her.

In this she was no different from other major stars. It would have been the same with Betty Grable.'

Hall paid the actress and sent her home. The affair might have ended right there; there were plenty of extras to fill out the shopping sequence (particularly since none of them could be seen in the film taken of that sequence).

But Cukor apparently decided to make an issue of it. With Monroe ready to go, the director shut down production for the morning and ordered casting to replace the blonde with a brunette. This process took four hours.

The whole incident was suspect. In the first place, there was a standing rule on all Marilyn Monroe films: 'No blondes'. As early as *Niagara* eleven years earlier, a blonde bit player had been removed from the motel sequence and replaced with a redhead. '*Something's Got to Give* Gene Allen had had a similar experience on the set of *Let's Make Love*.

'We were setting up a lobby display in the theatre sequence,' Allen remembered. 'We got a bunch of stills of actresses and put them up in the foyer as part of a tableau of former actresses who had worked this particular theatre. Marilyn objected to one of the pictures of a blonde actress. I said, "That's the simplest thing in the world, Marilyn." So I replaced it.'

At the start of *Something's Got to Give*, a memo from Weinstein was delivered to Cukor, the Fox casting department and all the assistant directors stating that no blonde actress was to be cast for any scene. This guarantee had been honoured on every other Monroe film.

So Cukor's costly manoeuvre must have been deliberate. 'The gal looked so much like Marilyn it was uncanny,' Snyder recalled. 'But there was one difference – this girl was fifteen years younger and she looked it.'

Later, when the production collapsed, the Fox publicity department dredged up this incident and passed it along to all the major Hollywood columnists. They depicted a half-crazed Monroe accusing an extra player of stealing her hair rinse. They said the attack was intentional and that the girl hardly resembled Monroe at all.

'I absolutely guarantee you that it didn't happen that way,' Snyder said. 'It was open and shut. Marilyn said a few words to Hall, then they paid the girl off and let her go home. She got the same amount of money as if she had stayed there all day.'

This demeaning episode – added to the other discourtesies – alarmed Monroe. When she returned the next day, she was accompanied by her army of retainers. From that moment forward, she would never be without them. She told Paula Strasberg, 'Now it's them or us!'

Monroe's return to the set also signalled the revival of her social life after a hiatus of more than a month.

On Tuesday, May 15, she left the studio wearing a black Norman Norell dress and an upswept hairstyle by Sidney Guilaroff to attend a series of dinner parties, including an affair in the Hollywood Hills for onetime LSD guru Timothy Leary. When Monroe heard that the Harvard professor was in town, she wangled an invitation to the party.

When she arrived at the hilltop house, late as usual, she learned that Leary had gone to a back bedroom for a nap. She insisted on stepping down the hall to meet him.

Leary heard a rustle and noticed a scent of Chanel No. 5. Even in the darkened bedroom, he knew it was Monroe. The star slid out of her mink and sat down beside him, playfully rumpling his blond hair.

'So, you're Timothy Leary.' She held his hand and continued ruffling his hair. 'Listen, you've got to turn me on. I've never let anyone inside my brain.'

Leary suggested a Los Angeles professor. Monroe answered, 'I don't want to do it with anyone else. I want to do it with you.'

He demurred.

Monroe said disappointedly, 'You have people like me

hitting on you all the time, trying to get turned on, don't you?'

Leary nodded.

'So you never know whether people like you for yourself or for the drugs?'

He nodded again.

'I know that feeling well,' she said.

She was fascinated by the professor's vulnerability. 'You go around turning people on. But now that I've met you, I think it's you that needs to be turned on.' She reached into a pocket of her black mink and said, 'I've got just the magic pills for you. Something of my own, called "Randy-mandys" [the street name for the powerful sedative Mandrax]. They turn off your mind and turn on your body.'

Monroe handed Leary a burnt-orange pill shaped like a cough drop. He washed down the pill with two swigs from her bottle of Dom Pérignon.

'Where do these come from?' he asked.

'I dunno,' said Marilyn. 'London, France, Mexico. I get them from a dear friend south of the border.'

In less than ten minutes, Leary felt warm all over. 'Like a balloon filled with honey.' When he tried to stand up, his legs buckled under him. As he slipped to the floor and slowly lost consciousness, he could hear Monroe giggling far off in the distance. 'Then I fell into a deep sleep,' he recalled.

When he awakened twelve hours later, Monroe had already telephoned his hostess with a luncheon invitation. Later that day the two of them walked together, unrecognised on the sands of Venice Beach, and discussed their drug experiences. 'I found her full of contradictions, funny and playful, but very shrewd,' Leary said in an interview.

Monroe renewed her plea for LSD 'then and there'. As they walked up and down the sand, she said, 'I've tried almost everything – at least once.'

In the end, the drug guru turned her down and they

parted. 'But it was a joyous walk on the beach with her,' Leary said wistfully.

Like most others who saw Monroe that spring, Leary found her remarkably sharp-witted and in complete control of herself.

– Chapter 10 –

A Matter of Adultery

On May 15, the day after Monroe returned to the set from her sickbed, 319 angry shareholders jammed into the conference room at Fox's Manhattan headquarters for the most contentious annual meeting in corporate history.

A bitter proxy fight had broken out – a battle that would eventually topple the corporation's leadership. Though the price of Fox stock had been falling steadily for two years and the quality of the studio's product had been deteriorating since 1959, it took an international scandal on the set of *Cleopatra* to mobilise large numbers of investors.

Since February, when Elizabeth Taylor and Richard Burton had begun their adulterous affair, the scandal had grown into a public relations disaster that had attracted the ire of women's clubs, religious leaders and members of Congress.

'*Cleopatra* came to symbolise all that was wrong with Fox,' said film scholar Brad Geagley. 'And the Taylor–Burton affair became a symbol that studio executives could no longer control the stars who worked for them.'

When the Fox leadership made the mistake of putting a colour photograph of Taylor and Burton on the cover of the 1961 annual report, which was mailed in early May, it was like waving a red flag before the already dissatisfied shareholders.

At the three-hour annual meeting, with proxies in their clenched fists, stockholders shouted Spyros Skouras down every time he mentioned *Cleopatra* and the scores of millions he expected the film to earn.

Getting nowhere, Skouras finally signalled a projectionist to dim the lights and show a compilation of scenes from the Egyptian epic.

As soon as Elizabeth Taylor's face appeared on the screen, beneath the black wig and heavy makeup, a chorus of hisses spread through the audience. When Burton appeared at her side, boos and catcalls were heard.

When the final frames of the Taylor film finished, the screen went black for a few seconds before Monroe appeared onscreen, moving languidly in the Jean Louis bikini. The test reel, the only edited film available from *Something's Got to Give*, was greeted with silence at first. Then the hisses resumed.

Skouras signalled for the lights to come back up and sighed with disappointment. Having pinned all his hopes on *Cleopatra* and the Monroe film, he now looked defeated. 'Monroe and Taylor will save Fox,' he had confidently predicted.

All Skouras achieved with these sneak previews was increased anger from the Fox shareholders. Taylor and Monroe would now be seen as twin symptoms of bad executive management. Journalists also saw them as twin disasters – two overindulged stars who were pulling the studio down around them.

At the time of the annual meeting, the angry shareholders didn't have enough proxies to unseat the board of directors. But the revolt continued into the summer.

As the board of directors would later discover, the Burton–Taylor affair actually began as a routine publicity stunt – one of those 'stars have eyes for each other' ploys that had been used by publicists since the days of the nickelodeon. A week before the first love scene between the stars, in early February, Skouras ordered the studio publicists in Rome, New York and Hollywood to make the first Burton–Taylor kiss an international event.

'Burton and Taylor were propelled into each other's arms,' said Geagley, whose dissertation on *Cleopatra* involved more than a hundred interviews. 'The studio expected them to fall in love.'

The first studio telegrams about the love scene described it as an 'electrifying moment'. 'Burton even forgot his lines,' Nathan Weiss, *Cleopatra* publicist said in a telegram to Harry Brand, Fox's Hollywood publicity chief. 'He was vulnerable. Elizabeth took his arm and looked directly into his eyes for almost a minute.'

Cleopatra director Joseph Mankiewicz later said about it, 'It makes a love scene much easier when your stars fall in love before your eyes.'

The earliest press releases by publicists Weiss and Jack Brodsky, and confidential memos from Skouras and other corporate papers, show that Fox planned for just a touch of love between the stars – a couple of kisses, a few nights out on Rome's Via Veneto and some titillating items for the gossip columns. Then Taylor was supposed to dutifully troop back to her husband, Eddie Fisher, and Burton to his wife, Sybil.

Unwisely, the Fox publicists had decided to contend with Sheilah Graham, the globetrotting doyenne of international gossip. Alerted by Weiss, she swooped down from London and closely monitored the set until the film was completed. The affair was soon front-page news.

Such 'first kiss' publicity worked as well in old Hollywood as it does today. Nobody, now or then, takes it seriously. Everyone knew, for instance, that Rock Hudson wasn't really in love with Doris Day, or Kim Novak with Frank Sinatra, but stories about them as off-screen couples were widely printed nonetheless.

But neither Skouras nor the Fox publicists had done their homework on Richard Burton. If they had, they would have discovered that he was the consummate homewrecker. Shortly before he made headlines in Rome, America's muckraking *Confidential* magazine claimed that it had found thirty couples, in the US and Great Britain, who had been ripped asunder by the amorous Welsh actor.

Burton showed more than casual interest in Taylor from his first day on the set. When Taylor arrived with a retinue of secretaries, hairdressers, maids and cosmetologists, Burton studied her glamorous procession for several moments. In an interview with the London *Times*, *Cleopatra* publicist Brodsky said, 'Burton stared at Elizabeth with greed and envy in his eyes. I had the sense that he was struck by the glamour of her stardom and that he wanted this kind of stardom for himself.' (Brodsky and Weiss later wrote the landmark study of the film, *The Cleopatra Papers*.)

Thirty-seven years old and with a series of cinematic failures to his credit, *Look Back in Anger*, *My Cousin Rachel* and *Prince of Players* among them, Burton viewed *Cleopatra* as his last chance for international stardom. Initially he lusted for that rarefied status far more than he did for the charms of Taylor.

He said as much to Eddie Fisher one afternoon. 'He drank my brandy, accepted my hospitality, and then said, "You're already a star. I'm not," said Fisher in an interview. 'Burton told me, "Your wife is going to make me a star."'

Tom Mankiewicz, housed in the Taylor villa, saw that 'Richard soon did whatever he wanted, and knew this was his big chance to become a movie star. He was clearly in love with her, but even that was part of his master plan.'

During the first six weeks of the affair, Taylor and Burton had a perfect alibi. Their romance was just a publicity stunt – everyone knew that. The studio said as much.

Hollywood's queen of scandal, Louella Parsons, was so

taken in that she refused to print the first reports of a more serious dalliance. Gossip columnists in Rome were no more savvy. The morning after Taylor and Burton were photographed necking at a sidewalk café, it was reported that 'the real affair is between Miss Taylor and Mr. Joseph L. Mankiewicz, her director. Her dinners with Mr. Burton are a ruse.'

The stories continued along those lines. When the stars were snapped by the paparazzi at the seashore, it was chalked up as another publicity coup.

The real dirt, however, was being dished on the set of *Something's Got to Give*. As artisans moved back and forth between the studio and the location in Rome, and later Egypt, they carried rumours back and forth – stories about Monroe to Rome, and about Burton and Taylor to Hollywood.

In March, when Burton marched onto the set of *Cleopatra* and announced, 'I finally fucked Elizabeth Taylor in the back of my Cadillac,' Cukor reported the story to designer William Travilla two days later.

Fascinated as she was by Taylor, Monroe was just as greedy for all the latest from the set in Rome. During breaks in filming, she would rush back to her bungalow for chats with old pals Travilla and choreographer Steven Papich. With Monroe on an old-fashioned slant board to protect the Jean Louis dresses, and Papich or Travilla on one of the lavender settees, they would pool the intelligence gleaned from all departments of the studio.

Monroe's closet source was publicist Frank Neill, a former newspaperman who had become indispensable to Harry Brand. 'The Neill Reports,' as Monroe called them, were remarkably accurate. And they were timely. In fact, the *Something's Got to Give* coffee klatch in Monroe's bungalow knew about the collapse of the Fisher–Taylor marriage before the front office did.

When Burton kissed Taylor before Fisher's eyes – which

eventually caused the singer to flee Rome – Monroe knew the next morning. 'The French kiss,' as it was dubbed at Fox, also caused Fisher to summon journalists to his side and go public with lurid details of the already public adultery.

'It started to go out of control at that point,' said Levathes, who was in Rome when the real hysteria started. 'I was in Walter Wanger's hotel suite at midnight one night when I got a call from Fisher.'

Fisher told Levathes, 'That S.O.B. Burton brought Liz back late tonight and then told me, "I like your wife, and I'm going to take your wife."'

Levathes didn't know how to comfort him. One of the studio chief's missions in Rome was to try to control the spreading scandal. 'I asked Eddie what he did about Burton's outrageous conduct,' Levathes recalled. 'And Eddie said, "Naturally, I sat down and tried to talk him out of it."'

While Levathes and fellow executives couldn't see that the *Cleopatra* scandal would soon taint the entire corporation, they feared it would destroy the film's chances at the box office. 'And we had almost everything riding on this one film,' Levathes admitted.

Fisher's first protests were not to his wife, but to the corporation. Perhaps he hoped that Twentieth Century-Fox, which had so blithely launched this affair, could edit it out as if it were a bad take.

But the 'publicity stunt' had strayed into real life. 'Elizabeth was besotted with Burton by late spring,' recalled Tom Mankiewicz. 'You could see in her every look that she was drunk in love.'

Fisher soon recognised the inevitable. 'If they had sent an engraved card telling them to keep their hands off each other, it wouldn't have made any difference,' he said in an interview. 'They couldn't stop it. They were powerless.'

By late April, there was a danger that Taylor would be expelled from Italy as an 'undesirable person'. First, Vatican

Radio, which beamed broadcasts to almost a million listeners, began editorialising against the affair, depicting Taylor as 'morally bankrupt'. Then, the weekly Vatican newspaper, *L'Osservatore della Domenica*, which had a circulation of more than a hundred thousand Catholic leaders, printed an 'open letter' to Taylor and Twentieth Century-Fox, in which she was accused of 'erotic vagrancy' and being an 'unfit mother'.

Since these editorials were personally approved by Pope John XXIII, Levathes was certain that the condemnation would spread around the world. 'It was so serious that we looked seriously at the morals clauses in the Burton and Taylor contracts,' he said.

The scandal was at its apex when Taylor filmed Cleopatra's entrance into Rome – in which 7000 Catholic extras portrayed the Roman masses of ancient times. Concern for Taylor's safety was so great that teams of sharpshooters from Roman SWAT teams were stationed on the rooftops of the *Cleopatra* set – while other troopers, in Roman wigs and togas, were hidden behind columns or positioned among the crowds of extras.

When a death threat was telephoned to Taylor's villa the night before the sequence was to be filmed, Fox thought briefly about moving the scene to another location, but soon realised that it was impossible.

A crew of 3 architects, 24 designers, 111 plasterers, and 200 painters had erected a Roman panorama that sprawled across 12 acres and included 60 sets. Other artisans – working in an aeroplane hangar – constructed a 22-ton rolling sphinx, atop which Taylor, dressed in cloth of gold, would ride triumphantly into Rome.

Aside from the death threat, Rome had accepted the editorials from the Vatican in silence. There wasn't a clue as to what the average Roman thought about Taylor's open adultery with Richard Burton. 'It was an entirely unpredictable situation,' Mankiewicz said later.

In her palatial dressing room, Taylor was apprehensive.

'Do you know that they spat at me on the streets yesterday?' she complained to *Cleopatra* costume designer Irene Sharaff as last-minute adjustments were made to the $6,500 cloth-of-gold costume.

Burton, resplendent in his Praetorian guard dress, burst in just as cosmetologists were completing Taylor's elaborate makeup, which included five shades of eye shadow.

Taylor said later that Burton had even had his Roman dagger sharpened. 'I don't know what he thought he could do with it,' she said.

An hour later, as the huge sphinx moved through a plaster triumphal arch and into the crowd of extras, they were, at first, stunned by the sight of her. First there was a buzz – a hum of voices. Then came a roar and strong rhythmic chants. 'Liz, Liz,' they cried. 'Baci, baci.' ('Kisses, kisses'.)

Several weeks later, on the second Monday in May, both Sybil Burton and Eddie Fisher went public with their abandonment. Just days before the Twentieth Century-Fox annual shareholders' meeting, Taylor called reporters to her Roman villa to issue the following statement: 'I am feeling terrible pain. But whether Richard existed or not, Eddie and I were just trying to hang on. The marriage was over.' Fisher and Taylor never lived together again.

Struggling to head off the public relations disaster before the annual meeting, Skouras told Mankiewicz, via telex, to keep Burton and Taylor home at night. 'The press of the world is now publicly reprimanding this romance,' Skouras told *Cleopatra*'s director. 'And I don't believe either Richard or Elizabeth fully understands the risks that they are taking.'

The same day, Skouras cabled one of the film's publicists, Nathan Weiss. 'Upon getting to Rome,' he wrote, 'you are to convince Wanger that Taylor and Burton must not be seen in public.'

At the close of the annual meeting, Skouras joked about the Burton–Taylor dilemma. 'Caesar was assassinated, Mark

Antony committed suicide, and Skouras will be dethroned. All by *Cleopatra*.'

'Privately, I was frightened for the future of the company,' said Levathes. 'The affair created an explosive situation.'

While the shareholders' meeting was still underway, Milton Gould, the financial lawyer who was head of the Fox executive committee, slipped out of the conference room to check on the progress of legal developments concerning Monroe.

Earlier, Gould had commented that 'we only need one more scandal before we really lose control.' He knew that just such a scandal was brewing.

A rumour had spread through the corporate headquarters that Monroe, though she had only been back for two days, was planning to leave the set on Thursday to make an appearance at President John F. Kennedy's birthday gala, set for Saturday, May 19.

Gossip columnist Dorothy Kilgallen had already reported to radio listeners Monday night that Monroe was to be the centrepiece of the forty-fifth-birthday celebration and that a 'spectacular dress' had been created for the star to wear.

Gould and the others on the executive committee instructed Frank Ferguson, the studio's chief counsel, to warn Monroe against leaving the set on Thursday for the flight to New York. Though the event was on Saturday, rehearsals were set for late Friday.

'If she had been well and appeared on the set regularly during the previous three weeks, we would have said, "God bless you . . . go ahead,"' said Peter Levathes. 'As it was, she had been absent for most of three weeks and had just returned to work.'

Corporate counsel Ferguson, who was headquartered at the Century City studio, spent most of Tuesday night working on a legal warning to Monroe. His two-page, single-spaced letter threatened the star with dismissal if she left the set of of *Something's Got to Give*. Ferguson also claimed that one of Monroe's legal representatives had informed Fox that she was planning to leave at noon on Thursday.

The attorney, who was both resident counsel and assistant secretary of the corporation, pointed out in the letter that scenes involving both Monroe and Dean Martin were scheduled for both Thursday afternoon and Friday. 'In the event that Miss Monroe absents herself . . . the same [action] will constitute a wilful failure to render services [as stated in her contract].'

Without specifically referring to Monroe's illness, Ferguson's letter also cautioned: 'In the event that Miss Monroe returns and principal photography of the motion picture continues . . . such recommencement will not be deemed to constitute a waiver [of Fox's rights to fire Monroe as stated in her contract].'

In other words, Fox could fire Monroe for leaving on Thursday and could also sue her for abandoning *Something's Got to Give*, if the studio so desired.

On Wednesday morning, May 16, Hedda Hopper called Harry Brand, Fox's Hollywood publicity chief, and asked him about the stories of Monroe's appearance at the Kennedy gala.

'Let me check with Cukor,' Brand replied.

Cukor said confidently that Monroe's appearance had been cancelled. 'Dean Martin bowed out [of the party] as well,' the director said. 'We're too far behind.'

Cukor was so certain of his information that he had scheduled a complicated fantasy sequence for 11 A.M. Friday. Perhaps the most expensive scene planned for *Something's Got to Give*, it was to feature Monroe, Dean Martin and Thomas Tryon.

The shot had to be planned at least twenty-four hours ahead, because an elaborate tropical tree hung with fake apples and boasting a thatch treehouse had to be painstakingly assembled. In addition, a limb had to be rigged to support Tryon, who was six foot two and 185 pounds.

'To say I was excited would be an understatement,' Tryon said. 'I was just getting started, and suddenly I had a chance to work with Marilyn Monroe!'

Late Wednesday night, Tryon was fitted with an abbreviated leopard-skin outfit – in which he was to appear as part of Monroe's daydream about the desert island she had shared with him.

Chapter 11

An Invitation From JFK

Just after noon on Thursday, a whining roar heralded the arrival of an enormous helicopter that set down in the cement courtyard adjacent to soundstage 14. A small tornado of dust and paper scraps whirled across the lot and into the faces of crew members on their way to lunch.

Borrowed from billionaire Howard Hughes by Peter Lawford, the spiffy chopper was the latest thing in the air – a chariot of royal blue entirely suitable for a space-age Cinderella.

While the propeller rotated slowly, Lawford, charged by JFK with getting Monroe to New York, jumped down and dashed through a back entrance to the set. A minute or so later he reappeared, hand in hand with Monroe. She was in her off-set uniform of Jax slacks, high heels, the big, almost platinum-coloured mink coat, and oversized sunglasses. Trailing several steps behind her were Newcomb and Strasberg.

The chopper's pilot saluted Monroe and helped her into a deep armchair. With Newcomb and Strasberg settled in, Lawford jumped aboard, glancing nervously behind him. His eyes locked on the soundstage doors as if he expected Cukor to bound out and reclaim his departing star.

But luck was with them, and with no sign of the mercurial director, the helicopter rose quickly into the air and headed for Los Angeles International Airport.

Production secretary Lee Hanna glanced at her watch. It was 12:40 on the dot. Monroe had been back on the set for three and a half days after three weeks of illness.

This splashy exit marked the start of an all-too-public escapade that sealed Monroe's fate at Fox – her historic appearance at President John F. Kennedy's birthday gala. Defying direct orders from New York, Monroe interrupted filming to catch a clipper jet for the East – where two days of rehearsal awaited her. It would eventually prove to be a costly declaration of independence.

Before the helicopter was out of sight, Cukor flew into a frenzy. 'Where the hell did she go?' he asked assistant director Buck Hall.

'To sing "Happy Birthday" to the President,' said Hall, shrugging in disgust.

'But we settled all that,' Cukor said. 'I said "No", the studio said "No". Period. She can't go.'

'I remember being with Cukor at the time, and we were both astonished that Marilyn had gone,' said screenwriter Bernstein. 'Cukor was particularly angry. He was starting to feel a kind of helplessness; a feeling that, regardless of what the studio said or did, Marilyn was going to get her way. But appearances were deceiving.'

For two weeks, Fox's New York office had used every means at its disposal to prevent Monroe from appearing at the star-studded Madison Square Garden gala. It became a bitter contractual dispute – with the Fox board of directors on one side and Monroe's lawyers and the fabled Kennedy brothers on the other.

Somewhat rashly, Levathes and Weinstein had given Monroe tentative approval to attend the gala back in February. But this was contingent on the speedy progress of *Something's Got to Give*, which was then ten days behind.

The grim telegram of warning was dispatched to Monroe, her attorney and even psychiatrist Ralph Greenson. In Beverly Hills, the star's law firm received a copy of the warning from the hands of a Fox courier.

The 120-line message, signed by Fox counsel Frank Ferguson, was couched in legal terms. To paraphrase, it said that if Monroe left the set for the gala, steps would be taken to have her fired.

The telegram's major wallop was contained in two key paragraphs: 'In the event that Miss Monroe absents herself on the dates of May 17 and 18, the same will constitute wilful failure to render services pursuant to her contractual agreements.' And, 'Such action will result in serious loss and material damage to Twentieth Century-Fox.' In a codicil, Ferguson hinted that 'termination' and a lawsuit would inevitably follow.

Monroe, who had spent $12,000 on a gown and a magnificent ermine stole to match, panicked. She quickly telephoned the White House. For some weeks, President Kennedy had been coaching her. He advised her on the choice of gown, and asked her to sing 'Happy Birthday' in breathless Monroe style. 'The President prefers my old, sexy style,' she giggled to costume designer William Travilla.

The actress read portions of the telegram to Kennedy, repeating the clause that promised 'dire consequences' if she interrupted filming for the trip to New York. Monroe later said that Kennedy promised to work it out.

When Monroe telegraphed a copy of the document to the White House, it ended up on the desk of Attorney General Robert Kennedy, a man already known in Washington circles as 'Mr. Fix-It'. In the past he had handled a number of similar political tasks with great adroitness. But he was also known for his rudeness and for a violent temper which erupted whenever he didn't get his way.

Bobby Kennedy, whose own relationship with the actress

was to begin later, was enthralled with the idea of having the world's sexiest movie star sing 'Happy Birthday' to the world's sexiest politician. But he must have been aware that this appearance would publicly announce the President's blazing affair with Monroe – a carefully guarded secret in both Washington and Hollywood.

Mickey Song, hairstylist to Jack, Bobby and Ted Kennedy, said it was his impression that Bobby wanted to make a statement through Monroe's appearance. 'I got the feeling that Marilyn was to be the centrepiece of the entire event. "Here's your present, JFK – the sexiest woman in the world!"'

'There was nothing like Bobby when he was crossed,' said Song, who as hairstylist for the event was privy to most of the negotiations. 'Bobby was determined to have Marilyn at this event – no matter what he had to do to achieve this goal.'

The Attorney General first contacted Levathes in Hollywood. 'I'd like you to make an exception for Marilyn Monroe,' he said. 'This is very, very important to the President of the United States.'

'I can't; not this time,' answered Levathes. 'The board of directors has already ruled.'

Bobby pleaded, 'I can't overemphasise the importance of this to Jack Kennedy.'

Levathes, who had been working closely with the Attorney General over the filming of his book, *The Enemy Within*, was in a difficult position. Shareholders were already complaining about Monroe's drawn-out illness and excused absences from the set of *Something's Got to Give*. The Hollywood press corps was likewise up in arms. 'The feeling was that we were about to have a second *Cleopatra* on our hands,' Levathes remembered.

Bobby finally went over Levathes's head to financier Milton Gould, then the most powerful man at Fox.

'The first time he called me he was fairly polite,' said Gould. 'He said that this appearance was of critical importance to the current administration. "The President wants it and I want it," said Bobby.'

Like Levathes, Gould said no. 'We can't afford to do it. Marilyn has just returned to the cameras and this appearance could end up costing us millions.'

'Think about it,' said the Attorney General, 'and I'll call you back later.'

The Attorney General called Gould back and this time he didn't bother to be polite. When Gould reaffirmed his refusal, Bobby flew into a rage.

'You'll be sorry for this, you fucking Jew bastard,' he screamed. 'You're dealing with the First Family in America.'

Gould replied, 'I don't know what I can do. The board has already decided on this.'

Bobby yelled back, 'I know what you can do. You can let her go.'

Always a gentleman, Gould continued to reason with the Attorney General. 'This actress has missed two weeks because of illness – an illness that isn't over yet. Don't you see that we can't afford to have her appear in public and on *television* as well?'

Again the Attorney General screamed, 'This is very important to the President and you'll end up being very sorry.' Then he slammed down the receiver.

Gould sighed. 'I knew then that the only one who would be sorry was Marilyn Monroe. I had already decided to fire her if she left Hollywood and appeared at that event. As I saw it, we only had one choice. That's how bad it was for the studio.'

Perhaps by design, Robert Kennedy never reported back to Monroe on his confrontation with Milton Gould.

'He led her to believe that the White House was taking care of it,' said designer William Travilla. 'Her impression was that the nasty telegram had been rescinded, so therefore, she ignored it completely,' setting in motion events whose consequences wouldn't be felt for weeks.

Henry Weinstein pointed out that Monroe was determined to go in any case. 'I mean, here's a girl who really did come from the streets, who had a mother who wasn't all there and a father who had disappeared; a girl who had known all the poverty in the world. And now she was going to sing "Happy Birthday" to the President of the United States in Madison Square Garden. There was no way for her to resist that.'

As Monroe flew to New York, a team of seamstresses in Beverly Hills was still working on her dress for the gala, readying it for Hazel Washington to hand-carry to New York on Saturday morning. Soon it would be one of the most famous gowns in American history.

Chapter 12

That Dress!

Work on the $12,000 gown had begun more than a month earlier. Monroe was secretive about it from the beginning.

At the first fitting, she balanced herself on a dressmaker's stool, naked except for a pair of beaded slippers. Despite a chill in the air, she stood there for four hours – fortified by an occasional glass of Dom Pérignon.

An army of artisans swirled about her: fabric cutters with their razor-sharp shears, pattern makers with thick black chalk and seamstresses with pockets full of thread and sequins. Standing aside, with her hand on her hip, was Rodeo Drive's most accomplished fitter, Elizabeth Courtney. And almost invisible in a corner sat the elegant designer Jean Louis, nibbling on Russian caviar.

The Frenchman was oblivious to the bustle, concentrating totally on Monroe as she turned and posed according to his instructions. He could already visualise the hang of the fabric and the swirl of brilliants on the completed gown.

'I want you to design a truly historical dress,' Monroe had told him, 'a dazzling dress that's one of a kind.'

'Where will you wear it?' the designer had asked.

'That,' she said, 'is the only thing I can't tell you.'

'Why?'

She smiled broadly. 'This time, Jean, it really is a state secret.'

Monroe had had only one other instruction for the designer. 'Let's make this a dress that only Marilyn Monroe would dare to wear.'

'I was completely mystified at first,' Jean Louis recalled. 'Marilyn wouldn't even give me a hint. At that time, I hadn't heard of her connection with the Kennedys. I knew nothing of the presidential gala.'

Sitting with inks and brushes in his Beverly Hills studio, Jean Louis abandoned design after design in his search for the perfect dress. He pored over thousands of still photos from Monroe's movies, hoping her previous gowns would give him an idea for this one. Then he hit on something. Why not trade on her sense of daring?

'Marilyn had a totally charming way of boldly displaying her body and remaining elegant at the same time,' he recalled. 'So I designed an apparently nude dress – the nudest dress – relieved only by sequins and beading.'

Monroe was delighted. 'That'll wake 'em up,' she said.

With only a month to assemble the dress, the Jean Louis organisation moved into high gear. It was a challenge even to obtain the fabric Jean Louis wanted – the lightest and sheerest soufflé in the world. Known as 'silk soufflé' or 'mesh', the cloth is woven on miniature looms from thread fifty times more delicate than ordinary thread. To be safe, Jean Louis ordered an entire bolt and had it flown to Los Angeles via Air France. With the soufflé in hand, the team descended on the Monroe house, beginning a process during which the dress was virtually sculpted onto her body. 'We used muslin and black chalk to create the pattern,' Jean Louis said. 'By draping the cloth over Marilyn's body, we then traced the contours, [creating] the pattern with the black chalk. The pattern was then cut out of the marked muslin.'

'It was like drawing her body onto pieces of cloth,' said Marge Plecher, who aided in the production. 'Jean Louis drew around her breasts, her nipples and the curves of her thighs and hips.'

Working from the muslin patterns, the designers cut the soufflé and stitched it into the basic gown. When Jean Louis helped Monroe into the unfinished gown for the first time, everyone in the room gasped.

Monroe took Marge's hand and said, 'Not bad for a thirty-six-year-old broad, huh?'

It was, however, only a shell of the dazzling 'Kennedy dress,' as it was later to be called. Jean Louis still had to construct a foundation to fit underneath it.

He leaned close to Monroe one afternoon. 'I take it you want this to be as nude as possible?'

'Completely nude, if possible,' she answered before collapsing into giggles.

Though the swinging sixties were on the horizon, this was easily the most daring gown yet ordered for a public occasion. When Jacqueline Kennedy heard of it, she murmured, 'Agggh. How typical.'

Because Monroe refused to wear undergarments, Jean Louis crafted a series of strategically placed panels, also made from soufflé, that masked her breasts and other delicate areas. It took as many as twenty individually sculpted layers to cover the breasts alone, and five hours of cutting and stitching so that the nipples could barely show through. A clear plastic zipper ran down the back from the neck, but Monroe had to be sewn into the dress as well.

More than 6,000 hand-sewn beads completed the effect.

'It was worth all the work,' recalled Jean Louis, 'because we achieved that marvellous illusion of beads over a nude body.' Political writer Arthur Schlesinger, Jr., later described the dress as 'skin and beads'.

One evening, while Elizabeth Courtney was completing tiny

stitches up the back of the dress, Eunice Murray interrupted the session to tell Monroe she had a phone call.

'Whoever it is, tell him I'll call back,' Monroe said.

Murray moved closer and whispered, 'But it's Hyannis Port.'

'I'll take it in here,' Monroe said.

Her answer surprised Murray. All previous calls from the White House or Hyannis Port had been taken in Monroe's locked bedroom.

As Elizabeth Courtney continued basting the back of the dress, she heard Monroe say, 'I'm wearing it now.'

The star began singing the birthday greeting she would sing to JFK. When she got to the words 'Mr. President,' she stopped. 'Uh-oh,' she giggled. 'I shouldn't have sung that.'

The actress blushed and looked up at Courtney. Later, when she had completed her chat with the President, she told the fitter, 'Well, I guess the cat's out of the bag now.'

'I'll never tell,' said Courtney, who described the encounter in a 1981 interview. 'But I had already heard about the dress and its purpose from Walter Winchell.'

After that last fitting, eighteen seamstresses worked on the gown for seven days straight, racing the clock as the gala approached. With the gown rushing to completion, Monroe began spending her evenings rehearsing what would become her inimitable, show-stopping rendition of 'Happy Birthday', for which Fox music director Lionel Newman was secretly coaching her during lunch breaks on *Something's Got to Give*. Just as they had collaborated on the sexy 'Diamonds Are a Girl's Best Friend', they were determined to infuse the simple 'Happy Birthday' with sexuality.

Monroe again imported hair colourist Pearl Porterfield to brew the hottest hair colour yet – a tint that *Vogue* magazine, after the gala, dubbed 'pillow slip white' and predicted would set a national fashion.

None of the artisans who were gilding this Hollywood

lily had a clue that Monroe was devilishly determined to offer herself up as the very antithesis of Jacqueline Kennedy. In place of Jackie's usually sedate Balmain gown would be Marilyn's extravagant Tinseltown costume; in place of Jackie's tame coif would be Marilyn's expanded page boy with understated wing flaring to the side. It was to set an international fashion.

'Marilyn considered Jackie her rival at this point,' said choreographer Steve Papich.

In a way, Monroe's extravagant display at Madison Square Garden was a misguided declaration of war. It was also a violation of all the rules laid out for her by the organisers of John Kennedy's forty-fifth-birthday party.

New York director-composer Richard Adler, chairman of the event, was the man who chose Monroe as the focal point and finale of the celebration. But when he had approached her in November 1961, he had had no way of knowing that her affair with JFK was just beginning to heat up.

He pursued the star to her Actors Studio class one night and came up to her during a coffee break. During his appeal, her eyes widened and misted over.

'Yes, of course, I'd love to,' she said, kissing him on the cheek.

Adler cautioned her, 'And, Marilyn, I not only want you to be there on time, I want you to actually be there.'

'Then I spoke to her of something even more delicate,' said Adler. 'I told her I wanted her to sing "Happy Birthday" straight and clear-voiced. And I told her "I mean *straight*."' Monroe nodded vigorously.

Then there was the choice of gown. Monroe leaned close to Adler and said soothingly, 'Dick, I have this beautiful Norman Norell dress – black and flowing, with a high neck. Will that do?'

'Perfectly,' said Adler.

Now that was easy, the composer thought. Marilyn was hardly as difficult as he'd been led to believe.

In late spring of 1962, however, Adler began hearing disturbing rumours from the West Coast about a revealing couturier gown and bawdy rehearsals in the Fox recording studio.

Adler went into a Broadway recording studio and sang 'Happy Birthday' the way he wanted Monroe to sing it. It was sent to her with the message: 'You should sing this precisely as I did. Full out. No baby-voiced breathlessness, *please!*'

During Monroe's last fitting with Jean Louis, she offered up her own all-stops-out breathless rendition. 'She wound up by singing the breathiest "Happy Birthday" I had ever heard,' said Jean Louis. 'She even included the word "President". Then she said, "Oh, I wasn't supposed to say that."' The designer remembered the whole effect as terribly charming.

As Monroe, Newcomb and her crew were airborne to New York, publicity about the star's appearance broke all over the East Coast. Adler was suddenly besieged with angry calls and telegrams protesting Monroe's appearance at the President's birthday party. 'Even the chairman of the Notre Dame Committee, a friend of the Kennedy family, demanded that she be removed,' Adler remembered. When the chairman of the Democratic Party called as well, Adler caved in. 'The show-biz side of me wanted to go with Marilyn, but the other side was racked with insecurity.'

So the composer called President Kennedy.

'Forget it,' said the President. 'It's a great idea for her to sing "Happy Birthday". It'll be fine. Everybody'll love it.'

Monroe then staged a private rehearsal for Adler at her apartment in New York. Sitting atop an upright piano and with jazz great Hank Jones accompanying her, she sang her version of 'Happy Birthday'.

'A bitter argument erupted between Marilyn and Adler,' said Ralph Roberts, who attended the rehearsal.

'It was pure baby-voiced breathiness, the very thing I feared,' Adler recalled. 'I went home certain we were headed for one of the most embarrassing disasters of all time.'

– Chapter 13 –

Birthday Blues

Early on the morning of May 19, Richard Adler decided to cancel Monroe's appearance at the gala. Haunted by her Tinseltown performance the night before, he had tossed and turned all night in his Manhattan apartment. 'I was certain I had made a terrible mistake that would ruin the gala,' he said.

But before Adler could fire Monroe, fate and a series of mishaps intervened.

When she awakened, Monroe intuitively knew that something was wrong. Trailing a long chiffon scarf and camouflaged by a car coat, she made a sullen appearance at the technical rehearsal. She chatted briefly with Peggy Lee, introduced herself to Ella Fitzgerald, and posed for a perfunctory photo with Adler.

In her coolest manner, she refused to sing. 'Mr. Adler has already heard me,' she said archly.

Peggy Lee later said that she noticed Monroe carefully surveying the stage, the lighting, and the seating arrangement in a sort of mental rehearsal.

Adler himself ran out to consult with his old friend Jack Benny. After hearing Adler's imitation of Monroe's performance, Benny erupted in anger. 'Get somebody else. What kind of a schmuck are you, anyway, getting Marilyn Monroe to sing "Happy Birthday" to the President of the United States?'

That did it for Adler. He decided to pull Monroe from the show. Seeking a replacement, he appealed to Shirley MacLaine, an old friend and a cast member of Adler's *The Pajama Game*. 'I don't think it will work and I've got to do something about it in a hurry,' he told her. 'Can you work up a rendition of "Happy Birthday" this quickly?'

MacLaine, a confidante of the Kennedy family as well, had a cooler head than Adler. 'It'll be okay, Dick. Marilyn is only one part of a long evening full of stars.'

'But it's the finale,' Adler lamented. 'I want you to sing it.'

MacLaine said she would sing the greeting as a favour to Adler. But as a member of Frank Sinatra's 'rat pack', she had heard all the inside talk about Monroe and JFK, and warned Adler against firing *Monroe*. 'Think of the repercussions – both public and private.'

Unknown to Adler, Monroe had called the President even earlier that morning to coo and sigh her way through the tribute. Hazel Washington remembered laughing as Monroe accompanied the telephone performance with the sexy gestures that would later prove so effective on stage.

'She did enjoy singing "Happy Birthday" to that man,' Washington remembered.

For his part, the President roared with laughter. Monroe needed no further approval.

Adler was trying to reach John Kennedy at the same time. He called the White House and was referred to the President's suite at the Carlyle Hotel.

'It took a good fifteen minutes for the President to come to the phone,' Adler said.

'Mr President,' said Adler, 'she's going to sing "Happy Birthday" in the slow, breathy tone, just like she did in *Gentlemen Prefer Blondes*.'

The President was soothing. 'Believe me, Dick, it'll be all right.'

Adler, who wrote the music for *The Pajama Game* and *Damn Yankees*, whose songs included 'Steam Heat' and 'You Gotta Have Heart', was an intuitive artist, but there was no way he – or anyone – could understand the turbulent emotions surrounding Monroe's sexy serenade.

To the driven, ambitious Robert Kennedy, Monroe was the ultimate birthday present. Gorgeously wrapped in her Jean Louis cellophane, she was a living doll, offered up as a kind of sacrifice.

To the President, Monroe's appearance validated the image of the most swinging White House ever. His lusty courtship of her (and hers of him) meant that he had finally topped his father, the grand old rake Joseph P. Kennedy, who had bedded the most sensual star of his era, the mercurial Gloria Swanson.

Rather than banish Monroe from the ceremony, the President sacrificed the First Lady. According to Jacqueline Kennedy's biographers Kitty Kelley and C. David Heymann, Jackie issued an ultimatum. It was Monroe or her. When the President chose, the First Lady quietly absented herself.

To Monroe, this was a command performance. 'She was implying that she was everyone's dream of Democratic success,' said Carl Rollyson, whose scholarly book *Marilyn Monroe: A Life of the Actress* dealt at length with the gala. 'She felt the event ratified her existence and defined her as both a star and as "one of the people".' Eunice Murray put it more colourfully: 'She would have come back from the dead to be there.'

As usual, Monroe suffered last-minute jitters. Besides phoning both the President and the Attorney General, she also sought reassurance from Joan Greenson, her psychiatrist's daughter, and from Ralph Roberts. Just before leaving for Madison Square Garden, Monroe telephoned Joan in California and repeated her performance, one that Joan had heard more than ten times. 'Marilyn was in Manhattan and I was out in my little room near the garage. It was the strangest feeling listening to her sing the song that would become so famous only a few hours later.'

Joan had functioned, along with Adler and Lionel Newman, as one of Monroe's coaches as she developed her sultry version of 'Happy Birthday' and as she carefully choreographed the body language to go along with it.

'She was over at our house one afternoon putting on makeup,' said Joan Greenson. 'And I was sitting right next to her. She said, "I'm going to be singing for the President. Listen and tell me what you think."'

As Monroe sang the first stanza, she dropped the makeup brush, and with her right hand traced her figure from the curve of her hip to her waist. As she sang the final chorus, she cupped her right breast gently with her fingers.

'It was enormously sexual,' Joan remembered. 'I said to her, "Gee, look at the sexy dance you're doing just standing there." I don't even think Marilyn was aware she was doing it.'

The last-minute plea for reassurance came at 6 P.M. New York Time, 3 P.M. on the West Coast. 'I told her that I absolutely thought she was doing it perfectly,' Joan recalled. 'She seemed to need those last few words.'

Ralph Roberts was equally supportive. 'I could tell it would be an historic occasion; that Marilyn knew of the opposition to her sexy interpretation. I told her it was absolutely the right thing to do.'

Then there was a second call from Robert Kennedy – seeking another favour. Because his relationship with Monroe was still formal (they had met only twice), Bobby was usually a bit gruff. But this time, he poured on the charm.

'Miss Monroe, I know that your hairstylist, Sidney Guilaroff, is unavailable. Would you, as a favour to me, allow our stylist to do your hair? He's the best, I can guarantee it.'

There was a strained moment of silence. Marilyn later told Steven Papich, 'I sure as hell didn't want to look like Jackie Kennedy.' Bobby described her reaction as 'frosty'.

'Look, he's a real nice guy,' Bobby stammered. 'I would consider it a personal favour if you did this.'

Finally, Monroe agreed, thereby helping to launch the career of a young stylist named Mickey Song, whose client list later included Ali McGraw, Raquel Welch and Cybill Shepherd.

'I'd never asked the Kennedys for anything,' Song remembered. 'But I'd been a fan of Marilyn's for years and I asked Bobby if it was at all possible. He agreed instantly. Bobby was always the man in charge. I knew he could fix it if anyone could.'

When Bobby Kennedy called the last time, Hazel Washington was sewing Monroe into the gown, a process that required more than five hundred small stitches up the side of the dress, under the arms, and down a front panel over the breasts.

'She was encased in that dress when she finally arrived at Madison Square Garden,' said Song. 'There was only a small slit, a few inches long, at the bottom [that] allowed her to walk in very small, gliding steps.'

Song was the first to observe the incredible optical illusion Jean Louis had designed.

A blast of cold air rushed in as Secret Service agents pushed open the double doors and helped Monroe down two flights of stairs. The Feds had to hold her by the elbows and virtually carry her down the steps. As she slowly glided beneath beams of light from the antique ceiling fixtures, Mickey Song was transfixed.

From a distance of five hundred yards, it looked as though she was nude except for the spider web that covered her from shoulder to ankle. Moving down the long hall almost in step with the languid vocal that Peggy Lee was singing above, Monroe took several minutes to reach the door of the dressing

Marilyn Monroe looked 'radiant' according to one Fox studio executive in these costume-test shots for *Something's Got to Give* taken on 10 April 1962.

Marilyn Monroe and Joe DiMaggio at the première for *The Seven Year Itch* in 1954.

Monroe with George Cukor who first directed her in 1960's *Let's Make Love*. Arthur Miller is on the right.

A still from *Some Like it Hot*.

A publicity shot.

On the set of
Something's Got to Give

Monroe with director
George Cukor and the
child actors who play
her children,
Alexandra Heilweil
and Chris Morley.

Heilweil, Monroe and
Morley.

Monroe with Paula
Strasberg, her drama
coach and close friend.

Monroe and 'Tippy'. The dog's failure to respond to cues resulted in over three hours of filming and at least twenty takes. From left, a propman, Monroe, Agnes Flanaghan, Monroe's hairdresser, 'Tippy' and Rudd Weatherwax, the dog's trainer.

Monroe recovering from her gruelling scene with 'Tippy'. Clustered around her are Strasberg, Whitey Snyder, her make-up man and close confidant, and Flanaghan; behind is her stand-in, Evelyn Moriarity.

Monroe with Murray Schumarch,
the *New York Times* reporter who covered Hollywood.

Monroe with Cukor and Fox executive, Phil Feldman.

Above Elizabeth Taylor as Cleopatra.

Right Taylor with husband, Eddie Fisher.

Below right Taylor with lover, Richard Burton.

Peter Levathes, Fox's chief of production (left) and Walter Wanger, *Cleopatra*'s producer on the film's set. Rome, 1961.

John F. Kennedy and Robert F. Kennedy during the steel crisis in April of 1962.

Arthur Rickerby/*Life* magazine

Marilyn Monroe singing 'Happy Birthday' to JFK at the Madison Square Garden gala. Monroe wore a 'nude' designer gown that had to be sewn onto her body. 19 May 1962.

Yale Joel/*Life* magazine

Bill Ray/*Life* magazine

room where Song stood, directly beneath the presidential box.

'Of course, you couldn't see a thing,' Song said. 'The sprays of brilliants were just in the right places.'

Only when Monroe was standing directly before him could Song appreciate the silk and bead collage that Jean Louis had fashioned using two hundred different patches of silk. Song was tongue-tied and Monroe was cool, apparently having second thoughts about placing herself in the hands of a new hairstylist.

'I remember it as a kind of daydream,' said Song. 'Marilyn's hair was pre-set in curlers and protected by a large scarf. I remember that she was trembling violently and that she seemed very vulnerable.'

Luckily, Song was both shy and diplomatic, qualities the star immediately sensed and liked. 'I wanted to do something that hadn't been done before,' he said. 'An original style for an historic occasion. Her hair could have been done exactly like Jacqueline Kennedy's, but I definitely wanted to stay away from that because of the situation between the two women. And that situation had been made abundantly clear by the First Lady's refusal to attend the party.'

As stylist and star tried to get acquainted, Bobby Kennedy paced back and forth, his hands jammed into the pockets of his tuxedo pants. When Song tried to comb the right side of Monroe's hair into the flip that became a worldwide craze after the gala, she snapped at him.

Bobby, tired of Marilyn's temperament and worried about the passing time, stalked over to the hairdresser and said, 'Mickey, would you excuse us, please?' From the hall Song could hear raised voices and expletives, the Attorney General's voice growing louder and louder.

Bobby came out, readjusting his white tie. 'It'll be okay now,' he said.

Almost as an afterthought, Bobby grabbed Song by the arm and asked him, 'By the way, do you like her?'

Song nodded enthusiastically.

Yelling over his shoulder as he bounded down the hall, Bobby Kennedy had the last word: 'Well, I think she's a rude, fucking bitch.'

In the dressing room, all smiles, was a purring Monroe. 'Mickey,' she said, taking his hand, 'go ahead and do your *something historic*.'

– Chapter 14 –

For the World to See

Now completely gilded for the gala, Monroe stood in the darkness at the very edge of the Madison Square Garden stage. Just behind her, also lost in the blackness, was the five-foot-high birthday cake, so heavy it took six waiters to lift it.

In centre stage, ringed by 20,000 Democrats, was the President's brother-in-law, Peter Lawford, delivering a drawn-out introduction of Monroe. He was also teasing the political crowd with an in-joke about a secret they all knew – that she was the President's lover.

Mickey Song caught one last glimpse of Monroe just before she stepped into the brilliant lights. She sighed and straightened her shoulders. The burden of so much glamour seemed to weigh her down. 'To John and Bobby, she was just a beautiful and glamorous party girl, but Marilyn didn't want to be the party girl any more,' said Song. 'Now she wanted a real relationship with the President.'

In fact, this would be Monroe's final appearance as the white-hot party girl – the available blonde, forever defined by the chauvinistic standards of a world ruled by men. Despite Song's closeness to the President and his brother, he resented their cavalier treatment of Monroe. 'You couldn't escape the impression that Marilyn was John's birthday present. And from what I understand, later, Marilyn was just that.'

He watched the actress move deliberately into the light – cutting short Lawford's sappy monologue. Just as Lawford said, 'Mr. President, never in the history of the world has one woman meant so much . . .'

A gasp that built into a roar greeted Monroe as she danced through the circles of light. She coyly clasped the ermine wrap about her, masking the dress beneath. She paused until the roar quieted, then shrugged out of the fur, letting it fall backward into Lawford's hands. Whistles and shrieks followed.

Up in the Presidential box, John Kennedy looked over his shoulder at writer Gene Schoor. 'Jesus Christ, look at that dress,' he said.

Schoor noticed that the President was staring at every undulation. 'What an ass, Gene,' Kennedy said. '*What* an ass.' Seated next to him, Bobby betrayed no trace of emotion.

Just behind the President in the director's control booth, Richard Adler took a long look at the transparent dress. 'It was everything I feared,' he said. Just before show time, he had received a last-minute flurry of calls protesting Monroe's appearance. Some came from Cabinet members, one from a senior member of the President's White House staff, and some from the highest levels of the Pentagon.

As she began the first husky chorus, Monroe seemed energised, perhaps from the Dexedrine prescribed by the studio doctors. Robert Slatzer remembered that she was also pumped up with megavitamins and antibiotics. 'The effect was just hair-raising, it was so beautiful,' said Ralph Roberts, who saw the performance from the VIP box. 'You couldn't hear yourself think for the screaming and yelling.'

'It was like mass seduction,' Adler recalled. 'With Marilyn whispering "Happy Birthday" and the crowd yelling and screaming for her, I realised then that the President was a better showman than I was.'

Monroe later told *Life* magazine that the 'approval of the crowd was like an embrace. Then I thought, by God, I'll sing this song if it's the last thing I ever do. And I did it for the people as well. I remember when I turned to the microphone, I looked all the way up into the stands and I thought, "That's where I'd be – way up under those rafters."'

The actress also talked of trying to sing her way into every heart in Madison Square Garden – with the hope that her audience understood her sensual message.

The dress and the occasion would etch themselves into the history of the Kennedy years, along with other film flashes of Camelot – JFK hatless at his inauguration; Jacqueline Kennedy arriving in Paris; John-John's salute to his father's coffin. Monroe's performance has been playing ever since.

From the moment the extravaganza began, the eyes of the world's press were focused on the one empty seat that mattered – the seat meant for the First Lady. 'Jackie knew about the affair by then,' said Los Angeles mayor Sam Yorty, a national figure in Democratic politics. 'That's why she stayed away.'

'The First Lady wanted complete control over social situations,' said biographer Kitty Kelley. 'She avoided any invitation where she would publicly have to tolerate any flirtations involving her husband. As soon as she found out that Monroe was going to sing, she took the children to Virginia for a weekend of horseback riding.'

Behind the public show, a poignant private drama played out as Monroe prepared to share President Kennedy's bed for what would be the last time. As soon as the spotlights were dimmed, she was virtually carried back to the dressing room, where she collapsed against the door, feeling dizzy. Despite the studio amphetamines and an entire split of champagne, the sinusitis had caught up with her. Her fever rose dangerously.

Hazel Washington tried to coax her back to the 57th Street apartment, with no success. Monroe insisted on attending the two parties that followed the gala – the public one at the penthouse of theatre magnate Arthur Krim and the intimate one at the President's penthouse.

During the two hours it took Monroe to recover from her seven-minute appearance, she was carefully snipped out of the dress so that it could dry, and was bathed with cool hand towels in an attempt to lower her temperature. 'I was very worried about her,' said Hazel Washington. 'From that evening on, Marilyn just kept getting sicker and sicker, but she wouldn't stop.'

Finally, back in the gown and with her hair combed out, she entered Arthur Krim's party on the arm of her former father-in-law, Isadore Miller. The crush of people, including two hundred of the most powerful men in America, were electrified as Monroe moved from group to group.

After an hour, President Kennedy couldn't wait any longer. He pulled Monroe away from the other guests and into a corner, where they were soon joined by Robert Kennedy. The three huddled together, talking animatedly for about fifteen minutes.

Monroe's vulnerability as she moved timidly through the crowd had ignited Robert Kennedy's interest. Dorothy Kilgallen later reported that Monroe and Bobby Kennedy danced five times during the evening, while an angry Ethel Kennedy looked on. Walking arm in arm from the small dance floor, they ran into White House journalist Merriman Smith. Somewhat annoyed by the reporter's presence, Bobby introduced Monroe.

Later, the Attorney General appeared uneasy as Smith chatted with Monroe and Isadore Miller, writing in a small notebook at the same time. When Bobby was informed by a Secret Service agent that a candid photo had been taken of Monroe and the Kennedy brothers, his face grew stormy.

Shortly after 1 A.M., Secret Service agents escorted the President, Monroe and a handful of others through the crowded apartment and into a private elevator which descended to the basement of Krim's apartment house. From there they moved through a series of tunnels that connected the Carlyle Hotel with nearby apartment houses. The crush of reporters in the hotel lobby never saw the private band of revellers who crowded into the penthouse, where some of them remained until dawn.

Politician Adlai Stevenson noted a bit of envy in Bobby's eyes as Jack squired Monroe through both gatherings. 'I don't think I had ever seen anyone so beautiful as Marilyn Monroe that night,' said Stevenson. 'But my encounters with her only came after I broke through the strong defences of Robert Kennedy.'

Arthur Schlesinger, Jr., later one of Bobby's biographers, also noted the interest: 'There was at once something magical and desperate about her. Bobby, with his chivalry, his sympathy and absolute directness of response, got through the glittering mist surrounding Marilyn as few did.'

But Jack was still the one she went to bed with. 'I learned from an FBI agent that they remained in the suite for several hours,' said columnist Earl Wilson in an interview. 'It was the last prolonged encounter between them.'

The motivation that kept them locked inside the bedroom suite wasn't sex. Monroe complained to both Slatzer and Roberts that Kennedy was both brutal and perfunctory in bed.

'He was in and out in a few seconds,' recalled Slatzer. 'She insisted that he made love like an adolescent.'

To Steven Papich, Monroe described the President as 'less than inspired' as a lover. She also told Slatzer, 'Many times, due to his weak back, nothing happened at all.'

The President apparently liked sharing his bed with the world's sexiest woman and enjoying his sense of power, both in the corridors of Washington and behind the closed doors of Hollywood. By all accounts, the two gossiped for hours – on the phone, at Lawford's Pacific coast mansion, and at the Carlyle. With the double doors to the private suite guarded by the Secret Service, Monroe and the President wound down from the dazzle of the gala. Outside, strong winds blew across the city, misting the picture windows in the penthouse.

Elsewhere, a related drama was occurring.

Journalist Merriman Smith was awakened at 2.30 A.M. by loud banging on his apartment door. He was confronted by two Secret Service agents who grilled him for an hour about his surprise appearance at the private party. 'They wanted to make sure I didn't write about Marilyn and Bobby,' he told Adler, who had got him into the private affair. 'I wasn't going to write about them anyway. I'm not a gossip columnist.'

Adler was horrified. 'I hadn't any idea that the Secret Service was involved in that kind of censorship.'

Agents also appeared at 8.30 the next morning in the photo lab of Time and Life Incorporated and demanded the negatives supposedly showing the Kennedys with Monroe at the Arthur Krim party. 'No such thing exists,' the director of the lab told them.

Monroe herself arrived at her East 57th Street apartment shortly before 4 A.M. Ralph Roberts was waiting there to knead away her tension. As they chatted about the parties, Monroe had enthusiastic praise for Robert Kennedy.

Although he had been on the sidelines during her affair with JFK, Monroe had never mentioned the Attorney General until the gala. He had startled her by discussing politics with her, acknowledging that there was more to Monroe than her glossy image.

But she told Roberts there was no chance of an affair between herself and the Attorney General. 'He's not my type,' she said. 'I think the word she used was "puny",' Roberts recalled.

Chapter 15

A Midnight Swim

Monroe flew back to Los Angeles early Sunday afternoon, May 20, with the Jean Louis gown in a garment bag slung over one arm.

As she swept through the New York airport, she noticed a heightened interest in her. Having dispensed with the usual disguise of sunglasses and a scarf, she seemed to enjoy the new dimension of fame.

Those who hadn't seen the sexy birthday serenade on the network news shows had probably seen photos of the gala on page one of their Sunday morning newspapers. One photo in particular had attracted the eye of editors. It showed Monroe from above and to the side, leaning toward President Kennedy, with her left hand caressing the bottom of her breast.

The gala, and the now indelible affirmation of her association with Camelot, gave her a fix of fame, a rush of power that overrode the residual traces of her illness and caused her to lay aside the feud with George Cukor. 'Energised' is the word Evelyn Moriarity and Henry Weinstein used to describe her.

But when she stopped at the old Pico Boulevard newsstand on her way home from the Los Angeles airport, she saw something that displeased her. The jammed racks of periodicals and international newspapers formed a tribute to Elizabeth Taylor, whose insolently beautiful face stared out from the covers of a score of magazines.

What Roman columnists now called 'the most public adultery in the world' had only whetted the appetite for gossip and fresh photographs of Taylor. Until the gala, Monroe, once America's favourite cover girl, had been off the front pages of the world for a year.

It isn't known whether or not Monroe had already conceived what would be her ultimate publicity stunt. But everyone noticed a new determination in her approach to *Something's Got to Give*.

At 6.05 A.M. on Monday, May 21, thirty-three hours after the gala, Monroe reported for work on soundstage 14. She sent word to Cukor that she was prepared to film any one of seven upcoming scenes, but close-ups, she said, were ruled out. Not even makeup artist Whitey Snyder could erase the traces of exhaustion from the whirlwind trip to New York.

As messengers ran back and forth between Monroe's bungalow and Cukor's office, the company was suddenly thrown into a turmoil by Dean Martin, who reported for work despite a bad cold and a temperature of 100 degrees.

Since Cukor had scheduled scenes of dialogue between the two stars, Monroe summoned studio doctor Lee Siegel to determine whether it was safe for her to work with Martin. She also had a telephone conversation with a nose-and-throat specialist at Cedars of Lebanon – the hospital that had diagnosed her sinus infection. Both advised her not to work with her costar.

Cukor was furious, claiming that there was no possible danger to Monroe. 'He's no longer contagious,' the director told assistant director Buck Hall.

A stalemate followed. Cukor fumed; Monroe locked herself in her dressing room. Weinstein tried to break the impasse.

Finally, the actress informed Weinstein that she wouldn't set foot on the soundstage if Martin was on it.

Plans were shifted. Cyd Charisse and the two children were called in, and the huge set was lighted.

The angry director expressed his displeasure once again by slowing down the pace, leading to Paula Strasberg's later claim that 'even when he had his star back, Cukor refused to make use of her. Only twenty-six short takes were completed on Monday – all of them variations of a single intimate moment between Christopher Morley and Monroe.' There is no noticeable variation in the takes.

On Tuesday, May 22, with Martin still sick in bed, Monroe sent a memo to Cukor and Weinstein informing them, 'I cannot work with Mr Martin until he's well. I take this action upon the advice of my physicians.' Monroe filmed for half a day with Cyd Charisse before leaving the stage in the early afternoon.

Then Cukor cleared everyone off the set to prepare for an important sequence to be shot on Wednesday morning. As soon as soundstage 14 was empty, about 2 P.M., construction crews and electricians moved in – along with half a dozen spotlights from a warehouse on the other side of the lot. Later, a series of wooden platforms was carted onto the set.

Just before Monroe left for the day, Cukor bustled into her dressing room for a private conference – and both of them talked with great animation. They may have had a second conference via telephone later that night. Eunice Murray vaguely remembers the call – the first one since production had started.

At 5 P.M., Newcomb called photographer Lawrence Schiller at home. 'I would plan to be on the set all day tomorrow if I were you, Larry,' said the publicist. 'And bring plenty of film. Marilyn has that swimming scene tomorrow and, knowing Marilyn, she might slip out of her suit.'

Lawrence Schiller was just making a name for himself

as a celebrity photographer and worked for *Paris Match* and *Life* magazine, among others. He would later become a major producer and director of the television movies *The Executioner's Song* and *Marilyn: The Untold Story*.

Schiller realised that this footage – the first nude scene by a major American star – would be historic. He also realised that he would only be allowed a few brief minutes with the star – while she was rehearsing. He brought another photographer, William Woodfield, into the deal so that they could get shots from several angles.

Cukor had the same idea. He ordered a second movie camera for the swimming scene. Two cinematographers, Billy Daniels and an unnamed assistant, would photograph Monroe at the same time. One camera was to shoot head on, the other from the side and slightly above. At one point, Cukor put a camera on a riser, built by carpenters working overnight, so that the lens could look down at Monroe as she clung to the side of the pool.

Both Monroe and Cukor wanted the stunt to appear unrehearsed and spontaneous – even though it was intricately choreographed. 'This needs to be a spur-of-the-moment thing,' Monroe told Cukor. (In 1980, Cukor took credit for the idea. 'I suggested she do the scene totally nude, and she agreed instantly,' he said.)

The script provided the ideal opportunity – a midnight swimming sequence in which Monroe, in the buff, would lure Martin from Cyd Charisse's bed. But no actual nudity was planned. There was only to be the illusion of a skinny-dip. To that end, Jean Louis designed an invisible swimsuit that was part body stocking and part silk bikini – fashioned from the same bolt of silk soufflé used for the 'Kennedy dress'.

On Wednesday morning, Monroe, faithful in her conversion to Method acting, consulted Paula Strasberg with the question: 'What if I played that scene totally in the nude?' The coach re-read the scene and answered, 'I'm sure, in this case, it would be charming. This is exactly as Ellen Arden might have done. After all, she had been swimming nude in the island lagoon for years.'

To lend a touch of authenticity to the stunt, Cukor directed Monroe to enter the pool wearing the mesh bikini. 'Don't take the suit off until I give you a signal,' he said. As part of their clever ruse, cinematographer Billy Daniels was cued to say, 'I'm sorry, darling, but the lines in the swimsuit are showing up.'

Monroe then executed a water ballet as she slipped off her top and bottom and deposited them at the edge of the pool. (The negatives and all prints of the star shedding the suit are missing from the Fox archives.)

Forewarned, Schiller and Woodfield both packed photographic arsenals, including brand-new motor-driven Nikons capable of taking dozens of frames per second.

'Nobody knew how carefully planned this was,' said associate producer Gene Allen. 'It would have been a big publicity boost for the picture – a sensational way to help sell the film when it was released.'

Monroe was giddy with anticipation of the frolic. She had obtained publicity proofs of Taylor's ersatz nude scene on the set of *Cleopatra* and noted that you could see the body stocking just below the water. Besides, the fleshy shoulders and arms protruding from the Egyptian milk bath showed that Taylor was no competition for Monroe. 'She was aware that she still had a fabulous body,' Slatzer recalled. 'This was a way to show the world that she wasn't over the hill.'

Joan Greenson agreed: 'There was a part of Marilyn that was a daredevil and a show-off. She thought, "Why not? If this is what we're doing, why not do it nude?" She really enjoyed being a bit shocking.'

During the rehearsal, when Schiller and Woodfield took their first pictures, the nudity came in flashes – as Monroe bobbed up and down in the turquoise water, as she slipped in and out of Dean Martin's oversized blue robe, and as she clung to the rim of the pool with one leg thrown up onto the Spanish tiles. But, during one brief sequence, she sat still on the steps of the pool, her back facing the cameras. As she looked back over her shoulder in wide-eyed innocence, Schiller captured some sensational frames.

Monroe had positioned Whitey Snyder between herself and the two movie cameras, telling him to warn her if she showed too much. 'She was obsessed with the idea that she would look indecent, but there was no danger of that,' said Snyder. 'Mostly, there was merely the illusion of nudity.'

The actress signalled Cukor that she wanted to perform for the still cameras for half an hour. He slipped off the set, taking the cinematographers with him.

On the contact sheets in the Fox archives, Monroe can be seen teasing the lens, letting the robe slide over her shoulders and hang there for a few seconds. Then, seeming to glory in herself, she tilted her head back and blew a kiss to the electricians on a ramp high above.

With an enigmatic smile, she released the robe so that it slid over her breasts to her abdomen. She caught it again and performed a sensual pantomime for Schiller and Woodfield.

Soon, Schiller was on his knees, slowly moving around Monroe in a semicircle. Through the lens, he was startled by the radiance of her body – trapped in the platinum light which poured down from the ceiling.

When Monroe shrugged out of the robe and it fell away, Schiller gasped.

The gentle whir of the Nikon was the only other sound on the set. Cukor was on a catwalk high above, orchestrating the play of the blinding spotlights across the surface of the pool with its azure-tinted water.

Outside the soundstage, pandemonium swept the lot. From office to office, the word spread that Monroe was doing a nude scene – her first since the nude calendar shots fourteen years earlier.

'The reaction was incredible,' recalled Henry Weinstein. 'Everyone wanted to get on that set. It became a stampede.' The producer requested a flying wedge of security guards to cover the five entrances to the soundstage. Work came to a halt all over the lot as everyone speculated about what was occurring on the set of *Something's Got to Give.*'

The nude scene took everybody by surprise. Not even the members of the publicity department had been informed, and when they did learn of it, Cukor issued orders that the event would be publicised only with Monroe's approval. 'The nude scene will be made public as part of a prearranged plan,' he said. 'All press calls are to be referred to Miss Newcomb.'

Nobody on the set, least of all Monroe, stopped to think of the scene's effect on her delicate health. It was a punishing day. Beginning at 10.40 A.M. and continuing until late afternoon (lunch was taken on the run at the edge of the set), she completed twenty rehearsals, twenty actual takes, and twenty sequences staged for the still photographers. In all, she was in the water for four hours – dog-paddling or swimming for about ninety minutes.

She had been receiving amphetamine shots for slightly more than two weeks – bolstered by Dexedrine capsules. At this point, the methamphetamines and strong antihistamines were totally masking the symptoms of her sinus infection.

With her fever quelled by speed and her headaches eased by Demerol, Monroe slipped in and out of the pool more than fifty times. To offset the heat of the lights, strong blasts of refrigerated air were pumped onto the set. The pool's non-circulating water was approximately ninety-four degrees, the air about seventy-four.

Because the scene required Monroe to spend so much time in the chlorinated water, the hairdressing and makeup rituals were complicated. First Bunny Gardell covered Monroe's naked body with the gooey body makeup invented by Max Factor for MGM's swimming star, Esther Williams. Then came the hair spray, a varnish-like solution that made Monroe's hair stiff and brittle.

None of this preparation fazed Monroe. She seemed revved up – more like the Monroe of the early fifties. 'She was deliriously happy,' said Weinstein. 'What made that day different from any other day? I don't know. Maybe she was relieved because the scene contained only a few lines of dialogue. As I watched her, I thought to myself, "Maybe we'll get this project finished after all."'

Weinstein added that the nude scene 'made her feel secure. It was her happiest day. I think she was fully aware of the sensation she was creating. She had fabulous instincts, you know. They were better than mine. Better than the studio's.'

Schiller and Woodfield were overwhelmed by the scene unfolding before their cameras. Nude photos of Marilyn Monroe were almost priceless. Monroe had already convinced Fox to relinquish its rights to any of the stills in return for worldwide publicity. 'We could have made three hundred thousand dollars on those shots if we had retained the rights,' publicist Harry Brand later commented.

'Marilyn knew instinctively that the photos would be perceived as part of a crass publicity stunt if Fox itself released the pictures,' Schiller said. Later, in her bungalow, Schiller asked Monroe what she wanted in return for signing away her personal rights.

Monroe took his hand. 'Larry,' she said, 'the week these pictures are released, I don't want to see Elizabeth Taylor's face on any magazine cover in the world.'

'She was seeking a way to show that, at least in the public's mind, she was more powerful than Elizabeth Taylor,' Schiller said. 'She also needed to validate her international stardom.'

Two days later, on Friday afternoon, Monroe met Schiller in front of the old Schwab's Drugstore to decide which of the hundreds of frames could be released. 'I remember sitting in my T-bird with Marilyn, she with a bottle of Dom Pérignon and a pair of pinking shears. She used the shears to destroy the negatives she didn't like. I ended up shredding hundreds of pictures on the spot because I wanted to keep her absolute confidence.'

The stills eventually appeared on the covers of seventy-two magazines in thirty-two countries – some of them behind the Iron Curtain. Collectively, Schiller and William Woodfield earned $200,000.

But, instead of 'waking up the studio executives' as Monroe had hoped, the publicity surrounding the gala and the swimming sequence backed the Fox board of directors into a corner.

– Chapter 16 –

Lost Weekend

On Friday, May 25, Fox executives on both coasts viewed the unedited film of Monroe's midnight swim.

Everyone agreed that it was one of her best scenes – and that it ranked with the billowing skirt sequence from *The Seven Year Itch* and the 'Diamonds are a Girl's Best Friend' production number from *Gentlemen Prefer Blondes*.

Monroe had also been on the set all week – further cause for optimism. The outlook might have been better still if Cukor could have got Monroe and Martin in front of the cameras at the same time. But Martin's cold lingered through Friday, and, despite a personal plea from the director, Monroe refused to share a soundstage with him.

Cukor was convinced that Monroe was merely trying to delay her first close-ups in her love scene with Martin until the effects of the exhausting trip to New York had worn off.

Saturday dawned hot and dry as desert winds pushed the moist Pacific air out to sea. Martin's symptoms vanished and, on Sunday, Lee Siegel pronounced him well enough to work with Monroe.

Assistant director Buck Hall quickly reshuffled the shooting schedule and booked the first Martin-Monroe scenes for Monday and Tuesday. He had to move fast. Actor Wally Cox was to join the cast for those scenes, portraying a nerdy shoe clerk who is enlisted by Monroe to pose as the hunk who shared her desert island for five years.

Monroe and Cukor had tussled for several days over the casting of this key role. Cukor wanted newcomer Don Knotts to play the part. Monroe eventually won out – but only after going over Cukor's head to Phil Feldman. 'She does have *cast approval*,' Feldman reminded the director.

Walter Bernstein's new dialogue for Cox, still being written on Saturday, was photocopied and sent by messenger to the guest house in Marlon Brando's Bel Air compound where Cox was staying. An old friend of both Monroe and Cox, Brando had introduced them early in 1961.

Filming for the week was to open with an eight-minute scene that involved Monroe, Martin, Cyd Charisse, Tom Tryon, Cox and Phil Silvers, who was playing an insurance salesman.

Cukor decided to ease Monroe into the sequence by scheduling a single line of dialogue for the first day. But the director knew he was in trouble when Monroe almost stumbled down a short flight of stairs during her entrance.

Tryon also realised that something was wrong. 'What's the matter with Marilyn?' he whispered to Cukor.

The director shook his head. 'I've never seen her like this. She looks like she's falling apart.'

Both men sat in chairs just behind the movie camera; their eyes were riveted on Monroe as she descended the pink stucco staircase in the centre of the set.

She moved in slow motion, as if in a trance. Her face was unnaturally pale despite multiple layers of rosy Max Factor makeup.

Monroe and Tryon were in the midst of the dream sequence that transported them to a south sea island. In Monroe's vision,

Tryon suddenly appeared, lounging on the tree limb in a loincloth.

Since there was only one line of dialogue, the actress was expected to breeze right through it.

'But from the moment she came to the set, she looked like a piece of fine crystal about to shatter,' said Tryon. 'All of her moves were tentative and tenuous.'

The script called for Monroe to walk down the stairs and whisper a few words to Dean Martin, who was positioned offstage. Then she would see Tryon, almost as in an hallucination, and recoil in shock.

'She only had two words to say, which were "Nick, darling",' before the flashback began,' said Tryon. 'But she couldn't get the words correct no matter how many times we did it. My heart went out to her.'

Four times in a row, Monroe swayed into view and stammered, 'Darling, Nick.'

Cukor rushed up. 'This is very simple, Marilyn. Just say, "Nick, darling", and then smile.'

Monroe's eyes widened. 'That's what I did, George.'

'No, you didn't,' the director snapped. 'You've got it backwards.'

The actress looked as if she was going to faint. Tryon was so sympathetic he couldn't look Cukor in the eye. 'I don't know why he didn't move on and fix it in the sound laboratory,' he later commented. 'But he wasn't ready to give an inch.'

The director ploughed ahead, impervious to Monroe's troubles.

For the first time since filming had begun, Monroe seemed overcome by her emotions. 'We could tell that her nerves were shattered,' Weinstein said. 'But no one knew what – or who – caused it.'

When word of the trouble on the set ran through the studio rumour mill, Fox switchboard operators noted that

'Marilyn had been trying all day to reach Frank Sinatra.' Unable to locate him, she sent a telegram to Australia, where the crooner was performing on his world tour. It isn't known whether or not she reached him on Monday, but he did call her, from Monaco, a week later.

'She was in such a mess that only Sinatra could get her out of it,' remembered associate producer Gene Allen. 'Who else would you call on? Who's somebody who can move mountains?'

After ten torturous takes, Montroe finally ran from the set and through the streets to her studio bungalow. 'She almost knocked me over,' recalled Hazel Washington. 'Cukor was acting like a bully – making a bad situation worse.'

Washington wrung her hands as Monroe collapsed in her makeup chair and grabbed a scarlet lipstick.

'Frank, help me,' she scrawled across the mirror.

She sat still for a few seconds before she grabbed the lipstick again. 'Frank, please help me,' she wrote.

Ten minutes later, Dean Martin strolled in, booted everyone else out of the dressing room and talked with Monroe for almost half an hour.

When they re-emerged, Monroe had a sad smile on her face, but she appeared more composed. Once she was back on the set, however, her shell of confidence collapsed. 'She was trembling all over,' said Tryon. 'Something dreadful had happened to her.'

The drama playing out that Monday on the set of *Something's Got to Give* resembled a gothic Hollywood drama – an actress engulfed by personal heartbreak; a director who was unwilling to help; a movie that was crumbling apart; and a studio that was desperately seeking an excuse to fire its star.

Henry Weinstein was puzzled. When Monroe had wound up the previous week of filming on Friday, she had been in remarkably good spirits. She had several glasses of Dom Pérignon with designer William Travilla in her bungalow, and proudly displayed the press clippings from her appearance at the gala.

An hour later that same Friday, traffic jammed at the intersection of Sunset Boulevard and Fairfax Avenue, where Monroe and Schiller sat in his car in front of Schwab's, engrossed in the yards of negatives from the nude scene. Schiller found her 'vibrant and excited'.

With the sunset framing her head, she reclined in Schiller's convertible, her high heels pressed against the dashboard. Long strips of contact prints overflowed her lap and spilled onto the floor. She giggled at the physical frailties caught by Schiller's camera.

As she edited the pictures with her pinking shears, she put a hand on the photographer's arm. 'Do you think this is entirely honest? I mean, is it wrong to eliminate all these frames?'

Schiller smiled. 'You have to protect yourself!' he said.

The task completed, she hurried into her limousine and sped towards Brentwood.

As she waved good-bye, the photographer marvelled at her joy; she was turning this tedious film into an adventure.

Then she disappeared for seventy-two hours. Phone calls went unanswered. Luncheon dates were missed.

'This was perhaps the most mysterious weekend of Marilyn's life,' said Henry Weinstein. 'It was even more puzzling than the day of her death. Something terrible happened to her that weekend. It was deeply personal, so personal that it shook Marilyn's psyche. I saw it happen, and I blame myself for not immediately calling Dr. Ralph Greenson back [from Switzerland, where his wife was receiving treatment]. But I didn't.'

A curtain of secrecy still obscures the events of May 26 and 27. Was Monroe closeted in her house, in the grip of drugs? Or did she have yet another clandestine abortion? Both possibilities were rumoured at the time.

'I don't think we will ever know for sure,' said Weinstein.

Actually, the key to the mystery of those forty-eight hours involves a series of telephone calls which began with a lengthy conversation between Monroe and Sinatra.

'Marilyn told me that Sinatra called her with a warning, advising her against further intimacy with the Kennedys,' Robert Slatzer said. 'He particularly advised her to back off from John Kennedy.' Slatzer said that Sinatra was apparently becoming more and more concerned about Monroe's relationship with the President. 'It was obvious that he would drop her. With another election year coming up, what choice did he have?'

Sinatra undoubtedly knew that the President was about to cut Monroe off – now that he had wrung every drop of usefulness out of her. JFK had bedded her half a dozen times, had revelled in her aura of glamour, and had validated their affair through the public display at Madison Square Garden. But the presidential gala was to be her swan song. Sinatra himself had been dropped by President Kennedy and ostracised by the White House four months earlier.

After courting the multimillionaire singer for years and exploiting his name and his talent during the presidential campaign, the Kennedys banished him overnight. On February 28, just weeks before JFK was to make a spectacular weekend visit to Sinatra's Palm Springs hideaway, the President's political advisers declared that the singer was 'an undesirable person'.

At a state dinner, Bobby Kennedy blurted out, 'This man is involved with criminal elements; you can't afford to be seen with him.'

The President turned red and changed the subject.

FBI director J. Edgar Hoover had already prepared three reports on Sinatra – reports charging that he had 'personal ties to ten leading figures of organised crime'.

The President read the memos, filed them and refused to sever his friendship with Sinatra. He wasn't ready to swear off the heavy doses of glamour and gossip the entertainer brought to his life.

Then, at 9 A.M. on February 27, 1962, Bobby burst into the Oval Office with yet another Hoover memorandum – this one striking closer to home. During a Las Vegas mob investigation, FBI agents had discovered that Judith Campbell Exner, a sometime mistress of Sam Giancàna, was also sleeping with the President of the United States. The FBI director charged that Sinatra had 'fixed Kennedy up' with Campbell.

Still JFK wavered.

But Bobby was already in action. He called Peter Lawford away from the set of his television series. 'Tell Sinatra that the President can't stay at his compound in March,' said Bobby. 'And find another house for the Palm Springs visit.'

Lawford was frantic. He was the one who, as a favour to JFK, had enlisted Sinatra's considerable help during the presidential campaign. He also knew how much the visit meant to the singer. Lawford objected strenuously.

Bobby was adamant. 'It's too dangerous.'

Lawford appealed to JFK. 'Don't do it, Mr. President. You owe Sinatra.'

'I can't stay at Sinatra's,' JFK answered. 'Not while Bobby is investigating Giancana. Frank is too close to this man.'

'It fell to me to break the news to Frank and, frankly, I was scared,' Lawford told Kitty Kelley. 'Frank had built special cottages for the President and for the Secret Service,' spending $1.2 million to prepare for the visit.

So, instead of honouring Sinatra with his presence and thereby paying him back for his campaign activity, Kennedy stayed with the singer's archrival and enemy, Bing Crosby.

Since Monroe spent the night with President Kennedy in one of Crosby's guest bungalows, her interest in JFK overrode her loyalty to Sinatra – her friend and benefactor for almost ten years.

'The Kennedys damn near broke Sinatra's heart,' recalled

longtime Hollywood columnist Dorothy Manners. 'They cruelly dropped him overnight. Perhaps he knew they would do the same thing to Marilyn and wanted to warn her.'

Also from Lawford, Sinatra apparently heard that the President was about to drop Monroe. 'He tried to warn her,' recalled Hazel Washington. 'But Marilyn wasn't in a mood to listen.'

On May 25, Monroe tried calling the President on his private line, only to find that it had been disconnected. When she tried the White House switchboard, operators refused to put her calls through. 'She was angry when the phone connection was cut,' Slatzer recalled. 'It was a terrible shock.'

On Saturday, a week after the gala, Monroe received several long distance calls from someone close to the Kennedy family – probably a member of Kennedy's campaign staff. Eunice Murray remembered such a call, as did Robert Slatzer. 'It got too hot for Jack, politically,' said actress Terry Moore, one of Monroe's closest girlfriends. Moore heard from Monroe that Attorney General Robert Kennedy had been delegated to put an end to the affair.

'At first, the President failed to perceive the danger in his relationship with Monroe,' recalled Monroe's biographer Anthony Summers. 'When she began prattling on about her connections in the White House and the secrets they had told her, the Kennedy family saw the possible consequences.'

Leaders of the Democratic party had already expressed their outrage over JFK's association with Monroe, just before the birthday party. Richard Adler recalled that key members of the party leadership (he didn't remember the exact names) called him the day before the gala and begged him to cut Monroe from the ceremony. Six congressmen and three senators, all Democrats, sent him telegrams to protest the birthday serenade. At the time, Washington was teeming with gossip about the President's affair with the movie star.

Former CBS news producer Ted Landreth, who also produced and directed the British Broadcasting Corporation documentary *Marilyn Monroe: Say Goodbye to the President* (1985), said he found ample evidence that 'highly placed political leaders knew of the affair. The Washington press corps knew about it, as well,' said Landreth, who also uncovered evidence that JFK had to end the relationship suddenly.

And Lawford told two of his former wives that Robert Kennedy was charged with breaking the news to Monroe. Both Patricia Seaton Lawford and Deborah Gould Lawford have said repeatedly that Bobby was ordered to end the affair shortly after the gala.

Former Los Angeles mayor Sam Yorty, a national Democratic powerhouse during the Kennedy era, noted that Monroe was a threat to the family image. 'They wanted to stay pristine pure. Even though they had a lot of affairs, they didn't want any of them to come out.'

About the same time, Monroe discovered that Fox had not approved her appearance at the presidential birthday, as Robert Kennedy and Peter Lawford had led her to believe. And now, as she began the third week of filming, the studio buzzed with rumours that the paperwork to fire her had already been prepared.

It was hardly surprising that she was emotionally shattered. Her appearance at the gala now promised to destroy her career. And, in repayment, the First Family had cut her adrift.

Ralph Greenson had warned Monroe about the President's intentions before he left for Europe. During a session in March, Greenson had hinted that the President might just be another user – not much different from the Hollywood heels who had bedded and abandoned her through the years.

Monroe also told Slatzer that she had received orders to back off from the President 'in late May'. And she told Terry Moore that JFK had changed the number of his private line in the Oval Office. 'She was very proud that she was given that number and was devastated when he cut it off,' Moore told ABC news producer Sylvia Chase.

After the dire messages from the White House, Monroe shut herself in her bedroom and refused to open the door for anyone. Her 'lost weekend' passed in a haze of champagne, barbiturates and solitude, but she reappeared on Monday morning and was driven to the studio.

'She could hardly stand up,' said Hazel Washington. 'But she insisted on working.'

None of the rumours of trouble with the Kennedys reached Cukor and his circle. 'We just knew she was shattered and needed help,' said Tryon.

The director filmed ten more versions of Monroe's entrance. But on the last take, as Cukor looked through the camera lens, he whispered to cinematographer Billy Daniels, 'Give me those two reels of film. As far as we're concerned, they never existed.'

Then Cukor did the most chivalrous thing he would do during the making of the film. He refused to print the damaging scenes filmed on the morning of May 28. All traces of the fantasy scenes, except for a few shots of Thomas Tryon's legs, were destroyed. They weren't even listed on the daily production log.

'I remember that Cukor discussed scenes like this,' recalled Weinstein. 'He was certainly disturbed about them. I remember him stating that Marilyn "was acting as if she were under water".' Despite the tragedy and fury of that lost weekend, Monroe put herself back together by Tuesday afternoon and again reported for filming.

PART THREE
June

Chapter 17

The Party's Over

At dawn on June 1, Monroe stood before the wall of mirrors in her dressing room and took a brutal, calculated look at her nude body from her ankles to her hairline. Because of the slate-grey clouds outside, the light was blissfully, flatteringly diffused – as if it were filtered through gossamer layers of silk.

Eunice Murray saw her sigh in frustration as she turned from side to side and twirled like a fashion model. 'To me, she looked marvellous during *Something's Got To Give* – better than she had in years,' said Whitey Snyder – the one man who had always seen her close up and unadorned. 'But it was easy for her to find fault, to pick out the tiniest lines under her eyes.'

Monroe seemed unusually tense as, one by one, the signs of maturity were erased by the oils and powders blended especially for her by Max Factor.

Though she didn't really put it into words – couldn't put it into words – June 1, 1962, held special significance for the superstitious actress. At midnight, she had turned thirty-six – an age that had always been, inexplicably, a watershed for Hollywood glamour girls. The flaming sex symbol of the Roaring Twenties, Clara Bow, made her last film at thirty-six and then quietly descended into a twilight world of emotional collapse. Two months after her thirty-sixth birthday, the glamorous Joan Crawford was declared 'box office poison' by the nation's theatre owners, yet she later made a big comeback.

Even the ageless Greta Garbo, who had weathered the demise of silent films and the death of her mentor, Irving Thalberg, began work on her only flop, *Two-Faced Woman*, the day she turned thirty-six. She abandoned her film career after that film.

Monroe was afraid that she had already begun the descent into the maelstrom. She could feel the undertow which had pulled down the Hollywood sex symbols who had preceded her. Norma Talmadge and Gloria Swanson had both been has-beens by the time they reached thirty (although Swanson did make a comeback at fifty).

In the days after the nude scene, Monroe was afraid that her fans were predominantly interested in her sex appeal and her body. Her rejection by JFK reinforced this fear.

'Her despair was akin to that of a painter who discovers that he is going blind or of a pianist whose hands are becoming arthritic,' said playwright and diplomat Clare Boothe Luce, who visited the set in late May. 'Whatever else Marilyn had hoped – and failed – to find in her life, her "howling public" must have been what she most feared to lose. Surely she realised that the mob worship of her for her pure sexuality could not last much longer.'

At a Hollywood party several months earlier, Jane Fonda, who was herself in danger of becoming a vapid sex symbol, told Monroe wistfully that she looked forward to the time 'when all the superficial beauty is gone and I can begin to play character parts and rely on acting alone'.

Monroe looked at her fearfully and said, 'Oh no, I can't imagine surviving that way. I don't think it will be possible for me.'

Conventional wisdom in Hollywood only exacerbated

Monroe's deeply held insecurities. During the early weeks of *Something's Got to Give*, director Billy Wilder, who had directed her two greatest successes, *The Seven Year Itch* and *Some Like It Hot*, seemed to speak for the Tinseltown power structure when he exclaimed, 'The question is whether Marilyn is a person at all or one of the greatest DuPont products ever invented. She has breasts like granite and a brain like Swiss cheese – full of holes.'

Monroe's birthday reverie before the mirror soon ended as she slipped into the mink and wool suit Jean Louis had designed for the final scenes – scenes of high comedy and playful banter involving both Dean Martin and Wally Cox.

As she stepped from the darkness into the now-familiar replica of George Cukor's courtyard, she couldn't have known that a brief champagne toast and a frustrated director's rage were about to bring down the curtain on *Something's Got to Give*.

Between May 21 and June 1, (except for the May 25 ordeal), Monroe had worked nine straight days and completed ten key scenes. Not even Cukor's sluggish pace, it seemed, could impede the film's forward movement.

Almost inexplicably, she had recovered from the Kennedy rejection and raced back to the set with seeming enthusiasm. Suddenly *Something's Got to Give* was making real progress – until Cukor derailed it, this time permanently.

During a short break on Friday afternoon, Cukor rose from his chair and glared as Monroe's publicist, Pat Newcomb, crossed the stage with two crystal glasses and a bottle of Dom Pérignon.

Cukor called over an assistant director and snapped, 'Get that champagne off the set. I don't want them to take even one sip. Miss Newcomb should act like a publicist and not like a social director.'

'He was furious about those few sips of champagne,' said

stand-in Evelyn Moriarity. 'And he was angry that a birthday party was being planned for later that day.'

Because Monroe's thirty-sixth birthday had been announced in the gossip columns, many members of the crew tried to lighten the mood on the set. But Cukor seemed intent on dampening all attempts at celebration. When the director was asked to help with a surprise party, he said, 'Not on this set; not now.'

'We needed to get a full day in,' recalled Gene Allen. 'It wasn't a personal slur.'

When Evelyn Moriarity realised that there would be no official birthday celebration, she sneaked around behind Cukor's back with a huge card, soliciting signatures and money for a birthday cake.

Discipline crumbled as tributes poured in from some of the most important figures in the 'new Hollywood', a wave of young artists who viewed Cukor as hopelessly passé. Marlon Brando, Robert Wagner and Jack Lemmon sent armloads of flowers; Peter and Pat Kennedy Lawford sent a case of champagne; MCA super-agent Lew Wasserman and Frank Sinatra sent gift baskets; and a *Who's Who* of the acting community dispatched a mail sack full of telegrams.

When Pat Newcomb and her champagne were guided off the set, Monroe gave Cukor a look of anger and disdain.

But the director wasn't alone in shunning the birthday celebration. To a man, Fox's executive corps refused to become involved. Of course, they had a hidden agenda. Since they had already activated the machinery to fire Monroe, it wouldn't have been wise to share her birthday cake in front of a regiment of photographers.

Monroe, terribly sensitive to any slight, must have viewed this as a clear indication that something was wrong.

Superstar birthdays are usually extravagant events. Huge cakes are assembled, groaning buffet tables are carted onto the set, and smiling executives come down from the front office to deliver glittering presents.

Over the years, Twentieth Century-Fox had raised this tradition to an art form. Shirley Temple once received a life-size gingerbread house, and Betty Grable's pin-up pose was depicted in frosting on a five-foot cake. Ice skater Sonja Henie found a diamond bracelet inside an ice sculpture.

Twentieth Century-Fox's celebration of Elizabeth Taylor's thirtieth birthday, earlier in 1962 in Rome, offered an interesting contrast to the undercover doings on the set of *Something's Got to Give*.

In Rome, Mankiewicz called a halt to the filming at 3 P.M., signalling the arrival of an enormous cake – a confection in Egyptian colours that was borne onto the set in a sedan chair. Taylor's gifts included a golden charm from producer Walter Wanger, a case of wine from the cast, and a $2,600 gold compact from Fox. Mankiewicz, Wanger and most of the production crew later attended a soirée in the Borgia Room of the Osteria del Orso, where a table full of orchids provided the centrepiece, courtesy of Spyros Skouras.

Fox's records prove that the company spent almost $5,000 on two birthday celebrations for Taylor – the first having been on the London set of the aborted Rouben Mamoulian version of *Cleopatra* in 1961.

The spread for Monroe included a five-dollar sheet cake, champagne courtesy of Dean Martin, and a large urn of coffee from the Fox snack bar. The last was later billed to Monroe's estate.

'Finally, after I had collected nearly all of the money, Henry Weinstein agreed to pay for the cake, so I returned the cash,' Moriarity said.

The cake depicted Monroe's midnight swim, featuring a small doll with platinum hair and a bikini.

'The morning of June first,' recalled Moriarity, 'I was still climbing the rafters to get all of the signatures, and had persuaded a studio artist to paint a caricature of Marilyn in a bikini. The card said "Happy Birthday Suit".'

Moriarity slipped off the set before the lunch break to pick up the cake at the fabled Los Angeles Farmers' Market. But when she tried to carry it onto the set, two assistant directors stopped her.

'You take that cake and hide it,' said one of the assistant directors. 'Cukor intends to get a full day's work out of that dame. Do you understand? You are not to bring that cake out until six P.M.'

'Marilyn felt all of the bad vibes,' said Joan Greenson. 'She told me they kept putting it off and putting it off. When she tried to share some of her gifts with crew members, someone told her, "We want you to *work* today!"'

Greenson remembered that 'even on her birthday, they treated her like a bad child. They had the idea that she should be treated as if she were naughty. They seemed to be saying, "We're going to be as nasty as we can".'

With the shabby celebration waiting in the shadows, Monroe, Dean Martin and Wally Cox completed the most difficult and complicated scene in the film. The day before that, Monroe and Cox had enacted a shoe store sequence that was so incandescent that it was edited and immediately sent to the New York office.

'She was wonderful in those last scenes,' recalled editor David Bretherton. 'She had never been better, or displayed more perfect timing. I did a comprehensive editing job of the scene in which Marilyn woos a timid Wally Cox, and I thought to myself then, "This is the most brilliant thing she's ever done".'

The scene being shot on June 1 was more complicated. In a lightning-fast series of quips, Monroe tried to pass off Cox as the man who had shared her desert island for five years. What she didn't know was that Dean Martin had already met the real island mate, played by the hunkish Thomas Tryon.

Filming began at 9.37 A.M., with Monroe positioned at the top of a towering staircase and Cukor glowering in the darkness below. With six white-hot spots directed at her face, the actress danced down twenty-two steps and leaned over a fretted iron railing.

'Nick, darling!' she whispered – flawlessly this time.

Having caught Dean Martin's attention, she dragged an unwilling Wally Cox down the flight of stairs. As he slowly emerged into the light, he was the very picture of the egg-headed nerd. His shoulders sagged in an ill-fitting suit and he peered out through glasses with Coke-bottle lenses.

This sequence, one of the longest, most complicated comedic turns in Monroe's career, involved six long shots, six medium views and six extremely intimate close-ups – all punctuated with what was left of the Nunnally Johnson patter.

At one point in the scene, Monroe and Cox attempted to describe the desert island that Cox had never seen. They delivered a burst of witty, rapid-fire repartee reminiscent of the Jean Harlow films of the thirties. In the Fox archival footage, all three actors frequently dissolve into laughter – at one point hugging one another.

Once, when the camera zoomed in on Monroe's flawless rear, Martin playfully formed his right hand into a gun and pointed a finger right at her curves, saying, 'Haven't I seen that some place before?'

Ironically, these sparkling final scenes were later described by Cukor as 'unusable. Marilyn was acting as if she were underwater. There is an insane, hypnotic quality to them.'

Fourteen versions of this scene remain in the cinema vaults at Fox – all but one of them perfect. And even in that one flawed take, it's Wally Cox who fluffs the line, causing Monroe and Martin to collapse in laughter.

Filming on the sequence included a series of close-ups that weren't completed until 6.05 P.M.

Now convinced that there would be no party, Monroe

had to be retrieved from her dressing room to attend the meagre celebration. In a silk blouse and slacks, the mink beret still pinned to her head, she was immortalised on film by Lawrence Schiller.

On the dark edges of the soundstage, Evelyn Moriarity had arranged the birthday repast on tables rushed over from the property department. Using the cake and its naughty bikinied doll as a centrepiece, she propped up a small card next to it, signed by the entire crew. Only one crucial signature was missing – and that belonged to the increasingly angry director. 'There was tremendous support for her from the entire crew – indeed, from all the craftsmen on the lot,' said Fox special effects wizard Paul Worzl. 'We all knew the score.'

Though Cukor's petulance was evident (he had also denied Monroe a party on the set of *Let's Make Love*), the script girls and the electricians, the prop men and the carpenters gathered around the table – each with a Fourth of July sparkler in hand.

Arm in arm with Weinstein, Monroe walked through the darkness to the table – giggling when the sparklers were all lit at once. Schiller captured her transfixed by the flickering light – a bittersweet tableau of the star's last birthday.

Monroe's gaiety seemed appropriately artificial as she gamely fed a piece of cake to Cukor.

Later, when Joan Greenson admired the pictures, Monroe said, 'But look how forced it was. Look at the eyes; the eyes are dead.'

'It was only a pretend celebration,' said Weinstein. 'There was a real pall over it. I don't know why. Perhaps it was because we had all gone through so much.'

Soon the party, sans Cukor, adjourned to the more congenial surroundings of Dean Martin's dressing room, where the actress tumbled playfully into Wally Cox's lap.

'Thirty-six, huh?' said Cox. 'Do you feel thirty-six?'

She nestled her head against his shoulder. 'I feel thirty-six and then some,' she said. 'And each day on this movie makes me feel older and older.'

'That's nothing, honey,' said Martin, swinging one of his omnipresent golf clubs. 'Wait'll you hit forty. That's the tough one.' (Martin was forty-five.)

A surprise call came in on Martin's private line from Cox and Monroe's pal, Marlon Brando, who offered personal birthday greetings. Monroe was later to celebrate her birthday more festively with Cox and Brando at Brando's matching Bel Air mansions.

While Martin and Cox talked, Monroe moved across the couch and whispered to Henry Weinstein, 'Honey, can I borrow the Jean Louis suit? I've got this appearance at Dodger Stadium tonight; the suit is the only thing I've got that's warm enough.'

Weinstein reacted with astonishment. 'Marilyn, you're not going through with that – the night air will kill you,' he said. Two days earlier, a cold front had moved down from Washington State, wrapping Southern California in a blanket of clouds, turning the nights frigid and windy. 'I knew if she went out in that weather she would turn sick,' Weinstein recalled. 'I also knew I was powerless to stop her.'

The producer appealed to Lee Siegel. 'Can you say something to stop her? I have a feeling that she will have a relapse, and that it will all collapse . . . all the work down the drain.'

Siegel agreed. Tests from Cedars of Lebanon Hospital showed that Monroe still had a lingering sinus infection and that it was in danger of flaring up at any time. He warned Marilyn, 'Honey, I wouldn't go out tonight. You're not out of the woods yet. When you made that commitment to the Dodgers, you had no idea the weather would turn bad.'

Monroe shook her head. 'I have to go. The people from the Muscular Dystrophy Association have sold thousands of tickets. Besides, I promised to take Dean Martin's son.'

Weinstein just shook his head.

As Rudy Kautsky and Wally Cox helped Monroe into the limousine, a light mist had begun to fall, and the temperatures had already dipped into the fifties. 'A Gloomy, Gloomy June Is Ushered In', lamented a headline in the afternoon newspaper. 'Brrr', the story began.

Schiller recorded Monroe's exit in a series of photographic cameos as the limousine pulled out of the Pico Boulevard gates. In one shot, Monroe, her left hand entwined with Cox's, looks straight ahead – apparently lost in her thoughts.

Monroe spent an hour on the field of Dodger Stadium that evening. She ignored the light mist to pose for news and television cameras, and to throw out the first ball. In newsreels of the charity event, she is particularly touching as she chats with several children in wheelchairs.

At one point, the wind caught her mink hat and lifted it off her head. The last photograph ever taken of Monroe in public shows her holding the hat with one hand and waving to the crowd with the other.

Later, as the limousine drove her home, her head began throbbing. The sinus infection had returned.

Chapter 18

Off With Her Head

On the afternoon of June 1, Peter Levathes arrived in Rome with orders to fire Elizabeth Taylor.

Frightened by the worst stock-market slump since the Great Depression, the Fox executive committee had empowered Levathes to inform Taylor that her last day was to be June 8, and that all filming on *Cleopatra* was to cease on June 30.

Because Taylor and Mankiewicz were expected to fight these edicts, Levathes was accompanied by two senior vice-presidents, Joseph Moskowitz, who functioned as a corporate troubleshooter, and attorney Otto Koegel, who was Frank Ferguson's New York counterpart.

All three men stepped from a Rolls-Royce limousine just before lunchtime. As they walked up a re-creation of the Imperial Highway, they were engulfed by hundreds of extras in Egyptian dress and by lines of Roman centurions in gilded armour and towering helmets.

Taylor met them on the sun-dappled terrace of the Cinecitta Studior's commissary. She was wearing a turquoise dress of silk chiffon and a small golden crown in the shape of a coiled cobra. Lobster salad, fresh rolls and champagne had been set out for the guests. Tea roses decorated the tables and all the stars were present, including Burton, Rex Harrison, Cesare Danova and Hume Cronyn.

Word of the planned dismissal had reached the set on May 28, and the superstar lunch was the first of a round of divertissements staged by Taylor and Walter Wanger to distract the visiting executives – dubbed by Taylor 'the Big Three'.

One of the film's New York publicists, Jack Brodsky, had written Nathan Weiss, his counterpart on the *Cleopatra* set, that 'the real madness here – the spirit of let's-shut-down-*Cleopatra*-before-they-shut-us-down – is at a feverish high.*

On May 28, Taylor enacted Cleopatra's suicide by holding a rubber cobra to her breast. Weiss cabled the New York office: 'WE HAVE IT. SHE IS DEAD!'

There was jubilation at corporate headquarters. Milton Gould and chairman of the board Samuel Rosenman were confident that Taylor could be dismissed – now that the movie's ending had been filmed.

The Fox board of directors had finally had enough of her $10,000 per day salary, her pink villa and her affair with Richard Burton.

Hoping to avoid a nasty proxy fight among Fox investors, the board planned to hold a press conference on June 8 to tell the world at large, and the shareholders in particular, that Taylor was off the payroll. The Big Three also had a hidden agenda. They wanted to get Taylor out of Rome and away from Burton.

---

*Brodsky and Weiss later edited their *Cleopatra* letters and memos into a book, *The Cleopatra Papers*. Published in 1963 by Simon and Schuster, it was the first inside look at the studio system in Hollywood history. From his post in New York, Brodsky was also conversant with the Monroe situation. His immediate boss was E. Charles Einfeld – a key player in the Monroe matter. Ironically, Brodsky is now a producer at Twentieth Century-Fox.

They came to Rome armed with facts and figures from a secret report commissioned by Fox president Spyros Skouras – the man who had initiated the remake of the 1917 Theda Bara film. 'We were seriously thinking of using the morals clauses in Taylor's contract,' said Levathes, referring to a clause stipulating that Taylor, or for that matter, Burton, could be fired for amoral conduct. 'At that point, Taylor had given us ample cause to invoke the clauses.'

Skouras had this in mind when he asked several junior executives – whose identities are now unknown – to catalogue the misdeeds of *Cleopatra*'s stars. Although the original reports do not appear in the Fox archives, Skouras summarised them in letters to Darryl Zanuck, telegrams to Walter Wanger, and memorandums to Levathes.

Judging from the Skouras letters, the Taylor-Burton affair was wilder and more dangerous than the gossip columnists had known. The letters describe two suicide attempts by Taylor; a lover's quarrel that left Taylor badly beaten and unable to work; and an on-set dictatorship in which Taylor sometimes held sway over Wanger and Mankiewicz.

Skouras was also able to document Taylor's repeated tardiness and absences, which far exceeded Monroe's. Taylor was appreciably late or absent 99 of the 101 shooting days in Rome, including the 22 days she missed because Burton had beaten her black and blue. The attendance report still exists in the Skouras archives – written in pencil and underlined with a red pen.

Perhaps the most interesting revelations in the Skouras papers concern the 'Liz and Dick' affair, which Skouras speculated could cost 'millions of dollars in ticket sales'. The secret report was a testimonial to the skills of *Cleopatra* publicists Jack Brodsky and Nathan Weiss, who repeatedly camouflaged the nastiest episodes.

The April 24 lovers' quarrel and beating is a case in point. Weiss convinced the press and the paparazzi that Taylor and

Burton had been in a minor automobile accident. The New York newspapers reported that Burton's car had jumped a kerb, resulting in 'minor injuries to Elizabeth Taylor'.

'Actually, Burton beat the hell out of her,' Skouras wrote to Zanuck in the fall of 1962. 'She got two black eyes, and her nose was beaten out of shape. It took twenty-two days for her to recover enough to resume filming.'

Later, Taylor's abandoned husband, Eddie Fisher, lamented, 'That wasn't the only time he beat her up. Why did he do it? Because that's the kind of man he is.'

Taylor's two suicide attempts were more serious. All insurance carriers had refused to risk money on her delicate health: if she had died, Fox would have lost all of its $42 million investment.

Though Brodsky and Weiss successfully sold these incidents as 'minor illnesses', Roman reporters questioned those versions from the start. After the first attempt in March, *Il Tempo* scoffed when Fox claimed that its star had been laid low by a case of food poisoning. The newspaper noted that 'police stormed the villa to investigate suicide charges'. Wanger jumped into the fray, noting that he also had been made ill by spoiled food. 'It was the bad bully beef we ate at lunch,' he said.

'I recall that incident,' said Lee Hanna, who was production secretary for *Something's Got to Give*. 'We got word in Hollywood that Elizabeth had died in Rome. Everyone was frightened for a while.'

Taylor apparently tried to kill herself again in early April after Burton threatened to return to his wife. According to the Skouras reports, Taylor took a massive dose of sleeping medication – probably Nembutal and Seconal. In Burton's diary, released in 1988, the actor said that Taylor had told him, 'I love you so much, I'm prepared to die for you.'

'Go ahead!' he told her.

This second attempt was probably half-hearted. Tom Mankiewicz said later that the actress had swallowed seven pills – slightly more than a normal dose of Nembutal for Taylor.*

The two suicide attempts, one of which was apparently a very close call, still weren't as frightening to studio executives as the scandal itself. 'The worst of all the *Cleopatra* troubles was Elizabeth's love affair with Burton,' Skouras wrote to Zanuck. 'The terrible publicity surrounding it, plus the beating Burton gave her at San Stefano [a small Italian resort], cost us dearly.'

Levathes also brought producer Walter Wanger documentation of a financial scandal, including accounting ledgers showing that countless millions had been squandered during the chaotic months in Rome from September 1961 through July 1962. 'Countless thousands of dollars disappeared,' Levathes recalled. 'And many corporate expenses which had nothing to do with *Cleopatra* were charged to the project. It was a nightmare.'

Levathes and his companions didn't get down to business until Saturday, June 2, when they summoned Wanger to meet with them. When the producer arrived, he found the three executives seated side by side behind a table. They presented an ultimatum from the executive committee. The document stated that Wanger was to be fired immediately, and Taylor a week later. Wanger was handed two consent forms – one for him, the other for Taylor.

Wanger slid the documents back across the table. 'You are obviously unaware that Miss Taylor is still needed for thirty-one additional scenes,' he said. 'And without these scenes, you will not have a coherent movie.'

Before he left, Wanger warned, 'You will have to present the conditions to Elizabeth Taylor yourself.'

---

*Because of the high tolerances, stars like Monroe and Taylor had built up, they consumed as many as ten Nembutals a night, usually washed down by champagne and combined with Demerol and Librium.

The 'Big Three' didn't fare any better with Mankiewicz. He was amused by the ultimatum. With most of the outdoor sequences still to be shot, there was little chance that Taylor could be fired. 'We would have the only 'interior' epic in film history,' the director chided Wanger. And they had yet to film the sumptuous 'night of love' during which Burton was to be seduced by Taylor on the deck of her golden barge.

While the executives were still in Rome, Mankiewicz sent a cable to the executive committee in New York. 'If Miss Taylor is not made available to me, we cannot film their meeting [on the royal barge]. That is the night that Antony first beds the Egyptian queen and becomes emotionally ensnared. If Miss Taylor is not available, the ensuing scenes would result in the most expensive coitus interruptus in history.'

A second meeting between Taylor and the Levathes delegation was held on Monday, June 4. This time tea was served. With huge golden sphinxes spread out before the windows and the columns of the Roman forum soaring skywards, Taylor bantered with the executives. All four of them made small talk and nobody mentioned the real reason for the visit.

There was a moment of discomfort when Burton strode in, his armour clanking, and kissed Taylor on the cheek. No attempt was made to introduce him to the members of the party. In a flash, he was gone – back to the set with Martin Landau and Cesare Danova.

Taylor had been gracious and charming. But this silken facade hid an iron will. She had already deployed a team of lawyers to protect her own corporation's sizeable financial stake in *Cleopatra*. (In addition to her $2 million salary, she was to receive 10 per cent of all net profits.) On Monday evening she met with Wanger and Mankiewicz to see whether, as she put it, 'we can take over the film and fire Twentieth Century-Fox'.

Taylor, Mankiewicz and Wanger were all partners with Fox for *Cleopatra* through their own personal production companies. Lawyers eventually advised that, technically, the studio couldn't fire her and that if it did, she could sue and tie up the film for years.

Taylor also used the press to fight Fox. Realising the power of the industry trade newspapers, *The Hollywood Reporter* and *Daily Variety*, she telephoned Amy Archerd of *Variety* and Mike Connolly of *The Reporter*. 'The studio did its best to stop this picture and to eliminate as many of the best scenes as possible,' she told Archerd. 'I will sue if I have to in order to finish this film.'

The Big Three sat through marathon screenings of the unedited epic on Sunday, Monday and Tuesday nights, frequently nudging each other to stay awake. There were two hours of the entrance scene alone.

Before the executives departed on Wednesday morning, Mankiewicz had convinced Levathes to pay Taylor for another month; *Cleopatra* itself was to continue for another nine weeks.

'It was like building the Golden Gate Bridge,' Levathes said almost thirty years later. 'We couldn't stop when we were already three-fourths across. In order to get the forty million dollars back, we had to finish it.'

Today Levathes still can't say how the film veered out of control. 'It began long before I became production chief, and was handled so unprofessionally. The inmates were running the asylum.'

In searching for causes, Fox executives overlooked one obvious factor – drugs. A chemical haze hung over the *Cleopatra* set. Taylor abused Nembutal, Seconal and Demerol; Burton was frequently drunk on brandy and vodka; Mankiewicz was high on amphetamines during the day and required a tranquilliser to sleep.

Mankiewicz later admitted that he received his first shot at 5 A.M., a second at noon, more at 5 P.M. and a tranquilliser injection at midnight – all administered by the company physician.

'I'll never forget the image of my father in a little place outside of Alexandria,' said Tom Mankiewicz. 'He was dragging his legs through the sand because they had hit a sciatic nerve with one of the shots. He had had so many shots that they had to find new places in which to stick the needle.'

Film scholar Brad Geagley discovered that the director collapsed with paralysis in Egypt.

'Mankiewicz's personality was completely altered by the drugs,' sai' ' Geagley. 'All the amphetamines gave him an air of manic grandeur. And there were massive side effects.'

Taylor's pharmacological habits were equally draining. Eddie Fisher said in an interview that he became her nurse early in the production. 'I was giving her shots of Demerol,' he said. 'I didn't want the doctors to come. I even felt sorry for them by this time. The whole *Cleopatra* thing went almost beyond alchohol and drugs to obsession.'

One morning, Fisher reached for his wife's glass of Coke and found that it was heavily spiked with brandy. 'There must have been an ounce of Coca-Cola and seven ounces of brandy. We had all thought she was drinking Coke.'

There was no way to tell how much Demerol Taylor was ingesting. 'I watched her take it and it didn't even seem to affect her that much,' said Fisher. 'The only way I could judge was when I took one of them. When I took even one of the pills she was taking, I couldn't even get out of my director's chair to go to the bathroom. Elizabeth could take an enormous amount of drugs. She was even written up in the medical journals. She showed the article to me one afternoon in Rome.'

Burton's drug of choice on the *Cleopatra* set was alcohol, a geyser of it. He was fond of saying, 'I only drink when I work.' But when he worked he drank prodigiously. Quaffing brandy at sunup, Vodka at midmorning, and beakers of wine during the sodden Italian lunches, he pressed his habit on anyone within reach. Within days of their famous love scene, Taylor was returning to the set, in the words of one executive, 'sloshing in wine'. A very light drinker until she met Burton, she now had as many as six glasses of wine at lunch and even more at the villa in the evenings.

'It was obvious that Elizabeth wasn't used to drinking at all during the day,' recalled Tom Mankiewicz. 'She returned from lunch with slurred speech and swollen eyes. I kept waiting for my father to say something about it, but he never did.'

A legend for his enormous tolerance of alcohol, Burton remained word-perfect most of the time. 'I remember Richard going into makeup at 6 A.M. and having a triple brandy,' said Tom Mankiewicz. 'On walking in, he'd whap it back and then say, "Good morning, luvs".'

The Fox executives had to bear these transgressions in silence.

At 5 A.M. Roman time, on June 2, Levathes was awakened by Phil Feldman, the man delegated to oversee *Something's Got to Give* in Hollywood while the production chief was in Rome.

'Monroe didn't report on Monday,' Feldman told him.

At that point, the studio only had $2.1 million invested in the Monroe film. 'There was paranoia that *Something's Got to Give* could veer out of control as well,' Henry Weinstein said.

Monroe was also in a more vulnerable position than Taylor. Her corporation was not an investor in *Something's Got to Give* and she did not own a percentage of the film. Marilyn Monroe Productions received her salary and served solely as a tax shelter. In addition, Taylor owned the wide screen Todd-A/O process, a main creative element of the Egyptian epic. Taylor had inherited Todd-A/O from Mike Todd and merely rented the cameras and lenses to Twentieth Century-Fox.

Monroe had already violated her contract by attending the presidential gala after being threatened with dismissal.

Feldman and Levathes consulted by phone five times as the production chief flew from Rome to London, and then on to New York. He also talked with 'one of Marilyn's advisers, who told me that she was in good health and that she simply did not feel like going to work'.

Feldman was told to consult with George Cukor; the director was told to take a good look at all the Monroe film and assess its quality.

What would Fox be losing if it fired Monroe?

Chapter 19

Power Plays

The firing of Marilyn Monroe was a high-stakes game in which lawyers, financiers, studio executives, agents, and even a psychiatrist competed with each other to determine the artistic future of an actress who was all but shut out of the negotiations.

The dealing, some of which might be termed double-dealing, involved players in three cities – Rome, New York and Los Angeles. It soon became a nightmare of miscommunication as Levathes in Europe, Milton Gould in Manhattan and Philip Feldman in Century City directed the campaign to fire one of the most financially successful stars in Fox's history.

Last-minute negotiations took place via international conference calls, over lunches in the studio commissary and in closed door sessions in the Darryl F. Zanuck Building.

Monroe and her closest advisers, Pat Newcomb, Paula Strasberg and public relations man Arthur Jacobs, were only incidental players.

The process was set in motion at 5.55 A.M. on Monday, June 4, when Eunice Murray, at Monroe's direction, telephoned Weinstein and told him that the star's sinus infection and bronchitis had flared up again. The appearance at Dodger Stadium, as Weinstein feared, had caused a relapse. All day

Monday, Monroe's temperature hovered at 100 degrees.

Five minutes after Murray's call, Weinstein notified Buck Hall and Cukor. Weinstein remembers feeling that this might be one sick call too many.

At 8 A.M., Lee Siegel drove to Brentwood to certify Monroe's condition. A few minutes later, he called Feldman from her kitchen and reported, 'The illness has flared up again.' Pat Newcomb remembered that Dr. Siegel told Monroe to stay home. His official verdict: 'Monroe is too ill to work.'

In the *Something's Got to Give* production offices, Hall cancelled Monday's filming and wrote the following on the weekly production log: 'Monroe's absence was *excused* due to illness.'

However, Feldman and Frank Ferguson described it differently in communiqués to the New York office. 'Monroe had no possible excuse for not appearing the morning of June 4th,' Feldman cabled Gould. Cukor and his staff forwarded a similar opinion. Gene Allen explained recently, 'We didn't believe Dr Siegel. By this point, Monroe was manipulating all of these doctors. We all believed she was malingering.'

In New York, Gould gave the word; plans to dismiss Monroe were put into effect. 'It had to be done,' said Levathes, who also claims that 'one of Monroe's advisers' told him, 'Monroe isn't ill, she just doesn't feel like coming in.'

'We made the decision when she left the set to attend the gala,' said Gould. 'Now it was time for action.'

Still, Fox proceeded cautiously.

At 11 A.M. on Monday, Feldman telephoned Monroe's attorney, Milton Rudin, and asked him whether Monroe would be on the set Tuesday morning.

Rudin couldn't guarantee it. 'I'll have to call you back,' he told Feldman.

Feldman cabled New York. 'Monroe's status for tomorrow is undetermined.'

At the Brentwood house, Monroe received massive antibiotic injections laced with megavitamins. Murray noticed that 'her headaches had returned – shortly after 3 A.M.'

Unfortunately, word of Monroe's illness never reached the man who was negotiating for her. 'I wasn't aware of any respiratory problems,' Rudin remembered. 'I knew of some emotional troubles.' Studio archives indicate that Rudin and co-counsel Martin Gang described their client's troubles as 'exhaustion'.

Despite Siegel's ruling and Monroe's treatment for sinusitis at Cedars of Lebanon Hospital on Sunday, June 3, Monroe never communicated to Rudin that she was ill. So it was on the basis of 'exhaustion', and Fox's definition of that term, that the star's fate was decided.

For the next five days, Rudin and, to a lesser extent, Gang were pitted against three of the best legal minds in the film industry. Besides chief counsel Ferguson, Gould, Levathes and Levathes's adjutant, Feldman, all specialised in entertainment law.

Gould, who had conceived the threatening letter to Monroe two days before the gala, had been elected to the Fox board of directors because he held thousands of proxies from angry stockholders. He had a reputation for rescuing troubled corporations. That same year, the *New York Times* described him as 'Dr. Gould, the man who provides intensive care for sick corporations.' In 1961, he had saved Curtis Publishing Company from bankruptcy by overhauling and greatly reducing the firm's corporate staff.

A native New Yorker with a law degree from Cornell University, Gould had begun his career as a special attorney for the United States Justice Department. He liked to say that he had never lost any of his 'prosecutorial zeal' when he crossed over into private commercial law in the forties. 'I'm a litigator, a trial lawyer,' he promised the investors who hoisted him onto the Fox board. 'I will use the same techniques in the boardroom that I use in the courtroom.' He was to prove this during the campaign to fire Monroe.

Levathes, a prize-winning scholar at Harvard, George Washington University and Georgetown University, soon formed a bond of understanding with Gould. 'We both thought the film studio should be run like a business – with an eye to the profit and loss columns. And the progress of *Cleopatra* and *Something's Got to Give* had broken all the rules of professional conduct.'

Levathes was just out of law school when he was interviewed by Spyros Skouras, who was seeking an executive assistant with a grasp of entertainment law. Though Levathes had already received a job offer from a prestigious Washington law firm, he was fascinated by Skouras – the immigrant who had worked his way up from busboy to theatre owner to distribution magnate to head of Twentieth Century-Fox. At the close of the hourlong interview, Skouras hired him.

Feldman was legally savvy as well. With Levathes in Europe and Gould distracted by the continuing power struggle within the Fox board of directors, Feldman, a graduate of both the Harvard Business School and the Harvard Law School, was the architect of the machinery to fire Monroe.

Phil Feldman had risen from law clerk to legal counsel for Hollywood's Famous Artists Corporation – in less than four years. As senior vice-president for Fox's West Coast operations, he was already renowned for his grasp of the intricacies of corporate law. Just a year before, when 50 per cent of all West Coast employees had been dropped for the sake of economy, Feldman had justified his reputation for ruthlessness when he booted out hundreds of major producers, directors and executives in less than three weeks.

He was particularly adept at breaking contracts. 'He was a new face at Fox in the early sixties,' said designer William Travilla. 'Since he had no ties to the past – no loyalties, so to speak' – he became the hatchet man.

From the outset, it was Feldman's opinion that Monroe

had violated both the letter and the spirit of her 1956 contract.

Rudin had the reputation of a bulldog when it came to client's rights and had negotiated airtight pacts for such clients as Frank Sinatra and Dean Martin.

But now he was hampered by lack of access to Monroe – the inability to penetrate the wall of publicists, physicians and assistants around her. 'Often not even her closest friends could get her on the phone,' recalled Ralph Roberts. 'They isolated her from the world.'

Rudin's disadvantage surfaced early in his campaign to save *Something's Got to Give*.

Four hours after Monday's filming ended, Feldman called Rudin to ask again about Tuesday's schedule. Rudin finally admitted that he couldn't get a definite answer. 'I can't get through to her.'

'That's too bad, because we need an answer right now,' said Feldman.

'I might send her a letter pointing out what the consequences might be if she continues on her present course,' Rudin said. 'That's as much as I can do at this point.'

Monroe's attorney had better news on Tuesday morning. At 9.40 A.M., Rudin held a conference call involving himself, Martin Gang, Weinstein and Feldman. 'Monroe could come in this afternoon,' Rudin offered. 'She is feeling much better.'

Feldman answered, 'Too late, we have already dismissed the company for today.'

Rudin reiterated his position. 'Monroe is ready and willing to work – this afternoon and all day tomorrow.' He also disclosed that his client had assailed him earlier in the day. 'She accused me of being "with them",' the lawyer said.

Feldman, charged by Gould with establishing firm legal grounds for the dismissal, was encouraged by Rudin's latest conversation. '[Rudin] did not at any time say that Monroe was "exhausted",' Feldman noted in a report for the legal department and the New York office. 'I inferred from what he said that she had no possible excuse for her actions.'

This opinion caused Levathes and Gould to set the firing in motion. 'Start looking for a replacement,' Levathes said from Rome.

Even though Rudin guaranteed Monroe's appearance on Wednesday, Feldman directed Owen McLean, senior vice-president for casting, to approach Shirley MacLaine, Kim Novak, Doris Day and Brigitte Bardot about replacing Monroe. Novak, a sultry star at Columbia Pictures, was the first choice.

But Rudin expected the crisis to end when Monroe reported to the set on Wednesday morning. He was confused when Buck Hall and Henry Weinstein didn't issue the traditional company call to Monroe at 4 P.M. on Tuesday for the Wednesday sequences. This created panic among members of Monroe's circle.

Rudin called Feldman at 4.20 P.M. 'Why hasn't the Wednesday call been issued?' he asked.

Feldman replied, 'Miss Monroe has not shown up for two days, and we are now concerned as to whether she can complete this film.' The company was to shoot without her until the executives could make that determination.

Rudin controlled his anger. 'Are you seeking a replacement for Miss Monroe?' he asked.

Feldman hedged. 'We haven't decided on a course of action.'

Monroe's attorney was suspicious. 'It appears to me that you are planning to replace her.'

In truth, Novak and MacLaine had already been approached through their agents.

Early Tuesday evening, Feldman and Ferguson began formulating a compromise by which Monroe's job would be saved and Fox would achieve its goal of showing the investors that the studio could indeed control its talent.

If Dr. Ralph Greenson would guarantee that his famous patient would show up every day, and if Monroe would abrogate all her artistic controls – and make a public apology – then she might be allowed to finish *Something's Got to Give*.

Monroe had already phoned Greenson, asking him to return from Europe as soon as possible. Now everything would be held in abeyance awaiting the psychiatrist's arrival late Wednesday afternoon.

Feldman confidently cabled Gould and Levathes: 'Perhaps Greenson can accomplish something for Twentieth's sake that Monroe's lawyers could not.'

To achieve the studio's public relations goals, Ferguson composed a set of humiliating conditions Monroe would have to sign if filming was resumed. They rescinded all the rights and privileges she had achieved after becoming a superstar. The document revoked her power of approval of costars, directors, cinematographers and screenwriters. Her publicists, drama coach, agents and lawyers would be barred from the lot 'without express approval of the Executive Head of Production at Twentieth Century-Fox'.

The tone of the document was extreme. The worst of the ten 'surrender' conditions was the fifth – which addressed her absences and tardinesses. In part, it said, 'Miss Monroe will be prompt in observing the work calls issued by us and will report on the stage at the times that we designate. She will also take her luncheon breaks only at times specified by us.'

It even addressed her memory lapses: 'When Miss Monroe reports for work every day, she will be fully prepared in connection with the scenes designated for photography on that day.'

This degrading document, which Fox intended to make public, was to be accompanied by a press release on Monroe's public apology. She was to have been forced to read it for newsreel crews. She didn't, of course, and it has disappeared.

Given this callous stand by Fox executives, Ralph Greenson faced an almost impossible situation when he flew home from

Europe early Wednesday evening. By then, Feldman had received a report from George Cukor that would further tarnish the studio's image of Monroe.

– Chapter 20 –

A Professional Opinion

When he finally viewed the unedited film from *Something's Got to Give*, George Cukor was troubled by what he saw on the screen.

During the first six weeks of production, the director had screened the daily rushes sporadically. The only scene that interested him at all was the nude bathing sequence – which he savoured with pride, watching it again and again.

Most weeks, Cukor had sent associate producer Gene Allen to the sessions. Allen took careful notes on each take and reported to Cukor each morning. Even before the director was ordered to look at the Monroe film, Allen had warned him about it.

'I'm very disturbed by Marilyn's scenes,' he said. 'I'd like to know what you think.'

At Phil Feldman's direction, Cukor sat down Wednesday morning and watched all the Monroe film – in chronological order – from the first costume tests through her final work.

David Bretherton had already roughly edited several of the sequences – most notably a hilarious meeting between Wally Cox and Monroe: He tries to sell her shoes; she tries to pick him up; both end up on the floor in a heap.

Today, this bit delights audiences. But when Cukor saw it, mixed in with four hours of completed film, he saw something that nobody else had perceived.

'There's no performance there at all,' he told Allen, who agreed with him. 'Monroe seems to be acting as if she were underwater. I honestly don't think we have anything at all.'

To double-check, he took a second look at Monroe's close-ups. 'She's going mad; you can see it happening,' he said.*

The director felt obligated to share his opinion with Feldman and to recommend that Monroe be replaced – he hoped with Kim Novak. While Cukor had been directing *Let's Make Love* two years earlier, Monroe had made light of all the on-set agonies on that film by chiding him, 'Remember, George, it's what's up on the screen that counts.'

It became a running joke between Cukor and Allen. As *Let's Make Love* became a nightmare, they were still able to laugh by repeating Monroe's dictum.

Now it wasn't so amusing. Cukor hated what he saw. Today it's hard to see what disturbed him so badly. As edited together by Henry Schipper and the Fox Entertainment News crew, the film seems enchanting. A majority of television critics agreed with Schipper that 'it compares to her best work'.

Patrick McGilligan, Cukor's most recent biographer, shares Cukor's opinion that they 'may not have had anything on the screen to fashion into a coherent film. He had a firm grasp of what he needed.'

Though not everyone involved with *Something's Got to Give* agreed with Cukor, including Bretherton and Weinstein,

---

*In 1979 Cukor told Peter Harry Brown that he had learned nothing to change his view that Monroe had been going insane. 'There was no chance that *Something's Got to Give* could be completed,' he said in an interview for the *Los Angeles Times* Calendar section. 'She should have been in an institution instead of on a soundstage.'

it was Cukor's opinion that counted. Executives trusted him. In an era of unwelcome 'new wave directors' who decked themselves out in jeans and T-shirts, Cukor still wore stiffly tailored clothes from London's Savile Row. Besides, he was a gentleman of the old school; he still deferred to the power of executives such as Louis B. Mayer and Darryl F. Zanuck.

This deference, however, was only a pose. Like many directors, Cukor hated the money men in the front offices and their attempts to exert authority over him. But he had rarely been so resentful of the moguls as he was during the making of *Something's Got to Give*.

After forcing him to make a film he did not believe in, Levathes and Feldman foisted Weinstein on him, revoked his casting authority, instead allowing Monroe to make all such decisions, and interfered with his attempts to rewrite the screenplay. These conditions may have coloured the director's opinion of the film and Monroe, whom he described as a two-faced manipulator. (All her requests and demands were relayed through Levathes.)

Wednesday afternoon, June 6, Cukor appeared before Feldman, Frank Ferguson and Stanley Hough, another vice-president. Cukor passionately urged them to shut down the film until a replacement for Monroe could be hired. His arguments were convincing.

'I thought it was a mistake to fire Marilyn Monroe,' recalled Tom Tryon, one of the few people Cukor confided in. 'I think the film should have gone forward. But George believed he could not get a performance out of her. The rest of his behaviour was based upon that feeling.'

Several days after Monroe was fired, Cukor admitted to Tryon that Monroe 'could have completed the film if the studio had given her time to rest. But Fox would not consider that suggestion.'

In this and two subsequent appearances, Cukor, perhaps unwittingly, became a participant in the plot to fire Monroe and to discredit her in the eyes of the Hollywood power structure. 'She is not capable of giving a performance at this point,' the director said.

The publicity surrounding the gala – and the midnight swim – placed the studio in a very embarrassing position. In the newsreel photos of the Kennedy party, and Schiller's stills of the midnight swim, Monroe appeared glowingly healthy. This came at a time when studio officials were telling investors how ill she was.

Fox executives were stunned by the fierceness of Cukor's statements. Of course, the director would not know for weeks that he, like Monroe, was a disposable pawn in the bitter corporate wars. For now, he was the front man who legitimised the studio's extraordinary action against Monroe.

The executives must have known that Cukor's reports were overstated. On June 1, Feldman and Hough had screened ninety minutes of *Something's Got to Give* and had been impressed by what they saw. They were so impressed, in fact, that Feldman ordered an internal investigation to determine whether there was enough good Monroe film to complete the film using a double for the actress.

But the corporate need to fire Monroe soon outweighed all other considerations.

Bu Thursday afternoon, when papers had already been drafted, Feldman's internal investigations showed that the Monroe film was so rich and so plentiful that it could probably be completed using a double.

As a backup plan, Philip Feldman and story editor Theodore Strauss met with veteran comedy writer Hal Kanter and hired him to fashion a complete screenplay around the scenes that Monroe had already shot. 'They wanted a finished film without ever shooting another frame of Marilyn Monroe,' Kanter recalled.

'I was told that I could use a double in a handful of scenes – shot from a distance and from behind – as MGM had done for *Saratoga* after Jean Harlow had died, leaving the film uncompleted.'

Kanter, best known as the screenwriter of *My Favourite Spy* and *The Road to Bali*, spent several days screening the rough takes from *Something's Got to Give*. 'I found much of it delightful,' he recalled. 'And I did come up with a screenplay that would have allowed them to release the film. Monroe had actually completed most of the important scenes.'

But Fox executives did not share their admiration of Monroe's completed work with attorney Milton Rudin, who was negotiating for Monroe, or with Ralph Greenson, who was flying home from Europe.

Since they had received only negative reports on *Something's Got to Give*, the attorney and the analyst would be at a great disadvantage in the last-minute bids to save Monroe's career.

– Chapter 21 –

Double-Dealing

On June 6, Ralph Greenson stepped off the plane exhausted. He had been in the air, or waiting in airports, for seventeen hours. But, instead of driving home to Santa Monica, he drove directly to Monroe's house – where she had retreated to her bedroom.

Greenson had to deal with a dilemma he himself had created when he had ordered Monroe to make *Something's Got to Give* in early January. At the beginning of April, when he had left for Europe, Monroe had been physically fit and, Greenson had believed, emotionally ready to finish this film, and thereby cancel her obligation to Fox, as painlessly as possible.

But the support system he had left behind – including Weinstein, Eunice Murray and a substitute analyst named Milton Wexler – had crumbled under the weight of Monroe's sinus infection and the emotional turmoil caused by the collapse of her affair with President Kennedy.

Greenson arrived at the Brentwood house just before dark and conferred privately with Monroe for two hours, attempting to determine whether she was strong enough mentally to finish the film.

Greenson apparently decided that it was worth the risk, since it would end her obligation with Fox. 'He felt that the Fox contract was holding her back,' said the analyst's daughter, Joan. 'She couldn't get on with her life and her career with this hanging over her head.'

Like Rudin, who was Greenson's brother-in-law, Greenson decided to withhold the news that the studio was ready to fire her and sue her for millions in lost revenues. Rudin had already informed Feldman that he was holding up Feldman's letter to Monroe informing her of the dire consequences of further absences. 'I have too much compassion for Marilyn as a human being to send that message,' Rudin told the executive.

Most of Thursday was devoted to conferences among all the players. Feldman was on the phone for most of the day – with Gould in New York, corporate attorney Otto Koegel in Rome, and Fox president Spyros Skouras, who was in a Manhattan hospital recuperating from prostate surgery. Rudin met with Greenson to devise a series of 'guarantees' to the studio if *Something's Got to Give* continued filming.

At 8.10 A.M. on Friday, June 8, the day Levathes was supposed to announce that Elizabeth Taylor had been dismissed from further work on *Cleopatra*, Rudin relayed the following message from Greenson: 'He thinks that Marilyn is ready to go back to work Monday morning,' and that she would finish *Something's Got to Give* 'in normal course'.

Rudin asked for a luncheon meeting that day involving Rudin, Feldman, Greenson and Frank Ferguson.

Meanwhile, in New York, a series of newspaper articles forced Fox's hand.

Murray Schumach, the Hollywood correspondent for the *New York Times*, wrote a series of articles on what he called 'the Fox dilemma', in which he depicted the studio executives as spineless men who were paralysed by the difficult decisions facing them.

Under the headline 'Weakness Seen in the Film Industry',

Schumach reported that 'the case of Marilyn Monroe is proof of how little authority even the very top executives have in Hollywood today.' The article had an immediate effect on Gould and the others on the corporation's executive committee. The *New York Times* was the bible for the financiers and Wall Street lawyers who were then challenging the entire Fox administration.

Schumach's series was to run through Sunday.

At noon on Friday, a catered lunch was served in the executive conference room for Feldman, Ferguson, Rudin and Greenson. Over salad, Feldman made the following announcement: 'I have to advise you that we have not departed from our position that Monroe is already in breach of contract.' Gould, in an interview for this book, said that in the opinion of the corporation's top executives, 'Monroe was as good as fired by this point.'

'Mr. Ferguson and I are here in the spirit of listening,' said Feldman, 'and to be convinced that Miss Monroe can actually continue this film.'

Fox also presented another condition to be met before filming could resume. 'Paula Strasberg and Pat Newcomb must be removed from the set for the duration of this film.'

The executives also asked whether Monroe would sign the set of conditions which had been prepared – and which would have reduced her to the status of a starlet.

Sadly, Rudin agreed that all creative decisions would be made by Fox alone, adding that the removal of Newcomb would be no problem.

'But what about Paula Strasberg?' Feldman asked.

Greenson thought for a moment before he said, 'I'm not sure anyone can get Marilyn to go along with this. I don't know if I would even suggest it.'

Rudin promised to raise the question to Monroe when he presented the Fox demands to his client. But Rudin also said that the actress was very loyal to her drama coach. The attorney also asked the studio officials if now 'is the right time to present all of your demands to Miss Monroe'.

Feldman seemed to panic. 'Please don't present these official conditions until I can confer with the New York office,' he said.

Towards the end of the luncheon, Greenson became expansive. 'I can persuade Marilyn to go along with any reasonable request,' he said. 'While I don't want to present myself as a "Svengali", I can convince Marilyn to do anything I want her to do.'

Feldman was amazed by Greenson's certainty. 'Would you then determine what scenes Marilyn will or will not do, and decide which takes were favourable or unfavourable?'

'Yes,' Greenson agreed. 'If necessary, I'll even go into the editing booth.'

Then Ferguson threw Greenson and Rudin off balance by asking that 'another psychiatrist, one chosen by Fox, would be brought in to consult on Monroe's sanity'.

As demeaning as this sounds, Greenson tentatively agreed and even suggested several names.

Over coffee, Rudin again pressed for the right to present all the Fox demands to Monroe for her approval. Feldman asked him to put the proposal on hold until later Friday afternoon.

The luncheon wound up at 1.45 P.M. As Rudin and Greenson walked to their cars, both admitted that the studio's attitude seemed promising.

Exactly two hours later, at 3.45 P.M., Feldman called Rudin – who was back at his Beverly Hills office. 'Fox is not interested in going any further with this,' Feldman said. 'We consider Marilyn Monroe to be in breach of contract, and we are going to pursue whatever remedies we can in that regard.'

Gould, Levathes and the executive committee had given the final word: there was to be no 'second chance'.

Judging from the documents that have survived, it almost

seems as if Fox toyed with Rudin and Greenson. Hours before the Friday luncheon, corporate lawyers – both in New York and Los Angeles – were hurriedly drafting a lawsuit against Monroe. In addition, Levathes had hired the Los Angeles law firm of Musick, Peeler and Garrett – one of the best firms in the country for cases involving theatrical contracts – as consultants on what would become a precedent-setting case. James R. O'Malley of that firm originally set damages at $500,000. He told the *New York Times* that the amount would probably increase to more than $1 million.

While Feldman was still negotiating with Rudin, law clerks at Musick, Peeler and Garrett were duplicating copies of the suit so that it could be filed with the clerk of Santa Monica Superior Court before the 5 P.M. deadline. The careful timing of this action betrays the calculation behind Fox's actions.

Levathes called Ferguson from London and told him to file the lawsuit on Friday. When Ferguson protested that there might not be enough time, Levathes answered, 'If you cannot do it that rapidly, hire another firm to help.' Thus James R. O'Malley was brought into the conflict.

Thirty years later, Levathes defended that action. 'There was so much gossiping going on,' he recalled, 'that I didn't want the suit to be reported surreptitiously. I personally charged the attorneys that this was not to be leaked to the press so that they could rhapsodise on it and make it into a big deal.'

Levathes didn't want to turn Monroe into a martyr.

Weinstein was told about the lawsuit and firing early Friday afternoon and submitted his resignation as producer of *Something's Got to Give*. 'This was a purely political move, and I wanted no part of it,' he said. 'They couldn't get rid of Taylor, so they decided to show they were strong men and fired Monroe – in Taylor's place.'

As soon as Rudin and Greenson learned that the lawsuit had been filed, they knew that Monroe had to be told immediately. They had to reach her before the press did. The New York journalists – with their early deadlines – had already been tipped by publicists in the New York office.

Because Rudin, out of kindness, hadn't mailed his letter to Monroe warning her of the consequences of her absences from the set, she had no idea that Twentieth Century-Fox was really going to fire her.

But she had heard rumours.

That same Friday, Ralph Roberts was at the Brentwood house giving Monroe a massage. He noticed that everyone was tiptoeing around the house – avoiding Monroe.

As he dug his hands into the muscles at the base of her neck, he realised that he had rarely felt her this tense. He indulged in some small talk with the actress, but both of them avoided the subject that was on their minds – the rumours that her firing was imminent.

She finally brought it up. 'I hear Cukor is trying to get me fired,' she said. 'I hear it's in the works.'

Roberts noted that he had heard the gossip as well. 'She had strong suspicions, even though nobody had told her directly,' he said. 'But she couldn't figure out why Cukor was doing this to her.'

Perhaps her doctors and publicists protected her too diligently. Abandoned by her erstwhile friends in the media and isolated by the rigours of her illness, Monroe was in the eye of a corporate hurricane.

She was also cushioned by a false sense of security.

Until Roberts confirmed the rumours, Monroe viewed this as just another tiff with Fox, one of a series of such battles stretching back to the early fifties. She had caused far more trouble – and missed more shooting days – during the making of *Let's Make Love*. Yet that film had eventually been completed. With her box-office power to back her up, Monroe was confident she would eventually win the battle over *Something's Got to Give*.

She also had a key ally in Lee Siegel, who stood firmly

behind her decision to remain at home until her sinus flareup subsided.

Her suspicions had been aroused late on Wednesday when the studio shut down production without even informing her.

As recently as *Let's Make Love*, Monroe had fought her own battles with the studio. But now her cadre of protectors dealt with the studio executives. Since most of them were afraid of Monroe, and of Fox, and since all of them were paid by Monroe, a combustible situation existed.

Around 5 P.M., when Greenson finally told Monroe she had been fired, Monroe reacted with anger. 'Perhaps I should get rid of these people,' she later told Slatzer. 'They seem to have done more harm than good.'

The members of Monroe's support group – her 'substitute family' as writer Lucy Freeman described them – had ceased communicating with each other. For instance, Paula Strasberg and Greenson had become enemies, and the psychiatrist now believed that the coach exerted an unhealthy influence over Monroe. Pat Newcomb didn't interact with any of the others, and Eunice Murray was secretive, communicating only with Greenson.

With the exception of Greenson, none of them was aware of the seriousness of Rudin's negotiations with Fox.

They couldn't have known that the five days of meetings and telephone conferences were a sham, nor could they have known that no one could have prevented the dismissal.

When Feldman told Rudin that the studio was simply waiting for Greenson's return, Monroe believed filming would resume no later than Monday, June 11. After all, Greenson had been negotiating with Fox on Monroe's behalf since *Something's Got to Give* had been conceived in the fall of 1961.

Joan Greenson said that her father was furious when he heard of the dismissal – on his car radio. 'Why did they make him come back from Europe when they obviously intended to fire her anyway?' the analyst's daughter wondered.

Newcomb was even angrier. 'The studio doctor examined her early in the week and told her to stay home,' she recalled. 'And when she did, they fired her.'

After he heard the radio bulletin, Greenson raced over to Monroe's house, took her into the bedroom and shut the door. He stayed there for more than an hour. He told Murray that no one was to reach Monroe by phone. 'Tell them that Marilyn is in conference and cannot come to the phone.' That unfortunate ruling cut the actress off from dozens of calls from Rupert Allan; Sidney Guilaroff; Nunnally Johnson (who called from Rome) and Darryl Zanuck (who called from Paris).

'I knew how Marilyn would react,' recalled Allan. 'I knew that she would be devastated, so I called repeatedly to offer support. I was unable to reach her all weekend.'

After giving Monroe a tranquilliser shot, Greenson lashed out at Fox in conversations with Eunice Murray. 'You know, it isn't as if she were goldbricking or out partying. They have acted in bad faith.'

Whitey Snyder and Marjorie Plecher tried a more direct approach, appearing at Monroe's door shortly after 6 P.M. 'She had never been fired before, so she was devastated,' Snyder recalled. 'She couldn't understand it.'

Monroe's hurt quickly turned to anger as she learned of the publicity campaign Fox launched to capitalise on her dismissal.

Chapter 22

The Media War

Milton Rudin and Philip Feldman had a gentleman's agreement to withhold any publicity surrounding Monroe's dismissal.

Early Friday, when Arthur Jacobs, whose public relations firm handled Monroe, wanted to go on the offensive, he was restrained by Rudin. 'Fox won't move on this if we don't,' Rudin said.

By early afternoon, Fox had already broken its word.

At about 2 P.M., columnist Earl Wilson telephoned Monroe from New York, seeking her 'reaction' to what he described as 'disturbing news from corporate headquarters in New York'.

'I've just gotten a tip that Fox has fired you from *Something's Got to Give*,' said Wilson. 'I'm anxious to hear your side of it.'

Still confident that Greenson and Rudin had contained the damage, Monroe laughed it off, saying, 'I haven't been fired, Earl. This is just a rumour. In fact, I'm now ready and eager to get back to the set on Monday.'

'Are you ill?' asked the columnist.

'I have been,' she replied. 'But I'm feeling a lot better. I'll be on the set Monday morning.'

Wilson was doubtful. His tip had come directly from an

old friend, E. Charles Einfeld, Fox's senior vice-president of marketing and advertising. Though the source was impeccable, and despite the fact that he had quite a jump on the entertainment story of the year, Wilson decided to go with Monroe.

His copyrighted story hit the streets at 10 P.M. Eastern time on June 8. In the early editions, Wilson's column ran on page one under a banner headline: 'Marilyn Will Return to Work on Monday'. Wilson's lead paragraph was generous and overly optimistic. 'Marilyn Monroe, insisting that she has not been fired by her studio, said today that she will leave her sickbed Monday and return to the set of *Something's Got to Give*.'

Across the Atlantic in London, film fans awakened to Sheilah Graham's scoop that Monroe had already been fired. 'When Marilyn shows up for work on Monday, she will find that she has been fired and replaced – perhaps with Kim Novak,' Graham wrote. 'Twentieth Century-Fox doesn't want her any more.'

Alerted by Einfeld as well, Graham phoned the Fox publicity department in Hollywood and persuaded her old pal Perry Lieber, then deputy chief of Fox's Hollywood publicity office, to confirm that Monroe had been fired and to provide her with a quote from someone in the front office.

Graham quoted the unnamed executive as saying, 'Marilyn hasn't shown up for days, even though she's been out on the town doing the night spots.'

Wilson and Graham obtained their respective scoops at about 3 P.M. California time, as Rudin was still negotiating with Phil Feldman – this despite the fact that the press blackout was to have lasted through Monday at least, when Levathes returned to Hollywood.

However, Feldman must have known that the Fox publicity men on both coasts were gearing up for one of the most extensive negative campaigns in Hollywood history.

This time, instead of selling a star, they were destroying one.

The campaign would prove remarkably successful.

The three men who directed this media blitz were masters of the game who had come to Hollywood during the fading days of silent films. They had helped invent the art of Tinseltown ballyhoo.

Einfeld was charged with turning Monroe's dismissal into a publicity coup – a message to the world that Fox could control at least one of its recalcitrant stars. He had been vice-president for advertising and publicity for Warner Brothers before coming to Fox. Brodsky and Weiss described him as possessing 'a driving, almost demonic, round-the-clock obsession' for his craft. Einfeld was the man who helped draft the demeaning set of conditions Monroe was to have signed.

Jack Warner, the feisty president of Warner Brothers, once called Einfeld 'the man who kept the secrets'. When Einfeld saved Mary Astor's career after her 'love diary' was made public, he earned the respect of every publicist in town. (The diary documented, in lurid terms, Astor's affairs since coming to Hollywood in the early twenties.)

Harry Brand, who ran the anti-Monroe campaign on the West coast, must have experienced mixed feelings about his task. Known as the 'dean of Hollywood press agents', Brand had been the architect of Monroe's stardom – from her first shopping centre opening to the star-studded premiere of her greatest triumph, *Bus Stop*, eight years later.

'Early on, Brand knew that Zanuck disliked Monroe,' said writer Maurice Zolotow. 'So he looked out for her.'

A Los Angeles native, Brand had been a sportswriter for the *Los Angeles Express*, then executive marketing assistant to Los Angeles mayor Pinky Snyder, before joining Warner Brothers in the mid-twenties. In the early days, while publicising screen clown Buster Keaton and silent glamour girl Norma Talmadge, he became known as 'the herald of hyperbole' because of his effusive press releases. When Zanuck and Joseph Schenck formed Twentieth Century-Fox in 1935, Brand came aboard as publicity director.

Brand had promoted Shirley Temple as the first child superstar, made Betty Grable the supreme pinup girl of World War II, and helped sell Cinemascope to a doubting world. 'But Harry was perhaps proudest of his campaign for Marilyn,' recalled his widow, Sybil. 'It took years and involved scores of publicity stunts.'

There is no written record of Brand's feelings about the get-Marilyn project, despite Rupert Allan's claim that Brand 'had come to despise Marilyn Monroe'.

From the beginning, Brand turned it over to his assistant, Perry Lieber, who had come to Fox from RKO. At that studio, Lieber had captained a series of particularly lurid campaigns for Howard Hughes, the eccentric billionaire who owned RKO from 1948 until 1954. 'Lieber was a man who would do anything for a headline,' said Harriet Parsons, Louella Parsons's daughter and an RKO producer during Lieber's days as head of publicity for RKO. 'He didn't care whether the news was good or bad – as long as it promoted the film he was working on.'

In 1952, during a similar campaign, Lieber almost destroyed Monroe's career. Her stardom had just taken off when Fox loaned her to RKO for a dockside melodrama called *Clash by Night*, starring Barbara Stanwyck and Paul Douglas.

To grab front-page headlines to promote *Clash By Night*, Lieber alerted United Press International reporter Aline Mosby that Monroe had posed for a nude calendar in 1949 – when she was having trouble paying her rent. Lieber even supplied a copy of the calendar – decorated by a honey-blonde Monroe stretched out on a sheet of red velvet. Monroe had been paid $50 for the session, which she used to head off an eviction notice.

Mosby's story was front-page news in papers across

America. 'A photograph of a beautiful, nude blonde on a 1952 calendar is hanging in garages and barbershops all over the nation,' Mosby wrote. 'Marilyn Monroe admitted today that the beauty is she.'

Two days earlier, Fox executives had told her to lie about it, to deny that she was the girl stretched out on red velvet. Instead, Monroe held a press conference. She explained that 'I was a week behind in my rent at the Studio Club. I had to have the fifty dollars, and the photographer, Tom Kelley, didn't think that anyone would recognise me.'

After several panicked days, Zanuck and Skouras were surprised that Monroe's honesty turned the tide. Letters to Fox were overwhelming in their support for Monroe.

But it was a close call, and Monroe never forgave Lieber.

During the 1962 anti-Monroe project, Lieber waged a campaign that traded on rumour, innuendo and character assassination.

When he provided the first bulletins to Louella Parsons, the veteran columnist was shocked by the crudity of the revelations. Monroe was depicted as 'half mad', and was described as sitting before her dressing-room mirror for hours – totally nude. Parsons was also told that the famed nude swimming scene occurred when Monroe suddenly took off the Jean Louis bikini. 'Monroe was high and didn't even know where she was,' Lieber told her.

Parsons soon disproved the rumours by talking to a few key sources at Fox. But versions of the story appeared in the *New York Times*, in Hedda Hopper's column and in the *New York Post*.

Twentieth Century-Fox had a staff of twenty publicists on both coasts, supplemented by a fleet of still photographers and a sizeable support staff. This entire machine was fully engaged in the Monroe campaign. In addition to Brand, Lieber and Einfeld, the other publicists who were closely involved were former hard news reporter Frank Neill and John Campbell, both of whom had worked on the team that boosted Monroe to stardom.

Now, like Dr. Frankenstein disassembling his monster, Brand and company began a step-by-step destruction of their greatest achievement.

Though it wasn't widely known, the drive to turn Monroe into a star had begun as a bet between Brand and former Fox president Joseph Schenck. 'Harry and I were at a dinner party in 1950 when Schenck made a crack about the worthlessness of publicity departments,' said Sybil Brand. 'Harry replied that the publicity men were usually *the major factor* in the creation of a big star.'

'They could become stars anyway – if they're any good,' Schenck replied.

Brand said angrily, 'You're wrong, Joe. I can take any unknown starlet under contract to Fox and make her into a box office star. I'm willing to wager ten thousand dollars on it.'

Schenck took up the challenge. 'Okay, Brand,' he said. 'But you pick the starlet.'

'I immediately thought of Marilyn Monroe,' said Sybil Brand. 'Very few people knew who she was at this point, and both Harry and Joe agreed. And we all know the result. It was the easiest ten grand Harry ever earned.'

Several weeks later, Brand launched a storm of hype for Monroe. Soon, thanks to lavish layouts in fan magazines, she was a well-known presence. 'Harry made her into a celebrity before any of her major films made it into the theatres,' Sybil recalled.

'The Fox mail room kept a weekly check of the number of requests for pictures each star received,' said Maurice Zolotow. 'Soon Marilyn's name was at the top of the list.'

Zanuck was suspicious. He believed Brand was playing 'star maker' by giving Monroe favoured treatment over all the other starlets. Brand was summoned to the executive offices. 'I think that your department is secretly engaged in promoting Marilyn Monroe, and I want it to stop,' said Zanuck. But Brand somehow convinced Zanuck that Monroe was an overnight sensation and that, suddenly and surprisingly, the public couldn't get enough of her.

At first, the affection was mutual between Monroe and the publicity men. It was an inspired pairing of a willing star and a powerful department. Monroe made herself available for endless premieres and stunts – no matter how trivial or silly. Harry Brand's troops also rushed in whenever the star's career needed a lift. For instance, when Zanuck refused to believe that Monroe could sing and dance well enough to carry *Gentlemen Prefer Blondes*, Brand found a way to convince him.

He persuaded the brass at the Camp Pendleton Marine Base to make Monroe the main attraction at the base's anniversary celebration. She danced into an audience of ten thousand Marines and sang four songs, including 'Diamonds Are a Girl's Best Friend'. Since Brand had filled the audience with columnists, wire service reporters and still photographers, the appearance received wide coverage.

Zanuck was convinced: instead of Betty Grable, for whom *Gentlemen Prefer Blondes* had been purchased, he gave the role to Monroe.

'But Marilyn became so big that she didn't need all the hype,' said Rupert Allan. 'If anything, she needed "less press" by the mid-fifties. When it was time for her to escape the blonde sex symbol image, the department felt that she had turned against them.'

Allan also believed that Brand, and many of those who worked under him, 'had come to loathe Marilyn Monroe'.

This hostility surfaced for the first time in 1954, when Monroe went on suspension rather than make *The Girl in Pink Tights*, which she termed 'a cheap, exploitive film'. Brand unleashed a burst of negative publicity.

He released the following statement to the Associated

Press: 'No one can handle Marilyn Monroe any longer. No one can give her advice. We're getting two hundred letters per day demanding that we get rid of her.'

To Hedda Hopper, Brand provided a statement 'from a highly placed studio executive' who was quoted as saying, 'Marilyn is disgusting. She's had five years of training – enough to produce ten competent actors. But still she can't act.'

Three years later, when Monroe delivered her tour de force in *Bus Stop*, Brand devised a condescending campaign that centred around the phrase, 'Marilyn Acts'.

The romance had obviously faded. But these were only pinpricks compared to the explosion of negative press that accompanied her dismissal from *Something's Got to Give*.

Groundwork for the negative hype began in mid-May, when Lieber hinted to reporters that Monroe was a hypochondriac who was 'sleeping all day and partying all night', as he told Parsons.

In an adroit series of leaks, Lieber released word of Monroe's illness by hinting that she was an imaginary invalid. Though Brand and Lieber had copies of the 'sinusitis rulings' by Fox physicians, Lieber attributed her absences to 'unspecified illnesses', leaving the impression that Monroe was malingering.

When a *Los Angeles Times* reporter asked about the progress of the star's recovery, a Fox spokesman asked, 'Recovery from what?'

Most executives at Fox believed that the campaign was a fair one. With the exception of Henry Weinstein, the most powerful men at the studio refused to believe that the actress was ill. In one memo to Skouras in New York, the episode was described as a 'sick out', a ploy to get more money, as one publicist hinted, to force Fox into cancelling *Something's Got to Give*.

This was only a prelude. The full-blown campaign didn't begin until Wednesday, June 6, two days before the dismissal.

The department roared into action, working into the night to engineer a series of highly effective verbal releases to hand-picked journalists.

That afternoon, Frank Neill telephoned New York columnist Harrison Carroll with the news that 'some kind of drastic action is being considered against Marilyn Monroe'.

The next morning, the Associated Press received a series of quotes from an unknown studio publicist. It contained this statement from a highly placed – but unnamed – executive at Fox: 'Something has to be done with these unprofessional stars – Marilyn Monroe included. We have to sit down on them or forget it.'

The same source was quoted as saying, 'We had a finished script, but Marilyn herself insisted upon rewriting it every day.'

On Friday, Sheilah Graham, who was still in London, received the following statement by Henry Weinstein via telex. 'Marilyn is not ill – I have had no official notification of her illness. All I get from her is that she is not reporting for work. We can't take it any more – her absences have cost the studio more than a million dollars.'

'I never said that, never talked to anyone about it,' Weinstein said. 'Of course Marilyn was sick. I more than anyone else knew how sick she was, but they simply released these statements in my name. The guys in publicity were given a free rein. In fact, after June sixth, I was gone. I had already quit in protest and was working at MGM.'

The same afternoon, another supposed Weinstein quote was fed to Vernon Scott of the *Los Angeles Herald Examiner*. 'By her wilful irresponsibility, Marilyn Monroe has taken the bread right out of the mouths of men who depend on this film to feed their families.'

Weinstein laughed out loud at that one. 'I would never have talked in that manner.'

In New York the same evening, one of Einfeld's men released this statement to Murray Schumach at the *Times* (ostensibly from Peter Levathes): 'Miss Monroe is not just being temperamental; she is mentally ill, perhaps seriously.'

'I never said that, nor did I feel that way,' said Levathes, who was in London when he supposedly levelled those charges.

During the coming days, the studio flacks were relentlessly creative in discrediting the star.

On Thursday afternoon, they issued a statement on Monroe's dismissal ahead of time, so that the news could break big in more than two hundred weekend newspapers across the country.

In part, the release said, 'Miss Monroe has given no justification for her failure to appear on many occasions. This action was forced upon us by Miss Monroe's repeated wilful violations of her contract.'

When studio physician Lee Siegel protested this 'obvious lie', Phil Feldman told him to stay out of it.

Publicist Pat Newcomb tried to fight back. 'I said then, as now, that the studio physician examined Marilyn at the beginning of the last week, and then told her to stay home. He told her she was too sick to go to work, and then the studio fired her.'

The studio publicists also telegraphed a bulletin on the firing to the Associated Press and United Press International and had it hand delivered to seven Los Angeles television stations.

On his way to break the news gently to Monroe, Ralph Greenson was furious when news of the firing came over his car radio. Rudin and the analyst Feldman had promised that there would be no news breaks until Monday.

Lieber enlisted help from his old friend Joan Crawford, who had publicly attacked Monroe in the past. Lieber counted on Crawford to attract headlines around the world.

Crawford had met Monroe at one of Joe Schenck's parties in the late forties. After watching Monroe move through the crowd, the older actress came over and said, 'I think I could help you a great deal if you would let me. For instance, that white knitted dress you are wearing is utterly incorrect for a dinner party of this kind.'

Several weeks later, Monroe was at Crawford's Brentwood mansion for lunch when Crawford began to dictate what Monroe could and could not wear. Angry words were exchanged, and Monroe spurned all further contact.

Their mutual dislike became public at the 1953 *Photoplay* magazine awards. Monroe had made a spectacular entrance, stealing the show in a revealing gold lamé dress. Crawford could barely hold her anger in check.

Crawford held an impromptu press conference. 'Marilyn Monroe is making the mistake of believing her own publicity,' she said. 'But the public likes to know that, underneath it all, actresses are ladies. Moviegoers don't want sex flaunted in their faces. What happened at these awards was like a burlesque show.'

Monroe outclassed Crawford by saying very little to the press – except that she was hurt.

Crawford's anger must have festered over the years, because she responded eagerly to Lieber's call for help. 'Marilyn is a child,' she told reporters. 'She is of an age to be a woman, but she is not.'

Crawford's own history was less than pristine. In the mid-twenties, when she was still Lucille Le Sueur, her tantrums were frequent. In the late twenties Crawford, like Monroe, traded on her body and her sex appeal to win popularity. Later her own use of alcohol rivalled Monroe's drug addiction.

Cukor was also pressed into service and performed with unexcelled gusto. Calling in a thirty-year debt owed him by columnist Hedda Hopper, the director gave an impassioned interview that did more than anything else to destroy Monroe's professional reputation.

'The poor dear has finally gone around the bend,' Cukor confided in the rough copy preserved in Hopper's professional papers. 'The sad thing is, the little work we do have is no good. There's a certain ruthlessness about all of her actions. The studio has given in to her on everything.'

'What do you think will happen to her?' Hopper asked.

'I think, Hedda, that this is the end of her career.'

Hopper, a fan of Cukor's since the Roaring Twenties, considered him the ultimate source for this – Hollywood's hottest story.

Before signing off, the director insisted, 'Please keep my name out of this. What I have told you is strictly off the record.'

Forty-eight hours later, Hopper led off her column with a devastating sentence: 'Marilyn Monroe's career is over, and she knows it.'

Later that same Saturday, the publicists orchestrated what became known as 'the phantom press conference', an event that supposedly involved George Cukor, Henry Weinstein and Peter G. Levathes. The publicists knew that news editors would pay attention to a press conference, whereas they would probably ignore a routine press release.

They produced a special press kit that included details of the announcement and long statements from the three men. Cukor was quoted on the star's mental problems; Levathes was cited as saying he had fired Monroe because of the Kennedy gala; and Weinstein commented on 'Marilyn's non-illness'.

In those freewheeling days, nobody in the media bothered to check into the alleged press conference. If they had, they would have known that Levathes was in New York, Cukor was out of town for a long weekend and Weinstein was already attending meetings at Metro-Goldwyn-Mayer.

'It never happened,' Levathes acknowledged. 'The publicity departments pretty well ran their own show in those days.'

On Sunday and Monday, the publicity department administered the coup de grace. Knowing that Monroe prided herself on her ties with the common man working on the studio lot –

the electricians, the carpenters, the prop men – the publicists drafted an advertisement to appear in the upcoming issue of *Weekly Variety*.

Simply written and only a few sentences long, it thanked Marilyn Monroe 'for the loss of our livelihoods'. It was signed by the crew of *Something's Got to Give*.

Since the ad wasn't to appear until later in the week, the publicists waited until Monday to release the details on it.

But one of them jumped the gun. When Monroe heard the story on a Sunday-morning newscast, she burst into tears. 'Is it true? Do they really hate me?' she asked her friend Whitey Snyder.

'No, honey,' Snyder said. 'It's not true. In fact, I've never heard of it.'

'She was devastated by that, of course,' said Rupert Allan, who called her from overseas that same day.

In truth, the crew, for the most part, sympathised with Monroe. In research for this book, twenty-three of the thirty surviving crew members were surveyed by telephone. None of them was involved in a protest of any kind against Monroe.

'We placed no ad,' recalled assistant director Buck Hall. 'It came from somewhere else. Believe me, I would have known if the crew placed that ad.'

Monroe's own publicist, however, could not convince her that the studio had paid for and planted the ad. 'So she sent a telegram to each crew member,' said Allan. 'It said, in part, "This was none of my doing".'

Next the Fox publicity corps reached into its considerable biographical files in an attempt to use Monroe's own life story as a weapon.

Over the previous decade, the actress had poured her heart out to such publicists as John Campbell and Frank Neill, dwelling particularly on the childhood that had been much like an orphan's and her bouts with depression. From

1949 through 1957, Monroe had dictated more than a hundred thousand words to publicists and their secretaries – creating a stream-of-consciousness account of her terrifying road to stardom.

In addition, the department had access to the confidential legal files on all of Monroe's films. The cumulative record of her absences, her drug usage and her temperamental outbursts provided the journalistic fodder for this attempt to end her career once and for all.

'They set out to destroy her; they didn't give a damn,' said Rupert Allan. 'The ruthlessness started with Harry Brand. For some forgotten slight, he hated Marilyn. Despised her. He always said ugly, dirty things about Marilyn to me . . . vile jokes and sexual innuendo. He said these things knowing that I was her friend and that I represented her. Imagine what he told her enemies.'

The publicists dredged up two of Marilyn's most private heartbreaks – her fear of insanity and her long-hidden history of learning disabilities. Cleverly and insidiously, they turned these faults into a firestorm.

When it became clear how far Fox was willing to go, a chill descended on Monroe's supporters, who were gathered in Brentwood. When the first stories alluded to 'mental problems', Ralph Greenwood decided to keep this information from her as long as possible.

But his discretion only delayed a hysterical reaction that was inevitable, given Monroe's primal fear of insanity.

'She wasn't insane, but her fear was intense,' said writer Lucy Freeman, confidante of Greenson. 'She was deathly afraid of mental illness.'

More specifically, she feared that schizophrenia was a genetic trait that plagued her mother's family and that it was lurking deep within her ready to explode at any time.

This terror, which Monroe relived every night, was instinctual. In fact, her earliest memories were of psychotic episodes.

While most children remember warm, nurturing experiences of their grandmothers, Monroe's memories were bloodcurdling.

When she was eighteen months old, Della Monroe, her grandmother, tried to smother her during a rage. Marilyn's foster parents recalled that 'Della had the wild-eyed look of a madwoman'.

'They say I shouldn't remember that,' she told Ralph Roberts. 'But I do remember it . . . it was terrible.' By the time Marilyn – then known as Norma Jean Mortenson – was four years old, Della Monroe was locked in a mental ward, and Marilyn's mother, Gladys Baker, had suffered the first of her own psychotic episodes.

By the time Marilyn was ten, Gladys Baker was also locked away in the first of a series of private psychiatric hospitals. She would remain behind protective walls for the rest of her life.

Monroe also knew that her mother's breakdown began with a series of angry outbursts in her mid-thirties – rages similar to those Monroe experienced during the making of *Something's Got to Give*.

'She knew that somehow her anger had to be contained or she would surrender to the madness that put her mother and her grandmother in asylums,' said Harold Rollyson, one of Monroe's biographers. 'She feared that all of her therapy had been fruitless.'

Between 1957 and 1962, Monroe had spent more than $150,000 on psychiatric treatment and hospitalisation. Now she felt that all the money, and the time, had been wasted.

She also questioned her continued need for the daily sessions – some of which lasted for hours – with Ralph Greenson.

Slatzer noted that Monroe often tried to back out of sessions. 'Marilyn would tell the secretary she didn't need to come in. Several minutes later Greenson would call. "You have to come in," he would tell her.'

Monroe told many of her friends, including Ralph Roberts

and Rupert Allan, that she began spinning elaborate fantasies for Greenson. She even made notes about symptoms and feelings she thought Greenson would want to hear. These were recorded in her stash of spiral notebooks. She even taped 'fake monologues' on her small reel-to-reel machine and offered them to Greenson in lieu of an agonising session of analysis.

One June afternoon, Monroe complained to Slatzer, 'Bob, I don't have anything to tell him. I hate this; I hate being forced into these meetings.'

'What goes on when you have nothing to say?' Slatzer asked.

She smiled slyly. 'I fantasise. I tell him things that never happened. There's no way he can check on them.'

'She might have even been crawling out from under her dependence on psychiatrists,' theorised Rupert Allan. 'In my opinion, they did her more harm than good.'

Ralph Roberts agreed. 'Shortly after the Kennedy gala, I was giving her a massage. As I was working on her feet, she said, "Ralph, if you ever hear they are putting me in an insane asylum, come out and show them that all I need is a massage." It's a silly thing, but she said it with such heartfelt sincerity.'

The firing propelled her back into Greenson's office, just as the rumours of insanity spread by the publicists reawakened her insomnia and her night terrors.

Then Fox stepped up the campaign.

In a series of leaks, the studio allowed the story of the 'lost weekend' to seep out. In Rome, a publicist on the *Cleopatra* set told Sheilah Graham that 'Marilyn can no longer remember her lines; Cukor is piecing her dialogue together, word by word.'

The story of her 'Darling, Nick; Nick, darling' troubles was spread all over town as evidence that she was losing her grip.

Actually, Monroe's learning disability was a shared secret on the lot, stretching back to her earliest days as a star. As early as *Niagara* in 1953, she routinely transposed words in the typical dyslexic pattern. After she flubbed a single sentence twenty-two times on the set of *How to Marry a Millionaire*, Lee Siegel explained to Nunnally Johnson, 'She has a problem of word perception; there's nothing wrong with her memory.'

This transposition of words, which sometimes made her a laughing stock, continued throughout her career.

On the set of *The Misfits*, John Huston and the cast worked in 102-degree heat for five hours as Monroe repeatedly flubbed her entrance line.

She was supposed to rush up to Clark Gable and gush, 'Here we are!' On the first take she swayed in on her spike heels and burbled, 'We're here!'

Huston was patient. 'Marilyn, the line is "Here we are," dear.'

There was another flub, and another. Monroe later told Arthur Miller that it didn't make any difference if a line was scrambled. 'It's the meaning that counts.'

The solution wasn't as simple during the filming of *Some Like It Hot*. She was to toddle into one scene and say breathlessly, 'Where's the bourbon?' She was only able to achieve a sound like 'Where's the bonbon?' After four hours, director Billy Wilder pasted slips of paper onto a set of drawers the actress had to open.

Even then, she fluffed it. It was obvious she was reading it wrong. It was a classic fault in word perception – the tendency to reshuffle words and letters.

The studio was unaware that she also suffered from Ménière's disease, an ear ailment that caused slight vertigo and indistinct hearing. Monroe frequently misunderstood George Cukor's directions. 'Much of Marilyn's vagueness stemmed from this hearing impairment,' said Rupert Allan.

In addition, her general problems on the set fit universal learning disability patterns. Wilma Jo Bush and Kenneth Wough might have been describing Monroe in their book,

Diagnosing Learning Problems, when they described the symptoms as 'impulsive, explosive behaviour; a low tolerance for frustration; abnormally light sleep patterns; poor short-term memory; and confusion about instructions'.

Fox publicists used these physical flaws to make the case that Monroe was descending into an end-of-career crisis.

All these troubles, added to Monroe's notorious temperament, were the ingredients of an industry-wide condemnation.

The hurricane of disastrous publicity seemed unstoppable at first. On the fourth day of the 'flack war', Hedda Hopper told her assistant Jaik Rosenstein, 'This may finish her – personally and professionally.'

Even the staid *Los Angeles Times* ruled that 'the days of such superstar shenanigans are over.'

When the storm broke on Friday afternoon, Monroe played *Camille* for a few hours. Sobbing intermittently, she swooned on her white sofa while Eunice Murray supplied a fountain of Dom Pérignon.

Greenson was there for two hours of high-priced hand holding, and Pat Newcomb was buried in an avalanche of calls from the press.

Many writers have depicted Monroe as totally lost and alone, brooding in her Brentwood house.

Actually, her sadness gave way to anger as the evening wore on. The star had always had the ability to stand back and take a detached look at that overexposed entity, 'Marilyn Monroe'. In that context, it was unbelievable that *anyone* had dared to fire *her*.

'First and foremost, she had trouble believing it had actually happened,' recalled Allan. 'It had been threatened many times before, but it had always been averted.'

When Ralph Roberts arrived for the routine massage session on Saturday, he found the star ready to do battle. 'You know, don't you, that they fired me because of Elizabeth Taylor? It's not her fault; it's the company's fault. But they did fire me because of Elizabeth Taylor.'

Roberts agreed.

Later she was even angrier. 'If they can't make money off me, they want to wreck my career so that no one can,' she said.

Several hours later she was already fighting back. During a visit from Whitey Snyder and Marjorie Plecher, the actress called Darryl F. Zanuck in Paris to protest the unfairness of the studio's actions. Zanuck, her old nemesis, instantly agreed to help.

As the weekend wore on, Monroe received additional help from an entirely unexpected source.

Chapter 23

Clash of the Titans

Word of Monroe's dismissal was slow to reach the set of *Something's Got to Give* where the cast and crew were still standing by on Friday, June 8.

The first rumours didn't circulate until 3.30 P.M., a half hour after the Associated Press broadcast its first bulletin to America's radio stations. Nobody believed the gossip at first; similar stories had circulated on May 18, when Monroe was in New York for the President's gala.

At 3.45 P.M., Fox hairstylist Agnes Flanaghan knocked on Dean Martin's dressing room door to ask his opinion of the story that Kim Novak had been hired to replace Monroe.

'I don't think so, honey,' Martin said. 'I'd certainly have heard about that.'

But it wasn't long before Buck Hall made it official by posting a notice on the call sheet next to the main entrance to soundstage 14. 'Set Closed Until Further Notice – Per Instructions from the Legal Department.'

About the same time, Whitey Snyder got a tip from a source in the front office. Not only had Monroe been fired, but the studio had worked quickly to replace her. Lee Remick, who owed the studio two films, was already in wardrobe, being fitted for Monroe's costumes.

Snyder approached Martin, who was still in golf clothes from a noon game at the Los Angeles Country Club. 'Dean, I think they've fired Marilyn,' Snyder said.

'What?' Martin said.

'Then Dean had his assistant run to the production office to verify the story,' Snyder remembered.

A few minutes later, the asistant was back. 'Yep,' he said. 'Monroe has been fired and Lee Remick's going to be your leading lady.'

Martin put his putter down, grabbed his coat and headed for the Fox parking lot. Snyder walked part of the way with him. 'Whitey, I made a contract to do this picture with Marilyn Monroe,' Martin said. 'That's the deal; the only deal. We're not going to be doing it with Lee Remick or any other actress.'

When Martin arrived home half an hour later, Vernon Scott, the Hollywood reporter for United Press International, coaxed a brief interview out of him. Martin told Scott that he had walked off the set and didn't plan to return. 'I have the greatest respect for Miss Remick as an artist,' Martin continued. 'But I signed to do this film with Marilyn Monroe.'

Shortly after 6 P.M., the UPI wires broadcast this bulletin: 'Dean Martin quit the Twentieth Century-Fox film because Marilyn Mnroe was fired.' In a substantially longer article the next day, Scott announced that Martin had already notified Fox of his decision through his agent, Herman Citron of the Music Corporation of America (MCA), then the world's largest talent agency.

This was a body blow to Fox's careful publicity campaign and it crippled the studio's attempts to mollify rebelling investors – particularly when the Martin announcement got more play and bigger headlines than editors had given Monroe's dismissal.

The *New York Daily News* ran a banner headline: 'No MM,

No Martin'. The *New York Times* was a bit more sedate. They headlined the story 'Dean Martin Quits over MM's Firing'. Radio and television stations made much of the story, using film clips from the Kennedy gala and about thirty seconds of Monroe's costume tests from *Something's Got to Give*.

All week, Feldman had been desperately searching for a replacement with enough star power to please Martin.

First on the list was Kim Novak, the former department store model and beauty queen (Miss Deep Freeze of 1952), who was Columbia Pictures' answer to Monroe. Gould, Levathes and Skouras all favoured the enigmatic blonde star. Novak refused even to consider the offer. Since she had also been victimised by an insensitive film studio (Columbia) and a despotic boss (Harry Cohn), she had long sympathised with Monroe.

Spurned by Novak, Feldman approached Shirley MacLaine on Tuesday and Doris Day on Wednesday. Both were wary of replacing Monroe; both declined only hours after receiving the offers. By Thursday morning, Feldman was desperate. Since Remick owed Fox two films, Feldman offered the star $80,000 to play Ellen Arden. Suspicious that this was a publicity ruse, Remick insisted that the studio pay her $80,000 when she signed the contract. If Monroe should be reinstated, Remick would get the money and a guarantee that she owed Fox no more films.

The twenty-seven-year-old actress was neither a box office power nor a major star at this point, though she would be both soon, with the 1962 release of *The Days of Wine and Roses*. Several weeks earlier, she had signed to make *The Running Man* for director Sir Carol Reed. Though the film was not to begin shooting until July, Remick didn't cancel out. She had a hunch that she would never make *Something's Got to Give*.

It remains unclear whether or not Fox ever intended to replace Monroe with Remick. But it is clear that the studio wanted the press to buy that line. Before Martin was informed of the dismissal, Feldman and Perry Lieber had already whisked Remick to the studio, pinned her into several of Monroe's costumes, and taken several pictures of her with George Cukor. In one of the stills, they are sitting side by side, looking over the script. In another, Cukor is kissing Remick's hand.

'I was only involved with that film for about twenty minutes,' Remick recalled thirty years later. 'It was most unpleasant. I could tell that we were just going through the motions for the benefit of the press.

'I certainly wasn't interested in it,' she continued. 'Marilyn and I were as different as two actresses can be. But the studio told me, "We have a contract with you, and we want you to fulfil your obligation."'

While the stills were being taken, Lieber and John Campbell, the unit publicist on *Something's Got to Give*, released several statements to the press in Remick's name. Two of them were suspiciously similar to the statements Fox had disseminated to the AP and UPI in the name of an anonymous 'front office executive'.

In the first Remick 'quotation', Monroe was chastised for being 'very, very unprofessional. She refuses to view the film industry as a business. And a business will not tolerate such behaviour.'

The second so-called Remick statement was stronger.

'I feel that Marilyn should have been replaced,' Remick purportedly said. 'I don't believe actors should be allowed to get away with this type of behaviour. The movie business is crumbling down around our ears because of that kind of behaviour. After all, despite all the glamour, this is still a business. Other people get fired for behaving as Marilyn did.'

'I never said any of those things,' Remick recalled. 'Since it was a publicity stunt, they released all those statements in my name. It was all very degrading.'

By that time, Martin's angry quotes to the AP had made the Remick charade unnecessary in any case.

The studio spent most of Saturday trying to convince Martin to accept Remick, or at least to say publicly that he accepted her. Feldman wasted most of the day ferrying messages from the New York office to Martin. But it was a circuitous route through Martin's agent, Herman Citron. When the actor still wouldn't budge, Fox threatened him with a multimillion-dollar lawsuit. When that failed to impress him, Feldman went over Citron's head with an appeal to MCA president Lew Wasserman.

The most Feldman could achieve was Martin's agreement to meet with studio executives on Monday morning, June 11.

When *Something's Got to Give* was being planned in November of 1961, Monroe had insisted on Martin despite a nasty battle with Fox – which wanted to cast James Garner in the role.

Now Martin was repaying in kind. Monroe was touched by his loyalty. When she received a pile of New York newspapers later on Sunday which publicist Arthur Jacobs had had flown in, she showed the biggest headline to Joan Greenson. It was the 'No MM, No Martin' banner. 'She was thrilled by that,' Greenson remembered.

To Fox executives, Martin's action underscored all the problems which faced studios in the early sixties. 'This was bigger than just one film or just two stars,' said Peter Levathes. 'The big agencies like MCA were threatening the studio system. They packaged actors, writers, directors and even producers, and they shut the studio out. Because of this, costs kept escalating.'

MCA, which represented Marilyn Monroe Productions and Dean Martin's company, Claude Productions, had packaged *Something's Got to Give*.

'The agencies were taking over more and more power,'

Levathes said. 'The big agents now thought they knew better than the studios and, because of that, were running us out of business.'

Dean Martin never elaborated on his reasons for putting his career and his future on the line for Monroe, but it was typical of a man whose on-screen image as an easy-going good guy was identical to his off-screen persona. An ex-prizefighter and ex-cardsharp, Martin had been labouring in a steel mill when he began singing nights and weekends in small clubs. After he teamed up with frenetic comedian Jerry Lewis in 1946, he assumed the role of a handsome, not-so-bright straight man. The Martin and Lewis partnership endured for ten years, eleven films and a thousand appearances in nightclubs.

When the partnership collapsed in the mid-fifties, many Hollywood producers thought Martin wouldn't survive as a solo act. But half a dozen number one hits, including 'Volare' and 'Memories Are Made of This', smoothed his way to film and television superstardom. In 1958, his role in *Some Came Running* opposite fellow 'Rat Packers' Sinatra and MacLaine proved his value as a dramatic star.

However predictable, Martin's loyalty to Monroe was far from popular. 'Nasty sayings were scrawled on his dressing-room door,' production secretary Lee Hanna recalled. 'By insisting on Monroe, it seemed as if the film would shut down for good – with the loss of one hundred and four jobs.'

Hedda Hopper warned the actor in her *Los Angeles Times* column. 'The unions are taking a dim view of Dean Martin's walkout,' Hopper wrote. She quoted a union official as saying, 'Dean's putting people out of work at a time when we are all faced with unemployment.'

Hopper also reminded readers that in the old days, unions had used more obvious ways for dealing with such conduct. 'The actor would be performing his heart out when a crystal chandelier would come crashing down. It missed, *the first time*.'

Levathes, who flew back to Los Angeles on Sunday, was determined to change Martin's mind but, just in case, had Ferguson begin drafting a $5.6-million lawsuit 'for breach of contract'.

The three-hour meeting among Feldman, Levathes, Frank Ferguson, Martin and Herman Citron was an exercise in frustration. The executives were determined to sell Remick to the increasingly sceptical actor.

When Feldman tried to verbally recap Martin's 'rejection of Remick', Martin interrupted him, saying, 'I didn't turn down Miss Remick, I simply said that I will not do the film without Miss Monroe. There is a big difference between the two statements.'

Levathes countered, 'What kind of position does that put our investment in?'

Martin answered, 'That's not a fair question to ask me. I have no quarrel with anyone.'

Levathes forged ahead. 'We think Miss Remick is of adequate stature,' he said. 'After all, she has appeared with Jack Lemmon [in *The Days of Wine and Roses*], with James Stewart [in *Anatomy of a Murder*], and with Glenn Ford [in *Experiment in Terror*].'

Martin patiently explained that he had taken the role mainly because 'the chemistry between Miss Monroe and myself was right.' The actor also said that the whole point of *Something's Got to Give* was Martin's desertion of his new bride, Cyd Charisse, for Monroe, which was something which wouldn't happen, Martin said, 'with Lee Remick'.

The production chief disagreed. 'This story is a warm situation in which the husband, with his children, loved his former wife, but was caught in an embarrassing position because he had remarried,' said Levathes. 'This is not the case of a man who chucks one woman for a sexpot.'

Martin shook his head.

Levathes was starting to get angry. 'We have leaned over backwards to get this film done – even offering Monroe a bonus,' he said. 'We have put up two million, one hundred and nine thousand dollars. But now we are running out of time.'

'What do you suggest?' Citron asked.

'We think Mr. Martin should approve Miss Remick,' said Levathes.

Hoping for a way out of the impasse, Citron said, 'Perhaps if you suggested Brigitte Bardot.'

With that, Levathes went to another office to call Milton Gould, chairman of Fox's executive committee, in New York.

Fifteen minutes later, Levathes re-entered to repeat, 'We believe Mr. Martin should approve Miss Remick.'

Citron and Martin withdrew without further comment.

'These were business decisions,' said Levathes. 'And it made sense to go ahead with Lee Remick.'

At noon Citron called back. It was still 'No MM, No Martin.'

In the meantime, Monroe was gathering other powerful allies.

– Chapter 24 –

Reinstatement

By the afternoon of Monday, June 11, Monroe had begun to fight back, exhibiting a toughness that was surprising.

With Pat Newcomb taking notes, Monroe dictated 104 telegrams to the cast and crew of *Something's Got to Give*. She lamented the studio's decision to shut down the film and added, 'It was none of my doing; I hope you know that.'

She also dispatched two wires to Attorney General Robert Kennedy – one to his home in Arlington, Virginia, and the other to his office in the United States Justice Department – both of which were later billed to Monroe's estate by the Arthur Jacobs Agency, which processed them.

The cable to Arlington officially declined an invitation to a formal dinner for Peter and Pat Kennedy Lawford. It read: 'Dear Attorney General and Mrs. Robert Kennedy: I would have been delighted to have accepted your invitation honouring Pat and Peter Lawford. Unfortunately, I am involved in a freedom ride protesting the loss of the minority rights belonging to the few remaining earthbound stars.'

Monroe had discussed her dismissal at length with Peter and Pat Lawford and the Attorney General. She closed the message with this line: 'After all, all we demanded was our right to twinkle.'

That referred to a discussion she had had with the Attorney General during the February party at the Lawford mansion. 'She said they talked of how few really big stars remained,' said Rupert Allan. 'Marilyn was immensely flattered when Bobby told her that she and Elizabeth Taylor were the only stars left.'

The second message, which didn't survive in any form, was undoubtedly a summation of her troubles with Fox and a plea for help. Monroe knew that Bobby Kennedy had several 'family connections' on Fox's board of directors, namely Samuel Rosenman and Darryl F. Zanuck. Hazel Washington remembered that Bobby called midweek to offer his assistance.

For three days, Monroe hesitated to call Skouras, who had guided and protected her since their brief affair. Skouras's intense and personal interest was one of the reasons Monroe was so sure that Twentieth Century-Fox would not fire her; his influence was her trump card.

She finally conquered her pride and called her benefactor. After a series of calls, she tracked him to the private suite of a Manhattan hospital, where he was still recuperating from surgery.

Skouras explained that it was the executive committee, not he, who had fired her. He admitted that he was only a figurehead, that he still had the title of president, but not the power – which lay in the hands of the committee. Milton Gould, he pointed out, was actually running Twentieth Century-Fox.

This was the first Monroe had learned that Wall Street lawyers, controlling enormous blocks of stock, had seized control of the board of directors. She found out that she had been fired by a triumvirate consisting of Gould, who headed the executive committee, Peter Levathes, and Judge Samuel

Rosenman, the former Franklin Roosevelt speechwriter (and former New York Superior Court justice) who was also chairman of the board.

Skouras sadly informed her that he could be of no help.

Then Monroe remembered a recent series of articles in the Hollywood trade papers which had indicated that her old nemesis, Darryl Zanuck, was engineering a return to power – this time as corporate president. Zanuck had just held a series of press conferences in Paris, telling journalists about the lamentable state of Fox, a studio he had built from a small, grade B film factory into a major power.

Late Monday afternoon, during a visit from Whitey Snyder, Monroe called Zanuck in Paris, where he was editing *The Longest Day*, a brilliant saga of World War II's D-Day landings. Snyder recalled that Monroe explained the nature of her illness and told Zanuck that she was ready for work – that she had licked the infection.

'I only heard one side of her conversation with Zanuck,' Snyder recalled. 'But I got the impression that he agreed to help engineer her comeback.'

Robert Kennedy also went immediately into action. He called Judge Rosenman, who had been a close pal of Joseph Kennedy when the elder Kennedy was ambassador to Great Britain and Rosenman was writing speeches for President Roosevelt. A small personal note in the Skouras papers, and in the Zanuck collection, indicates that Bobby convinced Rosenman to reconsider Monroe's case. The Fox chairman was sympathetic. He had known JFK and Bobby as youngsters and had had further contact with John when the future President, then a navy ensign, served on Roosevelt's staff during World War II.

There is no record of the Attorney General's exact conversations with Rosenman. But Rupert Allan, who called Monroe on Tuesday from Princess Grace's office in Monaco, learned that Bobby had informed the board chairman that President

Kennedy would be grateful for any help Rosenman could provide.

But the only man who could single-handedly reinstate Monroe was Milton Gould – the man Bobby had called a 'Jew bastard' when Gould refused to approve Monroe's appearance at the gala. America's First Family could therefore expect little aid from Gould.

Monroe's best hope was Zanuck, who was furious over his own troubles with Gould and the executive committee. Once one of the three most powerful men in the film industry – along with Louis B. Mayer and Jack Warner – Zanuck was now forced to grovel before the committee to obtain sufficient post-production cash to complete *The Longest Day*, which had cost Fox $8 million and had taken two years to film.

A week before Monroe's call to Paris, Zanuck learned that the executive committee was planning to seize *The Longest Day* and quickly release it in a thousand theatres with little or no promotion. Zanuck had planned for a classy roadshow presentation and a series of glitzy premieres to showcase *The Longest Day*'s thirty-five stars, who included Peter Lawford, Richard Burton, Henry Fonda and John Wayne. There was also a juicy role for Zanuck's mistress, Irina Demick.

When Zanuck put *The Longest Day* aside to fight for Monroe's reinstatement, neither he nor Monroe could have known that the battle over *Something's Got to Give* would lead to the overthrow of the Fox leadership – a revolution that would drastically alter the future of Twentieth Century-Fox.

Zanuck had actually heard about Monroe's dismissal before anyone in Hollywood. At 1 A.M. Paris time on the previous Friday, June 8, he had been summoned from his editing chores to take a call from his old pal, Nunnally Johnson.

'What's up?' Zanuck asked his favourite screenwriter.

Johnson answered angrily, 'They're going to fire Marilyn Monroe from *Something's Got to Give*.'

'God damn it!' said Zanuck. 'How do you know?'

'Marilyn just called me,' explained Johnson. 'And she was warned by Louella Parsons.'

Zanuck sighed. 'What can be done? That film could be a bonanza at the box office.' He was in a position to know. He had just made a secret trip to the West Coast to view footage from both *Cleopatra* and *Something's Got to Give*. He had come away hating the Egyptian epic and loving the Monroe film.

Johnson was pessimistic. 'I have already cabled Pete Levathes. I asked him to consider carefully who sells the most tickets – Monroe or George Cukor. And then to fire Cukor instead of Marilyn.'

Zanuck was silent.

'It's Cukor's doing, basically,' Johnson continued.

'But I like the film I saw,' said Zanuck. 'Marilyn never looked better.'

Johnson agreed.

The screenwriter's call pushed Zanuck into the nastiest, costliest fight of his life – the battle to regain control of Twentieth Century-Fox. 'You know I never particularly liked Monroe,' Zanuck told Johnson. 'But I've got a hell of a high regard for her box-office value. The treatment of her on this film makes me terribly frightened for the future of Fox.'

Zanuck promised to get back to Johnson. In the meantime, he called Skouras and put his old adversary on the case.

By the time Monroe herself called Zanuck on Saturday, the former studio maven, who had been described recently as 'through in Hollywood', was organising an incredible corporate coup.

Apparently, Monroe gave Zanuck a verbal guarantee that she would return to *Something's Got to Give* rapidly if she were given the chance. And he expressed his willingness to restore the Nunnally Johnson script – which he also preferred. He even indicated that Johnson might be hired to replace Cukor.

Rumours that Monroe was returning surfaced Monday in corporate headquarters, along with reports that the collapse of *Something's Got to Give* and the mishandling of *Cleopatra* had convinced Zanuck to make a serious bid to seize the presidency of Fox. 'These disasters occurred because the studio is run by committee,' Zanuck told reporters in Paris. 'Rule by committee doesn't work in Hollywood. Just look at *Cleopatra*.'

But there were no such rumours in Hollywood, where Feldman and Levathes considered the matter concluded. Monroe's attorney, Milton Rudin, was told that it was too late for negotiation.

When he arrived at his Beverly Hills office on Monday, Rudin was furious that Fox had broken its word to him. During a call to Feldman, Rudin challenged the executive's ethics.

'I hear that you have filed a lawsuit,' said Rudin.

'True,' Feldman answered. 'We filed it just before 5 P.M. on Friday.'

Feldman's flippancy disgusted Rudin. 'You could at least have informed us about it,' he said. 'Instead, we heard about it on the radio.'

Rudin also blasted the 'get Marilyn' publicity campaign, describing it as a 'betrayal'. 'Why have your publicity boys gone so far as to mention Marilyn's lack of discipline?' he asked. And the public complaints about Monroe's sanity, he pointed out, had turned the contest into a dirty fight.

'There were only a couple of quotes from Henry Weinstein, one from Levathes, and a graph or two about Lee Remick's casting,' Feldman lied. Rudin would soon find out that Weinstein, Remick and Levathes had not spoken to reporters.

Rudin reminded Feldman that he and Monroe had kept their part of the agreement. 'I had to order Arthur Jacobs to issue no publicity about her,' Rudin said. 'But Miss Monroe can be provoked too far.'

This veiled threat might have alarmed Feldman, since a 'pro-Marilyn' backlash had already begun, with telegrams from fans and calls to the Fox switchboard. These contacts were running ten to one in Monroe's favour.

'Already there were rumours that she would be re-hired,' said Hazel Washington.

Chapter 25

RFK

On the third weekend in June, while the corporate turmoil over Monroe's dismissal was still raging, Robert Francis Kennedy arrived at Marilyn's house for a visit that was both personal and political.

He was driving a white convertible and was dressed like a college boy in an Oxford-cloth shirt and penny loafers.

Monroe was still occupied with her beauty ritual when he drove up, so she told Eunice Murray that she was expecting a guest and to offer him a drink. Murray had no idea that the visitor was the Attorney General of the United States until she opened the door.

'I greeted Mr. Kennedy at the door and showed him into the living room that June afternoon,' Murray told ABC news producer Sylvia Chase. She also told Chase that Bobby displayed the demeanour of an earnest young suitor.

The glittering flirtation with Monroe that had begun at his brother's birthday party drew Bobby to her side as her professional life fell apart.

Monroe was unusually prompt that day and emerged from her dressing room wearing a flowing Pucci hostess gown. Her hair had been styled by Guilaroff, and her makeup completed the effect. 'All of that signified that Bobby's visit was an important one,' said Fred Lawrence Guiles, author of the Monroe biographies *Norma Jean* and *Legend*. 'It was unusual for Marilyn to dress formally for such a visit to her home. She hardly ever abandoned the slacks and blouse which she normally wore on such visits.'

On this, their first private meeting, they walked hand in hand around Monroe's pool while Bobby tossed a small white ball for her small white poodle. Given to Monroe by Frank Sinatra, the poodle was named 'Maf' – short for Mafia.

Very little is known about that ninety-minute conversation, other than a bit of crafty advice that RFK gave Monroe. 'I'm a lawyer and a politician,' he said. 'And I live in my work. You're an actress, and you live in your work as well. Besides, your work is important to the whole world. Stick with it.' Monroe later repeated this quote to both Eunice Murray and Robert Slatzer.

Then he bounded back into the convertible, gave a jaunty salute and was gone, to quote Murray, 'like a mirage'.

It seemed to Murray that 'a romantic relationship was well underway'.

'He took a personal interest in her,' said Guiles. 'And this type of mental relationship was far more dangerous than a strictly sexual relationship would have been.'

But there was another reason for Bobby's visit. Though the President had changed the number of his private line to the Oval Office, Monroe now called the regular switchboard repeatedly, angrily giving her name when operators would not put her through. One time she said petulantly, 'This is Marilyn Monroe! And I expect to speak with Jack.'

Peter Lawford's former wives, Patricia Seaton Lawford and Deborah Gould Lawford, both claimed that the purpose of RFK's initial visit was to prevent Monroe from openly contacting JFK.

Columnist James Bacon agreed. 'Marilyn told me at the

time that her first serious conversation with Bobby occurred when he came west that June. And she said he was there to keep her away from the President.'

Sometime during their walk around the pool, the Attorney General sternly told Monroe to 'stop calling the White House'. Then, to compensate her for the loss of the President's secret telephone line, Bobby gave her his own private number, which rang through to his desk at the Justice Department.

'Judy Garland had that phone number as well,' said Ed Guthman, RFK's press aide. 'Bobby was an enormously sympathetic man. He was a good listener. Before long, Marilyn was calling him three to four times a week.'

Monroe had been fascinated with Bobby since February, when she had dazzled him at the soirée given by Pat and Peter Lawford at their informal Western White House in Santa Monica.

The party celebrated Bobby's and Ethel Kennedy's departure on what would be a triumphant around-the-world tour. Pat Kennedy Lawford summoned all the important members of 'young Hollywood' to the bash. But Monroe was to occupy centre stage. Glitzy stars like Kim Novak, in a red sequinned gown by Jean Louis, Janet Leigh, in a thick velvet creation by Adrian, and Natalie Wood, in a billowing Balenciaga cocktail gown, were all upstaged by Monroe, in a stark, clinging black dress by Norman Norell.

Before she walked down the steps into this crush of fame, her arrival was already the talk of the evening. Typically late, she drove up in a small Volkswagen, which was lost in a line of limousines, Porsches and silver Rolls-Royces.

At the wheel was a handsome Irishman in a sweater and slacks, Whitey Snyder. 'I had been at Marilyn's giving her the full makeup treatment,' Snyder recalled. 'And she said impulsively, "Why don't you give me a ride?"'

So he whisked her down from the hills of Brentwood and Pacific Palisades to the beach mansion. 'It was ringed by Secret Service agents,' he remembered. 'They gave me a funny look, but upon recognising Marilyn, let us in.'

A valet opened the door so that she could step out in a cloud of Chanel No. 5, a black mink hanging off her shoulders. The flash guns of the press popped like fireworks.

'Hiya, boys,' Marilyn said, as Snyder drove through the gates and back onto the Pacific Coast Highway.

'Who brought you, Marilyn?' asked a reporter.

The star let the mink fall about her shoulders. 'Oh, just a sailor I've been dating,' she said with a wink.

Later Snyder laughed as he recalled, 'The reporters spent days looking for the naval officer who had captured Marilyn's heart. She actually gave me that nickname years earlier, because of my boats and because of my passion for sailing.'

Monroe confronted the crowd of people in the Lawfords' living room.

In a flowing white dress, Pat Kennedy Lawford greeted her. 'I wasn't sure you would come, with this huge, huge crowd,' she said.

'Are you kidding?' said Monroe. 'I'm dying to meet Bobby.'

'Well, I put you on one side of him, and Kim Novak on the other. Is that close enough?' asked Pat Lawford.

'Thanks a lot for Kim,' Monroe said with a laugh.

It has often been claimed that Monroe just bumped into Robert Kennedy, and that they felt an instant attraction. It has been argued that their meeting was an accident – a coincidence of time and place.

Actually, Monroe had prepared for her introduction to Bobby as rigorously as she would have studied for a film role. She had read armloads of newspapers on the Attorney General's upcoming world tour. She had besieged Peter Lawford with questions about Ethel, about the Attorney General's children, about the Justice Department, and about Bobby's closeness with his brother, the President.

'This was an intellectual, and not a sexual interest,' said

Robert Slatzer. 'And, for Marilyn, these were the more danger-ous and more permanent attachments.' Slatzer was in a position to know. His status as a newspaper columnist and screenwriter had fascinated Monroe in the forties. He had introduced her to the worlds of philosophy and abstract ideas.

'Her relationship with the President was sexual, with power as an aphrodisiac. It was sex with JFK and almost nothing else,' recalled choreographer Steven Papich. 'With JFK, there was no intellectual hangover.'

Almost thirty years later, Hazel Washington described the President as 'just another man passin' through', but described Bobby as 'the real thing'.

To court Bobby's intellectual side, Monroe coaxed Ralph Greenson's son, Daniel, into tutoring her so that she could talk politics with her dinner companion. 'They came up with a series of erudite questions that Marilyn concealed in her small purse – crib notes for a courtship,' Slatzer remembered.

The shyest of all the Kennedy men when it came to women, Bobby still couldn't bring himself to start a conversation with Monroe, even after the lengthy question-and-answer session at dinner.

The actress was lounging on the floor atop her mink, her shoes off, when Bobby flopped down. He didn't even say hello.

Pat Lawford said, 'You remember Marilyn?'

Bobby remained mute.

'Bobby, this is *Marilyn Monroe*.'

Finally they sprawled side by side on the Lawford carpet, with Monroe writing questions with her lipstick on a large napkin. One of them was, 'What does an Attorney General do?'

Later she taught him how to dance the twist. They moved about the floor as 'The Peppermint Twist' and 'Let's Twist Again' repeated on Peter Lawford's record player.

Bobby was so starstruck that evening that he called a

college chum and introduced Monroe over the phone. 'Guess who I just danced with?' Bobby asked. Then he put the actress on the phone.

Toward the end of the evening, Monroe engaged in a little clever manoeuvring. Sitting between Bobby and his press aide, Ed Guthman, she opened her eyes wide and, showing the effects of many glasses of champagne, said, 'I wonder if I should drive home.' Neither man knew, of course, that she owned no car at the time.

'Gee, you can't drive home in your condition,' said the Attorney General.

Monroe just smiled.

Bobby grabbed Guthman by the arm. 'You've got to come with me. I'm not taking her home alone.'

So the three of them drove up from the beach, Monroe and Bobby in the front seat, and Guthman in the back.

They left her in the living room of her house and in the hands of Eunice Murray.

The next morning, Bobby and Ethel Kennedy flew away on their world tour, and Monroe reported to Fox to be fitted for the *Something's Got to Give* costumes.

But a tentative bond was formed – one that, more than anything else, would determine the course of Monroe's final days. To quote Hazel Washington, 'Bobby Kennedy, that was the serious love affair.'

After Monroe had been fired and publicly humiliated by Fox, she decided that Dr. Greenson and Paula Strasberg had failed her. They had failed to save her job and therefore, like many of her early champions, such as Milton Greene and Arthur Miller, they no longer merited her trust.

She needed a new white knight to rescue her. That was when Bobby Kennedy reentered her life.

Chapter 26

Cease-Fire

On June 14, the Thursday after Monroe was fired, Ralph Greenson escorted her to the Beverly Hills clinic of Dr. Michael Gurdin, a man world-famous for his expert and discreet plastic surgery on scores of Hollywood stars. Because gossip columnists kept a trained eye on the clinic to keep track of the rich and famous who availed themselves of its services, they used the rear entrance.

Gurdin's nurse guided Greenson and Monroe into the surgeon's private office and brought them coffee and cookies.

When Gurdin dashed in, he was startled by Monroe's appearance. She was dressed in a dark suit – the moderately priced, department store variety – and wore a flowing black wig and a pair of sunglasses. An oversized scarf was wound around her neck and even covered the tip of her chin.

Gurdin had performed minor plastic surgery on Monroe several times over the years, including a slight reduction of her jaw in the forties and some work on the tip of her nose in 1950 – just before she soared to stardom.

After Gurdin was seated, Monroe slowly unwound the scarf and removed the dark glasses. Her nose was black and blue, and an oval bruise covered her left cheekbone.

Monroe said nothing as Gurdin moved closer and ran a finger down her nose. She remained mute as he guided her to the X-ray room. Finally Greenson broke the silence. 'Marilyn had a small accident in the shower,' he explained. 'She fell and hit the tiling.' This despite the facts that there were no tiles around Monroe's bathtub and she hardly ever took a shower.

Greenson continued, 'I'm sure there's nothing to it, but I felt we should at least have it checked.'

While the X-ray was being processed, Greenson continued his solo narrative about Monroe's troubles – her sinus infection, her dismissal from *Something's Got to Give* and the publicity campaign being waged against her.

'It's been bad, very bad for Marilyn,' Greenson whispered to Gurdin.

To the plastic surgeon, Monroe seemed subdued by drugs – lost in a haze.

'Dr. Greenson did all the talking,' Gurdin recalled. 'He didn't seem anxious for Marilyn to speak.'

Monroe finally showed some interest when a nurse handed Gurdin the X-rays. 'Is my nose broken?' she asked almost frantically. 'How quickly can you fix it?'

The news was good; her nose was only bruised. Monroe threw her arms around Greenson's neck and said, 'Thank goodness.'

Then she put the glasses back on, wound the scarf around her neck and exited, still leaning heavily on Greenson's arm.

Gurdin remembered that the injuries were typical of a fall. But Robert Slatzer, who discussed all Monroe's troubles with her, believed that somebody 'beat the hell out of her'.

These injuries were only one sign of the chaos and depression that followed her rejection by Fox – troubles that were heightened by the pervasiveness of the publicity campaign being waged by the studio.

'She became a recluse for a week or so,' Murray told

Photoplay. By all accounts, the ten days after the studio's announcements were days of solitude, sleeping pills and champagne binges.

Then Monroe decided to enlist the help of her fans. Between June 20 and July 15, she scheduled a rash of interviews and photo sessions that reminded her friends of the media blitzkriegs she had staged early in her career.

She gave ten interviews during a twenty-four-day barrage, ranging from sessions with her friend and columnist Sydney Skolsky to extravagantly produced photo shoots with Bert Stern of *Vogue* and with Douglas Kirkland. During the interviews, reporters were surprised that no topics were off limits, and that Monroe guided the reporters to the subject of Fox and their mistreatment of her over the years.

Aided by Pat Newcomb, Monroe slowly turned the tables on Fox.

Her quotes were not only offered to the public, but were also aimed at the men who ran the studio. To *Life* magazine's Richard Meryman, she railed, 'An actor is not a machine, no matter how much they want to say you are. After all, creativity has to start with humanity.'

Later in the same interview, the message to Fox became more blatant. 'This industry should behave like a mother whose child has just run out in front of a car. But, instead of clasping the child to them, [the studio heads] start punishing the child. Like you don't dare get a cold – how dare you get a cold! The executives can get colds and stay home forever and just phone in. But not stars. You know, no one feels worse than the one who's sick. I wish they had to act in a comedy with a high temperature and a sinus infection.'

About the manner of her firing, she told Meryman, 'I'm there to give a performance and not to be disciplined by the studio. After all, I am not in a military school.'

Monroe's journalistic barnstorming – and the actions of Zanuck, Bobby Kennedy and even Skouras – were having an effect. 'It wasn't long before word came from New York that Marilyn was ready to negotiate and promised to return to work with a new attitude,' Levathes recalled. 'I got the word to try and negotiate from New York. I don't know whether it was from Milton Gould or Judge Rosenman.'

Ten days after her humiliating dismissal, the studio was asking her to return.

But first there was more sabre rattling by the West Coast executives. Again, the publicity troops were deployed first. On June 17, Harry Brand orchestrated another media blast; this time the target was Dean Martin.

A day earlier, Fox had filed suit against Martin for $3 million, citing breach of contract and an 'unprofessional attitude'. When 'Miss Monroe defaulted on her contract,' the suit charged, 'Dean Martin acted in bad faith by refusing to approve any actress other than Miss Monroe.'

The suit further claimed that, although Martin was guaranteed star approval, he did not have the right to insist on Monroe and on Monroe only.

On June 24, Martin himself became part of what the press called 'a Hollywood triangle of litigation' by suing Fox for damages in the amount of $6.8 million. He also claimed that his professional reputation had been sullied.

'The studio deliberately presented an inaccurate picture of the situation and blamed Mr. Martin in order to duck criticism from private shareholders,' the suit contended.

Five days later, an amazingly revitalised Monroe devised a delicious charade to woo and conquer Fox production chief Peter Levathes. She invited him to her home for cocktails and for the unveiling of a new, no-nonsense Marilyn Monroe. Whitey Snyder and Sidney Guilaroff worked all afternoon creating a startling, severe look for the actress, rounded out by an understated Normal Norell dress of sober beige.

Chilled caviar was waiting, along with trays of canapés from a Brentwood gourmet shop.

Monroe had written and memorised several speeches to impress the studio boss. Then she called up every ounce of her Method acting training in order to portray everyone's idea of a savvy superstar, one who was wise to the bottom line and to executive realities.

Apparently wanting to be seen as the chief executive of Marilyn Monroe Productions, she had banished all traces of the dumb, easily available blonde. With Dean Martin refusing to work without her and rumours flooding the lot that she was to be rehired, she jumped the gun by calling this summit conference.

What she didn't know was that Levathes and Philip Feldman were coming to Brentwood with a plan to reactivate *Something's Got to Give*. Later, in telephone conversations with the actress, Levathes even hinted that the studio was upping the ante and might agree to pay her half a million dollars if *Something's Got to Give* was completed on schedule.

In New York, Monroe's firing and the global publicity that had accompanied it had taken the heat off the board of directors. Now *Something's Got to Give*, always a political football, was back in Levathes's hands. Bobby Kennedy's initial call to Judge Rosenman was relayed down the line to the production chief.

'I don't recall how I received the message,' said Levathes. 'We were told that Marilyn was ready to deal and to return to the set with a new outlook. I didn't care how that was achieved. I was delighted.'

This time, Fox met the actress halfway by agreeing to hold the initial conferences at her house.

As Monroe waited, she added a typically paranoid touch; she hid publicist Pat Newcomb behind the door to her bedroom. Armed with a pen and a stenographer's notebook, Newcomb recorded the meeting word for word.

If there was a hero in this dark tale of corporate dishonesty and betrayal, it was Fox production chief Peter G. Levathes.

Standing apart from the civil warfare among the board members, he began negotiating to rehire Monroe immediately. 'As soon as I received the clear signal that she was earnestly ready to resume filming and was deadly serious about it, I began preparing for her return,' he said.

Even while the corporate lawyers were still facing off against the legal teams representing Monroe and Martin, Levathes and the actress had already begun the process of reconciliation.

'I found, surprisingly, that she was an astute businesswoman in many ways,' Levathes said. 'She knew how important it was to finish *Something's Got to Give*.

'She was very rational; you couldn't have had a better meeting with an actress. She had a kind of renewed interest in the project that was infectious,' Levathes continued. 'I was finally confident that the picture would be made. In fact, I had even authorised a new rewrite of the script incorporating Marilyn's ideas.'

But there were to be some trade-offs. Monroe abandoned Paula Strasberg and discarded Greenson as her 'agent and negotiator'. In return, Cukor was to be replaced as director.

As June slid by and Monroe's sinusitis retreated, the studio offered to radically renegotiate her contract into a $1-million deal: $500,000 for *Something's Got to Give* and an additional $500,000 or more for a new musical called *What a Way to Go*, which, not so coincidentally, was to be produced by Monroe's chief publicist, Arthur P. Jacobs. The discovery of this new contract in the Fox archives invalidates most accounts of the star's final dealings with Twentieth Century-Fox.

Monroe was often described as wallowing in sadness over the loss of the Fox contract and over the permanent cancellation of *Something's Got to Give*. The morning after the star died, her close friend Peter Lawford hinted that the cancellation of this film was the main motive for her alleged suicide.

Through most of the summer, a shroud of secrecy cloaked

the revival of what had been seen as a doomed motion picture, but a few publicity leaks occurred. In late June, Monroe was spotted leaving the offices of the studio lawyers, hand in hand with Levathes – both of them joking and laughing.

Levathes noticed that the publicity war waged by Fox and the brutal dismissal that followed had awakened Monroe to certain economic realities. 'Now she wished to resume filming as soon as possible,' he said.

But Monroe's fiercest foes, Feldman and Charles Einfeld, made a last move to humiliate her even further.

In New York, Einfeld, as the studio's director of marketing, ordered one of his publicists to write a new, toned-down apology for Monroe to release before she was allowed to resume filming. She was to confess her barbiturate habit, beg forgiveness for her tardiness and lack of discipline and promise to abandon her 'prima donna ways'. No copy of the confession exists, but Fox executive Stan Hough, who read the document, called it 'horrendous'.

Levathes rejected the apology out of hand. 'I would never have allowed this humiliation. We had an understanding by that time, Marilyn and I. She showed tremendous good faith.'

At the time, plans called for *Something's Got to Give* to go before the cameras for a second time the third week in July. If this had actually happened, it might have saved Monroe's life.

But for some unknown reason, Monroe's representatives apparently delayed the entire process, deliberately stalling the studio. According to one account, the new contract languished for weeks on a lawyer's desk.

New York columnist Earl Wilson claimed that attorney Rudin deliberately dragged his feet on the pact. Once the million-dollar contract was tentatively drawn up, 'Mickey Rudin was in no rush to ratify it,' wrote Wilson. 'He was afraid that Marilyn would never live up to her part of the agreement.'

According to Wilson's memoirs, Rudin told him Monroe was 'obviously deeply ill, mentally ill. She probably should have been in an institution.'

Rudin should have been in a position to know; his brother-in-law, Ralph Greenson, was Monroe's analyst.

But Greenson's wife and daughter insist that Monroe wasn't insane, although she was severely depressed. 'Mickey is a lawyer who expects people to be logical,' said Hildi Greenson. 'Marilyn, of course, was completely illogical. Perhaps he viewed that as a sign that she was mentally ill.'

'The woman I negotiated with wasn't insane,' recalled Levathes. 'Of course, there were major problems, the insomnia and the drugs. What impressed me at the time was her genuine enthusiasm for going back to work.'

Actress and writer Susan Strasberg, daughter of Paula and Lee Strasberg, who was particularly close to Monroe during those last years, concluded, 'You have to ask yourself, what's crazy in Hollywood? Sure, Marilyn was highly eccentric. She took drugs and was sometimes irrational. What Hollywood star is not?'

Strasberg remembered a 1962 conversation about the days Monroe spent in the Payne Whitney Psychiatric Clinic in New York. 'They mistakenly put Marilyn in a locked ward. She told me she sometimes thought she was crazy. But after Payne Whitney, Marilyn said, "Susan, those people in there are really crazy. Thank God, I'm not like that. Now I know I'm not crazy."'

But Rudin had his reasons for stalling the contract negotiations. In a February 1992 interview, Rudin admitted that he was stalling so that Marilyn could be 'fully rested and restored before she returned to the set of *Something's Got to Give*'. Greenson, he said, learned of the disaster which occurred when she reported in April (her being ill with the virus). 'By that time Monroe had told me, "I know I have to do the film, but I still have mixed feelings."'

So Rudin began a delaying tactic.

Unknown to him, Fox was ready to move faster.

– Chapter 27 –

A Summer Love

When it came to keeping the Kennedy family name squeaky clean, Robert Kennedy must have seemed almost invincible by the summer of 1962.

Because of his ability to manipulate FBI director J. Edgar Hoover, and by seeing to it that thousands of documents and phone logs were given top-secret classifications, the Attorney General had hidden all traces of JFK's affair with Mafia party girl Judith Campbell Exner.

Similarly, Bobby made sure a clandestine alliance between the Kennedy administration and the Mafia during the Bay of Pigs affair was buried deep within the FBI and CIA. To achieve this end, he openly courted key members of both agencies to hush the slightest rumours of the President's mob connections.

Bobby even functioned as a marriage counsellor to control the fights and hide the infidelities within the sprawling Kennedy family. He sniffed out a series of extramarital affairs and then broke them off to protect the family's image. For instance, Lawford received several warnings from Bobby, according to his former wives.

Because of his artistry, the public knew nothing about orgies in the White House, raucous cocktail parties aboard

Air Force One, and backroom gambling in Las Vegas. No whisper of these doings appeared in print for almost two decades.

For most of his life, Bobby was the family's repository of Victorian morality, clucking on the sidelines while JFK and Teddy frolicked through a series of increasingly lurid sexual adventures.

Once at a party, Teddy threw his arms around his brothers, beamed and said, 'We three'. Bobby backed away in distaste, saying, 'No, you *two*!'

Walter Winchell privately described him as the family's 'sexual policeman'. Obviously the matriarch, Rose Kennedy, considered him just that. Six months earlier, in the fall of 1961, she had designated Bobby to talk to his brother-in-law, Steve Smith, when rumours of philandering threatened to break up his marriage to Jean.

The Attorney General was so offended by novelist Gore Vidal's bisexuality that he yanked the author away from Jacqueline Kennedy while the two danced at a state dinner in 1961.

He also began screening his brother's sexual partners. When the Attorney General heard from the Secret Service that JFK had asked for an introduction to a young German socialite in Washington circles, Bobby launched an FBI investigation. Two days later he learned that the socialite had had an affair with a Soviet attaché. He saw to it that she was summarily deported before the President could get his hands on her.

And yet this man, the Attorney General who had sent Secret Service agents to threaten a reporter whose only 'crime' was seeing Bobby dance with Marilyn Monroe, was now embarking on a blazing love affair with the most famous woman in the world.

Kennedy family intimates have scoffed at the possibility of a serious relationship between Monroe and the Attorney

General of the United States. It has been called 'a fantasy' spun by a sick and lonely woman.

Actually, the bond was both more intense and more likely than her lusty, tempestuous affair with the President. Bobby and Monroe were soulmates from the beginning; she was attracted by his intellect; he was drawn by her incessant search for something beyond Hollywood superstardom.

Romantically, Monroe was moving into uncharted waters, and she knew it. With her most recent lovers, Arthur Miller, Yves Montand and Frank Sinatra, she had shared a common interest – show business and the fascinating power games of Hollywood. Her intimacy with RFK was based on other interests.

'There was a point in time when Marilyn could have named the head of every major Hollywood studio, but might not have been able to tell you who was the governor of California,' said Robert Slatzer. 'Now she began boning up on Cuba, the Missile Crisis and organised crime.'

Evelyn Moriarity, the star's stand-in, recalled the 'stacks of notebooks' that suddenly appeared in the Brentwood house and the dressing-room bungalow on the Twentieth Century-Fox lot. As Monroe's telephone calls to Washington proliferated, so did the notebooks – a powerful record of her affairs with the President and his brother.

Initially, RFK and Monroe courted each other over the telephone – an instrument that was, in some ways, Monroe's major connection with real life. She enshrined the phone, and many times slept with one arm cradling it. Once, when discussing *A Streetcar Named Desire*, she told Susan Strasberg, 'I can relate to Blanche's statement about relying on the kindness of strangers. Well, I rely on the kindness of the telephone and whoever is on the other end of the line.'

Bobby and Monroe's ninety-minute tryst in the garden of the Brentwood house the first week in June led to a long-distance relationship so intense and passionate that Hazel

Washington described it as 'making love over the phone. And I do mean making love.'

Within a few days, Monroe was able to reach Bobby anywhere – from Hyannis Port to Europe. Her calls to the U.S. Justice Department were relayed to him immediately, no matter where he was.

'He was a wonderful person to tell your troubles to,' remembered his press aide, Ed Guthman. 'And Marilyn called him a lot during the summer of 1962. But then, so did Judy Garland and other ladies in trouble.'

Their affair might have ended as the loving phone conversations slowly decreased under the relentless pressures of two high-profile careers. But fate intervened. The two tentative lovers were thrown together repeatedly during June and July by the press of Hollywood business – both his and hers.

The Attorney General often descended on the Fox lot in a no-nonsense blue helicopter borrowed from the military. Secret Service agents in beautifully tailored blue suits bounded out and looked right and left, as if checking for assassins on the deserted studio streets. Then Bobby would leap out and head for the production offices of *The Enemy Within*, where veteran producer Jerry Wald was preparing the film version of RFK's best-seller of the same name. The film was to profile Bobby's attempts to curb organised crime within the labour movement. Jimmy Hoffa was to be a main character. Sometimes Kennedy wore his politician's uniform of blue pinstripes. But more often he jumped from the chopper wearing a white T-shirt, faded Levis and sneakers.

No evidence shows that Bobby slipped out of Jerry Wald's bungalow – which was almost fifty yards from Monroe's – to meet the actress on the lot. But Monroe was in the bungalow three times in July. However, it is certain that the Attorney General and the movie star sometimes spent the night in the Presidential Suite at the Beverly Hilton, only three miles from Twentieth Century-Fox. Sources at the hotel recall that elaborate meals were brought in from the Kennedy family's favourite Los Angeles restaurant, La Scala.*

The sprawling Lawford beach house, with its fourteen bedrooms and heated marble pool, provided another lush setting for much of this incendiary nine-week affair. If the Attorney General tried to avoid Monroe, as some claim, then his brother-in-law Peter Lawford literally pushed him into Marilyn's arms.

Both were guests of honour at four parties, including a Fourth of July bash during which Bobby, bare-chested in Levis, and Monroe, in a Pucci caftan, strolled the water's edge as the sun set over Malibu.

'There was an affair, no doubt about it,' Lawford's neighbour Peter Dye told the BBC. 'Marilyn gazed up at him with wonder in her eyes. She was absolutely starstruck.'

Dye was one of the few guests at the numerous Lawford parties who recognised that Monroe and RFK were, at the very least, infatuated with each other.

The Lawford house, at 625 Pacific Coast Highway, occupied the single largest oceanfront lot in Los Angeles County. With its twenty-seven rooms, halls that resembled mazes, and hidden suites, it was perfect for the long, roving parties the Lawfords loved to give. Entire wings could even be closed off for private purposes.

Monroe and the President had pursued their on-again, off-again affair in one of these love nests. Later detectives would claim to have bugged that suite to obtain illicit tapes for the Mafia.

Monroe may have shared the same wing with the Attorney

---

*Margaret Burk, the longtime publicist for the Ambassador Hotel in Los Angeles, confirmed that the Kennedys kept a clandestine suite there. Burk noted that 'Bobby and Marilyn supposedly used that set of rooms. I know it was used by Marilyn and President John Kennedy.' Burk also said that Monroe kept an apartment in Hollywood that may have served as a secret rendezvous.

General. Lawford neighbours Lynn Sherman and Peter Dye were observers of many meetings with Bobby and Monroe. Both were convinced that overnight trysts were involved.

The romance should have set off alarms when Bobby and Monroe spent the weekend of June 26 to 29 more or less together. Designer William Travilla saw them having dinner at La Scala on Friday night. On Saturday, the Attorney General was feted by his sister at a barbecue for fifty guests. With Bobby's wife, Ethel, back east, Monroe was invited as his 'dinner companion'.

As usual, Monroe arrived late – after hours of preparation. 'I never saw her so nervous about a party,' designer Elizabeth Courtney recalled. 'We altered three dresses before we found the right one.'

When Monroe left the room during one of the fittings, Courtney asked Hazel Washington what was going on. 'A man, honey, a new man,' Washington answered.

'Who is it?' asked Courtney.

'Kennedy,' Washington said.

'You mean the President?' asked a shocked Courtney.

'No, the other one, the brother.'

Courtney was even more shocked.

'Most people didn't know about Marilyn and the Kennedys,' Washington said years later. 'It was shocking, even to me. We didn't think of our leaders that way.'

By any standards, the thousand-dollar Elizabeth Courtney dress was a success – a standout among the pyjama outfits and tropical suits that the Lawfords' female guests favoured.

The Attorney General made another trek to Monroe's house the next afternoon – the day Monroe had told Eunice Murray and the handyman, 'I want the house entirely to myself today.'

Murray stayed just long enough to notice 'that they looked very romantic together'.

Evidence indicates, however, that this was a business meeting. Monroe was to meet Fox executives again the next day to hammer out details of the new contract for *Something's Got to Give*, and Bobby offered some sage advice. He told her that, as he understood it, her reinstatement was a foregone conclusion and that she could gain major concessions.

But there is considerable evidence that their relationship was not only sexual, but turbulent as well. 'I got the impression that it was sexually driven,' said hairdresser Mickey Song. 'It may have seemed to others that there wasn't an affair. But I'm certain that there was.'

Monroe also told Robert Slatzer, Hazel Washington and half a dozen other friends about her affair with the Attorney General. To Slatzer, she gently ridiculed the Attorney General's performance in bed. Columnist James Bacon also recalled 'that Marilyn told me there were no niceties in sex with the Kennedys. It was in and out. No feeling, no foreplay, no romantic conversation.'

Intimating that she was speaking of her new 'political lovers', the actress complained to writer William J. Weatherby that 'my body turns people on – like an electric light – yet there is scarcely anything human in it. People expect so much of me I sometimes feel hatred for them.'

Members of the Kennedy clan and scores of 'honorary Kennedys' have always considered this affair an impossibility, an invention of the tell-all biographies of the seventies and eighties.

But there is plenty of hard evidence to prove its existence. When the Los Angeles District Attorney's Office reinvestigated Monroe's death in 1982, investigators unearthed proof of an intimate relationship between Bobby and the actress. 'But since we ruled that Marilyn didn't die by criminal means, it didn't matter whether she was sleeping with the Attorney General and the President of the United States,' said Deputy District Attorney Mike Carroll, director of the 1982 study.

Testimony given before the psychological autopsy hearings in which doctors and psychiatrists tried to find out if she killed herself also verified the existence of 'an intense, probably sexual relationship'.

'There was evidence of her intimate relationship with Robert Kennedy,' said UCLA psychiatrist Robert Litman, who headed the probe. 'But Bobby was no different than any other of the strong men she brought into her life as rescuers. He was another of those father figures who eventually betrayed her.'

Additional evidence emerged when television producer Ted Landreth embarked on his landmark BBC documentary, *Marilyn and the Kennedys*. A former CBS Television News producer, Landreth polled scores of surviving journalists from the Washington press corps during the Kennedy years. 'Almost all of them were aware of her affair with Bobby Kennedy,' he recalled. In addition, Senator George Smathers, a carousing buddy of JFK's, said in a BBC interview that the President spoke often about his brother's affair.

Monroe was becoming increasingly indiscreet about her personal ties to the Kennedy brothers. By confiding in a host of friends and associates, she added to the furore that was erupting over the President's morals among his top advisers. Political columnist and adviser Theodore Sorensen had already written, 'This administration is going to do more for sex than Eisenhower's did for golf.'

'With the protection of the Secret Service, the assistance of worshipful aides and the intercessions of brothers and sisters, the new President was able to continue his freewheeling lifestyle, which included sleeping with countless women,' wrote Kitty Kelley in her landmark book, *Jackie Oh!* 'While the First Lady was away from Washington, the President even amused himself with nude swimming parties in the White House pool.'

When Monroe began bragging about her JFK escapades, danger alarms must have sounded in top Democratic circles. During the last complete day of production on *Something's Got to Give*, she blatantly displayed her ties to the Kennedys. She placed calls to JFK and Bobby through the Fox switchboard and in the presence of friends and acquaintances. 'She grabbed the phone and told the studio operator to dial directly into the Oval office,' recalled Stephen Papich.

Monroe winked at Papich. 'I'm calling Jack.'

'Jack?' Papich said.

'You know, Jack Kennedy. The President,' she whispered.

Kennedy's secretary apparently answered. Monroe said softly, 'May I speak to the President, please? This is Marilyn Monroe.'

'There was no secrecy at all,' said Papich. 'She even left a rather complicated message.'

Earlier in May, Monroe had persuaded designer William Travilla to let her borrow a white ermine cape from the wardrobe department 'to impress the President'.

The danger of public exposure increased after Monroe was fired, causing the press to monitor her even more carefully. Now the Attorney General became the careless brother. 'There were many, many rendezvous in June and July,' said Lynn Sherman, who lived near the Lawford mansion. 'The official car drove up, and you knew Bobby Kennedy was in town. Sometimes Marilyn and Bobby would go through the patio and onto the beach for long walks.'

At one party in July, Chuck Pick, a twenty-year-old parking attendant, caught revealing glimpses of Bobby as he romanced Monroe.

A grey-faced Secret Service agent sidled up to Pick and hissed, 'You have eyes, but you can't see; you have ears, but you can't hear; you have a mouth, but you can't speak.'

On a trip to Mexico City back in February, Monroe had confided to a new acquaintance, American expatriate Fred Vanderbilt Fields, about her burgeoning friendship with Bobby Kennedy. 'She said they had a long talk, a long political talk. She said she had asked Kennedy whether he was going to fire J. Edgar Hoover.'

At the Lawfords' February dinner party in Santa Monica,

another guest, Gloria Romanoff, overheard Bobby as he called his father in Palm Beach. 'Guess who I'm sitting with – Marilyn Monroe. Wanna talk to her?'

Before long the Kennedy clan found out about Bobby's indiscretions. One afternoon before Monroe's death, Pat Kennedy Lawford dropped in on neighbour Lynn Sherman for a drink. While Bobby's sister complained about Peter Lawford's womanising, she also slammed her brother: 'But we all go through it – look what Ethel's going through.' There was no doubt that she was referring to the Attorney General.

Lawford himself told another neighbour, 'Marilyn was passed from Jack to Bobby in the most callous manner.'

To the Attorney General, exhausted from his around-the-clock drive against organised crime, Monroe must have offered an empathetic, undemanding intimacy. Coming from a family of speechmakers, Bobby was exhilarated to have a lover who listened – who hung on his every word. But Monroe wasn't at all subservient in this relationship. In many ways she was as brilliant as Bobby. Her former husband, Arthur Miller, spoke of her 'lightning quick mind', and Truman Capote described her as 'unschooled, but enormously brilliant'.

'Strangely enough, Bobby became very, very infatuated with Marilyn despite many warnings,' said Deborah Gould Lawford. 'Before long, he was trapped.'

The dilemma was particularly awkward for Bobby, his family's 'Mr. Fix-It'. Since his father had been sidelined by a crippling stroke and his brother was running the country, the Attorney General was acting head of the tempestuous clan.

If he was faced with a conflict between his heart and the political future of the Kennedy dynasty, his priority would be clear. Monroe was smart enough to know where she stood. 'She was fascinated by him and scared to death of him at the same time,' recalled the Lawfords' neighbour, Peter Dye. Dye watched the relationship mature during the early summer of 1962.

'She told me she was nuts about him; she loved that "mental thing" about him,' said Dye. As for Bobby, 'he was nuts about her as well'.

The sheer force of Robert Kennedy's political power worked like an aphrodisiac for Monroe, whose physical attraction to the Attorney General was slight. In fact, she was repelled by him at first. After Bobby had made his play for her at the parties after the gala, she had told Robert Slatzer, 'He's certainly not my type.' She also told Slatzer that Bobby lacked the compelling good looks and charm of his brother the President.

During those few romantic days in the summer of 1962, they conversed for hours, she imparting Hollywood's backroom secrets and he holding forth on the glories of the New Frontier.

They talked of Fidel Castro and the Bay of Pigs; of civil rights and the Peace Corps. And they talked of organised crime. Monroe apparently made notes about their political conversations and borrowed books on current events from Ralph Greenson and Pat Newcomb.

But the relationship was far from sexless. The two had at least two, and probably four, sexual encounters, the first in early June in the Kennedy suite at the Beverly Hilton, another late that month at Monroe's house, and one at the Lawfords' beach house. She described these flings to Slatzer, Jeanne Carmen, Terry Moore and Hazel Washington.

Later, when ABC's *20/20* asked Eunice Murray whether there had been sexual encounters between Bobby and Monroe at the Brentwood house, Murray said, 'That's something I don't know. There could have been, but I know nothing about it.'

When members of the BBC investigative team were probing the actress's death in 1985, they uncovered a strange document among her effects. A handwritten note, apparently from Jean Kennedy Smith, validated the affair.

Bearing the address of the multimillion-dollar Kennedy

retreat, North Ocean Boulevard, Palm Beach, it said:

> Dear Marilyn:
>   Mother asked me to write and thank you for your sweet note to Daddy [Patriarch Joseph P. Kennedy] – he really enjoyed it and you were very cute to send it.
>   *Understand that you and Bobby are the new item!*
>   We all think you should come with him when he comes back east.
>
> Love,
Jean Smith

Spokesmen for the Kennedy family refuse to discuss the bizarre note. But Hazel Washington, to whom Monroe showed it, said that the actress accepted it as an official sanction of the dangerous love affair.

Perhaps the Attorney General's openness and boyish enthusiasm convinced Monroe that he was serious about their love affair. In late June, she told journalist William J. Weatherby, 'Maybe I'll get married again. The only problem is, he's married right now. He's famous, so we meet in secret.'

It's easy to dismiss her dreams of matrimony as fantastic. 'But, then again, she had a way of making those fantasies come true,' said UCLA's Robert Litman, who had long interviews with Ralph Greenson after Monroe's death. 'She was always able to attract the highest level of men. She went out after them, and she got them.'

Monroe once told Greenson that one of her goals was to meet humanitarian Albert Schweitzer and 'then seduce him'. Litman noted, 'It was a realistic goal to her.'

Perhaps Monroe's 'sex and glitz' act wasn't enough for the Kennedy brothers. She complained to Weatherby, 'My body turned all these people on. Sex isn't wrong if there's love in it. But too often people act as if it were gymnasium work. They would be as satisfied with a machine from a drugstore as with another human being.'

At this same time, when her only romantic alliance was with Bobby Kennedy, she voiced a similar lament to Peter Levathes.

'I'm a failure as a woman,' she said. 'My men expect so much of me, because of the image they've made of me – and that I've made of myself – as a sex symbol. They expect so much, and I can't live up to it. They expect bells to ring and whistles to whistle, but my anatomy is the same as any other woman's and I can't live up to it.'

Perhaps the final verdict on Monroe's tangled alliance with the Kennedys came from psychiatrist Ralph Greenson. Before his death in 1979, he told several journalists about her 'destructive relationships with two powerful and important men in government'.

The analyst also told Litman, 'I am afraid that Marilyn was being badly abused in these relationships.'

He also explained that the affair with Bobby Kennedy had become one of the most powerful forces in the life of his troubled patient.

Later, Litman's official report on the death included the statement, 'Greenson had very considerable concern that she was being used in these relationships. However, it seemed so gratifying to her to be associated with such powerful and important men that he could not declare himself to be against it. He told her to be sure she was doing it for something she felt was valuable and not just because she felt she had to do it.'

In 1962, three months after her death, journalist William Woodfield asked Greenson, 'What happened the evening Marilyn died?'

Greenson snapped back, 'Why don't you ask the Attorney General of the United States?'

In July 1962, however, Monroe's crush on Bobby Kennedy offered her a warm, romantic Indian summer – a handful of sunny days before the chill set in.

PART FOUR
July–August

Chapter 28

Betrayal

Monroe woke up one late-summer morning in 1962 and found that her lover had disconnected himself from her life.

Frantic for Bobby Kennedy's advice about returning to the set of *Something's Got to Give*, she dialled the private phone line that bypassed the huge Justice Department switchboard and rang in the Attorney General's office.

She got a recording: 'You have reached a nonworking number at the United States Justice Department. Please check your directory and dial again.'

Panicked and furious, she ignored Bobby's longstanding orders and called the main switchboard.

She also disobeyed by using her real name. 'This is Marilyn Monroe,' she said. 'I'm having trouble reaching the Attorney General on his private line.'

A supervising operator was deferential. 'That line was disconnected on the orders of the Attorney General and I'm sorry, but there is no referral.'

When the switchboard put Monroe through to the receptionist in Bobby's outer office, she was told, 'Mr. Kennedy is in conference all afternoon.'

Thus Bobby casually ended Monroe's bittersweet romance

with the Kennedy family. He did it cruelly, like a rich college boy dumping a girlfriend from the wrong side of the tracks. She had been fun; she had been exciting. But she was used up.

Protected by their wealth, safe behind the walls of their compounds in Hyannis Port and Palm Beach and hidden behind hundreds of functionaries, the Kennedy family quietly locked Monroe out.

'She was angry and hurt – even outraged – that they cut her off overnight,' recalled Slatzer. 'She was finally feeling abused.'

This was the worst, as well as the last, rejection in a life filled with rejection. Monroe had allowed herself to believe that Bobby was serious about their relationship. 'With Bobby, she felt there was a real chance, that he would make her First Lady one day,' said Monroe's confidante, the actress Terry Moore.

'I tried to point out how impossible this was and that it would ruin Robert Kennedy's future,' said Slatzer. 'I said, "Marilyn, this is a Catholic family. Bobby couldn't possibly divorce his wife." But she wouldn't listen.'

Several days later, Monroe called Slatzer again. She was becoming angry. She had heard that Bobby had referred to her as 'a dumb blonde' during a dinner at the Lawfords' beach house.

'When I told you earlier that he wouldn't take my calls, I wasn't sure why,' she told Slatzer. 'Maybe he really does feel that I'm a dumb blonde. I said to myself, "Maybe he's avoiding me because of that, or maybe he just doesn't need me any more. After all, he got what he wanted".'

Never had Monroe felt more like a sex object; she had travelled as far up as possible, using her fame and beauty for entrée. She had made it all the way to the bedroom of America's First Family. But once there, she had found out that the President and his brother weren't really different from the

Hollywood hustlers she had bedded early in her career. There was one slight difference: the hustlers had at least kissed her good-bye.

'The affair with Bobby was Marilyn's most dangerous alliance,' Slatzer recalled. 'Because there was a mental attachment as well as a physical one, she was badly hurt when he suddenly vanished.'

When the affair with Bobby first heated up, Ralph Greenson told colleagues that he was afraid Monroe would be badly wounded in the end. He told her to make sure she was involved with these men 'not because she felt she should be,' but 'because she wanted to be.'

Peter Lawford later told the *Long Beach Press Telegram* that Monroe 'was badly treated in many ways'.

Subsequently his wife, Patricia Seaton Lawford, told a press conference that Bobby ended Monroe's affair with JFK in a particularly brutal manner. 'When he broke it off, Bobby intimated that she was just another of "Jack's fucks",' she said. 'There was no effort to let her down easily.'

Reacting to endless questions about her relations with the First Family, Monroe finally began talking, first to friends and confidants and then, alarmingly, to members of the press.

She told columnists Sydney Skolsky, Earl Wilson, and James Bacon, of her affair with Bobby, and gossip was rampant in Washington, D.C. Dorothy Kilgallen found out about it on her own from a source in the nation's capital. The Washington press corps was abuzz with it, as well.

In mid-July, the dangers inherent in courting Monroe had hit Bobby like a ton of bricks. With Bobby, Jack and their mother, Rose, all wrapped up in Teddy's senatorial campaign, the tarnished Kennedy name was suddenly big news again on the East Coast. Teddy, who had no experience in government, was running against the popular Massachusetts Attorney General, Ed McCormack, in the Democratic primary. Because the family's name was used as a rallying cry, the opposition was eager to find a way to tarnish it. Admittedly the family waged an arrogant campaign, including a brochure with Teddy's picture on the front beneath the headline 'From a Great American Family'.

Another rallying slogan was 'The Kennedys: Dedicated to Public Service for Three Generations'.

Young McCormack cornered Teddy at a key debate and said, 'If your name was Edward Moore, your candidacy would be a joke.'

Teddy answered, 'But my name is Edward Kennedy and nobody is laughing.'

Monroe and the family's history of sexual relationships with Hollywood figures seemed far removed from Massachusetts – until two things happened.

First reporters uncovered the story that Teddy had been kicked out of Harvard for cheating. Political journalists went on the attack. *The Washington Post* called Teddy 'a modest young man with much to be modest about'.

Then FBI director J. Edgar Hoover became loose-lipped about a file he was assembling on the Attorney General, an avowed enemy, and his relationship with Monroe. It was, Hoover told friends, 'especially hot'.

The clan's patriarch, Ambassador Joseph Kennedy, communicated with Bobby in a series of notes, as he had lost most of his ability to speak after his stroke the previous December. The messages effectively expressed the father's rage about the spreading scandals in his family. In no uncertain terms, he ordered some sexual belt-tightening.

With the senatorial primary looming on September 11, Monroe was a definite liability to the Kennedys' political aspirations. Bobby was told to drop her as quickly and quietly as possible. He immediately changed his telephone numbers, ignored notes from the star and curtailed his trips to the West Coast.

His heartless dismissal was a macho act of a sort highly

regarded within the Kennedy clan. Patricia Seaton Lawford told television viewers in 1989, 'It seems as though Joe Kennedy's children, and the men and women they married, have a history of emotional and physical abuse. The men have a tendency to use women sexually and then discard them. This masks their own inability to feel.'

But Monroe could not accept the fact that her affair with Bobby was over. She tracked him by phone, devoured news clippings on his public appearances and continued calling the Justice Department.

'Bobby's rejection reawakened her father's complete abandonment of her,' said writer Lucy Freeman, who interviewed Ralph Greenson several times for the *New York Times*. 'Because of her father's early desertion, she created the sex goddess, the one that no man could possibly abandon; the woman all men would desire. But "all men" stood for the one man she could never possess – the lost father,' said Freeman, who wrote a book on Greenson's treatment of Monroe.

But Bobby was eventually to pay heavily for his careless disregard of Monroe's feelings.

Chapter 29

All's Fair

More than a thousand still photographs were arranged in remarkably neat rows around Monroe's living room. She had organised them according to her own formula: nudes near the windows, black-and-white shots in front of the couch and high-fashion prints layered one on top of the other according to colour.

Towering over the pictorial parade like Gulliver was Twentieth Century-Fox production chief Peter Levathes. It was a hot summer night, but Levathes was in his studio executive's uniform – a flawless grey wool suit, red regimental tie and brilliantly shined wing tips. This visit, in late July, was Levathes's second trip to the house.

Sitting off to one side was studio executive Phil Feldman, brought along by Levathes 'to keep up appearances'. In tribute to her newly won relationship with the studio head, their hostess allowed him to see the natural Monroe: platinum hair lightly brushed, only a touch of lipstick, and her freckled ivory complexion unadorned. She looked girlish and at least ten years younger than her thirty-six years. A pitcher of margaritas stood ready, with Mexican appetisers. The executives, however, accepted only Cokes.

Monroe had invited Levathes over for an evening of serious business. In a gruelling two-hour session, the star prodded him into choosing from the thousand pictures the handful that would soon appear in *Vogue*, *Redbook* and *Paris Match*. Despite an unending demand for glamour portraits of Monroe in the early sixties, she had shunned high-fashion sessions for years. Now she had posed for three celebrity photographers in six exhausting sessions within twenty days.

First she posed for New Yorker Bert Stern in a series of sequined gowns in the penthouse suite at the Bel Air Hotel. On two other evenings, she allowed Stern to photograph her in furs, then a diaphanous scarf, and then completely nude.

'Marilyn had the power; she was the wind; that comet shape that Blake draws around a sacred photo [sic],' Stern later wrote. 'She was the space and the dream, the mystery and the danger.'

For George Barris, Monroe cavorted at the Lawfords' beach house in a bulky Mexican sweater and Jax slacks. The most famous of these 'Western White House' portraits shows her on a balcony – windswept and toasting the ocean with a glass of champagne.

In a pair of appearances at Douglas Kirkland's Hollywood studio, she posed in a white bedroom suite that sported satin sheets. One of these portraits, perhaps the most famous, captured her as she rolled up in the sheets and hugged a blanket.

'Marilyn sought to show that her body could graduate through sixteen years from *Laff* and *Peek* to the glossies of the sixties without losing allure,' Anthony Summers wrote in *Goddess*.

Levathes came to Brentwood in response to a rather mysterious request from Monroe on the afternoon of Friday, July 20. 'I need your help with some pictures,' she told him. 'It's very important because I know now I can rely on your judgment.'

'The pictures on the floor had little alleys between them so we could walk up and down the lines,' Levathes said. 'The whole house seemed full of pictures and we spent more than two hours yakking about them.'

Monroe took his hand, saying, 'Pick the pictures I should send to the magazines, please. I can't do it.'

'I selected them,' Levathes remembered. 'And she sent them. And they were the precise ones that were later published after her death.'

During four meetings between the production chief and his star – two of which were held at Fox – Monroe and Levathes had mutually agreed that *Something's Got to Give* would resume filming in late August, beginning with a series of Monroe close-ups. Dean Martin would return in early September, and photography was to wind up before the end of October.

At this meeting, she turned to Levathes and said, 'I would like you to approve everything I am supposed to wear, my casting decisions, and get guidance from you on rewriting the screenplay. I want you personally – not someone you delegate.' This was a swipe at Phil Feldman, whom Monroe had come to despise.

Levathes laughed and replied, 'Marilyn, if I drew up a contract that I was to personally approve your wardrobe and everything else, everyone in New York would say, "Levathes is sleeping with Monroe." '

'They would, wouldn't they?' Monroe said, laughing wickedly.

Levathes reflected thirty years later on how natural she had seemed that evening. He had the uncanny feeling that he had finally been allowed to glimpse the real woman hidden inside the glamorous image.

That was the last time he would see her.

During their lengthy conversation, neither mentioned the one subject that must have been on both their minds. Looming in three days was a corporate showdown that could rip Twentieth Century-Fox apart.

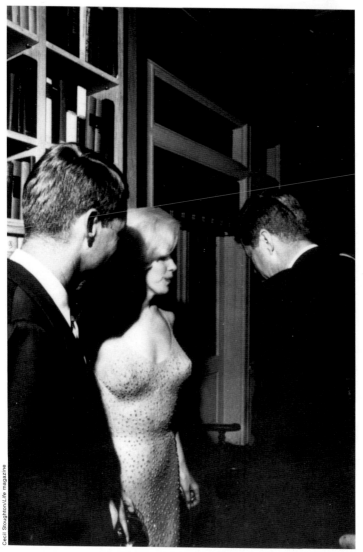

Monroe with JFK and RFK at
Arthur Krimm's birthday party
for the President. This is one of the
only shots of Monroe with both
Kennedy brothers.

Whitey Snyder touching up Monroe's make-up on the first day of
shooting following her 'lost weekend'. 28 May 1962.

Sydney Guilaroff adjusts Monroe's hairstyle. Strasberg is to her right;
Dean Martin and Marjorie Plecher stand in the background.

Monroe, Strasberg and Cukor in a rare moment of laughter. 21 May 1962.

A smiling star on the set.

Lawrence Schiller, a celebrity photographer, took these shots of Marilyn's swimming sequence in *Something's Got to Give* – the first nude scene ever done by a major American star.

Darryl F. Zanuck, the
former production
chief at Fox.

Zanuck, Spyros
Skouras, Fox president
at the time of
*Something's Got to
Give*, and President
Emeritus of Fox,
Joseph M. Schenk.

Schenk and Zanuck.

Top: Monroe on the final day of shooting for *Something's Got to Give.* 1 June 1962.

Centre: With Cukor and co-star, Wally Cox.

Right: With Cox

All photographs on this page: Lawrence Schiller

Marilyn Monroe at her
36th birthday party
given by co-workers at
Fox. The card features
a drawing of Monroe and
the slogan 'Happy
Birthday Suit'. 1 June
1962. From left,
Monroe, Flanaghan,
Moriarity, Eunice
Murray, Monroe's
housekeeper, Henry
Weinstein, producer,
and Bunny Gardel.

Marilyn Monroe
leaving the set of
Something's Got to Give
for the last time on 1
June 1962.

Angered at Fox's treatment of Monroe and frightened by the *Cleopatra* debacle, Darryl Zanuck was on his way to New York to regain control of the studio, if necessary by buying up huge blocks of stock. Milton Gould, John Loeb, another financier on the board and the rest of the 'Wall Street gang' had vowed a fight to the death to retain their seats on the board of directors.

'It was the only time in my life that I saw my dad frightened,' recalled his daughter, Darrilyn Zanuck. 'When he talked of the mishandling of the Monroe film and of *Cleopatra*, I could see that he was desperately concerned about the future of the company. Normally, my father was absolutely fearless.'

Spyros Skouras had turned his back on his former protégé, Levathes, and formed a secret pact with Zanuck to unseat the board. Zanuck's 280,000 shares of stock combined with Skouras's 100,000 gave them a head start in what loomed as a nasty proxy fight. Again, Monroe's fate was on the table. And again, she was seen as a box-office commodity, not as a woman or an actress. Zanuck had told Nunnally Johnson to assure her that *Something's Got to Give* would be completed 'to her satisfaction' and that the second film, *What a Way to Go*, would have priority under his new regime.

This two-picture deal was now the prime asset of the crumbling corporation. And it was a considerable asset at that. Marketing executives believed that the two Monroe films might bring $20 million to the studio coffers if they were handled properly.

Zanuck began his attack on June 6, two days after he learned that Monroe was to be fired by Milton Gould and Peter Levathes. The mogul shot off an angry telegram to the board, graphically describing their transgressions.

'He felt the dismissal of Monroe was a startling indication of the rudderless course Fox was pursuing,' wrote Zanuck's biographer, Leonard Mosley. 'Zanuck felt Levathes had decided to rid himself of this temperamental star, and this act convinced him of the man's poor judgment. He was the wrong person in control.'

The fact that the Fox board of directors decided to reinstate Monroe five days after receiving this cable may or may not be significant.

Monroe followed these developments with trepidation. 'Zanuck may be coming back this week,' she confided to Evelyn Moriarity. 'I don't know how I feel about that. It makes me kind of nervous.'

She had told Levathes earlier that she didn't really want anyone from that old group – the group nominated by Zanuck and Skouras – back in her professional life. 'She expressed dislike for all of them,' Levathes recalled. By now, however, Monroe realised that she needed both Skouras and Zanuck back in power if *Something's Got to Give* was to be made. Levathes was not aware that Monroe was wooing her former bosses.

Besides the *Cleopatra* scandal and the collapse of *Something's Got to Give*, Zanuck was concerned about the future of his own masterpiece, *The Longest Day*.

Gould and his fellow Wall Streeters were enthralled with the vigorous power of the unedited rushes from that film. Here was a certain winner. 'Suddenly, I saw a way for Fox to regain some of the millions lost on Zanuck's string of losers,' Gould recalled. 'We decided then and there to cross-collateralise *The Longest Day*, meaning we would apply the losses of Zanuck's other films to the profits of this blockbuster.'

When word of this was passed along to Zanuck in Paris, he commented tersely, 'That will never happen.'

'There developed a contest between Zanuck and myself,' Gould said. 'It was obvious that one of us would eventually lose. The winner would take the company and the loser would be vanquished.'

When Zanuck had fled Fox in 1956 because of career burnout, he had written himself a robber baron's deal. Each week, Fox paid him $2,885 for 'advisory services'. He was answerable only to his old friend, Spyros Skouras. He wasn't required to write a single memo or return a phone call. As the studio suffered the corporate calamities of the early sixties, Zanuck didn't raise a finger to help. No scrap of paper or phone transcript exists in the vast Fox archives to indicate Zanuck's interest in the twin disasters of *Cleopatra* and *Something's Got to Give* until the very last minute. Instead, he gloried in the scandals during long gabfests with his son Richard and friends such as Nunnally Johnson.

'He got all kinds of emoluments from the company,' Gould said. 'He was doing pretty well. We were losing money and he was making money.'

Zanuck, Skouras and New York attorney Arnold Grant 'spent weeks buying up thousands of shares of stock in order to win enough votes to unseat us', said Gould.

'But I had no knowledge that clandestine meetings between Zanuck, Skouras and Grant had occurred long before the showdown,' Gould recalled. Gould warned the board that he wouldn't remain 'if Zanuck is brought in as president'.

On July 25, three days after Monroe's photo selection meeting with Levathes, the Twentieth Century-Fox board met in a chaotic session at Fox headquarters in New York.

The Wall Streeters made Zanuck's private life the major issue. He was called to testify, and when he emerged from the boardroom, he was white-faced and shaken. 'What bastards!' he exclaimed. 'All my life I've never been so mistreated. They treated me like a schoolkid.'

'The bile just poured out of them,' Zanuck told his daughter, Darrilyn. 'And it was filthy stuff – mostly about my private life. What the hell did that have to do with my competence as president of Twentieth Century-Fox?'

Gould waged war during the stormy sessions, focusing on Zanuck's shameful attempts to make stars of a series of mistresses. In particular, Zanuck was accused of having squandered fortunes to pay his paramour Bella Darvi's gambling debts.

But this corporate muckraking didn't work, and Zanuck prevailed. The board voted nine to two to elect him president, and Gould exploded with anger. He resigned from the board that afternoon.

The biggest loser, however, was Monroe's ally, Levathes.

Before Monroe and Elizabeth Taylor had wrought their havoc, Peter G. Levathes had been the last, best hope of Twentieth Century-Fox. A week before Christmas 1961, while Monroe was still trying to find a way to avoid making *Something's Got to Give*, Levathes had been told he would succeed Skouras as president of the company. Summoned into the presidential offices in New York, Levathes had faced not only Skouras, but Otto Koegel, Fox's chief legal counsel, and new board member Milton Gould.

Skouras gestured stiffly towards Koegel, saying, 'Otto, you tell Peter.'

Koegel got up from his chair and put his hand on Levathes's shoulder, saying, 'I remember, years ago, this young law student coming to work here, and now it's my privilege and duty to advise him that the board is planning to elect him president of Twentieth Century-Fox next July.'

Levathes was stunned. Four months on the job as production chief and now this. The top job! Still, he couldn't shake the vague feeling that something was wrong. Skouras wouldn't look him in the eye.

Always a gentleman, Levathes instantly forgave his former mentor for turning against him at the July 1962 board meeting. 'I think Skouras was truly frightened at this point,' he later said. 'Not only was he afraid for his job, but he thought he might lose his place in the world.'

Remembering the warm promises of Christmas 1961, Levathes's wife, Christina, wasn't so charitable after Zanuck's election. 'Peter was marvellous about it,' she said. 'I stopped speaking to Skouras, but Peter would still have lunch with him. I just felt he portrayed Peter in an unforgivable manner.'

Chapter 30

The War Within

The walls protecting Monroe's home in Brentwood were more than two feet thick and seven feet high – a bulwark against the outside world. A towering stand of eucalyptus trees, imported as seedlings from Australia, acted as a rustling curtain.

Inside the gate and beneath the trees, a secret garden rambled over an acre of rolling lawns. Hillocks of baby's breath and veins of German moss stretched along a flagstone walkway. Brilliant bougainvillea vines made crimson splashes against whitewashed walls.

The house itself was built in the modified 'mission style', with handcarved wooden beams and massive walls. When the great windows were closed and the thick curtains were drawn, an eerie quiet pervaded. Eunice Murray, the veteran psychiatric nurse, added to the effect, walking silently in crepe-soled shoes and speaking in a soft voice that nonetheless echoed through the house.

The estate had a sense of permanence, from its handcarved doorways to the trees that dated to an era when it had been part of a Spanish land grant. As Monroe added flowering bushes, Oriental bulbs and sweet olive trees, the house slowly began to bear her personal stamp.

At night, when the coastal winds blew in from the sea, antique bronze wind chimes, a gift from poet Carl Sandburg, provided a soothing cadence from high in the trees.

But all this quiet and comfort failed to achieve its main purpose. The ebb and flow of the coastal breezes and the verdant garden could not lull Monroe to sleep.

Contrary to the rumours of her madness and hysteria during the period of her love affairs with the Kennedys, despite the hundreds of pages written about her so-called schizophrenia and her 'rejection syndrome,' Monroe's real illness during the summer of 1962 was insomnia.

Adding to her woes was a dangerous flirtation with anorexia – a creeping form of starvation that had begun with a crash diet to prepare for *Something's Got to Give*. Like the tragic heiress Barbara Hutton, Monroe was consuming fewer than six hundred calories a day in late June and early August. Some days she went without food altogether, living on champagne and pills. She lost twenty-seven pounds altogether.

Fox doctor Lee Siegel warned her on the first day of filming that she exhibited 'pronounced symptoms of hypoglycaemia' (low blood sugar) and that she 'was running on empty'. Her main meal was a 200-calorie breakfast of poached eggs and grapefruit juice.

After *Something's Got to Give* was shut down, she even gave up breakfast. Many days, according to Eunice Murray, she consumed nothing but a half dozen oysters and eight ounces of champagne. She craved the rush she got from gulping tranquillisers on an empty stomach.* On August 1, according to Murray, her diet consisted of three ounces of

---

*Monroe's insidious drug regimen was self-perpetuating. The methamphetamine shots at Fox made the Nembutal capsules necessary. The champagne magnified all the pharmacological effects. Monroe also experienced fake anxiety attacks that would be routinely recognised today as hypoglycaemia. She was so anaemic at one point that physicians administered dozens of vitamin injections.

steak, a Librium, a chloral hydrate, a Nembutal and two glasses of Dom Pérignon.

Photos taken in Malibu a few days earlier showed a rail-thin Monroe leaning lifelessly against a balcony with the sea behind her – the very portrait of a middle-aged anorexic.

Her constant insomnia, combined with her near-starvation, merely aped the symptoms of mental illness. Today a star in her condition would be rushed to the Betty Ford Clinic for ten weeks, put on a course of antidepressants and nursed back to a normal life. In 1962, before decades of sleep research and breakthroughs on anorexia, Greenson and the other physicians had few options. Instead of telling her to eat dinner, they gave her vitamin shots.

Makeup artist Whitey Snyder was the only one who described her problems succinctly: 'The girl couldn't go to sleep.'

Every night, with pills or without them, and with Ralph Roberts's massages, or without them, Monroe lay on her white satin comforter and trembled with fear. She undoubtedly suffered from what is now called 'sleep fright'. Scientists would say today that she was a 'sleep frantic personality'. The fear of not going to sleep was so powerful that all other mental problems melted into insignificance.

Shortly before her death, Monroe described her problem eloquently to Greenson. 'Last night I was awake all night again. Sometimes I wonder what the nighttime is for. It almost doesn't exist for me. It all seems like a long, long horrible day.'

Greenson shook his head as he sadly recorded her comments.

'Sleep became the real focus of her life and of my father's treatment,' Joan Greenson told Fox Entertainment News. 'She would do almost anything to get to sleep. But the more she tried the more she couldn't.' She had been afraid of the dark, and of going to sleep, ever since her brief stay in an orphanage as an adolescent. 'I didn't feel safe,' she said to Maurice Zolotow in 1959. 'People came and went during the night.

When the sun came up some of the kids weren't there any more. I never felt secure in the dark after that, as if I could still be spirited away.'

Her insomnia was so pronounced by the time she filmed *Gentlemen Prefer Blondes* that the studio doctors provided her with Seconal, the strongest barbiturate on the market. By the time she began *Something's Got to Give* she had been on barbiturates for twelve years.

In Ralph Greenson's view, insomnia was the major problem. The onset of night and darkness frightened Monroe, especially if she was alone. She would do almost anything to escape her bedroom and the terrible wakefulness that awaited her there. More than 80 per cent of her phone calls were made after 11 P.M. – a great many after 3 A.M.

One of the most reliable of her friends, and one she called again and again, was publicist Rupert Allan. No matter where he went, she would find him, even in Europe. Since his other major client was Grace Kelly, he was frequently in Monaco at the royal palace. The actress found him there several days after she was fired from *Something's Got to Give*.

'I was at Princess Grace's palace, and Marilyn was in Los Angeles, yet somehow she felt I could help her get to sleep. So we talked and talked and talked. Finally, she grew drowsy and hung up.'

Whitey Snyder was another member of Monroe's midnight club. 'I did what I could,' he remembered. 'I also tried to help Marilyn change her nighttime habits. She would rush home from the studio and jump into bed at six-thirty or seven P.M., sleep for a couple of hours, and then wake up at midnight for the rest of the night. I could never convince her to stay up until ten or eleven and then go to bed when she was tired like normal people.'

By late July, Monroe's life at the house on Fifth Helena Drive completely revolved around sleep. Her white-on-white bedroom was a shrine to Morpheus, the god of dreams. Shortly after she had moved to Brentwood, special drapery experts had installed 'blackout curtains' of a sort that hadn't been used, as Robert Slatzer said, since 'the U-boat scares during World War II'. They fitted over the windows and were attached to the walls with tacks in order to plunge the bedroom into blackness even at noon.

In the months before *Something's Got to Give* went before the cameras, Greenson had weaned Monroe down to a couple of chloral hydrates at night and a bit of champagne. The studio's methamphetamine shots effectively destroyed this regimen, replacing it with Monroe's old uppers-and-downers lifestyle of the fifties.

Most of her so-called 'suicide attempts' were actually mild to moderate overdoses. Because her speech became slurred and she seemed confused, friends often overreacted and summoned doctors. In reality, said Slatzer, 'Marilyn knew precisely how many pills it took to get her to sleep.'

Rupert Allan agreed, saying, 'Her knowledge of pharmacology was incredible. I think all, or at least most, of her flirtations with suicide were actually pleas for sympathy. Marilyn liked to be rescued. She would take a high dose of, say, Nembutal and then call somebody. But, even if she weren't rescued, there was no real danger.'

Allan also pointed out that Monroe made a great show of her arsenal of pills. She kept them out on tables – sometimes in the living room. 'They earned her a great sympathy value.'

As if her health problems weren't serious enough, Monroe was further devastated when a petty internecine war broke out among the people hired to help her.

The strife began when Greenson attempted to separate Monroe from her coterie of publicists, masseurs and coaches. He particularly targeted Ralph Roberts, Paula Strasberg, Whitey Snyder and Pat Newcomb.

'It must have been devastating to her,' said UCLA psychiatrist Robert Litman, head of the Los Angeles Suicide Team, an ad hoc group convened to investigate Monroe's death. 'Those people were an extended family to her. A civil war among the members of that family would have been terrible for her mental health.'

'I had to sneak around in order to continue our association,' recalled Roberts. 'Our appointments for massage usually were after 9 P.M. I had to come in without ringing the bell so Mrs. Murray wouldn't see us and report it to Greenson.'

At one point, Greenson told Monroe to 'give up Roberts and Strasberg, or stop analysis.' Both were banished for a time.

'There's no telling whether all these amateur psychiatrists and psychoanalysts she had around her, such as the Strasbergs, did any harm,' concluded Litman. 'Still, they were only trying to be helpful.'

But others saw Greenson's actions differently. 'I think he was jealous – obsessively so,' said Roberts. 'He could see that we were deep friends and that Marilyn trusted me completely. He was obsessed with her.'

During one session in June 1962, Greenson told Monroe that Roberts was an 'emotional leak'. The psychiatrist said, 'I'm trying to make you steady. And [Roberts] is a leak.'

By early August, Monroe was ready to banish Greenson instead. 'That last month she became convinced that he was doing her no good,' said Roberts.

Writer Lucy Freeman believed that 'Dr. Greenson's troubles began when he couldn't prevent Fox from firing her. You know, if one of the men in Marilyn's life failed her in a major way, he became suspect in her eyes.'

'Greenson wouldn't let her get out,' said Whitey Snyder. 'He was a money man . . . money, money, money.'

Greenson did have a sizeable economic stake. By midsummer 1962, he was earning $1,400 a month by treating Monroe with a *minimum* fifty-two hours of analysis per month though he charged Monroe only half of the fee paid by other patients.

The last two weeks of Monroe's life have almost always been protrayed as a countdown to tragedy – as if the black figure of death cast a shadow over her final days.

Each of her words and all her actions have been weighted with the gloom of her fate. Her friends and enemies alike have been depicted as larger-than-life heroes and villains, playing their roles under the glare of international fame.

Actually, Monroe's death interrupted a life and career that was in midpassage. Her last days were a time of exhilaration, activity, tears and laughter.

She had million-dollar deals to sign, including an $11-million pact with Italian filmmakers for four films in Italy; a film to complete; a garden to plant; and a house to finish.

She had planned lunches and dinners for the near future, as well as a three-day theatre trip to New York City. And like many a Hollywood celebrity, she maintained a degree of mystery and a touch of glamorous subterfuge in her life as she tried to keep her distance from an increasingly vigilant press.

Chapter 31

Danger Signs

Kindhearted Peter Lawford was about to pay the price for another crushed relationship involving the Kennedy brothers.

President Kennedy's betrayal of Frank Sinatra had already cost Lawford dearly. When JFK had abruptly and unapologetically cancelled his stay at Sinatra's Palm Springs mansion early in 1962, Lawford had lost both his professional and private access to the millionaire singer. He was even cut from the casts of the 'Rat Pack' movies that had financially supported him over the years.

Lawford was set adrift socially as well. No Hollywood hostess who valued her connections dared invite Sinatra and Lawford to the same party. Twice at public functions Lawford had walked up and held his hand out to Sinatra, only to have the singer turn away.

Lawford bore the humiliation gamely and hoped JFK would make it up to Sinatra.

Now Lawford had to cope with a twice-betrayed Marilyn Monroe, who felt abused by both Kennedy brothers. Straightforward as she was, Monroe could never understand why the President, and later the Attorney General, hadn't the courage or the gallantry to tell her themselves.

As Monroe continued to call Washington, Lawford, who considered himself JFK's official ambassador to the world of Hollywood, was ordered to cut her off from all contact with the First Family. The President had already dispatched Bobby to sever the ties with Monroe, but soon learned that the Attorney General had become seriously infatuated with the actress.

So now Lawford was to march on Brentwood and tell his longtime friend she was no longer wanted. And Monroe was already heartbroken by her treatment at the hands of the Kennedys.

First, Monroe called the Attorney General at his home, Hickory Hill in Arlington, Virginia, some time between July 22 and 27. She allegedly got the telephone number of Bobby's office at home from producer Jerry Wald, who was preparing to film *The Enemy Within*.

'Bobby was furious with Marilyn for taking this liberty,' recalled Lawford's biographer, James Spada. 'Bobby had orders to distance himself from Marilyn as quickly as possible.'

Second, an anonymous caller to Ted Kennedy's campaign headquarters in Massachusetts in late July threatened to reveal the Kennedy brothers' 'involvement with certain Hollywood stars'. The caller also warned that 'a picture of Marilyn Monroe and both brothers still existed', despite the Secret Service's sweep of Manhattan photo archives.

This same source wrote to Hollywood columnist Hedda Hopper on July 28 to impart similar information. 'I have already called the Kennedy offices about this,' wrote the source, who has never been identified. 'Why don't you tell the story of Marilyn and the President?' The postmark on that letter was Boston. Hopper believed the letter came from someone close to Teddy's senatorial opponent.

Third, a 'disgruntled employee' of Hollywood detective Fred Otash called the Justice Department in July 1962 and offered details of 'a major bugging operation' at Monroe's house. 'You will be fascinated by the voices you hear on those tapes,' said the private eye.

And fourth, Monroe telephoned Pat Kennedy Lawford on August 1 to confess her sorrow over Bobby's false promises. The actress was so shocked by what the President's sister told her that she repeated it later that night to Robert Slatzer. 'Pat told her that she should forget Bobby,' Slatzer recalled. 'She told Marilyn something like, "Bobby's still a little boy wanting to play like a little boy." Pat also told Marilyn that marriage was out of the question.'

Most importantly, Bobby's sister told Monroe that Rose Kennedy had ordered all her sons' sexual adventures to cease – 'immediately'. By then, Rose had been brought into Teddy's sagging senatorial race to shore him up with the power of her spotless image. 'It was smart politics, bringing Rose into the campaign,' said Bobby's confidant and later biographer, Arthur Schlesinger, Jr.

In Massachusetts, editorial cartoonists were having a grand time with the Kennedy name. One sketch showed a bumpkin-like Teddy gesturing towards the White House. The Attorney General was standing on the lawn introducing his brother: 'It's my great privilege to present a man who – uh – has a brother who . . .'

Another caricature showed all three brothers dancing hand in hand on the White House lawn. The caption read, 'Triplets! Now, ain't they cute!'

By then, Bobby was deeply involved in his younger brother's campaign. In the first of a series of debates with Massachusetts Attorney General Ed McCormack, Teddy visibly withered under McCormack's attacks. At one point, McCormack turned to Teddy and said, 'Mr. Kennedy, you have never worked for a living, you have never held elected office, and you aren't running on your qualifications, because you have none.' Teddy stood there for almost a minute, unable to answer.

Finally he turned to another question, ignoring McCormack's attack completely.

As he had done with JFK's presidential campaign, Bobby entered Teddy's senatorial bid at the last minute as a sort of political quarterback. He taught Teddy how to debate, how to deflect personal attacks and how to dissemble on the issues.

At that point, even the hint of scandal could destroy the delicate foundation of the Kennedy power base. After all, John F. Kennedy had been elected President of the United States by the narrowest margin in history. And the just-barely-defeated Richard M. Nixon was still politically active. All the Nixon supporters and most of the strategists of the Republican party were watching Teddy's senatorial campaign for signs of weaknesses in the great Kennedy machine.

Even the President remarked that this Massachusetts campaign 'was causing more trouble than the Bay of Pigs scandal'.

Into this cauldron of political turmoil was dropped yet another dilemma – Monroe's increasing hostility about her treatment by JFK and Bobby. No longer discreet, she told Skolsky that she intended to 'go public with the indiscretions of the Kennedy brothers'. Though no definitive report of the affairs surfaced, Monroe, as Anthony Summers noted, 'was prattling on about the love affairs'.

Now Monroe had disappeared from sight.

Despite her fame, she still had the ability to vanish for days at a time. She was, in fact, the least recognisable of all major stars. When she washed her face clean of makeup, covered her hair with a scarf and bundled herself in bulky sweaters, she was rarely unmasked – even on Rodeo Drive in Beverly Hills or Fifth Avenue in New York.

Besides, she had friends who could always be counted on to protect her anonymity. Susan Strasberg recalled walking beside her near Central Park without attracting a single second glance. With help from Pat Newcomb or Jeanne Carmen, Monroe's girlfriend, she would disappear into a

private clinic, a resort hotel or a hospital under a pseud-
onym.

Now, on July 19, she jumped into a limousine and eluded
a pair of private detectives who had been paid by Fred Otash
to follow her.

When she returned on the evening of July 21 – the day
before the picture-choosing session with Levathes – she looked
wan and exhausted.

Many of her friends and confidants hinted that she had
checked into Cedars of Lebanon Hospital under an assumed
name and aborted President Kennedy's baby. Still others
insisted it was Bobby's child.

'That is a definite possibility,' said publicist and close friend
Rupert Allan. 'I heard that she was pregnant and that it was
Bobby's child.'

Michael Selsman, a publicist who worked alongside Allan
in the Arthur Jacobs Public Relations Company, told him that
Monroe had admitted she was pregnant almost four weeks
earlier.

Detective Fred Otash learned of it as well. From what
he overheard on the audiotapes from Monroe's house, he
concluded that 'an American doctor went with her across
the border to Mexico for the abortion, making Marilyn safe,
medically.' Sources at Fox speculated that one of the studio
physicians might have been involved.

At first, Agnes Flanaghan, Marilyn's hairstylist at Fox,
was the only person she trusted with the details of the secret
operation. 'She told Agnes there was an abortion and that she
had checked into the hospital incognito,' said Allan. 'But this
is the sort of thing Marilyn wouldn't have shared with me.'

Other clues included a vial of morphine capsules with a
Cedars of Lebanon label and a frantic telephone call from
Monroe to her former gynaecologist, Leon Khron. The actress
told Khron's nurse that she needed 'an emergency appointment'.

'She might have been afraid that this quickie abortion had hurt her chances to have children, this time permanently,' said Robert Slatzer. 'You've got to remember that Marilyn was heartbroken over her inability to have children. And she was determined to keep trying.'

When Monroe fearfully called Bobby at Hickory Hill, she must have told him that she had just endured another abortion. The news apparently failed to shake his resolution to banish her from the Kennedy circle. Now all her calls went unanswered – even by a secretary.

As agonising days passed and Bobby remained elusive, Monroe spread bitter tales about her pregnancy. She told hairdresser Agnes Flanaghan, Laguna Beach realtor Arthur James and Rupert Allan all about it – though Allan and James understood that she had had a miscarriage. Flanaghan told Hazel Washington, 'Marilyn's looking so poorly because she had an abortion.'

'Those few who knew her secret were horrified,' said biographer Fred Lawrence Guiles.

She undoubtedly described the private agony of yet another abortion – her thirteenth – in her growing stack of spiral notebooks, where she was making notes for a projected autobiography.

Monroe's aborted pregnancy, combined with her rising outrage over her cavalier treatment by the President and his brother, caused great consternation in the offices of the posh Arthur Jacobs Public Relations Agency.* Publicist Michael

*Rupert Allan, British journalist Sandra Shevey and Hazel Washington believe that Monroe was carrying the President's baby, and that the pregnancy resulted from their series of trysts during the early history of *Something's Got to Give*. The Los Angeles coroner, Dr. Thomas Noguchi, said that he found indications of 'multiple abortions' during the autopsy on Monroe, but that there was no way to distinguish between a fresh abortion and one that had taken place years before.

Selsman interrupted a heated discussion between Pat Newcomb and Jacobs about the dire effects on Monroe's career
– and, more importantly, on the Kennedys' careers – of her
love affairs with the brothers.

'Nineteen sixty-two was a long time ago,' said Rupert Allan
many years later. 'If word that Marilyn had aborted a child by
one of the Kennedys reached the press – in those pre-tabloid
days – everyone connected with it would have been ruined.'

Now, in Hollywood, 'the Marilyn question' had become
a powder keg for the Kennedys.

The Attorney General apparently decided to let Lawford
handle this latest emergency. Kennedy wished to avoid an ugly
scene. Monroe had screamed at Justice Department operators
following Bobby's decision to eliminate all telephone contact.

Since Monroe had become intimate with Patricia Kennedy
Lawford, Bobby apparently prevailed on Pat Lawford to get
Monroe out of town during his visit to Los Angeles the week-
end of July 27 to 29. The Attorney General was flying in for
a public appearance and several conferences on the progress of
The Enemy Within.

Monroe later told Slatzer that the Kennedys had tricked
her into leaving Los Angeles. She also expressed considerable
anger at Pat Lawford. ' [Bobby] is doing all he can to avoid a
showdown with me,' Monroe told Slatzer in a long-distance
telephone call.

The Lawfords persuaded Monroe to accompany them on a
weekend jaunt to Lake Tahoe, ostensibly to attend Jack Jones's
opening at Frank Sinatra's lavish Cal-Neva Lodge.

Weak from the effects of the abortion and furious over Bobby's hypocrisy, the actress delivered herself into the Lawfords'
hands and, again, virtually disappeared until late Sunday night,
when the Attorney General was safely back in Washington.

When she reappeared, Hollywood was dizzy with rumours
of her abortion and a critical drug overdose on Saturday night.

Others perhaps heard of a midnight clash between Sinatra and Joe DiMaggio.

The passing decades have done little to dispel the myth of 'rehearsal for death', but some clues – however murky – have emerged to set the record straight.

In 1985, a mob-connected executive who supervised Mafia kingpin Sam Giancana's interest in Cal-Neva, made this enigmatic statement: 'There was more to what happened up there than anybody has ever been told. It would have been the big fall for Bobby Kennedy.'

At the very least, the comment must mean that the Attorney General, through Peter Lawford, orchestrated the strange events in Northern California. 'Bobby told Peter to inform Marilyn brutally and frankly that it was over,' Lawford's former wife, Deborah Gould, told journalists for ABC News.

Lawford's assignment was to tell Monroe that her relationships with John and Bobby Kennedy were over. There were to be no more phone calls, no more visits, no more cards and letters. Though Lawford and Sinatra were estranged, Lawford was still occasionally invited to nightclub openings – such as this gala weekend for Jack Jones.

Word of this ultimatum may have been relayed to Joe DiMaggio – who also rushed to Lake Tahoe late Friday night to console Monroe. When he found the Cal-Neva full, the night clerk booked him rooms in the nearby Silver Crest Motor Hotel. The former baseball hero asked Cal-Neva bell captain Roy Langford where Monroe was. 'Honestly, Mr. DiMaggio, I don't know,' said Langford.

Monroe's name never appeared on the Cal-Neva books. She was secretly installed in Bungalow 52, part of a complex permanently reserved for 'special guests' of Frank Sinatra. Bellboys who repeatedly delivered room service to the bungalow never saw her. The door was answered by Peter Lawford.

Monroe was a shadowy presence at the Cal-Neva. Because of her anger and her exhaustion, she was unable to attend Jack

Jones's opening. There were plenty of rumours, but only one dramatic sighting of the film star. Shortly before dawn on Sunday morning, a Cal-Neva doorman strolled outside as the fog began to blanket the lake. He was stunned to see Monroe, still in her white robe, dragging one bare foot in the ice-cold swimming pool. Her gaze was fixed on the foothills above the rustic lodge.

The clerk's eyes followed Monroe's to the edge of a granite ridge. Standing there, staring down, was Joe DiMaggio, another surreal vision in the mist.

Since Monroe was still carrying a torch for Sinatra, her host, the weekend couldn't have been carefree in any case. After her divorce from Arthur Miller in 1960, Monroe had rebounded into Sinatra's arms and the two indulged in a dazzling season of nightlife in Las Vegas, San Francisco and Manhattan. She also stayed at the singer's bachelor mansion in Coldwater Canyon for several weeks until she found an apartment. Apparently they fell in love in a matter of days – so much so that she spent $10,000 on new gowns, more formal and glitzier than usual, the way Sinatra liked her to dress.

She told her New York maid Lena Pepitone that she was considering marriage and showed off a pair of emerald earrings Sinatra had given her. Many of Monroe's friends blamed the early troubles on the set of *Something's Got to Give* on the sudden announcement that Sinatra was engaged to Juliet Prowse.

Years later, when Lawford was embellishing one story after another about Monroe's last days, he told detectives for the Los Angeles district attorney's office that she had overdosed at Cal-Neva. He described the incident as a blatant suicide attempt 'over her sorrow at losing *Something's Got to Give*'.

This highly unlikely account may have been part of Lawford's continual attempts to bolster his claims that Monroe committed suicide. 'She tried to kill herself the night of July twenty-eighth, and she finally succeeded on August fourth,' Lawford told the district attorney.

It seems more likely that Monroe learned that Bobby was in Los Angeles, as word of his speech to the National Insurance Association was broadcast on all three television networks, and flew into a rage. Lawford himself may have drugged her. A DiMaggio confidant, Harry Hall, reported, 'She went up there, and they gave her pills.' Ralph Greenson denied that she attempted suicide that weekend.

The drugs, coupled with the aftereffects of the abortion, were physically devastating. A single photograph survives from the weekend – a sad tableau of Lawford and Monroe leaning against each other. The other shots taken then were even worse. Biographer Anthony Summers found the Beverly Hills film processor who developed film from the weekend for Frank Sinatra. 'I suggested [Summers] burn them,' the technician reported. 'And he did.'

On Sunday, Pat and Peter Lawford and Monroe left Lake Tahoe in a private jet, Pat Lawford to catch a flight from San Francisco to Hyannis Port, and Peter and Monroe to head for Hollywood. En route from Los Angeles International Airport in a limousine, Lawford ordered the driver to stop at a pay phone just blocks from his beachfront mansion. He jumped out of the car and was on the phone for more than half an hour. Lawford didn't trust his own phones, and believed that his house was bugged.

'He was warning Bobby that Marilyn had begun making threats,' said Lawford biographer James Spada in an interview.

According to Robert Slatzer, it was then that the Attorney General of the United States, the nation's number-one law enforcement officer, learned that Monroe was planning to hold a press conference to talk about 'my many relations with the Kennedy family'.

Back home in Brentwood, the actress called Ralph Roberts.

As he kneaded her taut muscles, she raised her head and looked him in the eye.

'Have you heard the talk about Bobby and me?' she asked.

Roberts replied, 'All Hollywood is talking about it.'

The accumulated scandal of the Kennedys in Hollywood was reaching a critical impasse that could only lead to a violent explosion.

Chapter 32

A Woman Scorned

'No! I want Bobby to tell me himself. *In person*,' Monroe told an increasingly alarmed Robert Slatzer. 'I want to hear from him that it's over. He owes me an explanation. After all those promises I want to know what happened.'

This time, Monroe wasn't going to be shoved aside just because she had become inconvenient.

Two years earlier, the ambitious French actor Yves Montand had wooed her into a liaison during the production of *Let's Make Love*, which contained Montand's first major part in an American film. When they embarked on their affair, the lovers made a pact that it would be kept secret – to protect their careers. But Montand, desperate for Hollywood stardom, revealed the affair to Hedda Hopper, Louella Parsons and Sheilah Graham, unleashing a firestorm of publicity. In coy interviews with the columnists, Montand portrayed Monroe as a desperate femme fatale out to end his marriage to Simone Signoret. 'He used her shamelessly,' recalled publicist Rupert Allan, who had taken on Montand as a personal favour to Monroe. 'He parlayed the affair into a series of American film roles.'

Two days after *Let's Make Love* was finished, Montand

bolted – leaving Monroe to explain the indiscretion and to accept the blame. 'There was a lot Marilyn could have said and done, and I advised her to go public with her side,' Allan said. 'But she couldn't; in the end, she was just too kind.'

When Monroe's marriage to Arthur Miller collapsed less than seven months later, she again allowed the public to believe that *her* indiscretions had led to their separation. During the divorce proceedings which ended their marriage in 1961, she refused to reveal Miller's own flirtations. The day the divorce became final, she declined to respond to the stories Miller appeared to be spreading about her conduct on the set of *The Misfits*. 'Actually, Miller committed the first indiscretion,' said Jean Louis, who designed the costumes for the film. 'And Monroe was confronted with this betrayal.' Eighteen months later, Miller married one of the still photographers hired for the film.

Just as *Something's Got to Give* began filming, Monroe endured a similar situation when Sinatra became engaged to dancer Juliet Prowse without cleanly severing his amorous ties to Monroe. But again she suffered in silence.

As for President John F. Kennedy, he retreated into the safety of the White House without even the pretence of a good-bye. Instead, the President sent his younger brother to end his affair with the screen star.

But Monroe wasn't going to let Bobby Kennedy off so easily.

'What are you going to do if he never takes your call?' Slatzer asked.

'I might just hold a press conference,' she said blithely. 'I've certainly got plenty to say.'

Just after daybreak on Monday, July 30, a thick fog hung over Brentwood and swirled around the stores and boutiques lining San Vicente Boulevard, the main thoroughfare that cuts through the town's wooded neighbourhoods.

Monroe, bundled in a Mexican sweater, was feeding quarters into a pay telephone as she talked to Slatzer who was in Columbus, Ohio. 'She no longer trusted her own telephone,' he recalled. 'So she slipped off to a nearby phone booth several times a day to make her calls.'*

Slatzer felt helpless to stop what he believed would be a dangerous confrontation between Monroe and the Kennedys. He made her promise to call him before making a final decision.

An hour later, Monroe made another call to Bobby Kennedy's office at the Justice Department. The Attorney General finally took her call; the conversation lasted eight minutes. What was said is unknown, but afterwards, she began referring to him as 'that bastard'.

At 8 A.M. the same day, Eunice Murray found Monroe strolling up and down beside the brick wall behind the house, trying to decide how many bougainvillea vines to plant. In her hand was a lavish book on Mexican gardens, a present from the housekeeper. Monroe wandered across the property. 'There was a peaceful expression on her face when she was out there,' Murray later remembered. Later that week Monroe chose dozens of new plants for what she called her 'garden of colour'.

Between Monday, July 30, and Saturday, August 4, Monroe had three business meetings, spent eleven and a half hours with her analyst, ordered a $10,000 evening gown from Jean Louis, appeared on the cover of *Life* magazine, twice ordered deli food, and bought $100 worth of Chanel No. 5.

Two themes dominated these days: she told friends she

---

*During her final month, Monroe told friends she could hear clicks every time she used her private line – to her a sure sign that the FBI – or the Secret Service – had tapped her telephone.

One of Frank Sinatra's secretaries arranged for an 'intelligence sweep'. But even when it came up clean, Monroe remained unconvinced. Although she continued to make many phone calls from home, she made all her calls to and about the Kennedys from Brentwood phone booths.

was determined to force a personal farewell from the Attorney General, and her excitement at the prospect of returning to Twentieth Century-Fox in triumph with a million-dollar contract.

The fabulous new deal with Fox, including the personal protection of Peter Levathes and the corporate board, failed to assuage Monroe's desire to confront the Kennedys. After Bobby declined to meet with her, her sorrow turned to fury.

But the family still didn't perceive the danger.

'It was a crass and, in hindsight, a tragic brush-off,' said Rupert Allan. 'Marilyn wasn't really that unreasonable. If Kennedy had just confronted her one last time, everything might have turned out differently.'

Monroe asked Mickey Song, the Kennedy hairstylist based in L.A., to come to her house on Wednesday night for what turned out to be a private inquisition.

'I thought she needed her hair done quickly; that an emergency had come up,' said Song, who hadn't seen Monroe since he had styled her hair for the JFK birthday gala. 'So naturally, I brought along all of my gear.'

Instead, Song found Monroe dressed in a Pucci outfit and ready to serve him champagne and caviar. With Eunice Murray absent, they sat alone on the long white sofa.

Twenty-year-old Song, used to living within the charmed Kennedy circle, was accustomed to the presence of celebrities. As Bobby told him in the limousine on the way to JFK's inauguration, 'Kid, you'll never see the world from this vantage point again.'

Still, nothing prepared Song for Monroe's close-up star power: the voice heard in *Some Like It Hot*, the ivory and alabaster face seen in *How to Marry a Millionaire*, the innate sensuality felt in *Niagara*.

'You know, Mickey,' Monroe said, 'I never really thanked you for the gala.' She pressed another glass of Dom Pérignon on him. 'Your style was a hit, you know,' she said with a giggle. 'People all over the world are copying that little flip on the side. It was very ingenious.'

Song tried his best to relax, waiting for her to get to the point. Finally, between nibbles of caviar, she asked the first in a long series of questions about the Kennedy family.

'How close, really, are Jack and Jackie?' she asked. 'Is that a happy marriage?'

Song shrugged. 'I never get close enough to know anything. I don't see Jackie that often and I've never really seen them together.'

Monroe turned catty. 'What about Bobby and Ethel? I can't believe that's a happy marriage. What does he see in her?'

Again Song avoided answering. 'I rarely see Ethel.'

For the next hour, Monroe queried him about First Family secrets, occasionally picking up a grain of gossip.

'I got the uneasy feeling that she wanted information to use against the Kennedys in some way,' he remembered thirty years later. 'She was in a very analytical state – very alert and very determined. She wanted dish, and who else to get it from but the family hairdresser? But I wasn't about to turn on them, not even for Marilyn Monroe.'

She tried one more ploy. Laying a hand comfortably on Song's arm, she said, 'Don't you feel used by them?'

Song shook his head, saying, 'They've been wonderful to me.'

But she pressed on. 'Not even a little bit? They haven't abused you in some small way?'

'She was trying to make it seem as if the two of us were allies against the big, arrogant family. She wanted me to be a co-conspirator.'

The hairstylist again shook his head. Monroe's face turned flinty cold as she said, 'Well, *I do*.'

Song finally broke free and left the house – or, as he described it, 'I escaped as fast as I could.'

As his car turned around in the driveway, Monroe reached under the couch and pulled out a small ivory-coloured tape recorder. She flicked the machine off and unloaded the reel-to-reel tape. She labelled it 'M.S., August 2'. Then she hid it along with the cache of studio documents in her bedroom.

As devastated as she was by the course of her private life, Monroe, negotiating by herself, had achieved a stunning victory in her long battle with Twentieth Century-Fox. After she had a series of 'summit meetings' with Fox executive vice-president Philip Feldman – and a long telephone conference with him that last Monday – the studio officially put *Something's Got to Give* back into production.

Under the terms of the new two-picture deal, Monroe was guaranteed a million-dollar salary for the two films, a new director, a personally tailored rewrite of the script (by Nunnally Johnson), and a producer of her choice. 'Few people knew about the second film,' recalled Fox executive secretary Lee Hanna. 'It was controversial, and the studio kept it very quiet.'

On one of her final afternoons, Monroe journeyed to the studio and met for an hour with Feldman, who was then running the lot as Levathes battled to retain control of the corporation. She emerged arm in arm with the vice-president, laughing and joking.

Earlier, she had slipped into the screening room at Fox to view a pair of films made by British producer-director J. Lee Thompson, who had been proposed to guide the second Fox film. After watching *Tiger Bay* and *Flame Over India*, she told Feldman to proceed.

To be titled *What a Way to Go*, the movie, a big-budget musical comedy, would allow Monroe to play a woman who goes through many changes as seven husbands die – one after the other – usually days after the wedding. The film would take her from rags to riches and through a series of identities – from a singing and dancing superstar to a Bohemian artist on the Left Bank in Paris. Her costars were to be, among others, Gene Kelly, Dean Martin, Paul Newman, Dick Van Dyke and Frank Sinatra.

Shortly after Monroe talked to Slatzer on Monday morning, Feldman called her with some unpleasant news. As the last hurdle she must clear before the resumption of *Something's Got to Give*, the Fox leadership wanted her to fire drama coach Paula Strasberg and to exclude Ralph Greenson from further negotiations with the studio.

'We felt that it would go fine if we could get her out of the hands of all those advisers,' said Levathes. 'We wanted to work one on one with Marilyn.'

Monroe asked for a day to think about it. While Greenson was eager to be relieved, the acting coach was a tougher case. Rudin had warned the executives that it would be 'hard if not impossible for Marilyn to give up Strasberg'. Monroe still felt loyalty to Paula's husband Lee – though her affection for Paula had cooled.

For six years, since *Bus Stop*, the dour drama teacher had been on the sets of all Monroe's films. Week by week, scene by scene, Monroe's friends had watched Strasberg chip away at the star's small stock of self-confidence.

'She refused to let Marilyn stand on her own,' said Whitey Snyder. 'Marilyn felt she couldn't operate without Paula. But in actuality, Marilyn was fine before Paula came on the scene.'

Flapping her black cape and staring into Monroe's eyes, Strasberg put the star through excruciating emotional gymnastics before every take. John Huston, who suffered under 'the Strasberg treatment' during *The Misfits*, described her tactics: 'She would cough or throw whatever trick necessary to stop a shot she didn't like. When the director went crazy, and the star hid in her dressing room, only the witch was left to deal with the issues.'

Most of the cast and crew members interviewed for this book – thirty-two people in all – pointed to Paula Strasberg as the main reason *Something's Got to Give* collapsed. '"Witch" and "sinister" are harsh words to level against somebody,' said Thomas Tryon, who deplored the impediments Strasberg created by her meddling. 'But "black witch" and "sinister" describe her perfectly.'

When things were moving along smoothly, Strasberg would sweep onto the set and lure Monroe back to the dressing room. 'Then the set was, in effect, closed down for whatever length of time Paula desired,' said editor David Bretherton. 'Cukor would have loved to strangle her.'

Voicing Method aphorisms about 'pretending to be a cabbage' or 'remembering your first glass of champagne', Strasberg muddied the waters of every film she was involved in.

Sadly, her value to Monroe was as a stand-in for her husband, Lee, the founder of the Actors Studio. 'Paula was her bridge to Lee,' wrote Arthur Miller. 'She felt a nearly religious dependency on him – the more so, perhaps, because he was not present.'

One morning during *The Misfits*, Monroe turned on Paula. 'She doesn't mean anything to me,' she later told Miller.

'In effect, Paula was the mad mother all over again,' Miller theorised. 'She was a fantasy mother who would confirm anything Marilyn wished to hear.'

From the studio's viewpoint, Paula Strasberg was the biggest stumbling block in the attempt to revive *Something's Got to Give*.

Levathes and Feldman couldn't have known that Monroe had already decided to drop Strasberg. When Monroe learned of the charges levelled against Strasberg during attorney Milton Rudin's meetings with Fox, she was shocked. 'Marilyn truly wasn't aware of the demands Fox had made,' said Ralph Roberts. She agreed instantly to discharge the drama coach, adding that she no longer felt the need for one. Unknown to

Fox, she had already decided to cut the Strasbergs out of her will.*

In fact, Monroe had already given the drama coach a one-way ticket back to New York. 'I'm cleaning house,' she told Slatzer on August 3. 'I'm starting with Paula. She's gone.'

Since Fox had taken the first steps towards healing the rift, she decided to meet the studio halfway. The strong complaints registered against the drama coach finally opened her eyes to the rest of her circle of advisers. She relieved Ralph Greenson of his obligations to Fox and agreed to replace publicist Patricia Newcomb with Rupert Allan and to discharge Eunice Murray.

Monroe had fired staff members before, but never with such firmness. Despite her emotional turmoil, her old professionalism was returning.

Peter Levathes responded in kind. On Wednesday he hired Jean Negulesco, an old favourite of Monroe, to direct the reincarnated *Something's Got to Give*. A charming continental, Negulesco piloted his films with a finesse that had made *How to Marry a Millionaire* a picnic for Monroe, Lauren Bacall and Betty Grable.

Negulesco proved himself an ally from the start. 'We've got to retain the Johnson script – restored to its original form,' he told Levathes.

'Why should we?' asked Feldman. 'Marilyn has no script approval.'

Levathes protested as well. 'We spent a lot of time and money on the rewrite.'

'Perhaps, but Marilyn doesn't think it was worth it,'

*The changes were not made in time, so Lee Strasberg was one of the main beneficiaries of Monroe's will. After Paula died, Lee married actress Anna Strasberg, who now exercises the most power over the bequests, and who controls all the rights and licences negotiated for the use of Monroe's name.

Negulesco answered. The director wanted to move quickly. 'Let me go see her,' he said.

'You can't,' the production chief answered. 'Let the lawyers handle it.'

Negulesco assured Levathes that the visit would be an informal one. 'Mr. Levathes, I know Marilyn. I'll find a legitimate reason to see her. I'll take her a drawing I made of her in *How to Marry a Millionaire* for her new home. We'll have a drink. Maybe a laugh. I'll promise her that we'll go back to the script she liked, and you'll have the Monroe picture Fox so badly needs.'

Negulesco wanted to schedule his first conference with Monroe for late afternoon on Saturday, August 4.

'Maybe I shouldn't have listened to Levathes,' he later commented. 'Maybe this was the chance to give her the hope she so badly needed.'

Negulesco secured Monroe's last, and most important, concessions from Fox. The entire Cukor team, from the fawning assistant directors to the harpy-like secretaries, would not be re-engaged.

On Thursday afternoon, August 2, an ecstatic Monroe called Whitey Snyder and asked him to bring Marge Plecher over for cocktails and appetisers. 'We'll have a real celebration,' she said.

The purple glow of summer hung in the sky when Snyder and Plecher drove through the adobe gateway. Monroe, dressed in dark slacks and a raw-silk blouse, threw open the front door and greeted them with glasses of Dom Pérignon. Her conversation was gay and animated as she spoke enthusiastically about the return to the old script and her détente with the powerful forces that controlled Twentieth Century-Fox.

Just two nights earlier, she told her guests, she had received a call from her old nemesis, Darryl F. Zanuck, who after his successful coup had just been named president of Fox. Zanuck had assured her that *Something's Got to Give* would be given priority.

As she passed a tray of Mexican appetisers, Monroe declared, 'We're going back, Margie. *Something's Got to Give* is going to be finished after all.'

'She was excited and happy that night, which was the last time I ever saw her,' Plecher remembered. 'We were going to begin shooting in a matter of weeks.'

Actually, Monroe was to begin close-up work on September 4, with principal photography to start on September 16, after Dean Martin completed another film, *Toys in the Attic*.

The actress had one last conversation, on the phone, with Levathes the week she died. 'You won't recognise me,' she giggled. 'Imagine a Marilyn Monroe who actually comes to the set on time.' She dissolved in laughter.

'God bless you,' Levathes said. 'We're ready for you.'

Chapter 33

The Chase

Friday, August 3, 1962, must have been a bad day in the Kennedy compound in Hyannis Port. The weather was glorious and balmy as an offshore wind swept over the dunes of the Massachusetts Cape area. But bad news came to the Kennedy doorstep with the morning paper.

After weeks of chasing the story, New York gossip columnist Dorothy Kilgallen had finally reported on Monroe's affair with Bobby Kennedy.

Kilgallen had decided to run the story as a blind item, but still, it was a potent warning to the Kennedys. The column opened, 'Marilyn Monroe is cooking in the sex appeal department. She has appeared vastly alluring to a handsome gentleman. A handsome gentleman with a bigger name than Joe DiMaggio in his heyday – so don't write her off.'

For weeks, Kilgallen had been hunting for a way to break the news of Monroe's ties, romantic and otherwise, with the Kennedy brothers. She had interviewed dozens of sources in the Kennedy circle – from chauffeurs to society reporters. Her calls to Bobby at the Justice Department had begun the Wednesday before Monroe died, and she talked to members of his campaign staff, including Kenneth O'Donnell. Frank

Neill, one of the men who had proved so valuable in the 'get Marilyn' campaign earlier in the summer, provided Kilgallen with hints of the affairs, according to Robert Slatzer.

Interviewers for the 1986 BBC special *Say Goodbye to the President – Marilyn Monroe and the Kennedys* learned that members of the Kennedy family had heard that Kilgallen was getting closer and closer to completing a bombshell story.

Before the shock of Kilgallen's column wore off, a new dilemma arose. Monroe finally reached Pat Kennedy Lawford in Hyannis Port and asked for a phone number where she could call the Attorney General over the weekend. Whether or not Bobby's sister provided Monroe with the information is in question, but Pat Lawford was very close to the actress at this point. Eunice Murray described her as 'Marilyn's best friend.' Peter Lawford later admitted he had referred Monroe to his wife in Hyannis Port, but claimed ignorance of the outcome of her call.

Whatever her source, Monroe knew by midmorning that Bobby, Ethel and their children were on a jet headed for San Francisco. It was a combined business and vacation trip; the Attorney General was to address the American Bar Association in the Bay area, and the family was to stay at a friend's ranch outside the city. For his stay in the city, Bobby Kennedy had secured a top-floor suite at the lush St. Francis Hotel.*

Members of the press who covered his arrival noted that the normal 'Bobby jauntiness' was absent. *The San Francisco Chronicle* reported, 'He was without his usual flashy smile and shook hands woodenly with those who welcomed him. Perhaps the cares of the administration are weighing heavily on him.'

If his smile was wan as he arrived at the bustling St.

---

*Kennedy and his family spent most of the three-day weekend at the Bates Ranch in Gilroy, California. The bar association provided a suite at the St. Francis Hotel for use as an office and retreat during its convention.

Francis Hotel, it must have been erased completely by the time he reached the suite. The red message light was already flashing on the telephone. Excited switchboard operators told a Kennedy aide that Marilyn Monroe had called three times. Later, these same operators told William Randolph Hearst's top police reporter, Florabel Muir, that Monroe had continued to call and that aides had continued to pick up the messages. But Kennedy didn't return the calls – at least not from the St. Francis.

As he strolled through the airport corridors and drove through San Francisco, he couldn't escape images of Monroe. Sparkling scenes from *Something's Got to Give* decorated the covers of *Life* magazine and *Paris Match*. At the time, *Life* was involved in a special publicity campaign, displaying large cards featuring Monroe's nude swimming scene at newsstands and airport gift shops.

By early afternoon in Brentwood, Monroe was no closer to a confrontation with Kennedy than she had been earlier in the week. As she drove to her appointment with her internist, Hyman Engleberg, and to her therapy sessions with Ralph Greenson, she stopped at phone booths three times.

After receiving shots of an unknown substance from Engleberg, she called Slatzer at his home in Columbus, chatted with him for a few minutes, and also spoke with Slatzer's friend Lee Henry, a restaurateur.

After some small talk, she renewed her threats against the Kennedy brothers. 'If I don't hear from Bobby Kennedy before the end of the weekend, I'm going to call a press conference, and blow the lid off this whole damn thing!' she said.

'What thing?' Slatzer asked.

'I'm going to tell about my relationship with both Kennedy brothers. Everybody has been calling, trying to get the story anyway – Winchell, Kilgallen. And it's clear to me now that the Kennedys got what they wanted out of me and then moved on.'

Slatzer was increasingly troubled by these threats. 'Say you do hold a press conference, Marilyn,' he said. 'What will you get out of it? Why bother?'

'I told you I want to hear it from him,' she replied. 'I want Bobby to end it himself.'

Monroe also told her friend Jeanne Carmen and Elizabeth Courtney, Jean Louis's head fitter, that she was planning to stage a press conference – though it's more likely she would have made her point through a series of carefully structured interviews with columnists. Publicists Rupert Allan and Pat Newcomb usually favoured one-on-one talks with the media.

Later that same day the actress began looking for Allan, who had just returned from Monaco. She left a message with his Beverly Hills answering service saying that she had 'very important business to discuss'.

She even asked Ralph Roberts to find Allan for her. 'Tell him this is very important,' she told Roberts.

'Ralph reached me,' Allan rememberd. 'But I had jet lag after the flight from France and a bad case of bronchitis I had picked up in Monaco. I knew if I spoke one word to Marilyn, she would insist on coming over with chicken soup and aspirin. And I was really too sick for that.'

Allan soon found out that 'the very important business' Monroe wanted to discuss was a press conference of some sort concerning the Kennedys. 'I don't know how I would have handled that,' he said in an interview. 'Of course, I was angry and saddened by the way the Kennedys had treated her, but I think I could have talked her out of making it public knowledge. In my opinion, it would have badly hurt her career.'

The actress also called Elizabeth Courtney, saying she needed help finding 'a dressy suit' for a special occasion. She had already ordered an evening gown that was to be fitted the following Monday morning.

Courtney promised to help, adding, 'If we can't find anything right, Jean could work up something rather quickly.'

Even Slatzer doesn't know today whether Monroe would have gone through with the press conference. 'She felt like a spurned woman and that she had been deliberately used,' he said.

If Monroe had told her story to the media, she would have given the scoop to her old friend and protector, columnist Sydney Skolsky. Skolsky was already so alarmed by her confidences about the Kennedys that he had his daughter, Steffi, listen in on an extension whenever Monroe went into one of her 'Bobby and Jack soliloquies'.

Later, Lawford bore the brunt of another vitriolic attack when Monroe called to say that she had 'highly incriminating tapes of herself and Bobby' – tapes she intended to play 'if I have to'.

To defuse this time bomb, Lawford pleaded with her to go to dinner with him at La Scala. With a considerable show of poutiness, she allowed herself to be persuaded.

Two days after Monroe's death, Rupert Allan was told by a maître d' that she and Bobby Kennedy had been seen arguing at a back table at La Scala. Saddened by his friend's death and eager to place blame, Allan went to considerable trouble to track down the rumour. 'My friend at La Scala proved to my satisfaction that Marilyn met Bobby there Friday night,' he said.

The Attorney General, having received Monroe's increasingly strident messages at the St. Francis Hotel and the others from Hyannis Port, may have flown down to Hollywood to make a quick nonaggression pact with her. Since he was in San Francisco very early the next morning, he must have flown back to Northern California immediately after dinner. By jet, San Francisco was only a forty-five minute flight from Los Angeles.

Asked about that possibility, Peter Lawford later said, 'That's ridiculous.'

'I tell you he was there,' said Rupert Allan. 'I don't know

how they worked out all the logistics, but he was there.'

If so, Bobby may have tried the wine-and-candlelight approach to ease Monroe out of the picture. Failing this, however, he would have had no compunction about getting rough.

The Bobby Kennedy Monroe knew was not the mellow 'champion of the little guy' he became after his brother's assassination. She didn't know the passionate civil rights advocate of the 1968 presidential campaign. He wouldn't play any of those roles for several more years. In 1962, he was the ruthless troubleshooter of a family that could kick up plenty of trouble. Old Joseph Kennedy once said, 'Bobby's my boy; when Bobby hates you, you stay hated.'

'Bobby always spoke in commands and would use any means to get what he wanted,' said Thomas C. Reeves, one of John Kennedy's most recent biographers.

When Bobby uncovered some minor indiscretions on the part of Ed McCormack, Teddy Kennedy's senatorial opponent, McCormack asked him why he was fighting so dirty. 'This is an election you will win hands down, so why bother?'

Bobby answered, 'We're doing it because we *can*!'

In fact, the first family test that Bobby Kennedy ever failed was the Marilyn Monroe mission. He was sent to California to end the connection and instead became enamoured of the screen goddess. His error wasn't falling in love; his error was his failure to silence her.

Kennedy supporters often joked that Bobby would amputate his own arm if the family demanded it. How far would he go to silence Monroe?

– Chapter 34 –

The Silencers

On Saturday afternoon, August 4, a Fox security guard squinted through the morning fog to catch a glimpse of the huge government helicopter that hung in the sky above the studio. Waving a fluorescent orange flashlight, the guard directed the chopper towards some hastily drawn landing marks. The whirring of the blades echoed off the soundstage walls on the empty lot.

Once the helicopter was safely settled near Shirley Temple's old house from *The Little Colonel*, the guard jumped into his golf cart and headed back to the main gates. The chopper had been approved to land at just after 11 A.M., as duly noted in the studio's security log. A dark grey limousine was parked to the side, its driver standing at attention.

Studio publicist Frank Neill, whose office was near the landing pad, wasn't surprised to see the familiar figure of Bobby Kennedy leap from the helicopter and dash to the limousine. Neill was working with the Attorney General on publicity for *The Enemy Within*.

Neill later noted that Kennedy was preoccupied, gazing from side to side before sliding into the backseat. Through the open door, Neill caught a glimpse of the carefully tanned face of Peter Lawford.

The publicist and two baffled security guards were the only official witnesses to Kennedy's arrival in Los Angeles on that historic morning.

The limousine rumbled across the speed bumps at the security gates and swept down Pico Boulevard towards Santa Monica Beach.

'Although Bobby hesitated at first, he reluctantly agreed to see Marilyn,' said C. David Heymann, Jacqueline Kennedy's biographer. 'He flew to Los Angeles, and took the chopper from the airport to the Fox lot.'

Monroe was waiting in Brentwood with a buffet of Mexican food – guacamole, stuffed mushrooms, spicy meatballs – and her ritual Dom Pérignon.

Robert Kennedy had changed in the six weeks since he had been smitten by Monroe on the night of his brother's birthday party. A Twentieth Century-Fox newsreel summed it up just days earlier: 'Robert Kennedy is now looking as *presidential* as his brother.'

Among America's younger set, Bobby was on his way to becoming a legend. He had developed a national following among many of the same teenagers who worshipped James Dean. As he drove in and out of the White House gates in his spiffy blue convertible, girls begged for autographs. Fan letters poured in from adoring women. Strangers crowded around to shake his hand.

Newspaper reporters had quit using the 'brother of the President' tag line to describe him. *Esquire* magazine wrote, 'Bobby's own image was now so bright that people would sometimes mistake Jack for Bobby and rush up to congratulate him on his war against the Mob.'

In June, Bobby was named 'Father of the Year', focusing an intense glare of publicity on what was described as 'his Norman Rockwell family life'. The wire services ran photos of Ethel, Bobby and the children cavorting at Hickory Hill. An *Esquire* reporter was told, 'If you're writing anything about Bobby, you've got to meet Ethel. She's as responsible for his success as he is.'

Suddenly Bobby had a lot more to lose than the reputation of his dynasty. His own political future was at stake.

Other witnesses verified his presence in Los Angeles that day. The Los Angeles police chief at that time, William Parker, told Mayor Sam Yorty that Kennedy arrived by helicopter some time in the morning.

Considering the secrecy of his visit, the Attorney General couldn't have landed at his usual place – on the white sand in front of the Lawford mansion. On this scorchingly hot Saturday, fifty thousand sunbathers were packed onto the stretches of beach that surrounded the informal Western White House.

Most logically, Kennedy would have been driven west on Pico Boulevard to the breaking waves of the Pacific, then along the Pacific Coast Highway to the Lawford compound. Several neighbours saw him there in midafternoon. By the summer of 1962, however, a Kennedy sighting was of relatively little interest to the neighbourhood. In fact, the residents of the Santa Monica Gold Coast had become Kennedy jaded.

'It was Bobby all right,' said next-door neighbour Ward Wood. 'He was in khakis and a white shirt open at the neck.' Wood placed the time of Kennedy's arrival at midafternoon.

Other evidence places the Attorney General in Los Angeles that afternoon and for at least part of the evening. In interviews for this book, both former Los Angeles mayor Yorty and ex-police chief Tom Reddin, who followed Parker as police chief, said that they had seen confidential police reports on Bobby's movements that afternoon. 'What I saw in the intelligence reports absolutely proved to my satisfaction that he was here and that he probably saw Marilyn Monroe,' said Reddin. 'It is a riddle, isn't it?'

Louella Parsons, the top Hearst columnist, spent weeks

digging out the truth after Monroe's death. 'Bobby was here,' agreed Parsons's assistant, Dorothy Manners, who later took over Parsons's column.

Reddin, who was passionate about unsolved murders, read reams of classified documents on the Monroe case while he was police chief and had many discussions with William Parker, the police chief at the time of Monroe's death. 'On the basis of all the cumulative evidence I have seen,' Reddin said, 'both Bobby and Jack not only had relationships with Monroe, but Bobby was here that final day on some sort of mission.'

Is there a possibility that the Attorney General wasn't in town? Reddin shook his head and said, 'Chief Parker was close to the Kennedys and a friend of mine. He never would have lied to me.'

Before Kennedy took the extraordinary and dangerous trip to Los Angeles, he apparently realised the danger he ran from cutting Monroe off so brusquely. He made several attempts to calm her rage via long-distance telephone.

But a phone call wasn't likely to placate her. Like Kennedy, Monroe had changed drastically since the gala. When Fox realised that she couldn't be replaced and eagerly negotiated the terms of her return, she felt a new sense of power.

Twenty-four hours earlier, on Friday morning, Broadway composer Jule Styne had called from New York to offer her the starring role in a musical version of *A Tree Grows in Brooklyn*. Backers had already put up $1 million on Monroe's name alone. An $11-million film offer from Italy was equally flattering, since the leading lights of Italian cinema had offered her the right to select her own scripts, directors and costars.

Her bouts of insomnia had lessened. But these promising developments didn't relieve the 'quiet as a mouse' regime in the Brentwood house, which was geared, as ever, to the uncertain rhythm of the owner's sleep patterns.

Monroe had been up for hours when Eunice Murray and Pat Newcomb, who had spent the night, finally stirred at 9

A.M. Leaning against the kitchen wall in a terrycloth bathrobe, Monroe became cross with Newcomb before the publicist had said a word to her.

'I had been able to sleep all night, and Marilyn hadn't. While I had my door closed, sleeping, Marilyn wandered through the house,' Newcomb said. 'When I came out looking refreshed, it made her furious.'

The two combatants – whom Murray described as 'close as two adolescent girls' – patched up their quarrel just before Monroe received two phone calls. At 11 A.M., they began arguing again – apparently over those calls.

'Marilyn had calls that morning, and by the time I saw her she was in a rage,' Newcomb said.

The calls were undoubtedly from Lawford and Bobby Kennedy, in that order – with Kennedy strongly fighting against a trip to Los Angeles.

In his testimony before the Suicide Prevention Team after Monroe died, Ralph Greenson said, 'She recently had sexual relationships with extremely important men in government, men who were at the highest level. She was unhappy because, once again, she was alone on Saturday night.'

'Marilyn was expecting to see one of these men that night,' Suicide Investigation Team member Norman Tabachnick later recalled. 'Then she heard that the meeting was off.'

Monroe was angry, tired and vengeful on Saturday morning. She was not a woman to be trifled with.

She spoke briefly to photographer Larry Schiller about a *Playboy* layout, set up a fitting with Jean Louis for Monday morning, agreed to meet with Gene Kelly about *What a Way to Go* on Monday afternoon, and firmed up plans for ten days in New York. Because of her sleepless night, she moved through the day in a daze.

A series of disturbing calls on Friday night and early Saturday morning had kept her awake. They also kept her mind focused on Bobby Kennedy's betrayal. The first came at 11 P.M. on Friday. Marilyn answered drowsily.

A female voice screamed at her, 'Leave Bobby alone, you tramp! Leave Bobby alone!' Then the woman hung up.

A second call came at 12:45 A.M. It was the same woman. 'You'll be sorry if you ever see Bobby Kennedy again!'

The calls continued intermittently until 5:30 A.M.

'I don't think it was Ethel Kennedy,' Monroe told her friend Jeanne Carmen. 'But I think she had something to do with it.'

If Monroe had been angry before the phone calls, she was furious after them.

'She was capable of great rages when she was cornered,' said Slatzer. 'Anger was a rare emotion for Marilyn, but when she did get angry, almost anything could happen.'

But more than anger or rage shaped the events that occurred on that sultry afternoon in the house on Fifth Helena Drive.

The story of Monroe's last afternoon has come down to us in a series of glimpses, fragments of conversation, murky, unreliable confessions, and inept police work.

It seems certain that Bobby Kennedy, alone or with his brother-in-law Peter Lawford, drove to Monroe's house to quash the impending scandal that had alarmed the Hyannis Port contingency.*

'It was apparent to Bobby and Lawford that Marilyn had already downed quite a bit of champagne by the time they arrived,' said a Jacqueline Kennedy biographer, C. David Heymann. 'Lawford poured himself a glass and went out to the swimming pool so Bobby [and Marilyn] could talk.

---

*Apparently to protect himself, Bobby submitted an exhaustive report on his weekend to the FBI. And he willingly met with agents, describing, in great detail, his weekend at the ranch of attorney John Bates. The FBI also interviewed Bates and Bobby's aide, Ed Guthman. What makes this report so suspicious is its lack of censorship. It is virtually the only uncensored document in the bureau's voluminous file on Bobby Kennedy.

Within minutes, he heard shouting. Bobby said he was going back to Peter's, and Marilyn insisted he had promised to spend the afternoon with her.'

Sound recordings of that visit probably exist somewhere in the vaults of the Secret Service, the CIA or the FBI. J. Edgar Hoover was said to have made a copy for his own secret files, and apparently listened to it regularly.

What would these tapes tell us, if we could hear them?

According to Hollywood detective Fred Otash and writer Ray Strait, who claimed to have heard them, the tapes revealed a running quarrel between Monroe and Kennedy as they moved from room to room and topic to topic. 'I feel used,' Monroe supposedly cried at one point.

One government source told reporters for ABC's *20/20* that Monroe confronted Kennedy with 'his promise to marry her that weekend'.

Fred Otash, who was allegedly paid by the Mafia to bug Monroe's home and thereby gain evidence to be used against the Kennedys, put it more succinctly: 'The conversations were strident,' he said. 'Marilyn and Bobby had a very violent argument and she told him, "I feel used, I feel passed around." '

Then, said Otash, 'Marilyn ordered the Attorney General out of her house.'

Later the tapes supposedly recorded a call from Monroe to Kennedy, who was still at the Lawfords' beach house. Again, according to Otash, Monroe screamed, 'Don't bother me. Leave me alone.'

During the taping of the *20/20* segment on her death, which ABC later decided not to air, the following exchange occurred:

20/20: Did these tapes confirm that Bobby Kennedy
and Marilyn Monroe had an affair?
Otash: Of course.

20/20: Were the tapes running at the time of her death?
Otash: Of course.

Apparently Otash had already decided to withhold information about that portion of the tapes involving the actress's death.

But according to a source for this book who is in organised crime, somebody – either Kennedy or Secret Service agents – had already found the bugs in Monroe's house and pulled the wires.

Lawford's biographer, James Spada, said that Kennedy was frantically searching the house for any sign of a wiretap during his arguments with Monroe.

After the visit, Monroe was so distraught that she summoned Greenson for a ninety-minute session – which may or may not have involved an injection similar to that given to her by Dr. Engleberg on Friday afternoon. By 5:30 P.M., Greenson left Monroe with Eunice Murray and drove home. Monroe talked on the phone to Joe DiMaggio, Jr., Sydney Guilaroff and Jeanne Carmen – none of whom noticed that she was depressed or under the influence of drugs.

But the world's most beautiful woman *was* home alone on a Saturday night.*

Or was she?

---

*Many people believe that Bobby Kennedy returned just before dark – this time with a physician – perhaps to calm Monroe down.

In a taped interview with Robert Slatzer, a neighbour named Elizabeth Pollard said that the Attorney General and another well-dressed man came to the house some time *late* in the afternoon. Women at a card party were able to see the man from an upstairs window. One of them, referring to Kennedy, said, 'Look, girls, there he is *again*.'

Chapter 35

Dirty Business

Arthur Jacobs leaned back in his seat and looked up at the sickle moon hanging over the Hollywood Bowl. He sipped champagne with his fiancée, actress Natalie Trundy, and let the music drift over him.

Henry Mancini held the baton, guiding the orchestra through a lush medley of his movie hits. Chinese lanterns stretched up the foothills like giant fireflies. It was a perfect evening.

Then Jacobs caught sight of a uniformed page moving up the steps to his box. The boy leaned down next to the impeccably dressed publicist.

'Mr. Jacobs,' he said, 'We've got an urgent call for you backstage. They say it's an emergency.'

Jacobs jumped up, kissed his fiancée, and followed the usher's flashlight to the dressing rooms beneath the orchestra pit. He felt weak as he listened to the message from an unidentified caller – almost certainly a Fox publicity executive.

Then he bounded back up the steps and whispered to Trundy, 'This is serious. Marilyn is dead! I may be gone for quite a while, but I'll call you as soon as I can.' It was just after 10:30 P.M. on Saturday, August 4.

Six miles across town, the beach entrance to the Lawford mansion stood open, throwing beams of light across the sand. It was a hot, still night, and windows in the colony of million-aires on the Santa Monica Gold Coast remained open.

Most residents heard the groaning engine of the blue helicopter and saw the sandstorm it kicked up. An athletic young man, his hair tousled and his shirtsleeves rolled up, leaped into the helicopter and it headed off in the direction of Los Angeles International Airport, less than five miles away.

In West Los Angeles, Twentieth Century-Fox publicist Frank Neill was watching television when his call came. He listened for some minutes before pulling on a business suit and racing towards Brentwood.

In downtown Santa Monica, two federal agents and a Los Angeles police intelligence detective invaded the headquarters of General Telephone and approached the night supervisor. Within minutes, these 'men in dark suits', as the supervisor described them to reporter Florabel Muir, stalked out the door and jumped into a car with U.S. Government licence plates. They carried a sealed envelope containing the original toll call records for both of Monroe's telephones. This effectively wiped out all her telephone records for the previous six weeks.

Some time during this extraordinary sequence of events, Peter Levathes received a panicked request from Fox publicist Frank Neill that Twentieth Century-Fox security guards be rushed to the house on Fifth Helena Drive.

Perhaps the most sinister sign that Monroe was in serious trouble – or already dead – was the emergency call to Jacobs, whose powerful agency had been retained by both Monroe and Fox to help publicise the resumption of filming on *Something's Got to Give*.

Less than half an hour later, Los Angeles Police Chief William Parker was pulled from his bed by a call relayed through the main police switchboard downtown. Parker in turn called members of his new intelligence squad to attend a meeting at 7 A.M. the next morning.

All these forces were in play before 11:30 P.M. Saturday night. Then there was silence for five hours.

Shortly before midnight, Los Angeles slumbered under a stultifying heat wave. The air above the Pacific Ocean was still, allowing the hot desert winds to be sucked into the Los Angeles basin. Brentwood, which normally murmured with the sounds of ocean breezes in its towering trees, was so quiet that the barking of dogs penetrated the open windows. Traffic was almost nonexistent. 'It was so quiet and so still that it made your skin crawl,' Eunice Murray would later remember.

As Saturday slowly passed into Sunday, cars crept up and down tiny Fifth Helena Drive with their headlights off. The people moving in and out of Monroe's white gates walked softly and spoke in whispers.

First 1 A.M. swept by; then 2 A.M.; then 3 A.M. Unknown agents and publicists broke into Monroe's file cabinets and carried away all papers related to Fox. Three drawers of the cabinet were full on Saturday but empty Sunday morning. Hazel Washington later saw some of these letters being burned.

No one in the densely populated neighbourhood heard a sound.

The first call from the house on Fifth Helena to the outside world came five hours after Arthur Jacobs was called away from the Hollywood Bowl.

Police sergeant Jack Clemmons was on watch at the West Los Angeles substation, less than three miles from Monroe's house. It was a slow night, and Clemmons had his feet propped up on the desk. At 4.25 A.M., the telephone rang. 'West Los Angeles, Sergeant Clemmons,' he said.

At first the man on the phone was so agitated that Clemmons couldn't understand him. He was talking very fast and seemed to have a European accent.

'Slow down,' the sergeant ordered.

'Marilyn Monroe is dead,' the caller said. 'She just committed suicide.'

Now the man had Clemmons's full attention. 'Who is this?'

'I'm Dr. Ralph Greenson, Miss Monroe's psychiatrist.'

'Give me the address,' Clemmons said. 'I'll be right over.'

The sergeant's mind raced. If this call was on the level, a hell of a mess was about to begin. If it wasn't, somebody was in real trouble.

Surfers, raucous in their 'woody' station wagons and jazzed-up coupes, were already zooming through the darkness to the breakers. They dodged around Clemmons's squad car with Beach Boys' medleys blaring from their radios. It promised to be a glittering day at the beach, and the sandy coast near Malibu would shortly be full of life.

Sergeant Clemmons drove down San Vicente Boulevard, turned on Carmelita Drive and entered the short cul-de-sac known as Fifth Helena.

The small private road was surprisingly empty of cars. There was no light at all at Monroe's house. The porch and garage were dark and even the pool lights had been doused.

Clemmons nosed his squad car into the circular driveway. The calls from his police radio blared out in the silence.

He knocked gently on the door and gazed at the modest house, which somehow didn't seem a fitting residence for Marilyn Monroe. He knocked again. He could hear scurrying inside and what seemed like whispered conversations. A good minute or so later, the diminutive Eunice Murray opened the door. She was visibly shaken. As he followed her through the living room and down the hall, he realised that the housekeeper wasn't merely nervous; she was afraid.

'She seemed dishonest right from the beginning,' Clemmons remembered years later. 'I couldn't put my finger on what was wrong – not at first.'

She led Clemmons to the bedroom and gestured towards Monroe's bed.

'She was lying face down in what I call the soldier's position. Her face was in a pillow; her hands were by her side and her legs were stretched out perfectly straight.'

Clemmons thought to himself, 'She must have been placed that way. Nobody dies like that.'

He finally addressed the two doctors who were standing side by side in the hall. 'Was this body moved?' he asked.

Both men shook their heads.

The policeman looked at the two physicians – the tall, distinguished Hyman Engleberg and the short, dynamic Ralph Greenson. 'Liars, both of them,' he thought. Monroe had not died in that position.

The sheet had been pulled up over her head, leaving only a shock of pillow-white hair showing.

'She committed suicide,' volunteered Greenson, gesturing towards a bedside table full of vials and bottles, a veritable pharmacopoeia.

'Did you try to revive her?' Clemmons asked.

'No, it was too late; we got here too late,' said Greenson.

'That was the most obviously staged death scene I have ever seen,' said Clemmons. 'The pill bottles had been arranged in neat order and the body deliberately positioned. It all looked too tidy.'

The sergeant stood in the middle of Monroe's bedroom and looked long and hard at Ralph Greenson. 'Do you know when she took the pills?'

Greenson answered, 'No.'

'I strongly disliked Greenson's attitude,' Clemmons remembered. 'He was cocky, almost challenging me to accuse him of something.'

Then the sergeant turned to question Murray and saw that she had slipped away. He wandered through the house and finally discovered her in a room off the kitchen – where both the washer and dryer were running. She had already washed one complete load and was doing a second. A third load of linens had been folded and put on a counter. Clemmons realised that she must have been washing for several hours.

He began questioning her as she stood folding towels next to the washer. 'When was she discovered?' he asked.

'Just after midnight,' she said – somewhat tentatively. She also volunteered that Greenson had been there since 12:30 A.M.

Clemmons walked back to the bedroom to confront Greenson. 'I asked Dr. Greenson what had taken him three hours to call us.'

Greenson answered defiantly, 'We had to get the permission from the studio publicity department before we could call anyone.'

'The publicity department?' Clemmons asked.

'Yes, from Twentieth Century-Fox. Miss Monroe is making a picture there,' the analyst answered. Actually he might have put it another way. Not only had he called the studio publicity department, he had waited until the department's work was done before calling the police.

The heavy hand of Twentieth Century-Fox was everywhere: a sheath of studio documents on Monroe's coffee table had vanished; the notes Pat Newcomb had made of Monroe's meeting with Levathes were gone, as were all studio documents from the actress's personal file cabinet. Murray noted later that letters and memos and even phone messages had been spirited away.

But the Fox operatives were only a few of the shadowy figures who rifled the house that evening.

Clemmons, still angry after thirty years, stands by his statement to the press on that Sunday morning: 'Marilyn Monroe didn't commit suicide; she was murdered.'

Columnist James Bacon, the first reporter on the scene, lamented later that 'none of us knows what happened in the period between when she was discovered and when the ambulances were called. Because of what happened during that time, I don't think we will ever know precisely how Marilyn Monroe died.'

– Chapter 36 –

The Morning After

August 5, 1962, dawned spectacularly on the white sands of Santa Monica beach. Since 6 A.M., a Top 40 radio station had been broadcasting live from the sand, blasting rock and roll from a kiosk about five hundred yards from the Lawford house. Songs by Bobby Darin, Elvis Presley and Del Shannon echoed through the beach community.

Teenagers from Bel Air, Westwood and Beverly Hills had already settled into the 'in spots' on the beach, and gaily coloured umbrellas and legions of beach chairs spread across the dunes.

Suddenly the disc jockey interrupted a song and replaced it with the soft, outdated sound of Ray Anthony's 1953 tribute to Marilyn Monroe.

After a few seconds of silence, the jockey, in tennis shorts and Hawaiian shirt, broke the news: 'Marilyn Monroe is dead of suicide at age thirty-six. We grasp at straws as if knowing how she died will bring her back. Not since Jean Harlow have the standards of feminine beauty been so embodied in one woman. Marilyn Monroe; dead at thirty-six.'

For a while, the volleyball game slowed down. Some of the surfer girls had moist eyes. Many of them had copied the star's whiteout hairdo and her heavily structured makeup.

For the first time since the Bel Air fire in 1961, the *Los Angeles Herald* and the *Los Angeles Times* put out extra editions and rushed them to the newspaper racks. The beachcombers pooled their dimes to snatch up the special editions.

In huge black banner headlines, the message on the front page of the *Los Angeles Times* was simple: 'MARILYN, DEAD.' Just those two words in eighty-six-point type.

Nearby in the lush mansions of the rich, shock set in. Marilyn Monroe had been such a fixture on the Gold Coast during the Kennedy years that people were stunned. All eyes turned to the Lawford villa, where the curtains were still drawn. Surprisingly for this time of year, even the shutters on the huge picture windows were closed.

Inside, already half drunk on Bloody Marys, Peter Lawford was confronting friends, family and his own badly shaken conscience.

The first to get through to him on the phone was his mother, Lady May Lawford, the notorious 'Lady L', a leader of the British expatriate community in Los Angeles. She had just finished a long conversation with one of her son's next-door neighbours. 'I already knew that a dark helicopter, like the one the Kennedy boys used, had been parked on the beach,' she said in an interview. 'And I knew that neighbours saw Bobby dashing in and out on Saturday'.

'Why the hell didn't you go over to Marilyn's house when she called you?' she demanded of her son, having by this time heard news reports that Lawford had been the last person to speak to Monroe.

'I called her lawyer instead,' Lawford explained.

'How could you be so unfeeling when that girl's life was at stake?' Lady Lawford continued. When her son tried to explain his actions, she hung up on him.

'I felt Peter was awfully mean to Marilyn,' Lady Lawford recalled before her death in the late 1980s. 'After all, on the evening she died, she had called him on the phone and said good-bye to everyone there at his beach house. When I reached him on Saturday night, I heard the awful Boston accent of Bobby Kennedy. I wasn't surprised – Bobby was in and out all summer.'

Shortly after, a distraught Rupert Allan called, also seeking an explanation. 'At first he made no sense at all, and could barely talk between his sobs.'

Allan finally raged at him, 'What the hell happened last night? Were you really the last person to talk to her?'

'I think so,' said Lawford, continuing to cry.

'What happened? Can you explain it to me?' Allan demanded.

The normally voluble British actor offered Allan the same story he would repeat again and again over the years. His version rarely varied – not even when he gave the *Los Angeles Times* a tearful account four weeks before he died in 1982.

This, more or less, is the Lawford story:

Early Saturday afternoon, Lawford invited Monroe for an informal barbecue – set for 8 P.M. at the beach house. Supposedly, the star expressed interest and agreed that Lawford's friends, the Joseph Naars, could pick her up.

Then Lawford said he called Brentwood again and found Monroe in a morose state, refusing to attend. 'I could hear her depression; her speech was slurred.'

Monroe called again after 8 P.M., when most of the guests were there. 'She more or less told him she was at the end of her rope,' recalled Deputy Los Angeles District Attorney Mike Carroll, who grilled Lawford during the reinvestigation of the case in 1982.

Lawford also said that Monroe told him, 'Say good-bye to Pat, say good-bye to the President, and say good-bye to yourself, because you are a nice guy.'

Lawford called his agent, Milt Ebbins, who warned, 'You can't go over there, you are the President's brother-in-law.'

Ebbins then called Milton Rudin, who checked back with Eunice Murray. She supposedly assured him that nothing was wrong.

That, Lawford said, was the extent of his involvement.

Allan knew Lawford was lying. 'Marilyn would never have called Peter Lawford during an emergency,' he said. 'She hated him. Her only relationship was with Pat Kennedy Lawford, who Marilyn knew was at Hyannis Port.'

Nearly thirty years later, Allan shook his head sadly. 'Marilyn would only have called Peter Lawford if she were looking for Bobby Kennedy.'

To Allan, the master publicist, Lawford's story sounded as though it had been written for him by a public relations expert. It seemed more like an alibi than an actual event.

As further news bulletins dominated radio and television, and as friends called friends, heartsick members of Monroe's circle awakened to the most beautiful of summer days and the darkest of tragedies.

The morning sun had just begun to stream through the windows of Whitey Snyder's Malibu apartment when his phone rang.

'Are you awake, Dad?' said Snyder's son.

'I am now,' Snyder snapped.

'Have you heard?' his son asked.

Snyder sat up in bed. He knew instinctively what his son was about to say. 'Marilyn's dead, isn't she?' he asked.

His son answered, 'I'm sorry, Dad, really sorry.'

Snyder jumped out of bed and got dressed, only half believing that his friend was gone. He ran to his car and drove up the Pacific Coast Highway, past the Lawford mansion and up to the flatlands above.

'It hadn't sunk in,' he recalled. 'I wanted to see for myself. I wanted to know for sure.'

He drove down Fifth Helena Drive into media mayhem. Television news trucks, radio cars and clusters of paparazzi, some speaking French and Italian, all flooded together in a tide of rudeness.

Not much earlier, publicist Pat Newcomb had lost control and raged at them, 'You bloodsuckers! You vampires! You can't even let her die in peace, can you?'

Monroe's adored makeup man agreed. 'Bastards,' he thought as he crept through the crowd of cars in his Volkswagen. He tried to turn through the gates he had driven through so often. 'Sorry, buddy,' said a stern-faced policeman.

'But I'm Marilyn's makeup man,' Snyder explained. 'I need to come in.'

The policeman waved him off.

'I don't know what I was thinking,' Snyder recalled. 'Marilyn wasn't even there. I guess I had to see for myself that it had actually happened.'

On Snyder's car radio, United Press International was calling her death a suicide. 'Monroe died from a self-administered barbiturate overdose,' the bulletin said.

'No way,' Snyder thought. 'No damn way.'

He thought back ten years to the location shoot of *River of No Return*. ' [Marilyn and I] were riding in a locomotive of a narrow-gauge railroad, way out in the country,' he recalled. 'She was very upset over the DiMaggio dilemma. Joe wanted to take her away from the degrading, demeaning Hollywood life-style. He wanted to give her a family life: values, security, her own house. But Marilyn was afraid to leave her career – even though it brought her such turmoil.'

'I'd love to get off this train and just disappear,' she said, 'never to be heard from again.'

Snyder pointed towards the snow-covered mountains in the distance. 'Marilyn,' he said. 'Why don't you and Joe go up into the mountains, set up housekeeping, have some children and live there for the rest of your lives? You know, honey, Joe doesn't like the studio business either.'

The actress had tears in her eyes when she linked her arm in Snyder's. 'I know. I know what you're saying, Whitey, and I know you're right, but I just can't do this. I cannot run away from the stardom and the fame.'

Snyder shook off the memories and went home to fortify himself for what lay ahead. He had a big debt to repay – a bittersweet debt that would call on every bit of strength he had. Early in Monroe's career, just after she became a superstar, she had insisted on having Snyder promoted and designated by Fox as her personal makeup man. She saw to it that he received favoured treatment. And she made him a consultant on all of her independent productions. He had once asked her if there was a way he could repay her for all she had done.

'Whitey,' she said, looking him straight in the eye. 'When I die, don't you let anyone else touch my face. I want you to do that for me.'

So Snyder headed home to pack his makeup case.

Several minutes after he turned back to Malibu, Pat Newcomb was finally bundled into Eunice Murray's car by Greenson and Milton Rudin and driven through the gates into the swarming mob of reporters jammed into the small cul-de-sac. The reporters shoved their camera lenses against the car windows and thrust their microphones into Newcomb's face.

Still shaking and with tears running down her face, the publicist pleaded, 'Let us leave.'

A reporter from NBC News shouted one more question: 'How do you feel, Miss Newcomb?'

She looked him in the eye and said, almost in a whisper, 'When your best friend kills herself, how do you feel? What do you do?'

Stunned momentarily, the wave of reporters parted, allowing the car to pass through. Newcomb looked back over her shoulder, sobbing again.

Of all the players in this melodrama of Monroe's last hours, Pat Newcomb was the most mysterious. Because she was the only person to cry out in protest at the media circus, she soon became a controversial figure. Rumours swirled about her. It was said by journalist Frank Capell and hinted by a 1985 BBC documentary that she was a 'Kennedy plant' and that she was part of the coverup. Dozens of tabloid stories even suggested that she might have been present when Monroe died.

Actually, like Monroe's maid, Hazel Washington, Newcomb was little more than an innocent bystander who stumbled onto the scene too late to avert the tragedy.

She had been awakened at her Beverly Hills apartment by Milton Rudin at about 3.35 A.M. – an hour before Ralph Greenson called the police. She rushed out to Brentwood, where she was met by her boss, Arthur Jacobs. Though both were on the scene, they remained hidden from Sergeant Jack Clemmons. 'But I had the feeling that Newcomb, and others, were hiding,' Clemmons said later. 'It was just a sixth sense that I had.'

Eunice Murray described Newcomb's condition as 'hysterical'. Murray remembered, 'She wandered about the house for quite a while. In fact, the police had been ready to close the house for some time, but she wouldn't leave. They actually had to keep her out of the house.'

The housekeeper remarked that 'by the time [Newcomb] arrived, there were so many people in and out that she wasn't noticed'. In fact, Newcomb was on the phone most of the time – already dealing with the calls from reporters around the world. 'I talked to more than six hundred journalists on Sunday,' she recalled. 'It was my job to do what I could for Marilyn.'

The publicist remembered seeing 'more than five people on the scene when I arrived'.

By the time she left – at around 11 A.M. – the house was

swarming with people, including three Twentieth Century-Fox security guards, Arthur Jacobs, a General Telephone technician – who, inexplicably, was already disconnecting the phone lines – and reporters James Bacon and James A. Hudson of UPI.

Conspicuous amid this ragtag band were four men in dark slacks, white shirts and highly polished brogans. They were obviously representatives of the Secret Service or the FBI.

Shortly before noon, Hazel Washington and her husband, Rocky, a Los Angeles police detective, arrived to pick up a card table and chairs they had loaned to Monroe in February. They were told the house was being closed the next day. As Hazel Washington carted the furniture through the hall, she noticed one of the well-dressed men burning a pile of documents in the huge Mexican fireplace. The locks on Monroe's metal filing cabinet had already been smashed with a crowbar and the drawers rifled. Monroe's executors would have new locks installed ten days later, but the important documents – including all the studio papers – were already gone.

The maid paused for a second to watch the action around the fireplace. She noticed that Monroe's stenographic notebooks were already blazing, and that the legal papers related to her new $1-million Fox deal were sitting nearby. Also in the pile were several reel-to-reel tapes, parts of a datebook and a crumpled collection of loose pages in Monroe's handwriting.

Most significant were the stenographic notebooks. At the insistence of Peter Lawford, the actress had carried these pads on Air Force One as part of the 'secretary disguise' that she had assumed each time she met President Kennedy. What began as a subterfuge became a habit as Monroe began recording the political talk she overheard – from those who surrounded JFK and Bobby Kennedy. Though she didn't always understand what she heard, she had had ample opportunity to transcribe references to the Bay of Pigs, the plot to assassinate Castro, and Bobby's crackdown on the Mafia.

'She wrote all kinds of things on those pads,' said Evelyn Moriarity. 'It was her substitute for a diary.'

When Washington left, she noticed that the studio guards, dispatched by Fox chief Peter Levathes, now had full control of the house – giving Frank Neill and three other publicists an opportunity to purge Monroe's files of all documents related to the corporation. Among the missing documents were the originals and all copies of the verbatim notes taken by Newcomb during Monroe's 'reinstatement meeting' with Peter Levathes. After recording all the Fox promises from her hiding place in Monroe's bedroom, Newcomb had had the reports typed up and photocopied. After the burning, all that remained was an empty file folder labelled, '*Something's Got to Give*, July 1962'.

Four hours after Hazel Washington left with her furniture, federal agents, who had ordered a check on Rocky Washington's car, showed up at the couple's Baldwin Hills home demanding an interview. Rocky discouraged them, saying, 'She knows nothing.' The feds never returned to talk with Hazel.

Four hundred miles to the north, at 9 A.M. Mass in an antique Catholic church near Gilroy, California, Bobby Kennedy emerged into the brilliant sunshine and spoke to his press agent, Ed Guthman.

'Isn't it too bad about Marilyn Monroe?' Guthman said.

Guthman recalled, 'Bobby said, "Yeah, it's too bad." And we talked a little bit about it and that was that.'

In the Kennedy compound on the East Coast, family members were relaxing around the pool, where patriarch Joseph Kennedy was exercising, when the news of Monroe's death came over the radio. A complete and sobering silence fell over the gathering before family members slowly drifted away.

Pat Kennedy Lawford, according to her husband, collapsed from grief over the loss of her friend. A short time later, she rushed into her bungalow and started packing to fly back for the funeral.

Four miles from the Monroe house, in the towering pink mansion of another Fox movie star, Jayne Mansfield had a tearful, almost hysterical reaction to the news of Monroe's death. As Mansfield paced around her heart-shaped swimming pool, she pondered her own tenuous relationship with President Kennedy.

She grabbed the arm of her assistant, Ray Strait, and said, 'I may be next.'

'She was terrified of the Kennedys,' Strait recalled. 'She always believed they had something to do with Marilyn's death.'

Within hours, the media took over.

In the hurricane of telephone calls whirling around the globe, no reporter presumed to call the Kennedys. The connection between the movie goddess and the First Family would remain private.

Instead, the world's press was riveted on the single theme: 'It was Hollywood that killed Marilyn Monroe!'

Most reports agreed with Moscow's government newspaper, *Isvestia*, which declared, 'Hollywood gave birth to her and killed her.'

The Vatican's *L'Osservatore romano* declared her 'a victim of a mentality and a way of life of which she was forced to be the symbol. Her death transcends the limits of personal tragedy and acquires social reverberations.'

In the torrent of newsprint, a Stockholm newspaper, *Dagens Nyheter*, came closest to the truth. 'Marilyn was the victim of the glaring lights, the severe demands, the cracking whips, the cheers and the jeers and juggling in the big circus tent of the movies.'

While it's true that the movie industry took advantage of Monroe in a way that would be unthinkable for a star of her magnitude today, the studio system alone was not responsible for her death. Other, even larger, forces were at work.

Chapter 37

The Official Version

Arthur Jacobs was the consummate publicist, dedicated to detail and tireless in his attempts to seek out and impress every last reporter who covered Hollywood.

A graduate of the posh and private University of Southern California, Jacobs had risen from a job as a clerk in the Metro-Goldwyn-Mayer mail room to become head of a powerful public relations agency with offices in New York, Hollywood and London.

When he talked, people listened.

And he never talked more glibly or more impressively than in the forty-eight hours after Monroe's death. More than anyone else, he was the architect of the 'official version' of what happened in the small Spanish-style house in Brentwood on August 4, 1962.

When his wife, Natalie, later told the BBC in 1984 that Arthur had 'fudged the Marilyn Monroe story a bit', she was understating the case. Jacobs had put up a curtain of lies that concealed the real story of Monroe's last hours which held for two decades.

'It was carefully done and beautifully executed,' recalled Rupert Allan. Allan called a 'strategy meeting' on Sunday night in the Jacobs company offices on the Sunset Strip. Jacobs, Allan, Jacobs employee Michael Selsman and a delegate from the Kennedy family – 'a cousin or something', as Allan recalled it – hatched a sombre plan to keep the Kennedy name from being tainted by Monroe's death. Photographer Lawrence Schiller, who unwittingly stumbled in to pick up release forms for the nude swimming photos, remembers much shouting about how to 'keep the Kennedys out of it all'. Allan also believes that Peter Lawford had been there earlier in the afternoon to meet with Jacobs and present the Kennedy stance.

'It was decided to play up the "accidental death" scenario,' said Allan. 'But none of us believed it.'

Of course, the coverup was put into effect minutes after Monroe was pronounced dead. During the five hours – or more – between the time her body was discovered and the police were called, Twentieth Century-Fox publicists Frank Neill, John Campbell and Arthur Jacobs engaged in the wholesale destruction and removal of studio documents from her home. It was rumoured that Jacobs and Harry Brand, who talked to his men in Brentwood by phone, sought advice from Los Angeles Police Chief William Parker – the same man who destroyed all the police documents on Monroe's death, except for about seventy pages of heavily censored documents that would be released in the seventies.

'Honey, those agents burned documents in the fireplace,' recalled Hazel Washington.

'Indeed they did,' confirmed Evelyn Moriarity. 'No one knew precisely what was destroyed.'

By noon, when reporters were allowed to penetrate the wall of silence surrounding the scandal, the studio was ready with an obviously rehearsed version of Monroe's death.

It went like this: At 3:30 A.M., Eunice Murray noticed that Monroe's bedroom light was still on; the star didn't answer Murray's knocks on the door; Murray ran outside, looked through the window and saw Monroe on her bed 'looking strange'; she phoned Greenson in alarm; the psychiatrist arrived at 3:40 A.M., broke into the bedroom, and found his patient already dead; Dr. Engleberg was called and pronounced her dead at 4:00 A.M. A police spokesman also announced that no toll calls were made from GR(anite) 6-1890, Monroe's number.

All the early reports stated that Monroe committed suicide. When police first arrived, the first words out of Ralph Greenson's mouth were, 'We lost her; she committed suicide.' Police Chief Parker, in his earliest press statement, said, 'Marilyn Monroe accidentally took too many Nembutal capsules.'

Greenson, Parker and the Arthur Jacobs office explained that Monroe took a normal dose of sleeping pills and dozed off; she awakened a half hour later and took another dose; then a half hour later for another dose; and on and on as a lethal concentration built up in her system.

To the thousand reporters who called Fox and Jacobs in the three days after her death, the story was offered in a series of oral discussions – there were never any written press releases.

Through the decades, this story has showed remarkable tenacity. Most books and thousands of articles failed to challenge it. The job was done so well that it would be almost ten years before the Kennedy brothers were publicly linked with the scandal, and another ten years before major truths would emerge.

To quote television producer Ted Landreth, who produced the startling *Say Goodbye to the President – Marilyn Monroe and the Kennedys* for the BBC in 1986, 'Hollywood had the media story of the century – and missed it.'

But the morning after, several reporters chased after the story and made some spectacular finds.

First out of the gate, just after dawn on Sunday, August 5, was Florabel Muir, a crime reporter for the Hearst Corporation. After hearing reports of Monroe's death on the radio, she called her contacts at General Telephone, including a highly placed supervisor. 'Give me a rundown of Marilyn's phone calls for the last three days,' she said to the night supervisor.

'Can't do it,' the supervisor told her. 'The records are gone.'

'Who got them?' she asked.

'Federal agents, we think,' said the supervisor.

Veteran Hollywood reporter Joe Hyams was right behind her. Preparing a story for the *New York Herald Tribune*, he also sought the paper tapes (which recorded calls in those days) that contained a record of the star's most recent telephone calls. He was informed by sources at General Telephone that 'men in dark suits and well-shined shoes had confiscated them sometime before dawn.'

Unable to verify Monroe's calls to the far-flung Kennedys, both Hyams and Muir were stalled for the time being.

By Monday morning, August 6, when the actress was to have met with Rupert Allan to talk about exposing her affairs with the Kennedys, Jacobs' company was releasing its 'accidental suicide' version of her death. The press readily took up Jacobs's explanation, which most people still accept today.

Five days later, the Los Angeles County coroner determined the cause of death as 'the result of barbiturate poisoning, specifically of Nembutal and chloral hydrate.' After a further five days, the coroner finally released his verdict of 'probable suicide'. But some members of his department disagreed with that conclusion.

Police Chief William Parker, a close friend of both Robert and Ethel Kennedy, had been seeking the suicide verdict, apparently to protect the Attorney General. By August 10, he had turned the investigation over to his newly formed intelligence division. This meant that all details of Monroe's death were to remain secret permanently 'for reasons of security'.

While coroners, detectives and publicists tried to explain Monroe's death, Joe DiMaggio was planning his former wife's funeral. He made one thing clear: Hollywood was not to be included.

Of the twenty-four people invited to the small, sad ritual, DiMaggio was the only one whose name the public would have recognised. At the last minute, the legendary baseball star warned the funeral director, 'Make sure that none of those damned Kennedys come to the funeral.'

Also excluded was Frank Sinatra, who had been Monroe's staunchest ally during the last two years.

'I could understand those decisions,' said Rupert Allan. 'DiMaggio's marriage to Marilyn was ruined by the demands of her career. And he knew almost everything about her relationships with the Kennedys. He knew what they had done to her.'

But Pat Kennedy Lawford was already on her way from Hyannis Port, determined to represent her family at the funeral. She burst into tears when told that she specifically had been denied admittance to the tiny Westwood Memorial Park.

An initial finger of blame had been pointed towards the First Family. It would be more than two decades before the world finally understood DiMaggio's brusque treatment of the Kennedys.

Bit by bit, fact by fact, reporters began chipping away at a coverup that rivalled in every way the one that would surround the assassination of President Kennedy a year later in Dallas. Over the decades, books would be suppressed, magazine articles cancelled, witnesses sworn to secrecy and police reports hidden or destroyed. The power of a rich, proud family, the protective stand of a powerful film studio, and the secretiveness of the Los Angeles Police Department perpetuated the enigma of Monroe's death.

Chapter 38

Gag Rule

Shortly after dawn on Sunday, August 5, a woman ran from Monroe's house screaming, 'Murderers! Murderers! Are you satisfied now that you've killed her?'

Most reporters on the scene heard tales of this chilling event. Three neighbours actually heard it. In fact, it was the neighbourhood's only clue to the scandal hidden behind the star's white adobe walls.

The Hearst journalist Florabel Muir became obsessed with the incident. At first she thought the 'mystery woman' was Eunice Murray, hysterical over what she had witnessed. But Muir's four interviews with Murray convinced her that 'this lady is part of the coverup.'

Muir eventually suspected that the screaming woman was Pat Newcomb, who had stumbled onto what she believed was a murder scene when she arrived at 4:45 A.M. 'There had to be a reason why Newcomb was the last person called,' Muir said.

But Muir would never crack this case. The woman's identity is still a mystery.

This was the first time anyone used the word 'murder' to describe Monroe's death. The word wouldn't be used publicly in connection with the case for years to come.

From the outset, the Hollywood press corps covered the star's overdose as a 'soft story' – the sad suicide of a woman leading a life that was more than she could bear. In the meantime, clues to the murder were being erased day by day and key witnesses spirited away from Los Angeles one by one.

A week after the funeral, Muir led off her column with this cryptic item: 'Strange pressures are being forced on the Los Angeles Police Department. Sources close to the detectives on this case said that the pressures were mysterious and were apparently coming from persons who had been in close touch with Marilyn during the past few weeks.'

In New York, Dorothy Kilgallen told her editors that 'the last man to talk to Marilyn Monroe was America's Attorney General, but I don't have absolute proof.' She said her source was a photographer who was 'very, very close to the actress'.

Kilgallen went as far as she dared in a column published three days after Monroe's death.

'On Marilyn's last night, her plea for help was answered by a very powerful man. But the man let Marilyn slip away from him, which is probably what would have happened anyway with a little more time.'

A few months later, Kilgallen privately decided that Monroe had been murdered.

The Hollywood press corps, led by Hedda Hopper and Louella Parsons, heard strange stories of homicide and the Kennedy brothers. 'The rumours were there; the suspicions were there; but there was simply no proof. My mother tried for months to dig out the story, but, for once in her life, she couldn't,' said Harriet Parsons, Louella's daughter. 'It was very frustrating – the biggest story in Hollywood history and my mother couldn't even get close to it.'

As soon as the hysteria died down, Louella Parsons went after the two people she knew could tell her the truth – Peter Lawford and Pat Newcomb, both of whom she knew personally. But they had vanished. The fabulous Lawford beach house was temporarily closed up, and Newcombs' phone went unanswered. Parsons and her assistant, Dorothy Manners, finally learned they were at the Kennedy compound at Hyannis Port.

'All of my mother's calls went unanswered,' recalled Harriet. 'There was simply no one she could quote on the subject.'

The Monday after Monroe's death, not even police detectives could reach the President's brother-in-law. Lawford's Los Angeles office told them curtly, 'Mr. Lawford will not be back in town for some time. Leave your number and Mr. Lawford's secretary will try and work you in for an appointment later this year.'

Sergeant Robert Byron, who took over the Monroe case from Clemmons (by then it was a homicide case), tried to question Lawford, only to be repeatedly stonewalled. 'Mr. Lawford is unavailable because he has taken an airplane,' the actor's secretary told Byron. 'His exact destination is unknown at this time. But I will ask him to call you at his earliest convenience.'

As for Newcomb, who was crushed by her friend's death, she sealed herself off from the world – first in Hyannis Port and then on an extended tour of Europe.

Crusading right-wing journalist Frank Capell reported that the Kennedys had 'paid her off with this European jaunt'.

'It's true that I went back to the Kennedy compound,' Newcomb says today. 'Pat and Peter Lawford invited me; it was a rough time, but the Kennedys had nothing to do with my European trip. It was a business trip planned long before Marilyn's death.'

Hedda Hopper, who could play rougher than Parsons, had even less luck. Shortly after the Los Angeles Police Department closed the case – in a questionable move, only five days after Monroe's death – Hopper received a series of letters urging her to break the story of Monroe and the Kennedys.

One writer from Cape Cod, Massachusetts, wrote, 'You motion picture columnists do no credit to yourselves by shielding the Kennedys in the Monroe business. As you must know, Lawford is simply the fall guy for Robert and JFK. It was Bobby on the phone that night.'

However, Hopper lamented her lack of success. 'This has to be the most closely guarded secret in the history of this town, and that's saying a lot,' she told Rupert Allan.

Frustration soon overcame Hollywood's lightweight reporters, and they gave up the chase and settled on an accidental overdose as the cause of death. To make sure they got the point, Lawford later emerged from the Kennedy compound for a public-appearance tour. Granting exclusive interviews to handpicked journalists in New York, Boston and San Francisco, he said, 'I know that it was accidental. I know that the poor dear didn't mean to kill herself.' To bolster his point, Lawford told a convoluted story of Monroe's supposed overdose at Lake Tahoe the weekend before her death.

'The Lawford version' went out over the wire services and helped lay to rest many remaining doubts.

When the Los Angeles district attorney's office reinvestigated Monroe's death in 1982, detectives found that Lawford 'and the studio people' had been very busy rearranging the scene.

Fred Otash confessed that Lawford had called him at about 3 A.M., ninety minutes before Ralph Greenson called the police. Lawford asked the private eye to 'sweep the house of anything which would incriminate the President.'

Otash, who was paid by the Mafia to bug Lawford's house, along with Monroe's, quickly declined. ' [Lawford] was desperate because he realised he had only a few hours to finish the job,' Otash said later.

As precious minutes ticked by, minutes in which doctors might have been able to save Monroe, Lawford, who was hopelessly drunk, rushed to Brentwood the back way. When the actor left the house on Fifth Helena, a stash of tapes, notebooks and letters disappeared forever. 'Lawford took care of what he could,' said Los Angeles mayor Sam Yorty, a political power broker at the time. Yorty was one of the few who saw the full police report on Monroe's death.

'Peter was so enamoured of the Kennedy charisma that if Jack or Bobby asked him to, he would have done anything – legal or illegal. So it was with Marilyn's death – he had a major part in the coverup,' said his mother, Lady May Lawford. Some of the tapes stolen from Monroe's bedroom reportedly ended up in Bobby Kennedy's hands less than a week later. Hairdresser Mickey Song said the tapes were described in detail to him – by Kennedy.

Lawford's assignment must have been completed by mid-morning, because he called the President at the White House and was immediately put through to the Oval Office. When he hung up, he went to the airport and then to the Kennedy compound in Hyannis Port. Though withheld from the official presidential phone logs 'for reasons of national security', the record of the crucial call was uncovered by journalist Anthony Summers in September 1991 – automatically logged as part of a telephone security system.

Meanwhile, a parallel coverup was underway in the Los Angeles County coroner's office, where tissue samples – which could have proved how the drugs had been administered – were washed down the drain.

Deputy Coroner Thomas Noguchi, later to become world-famous as the coroner to the stars, had already decreed that Monroe died from 'barbiturate poisoning'. But he hadn't yet determined how the drugs had got into her system. Had she really gulped seventy pills in less than ten minutes? Or had she been given a massive injection?

Although he found no overt signs that she had received a shot, Noguchi also knew how hard it would have been to swallow that many pills. So he took careful tissue slices from her liver and kidneys and sent them upstairs to Chief Toxicologist Raymond Abernathy.

Two days later, when police detectives started to suggest that Monroe might have been murdered, Noguchi called for the test results. He was curtly informed by superiors that the samples had been discarded. An official memo said that 'further tests are unnecessary as the death has been declared to be a *suicide*.' Noguchi's carefully preserved tissue samples had been inexplicably discarded on orders of Chief Toxicologist Raymond Abernathy.

'That should never have happened,' said Deputy District Attorney John Miner. 'There should have been microscopic tests. I have no explanation for this.'

Fortunately for the conspirators, the press was asking few questions.

One reporter who tried to tell the truth was slapped down by his own editors. Ezra Goodman, Hollywood bureau chief for *Time* magazine, was coincidentally preparing a cover story on Monroe when she died.

Goodman plunged into the confusion surrounding her death and came up with a remarkable story linking the actress with the Kennedy administration. But no sooner had he filed it than top editors at *Time* not only killed the piece, but destroyed all copies of the article. According to sources at *Time*, editors thought Goodman's piece could have destroyed the President.

A rightly furious Goodman, who had written *The Fifty Year Decline and Fall of Hollywood*, converted his article into an outline for a comprehensive book about Monroe titled *Norma Jean Baker, a Venture into Mythology*. Macmillan Publishing, which paid an advance of $5,000, eventually refused to print the 356-page manuscript, which actually only alluded to the Kennedys. In all, fourteen publishers rejected it. At the time, a spokesman for Simon and Schuster told *Time*, 'This manuscript is dangerous.'

'I met a good many people I would much rather never

have met,' Goodman said at the time. 'Many of them were on the make and on the take. Marilyn Monroe knew many such people . . . nasty, mean, rotten, little people. And nasty, mean, rotten, *big* people, too.'

The publishing industry had effectively turned its back on the real Marilyn Monroe story. And despite the hints in *Photoplay* in 1968 it would be four years before another writer took up the challenge.

From 1962 to 1982, the FBI kept tabs on every word printed about Monroe's death. The secret file of clips, books, reviews and photos ran to thousands of entries.

In some cases, special agents were even deployed to study prospective articles and books while they were still in the galley stage. The clandestine readers prepared detailed critiques of the articles and books – particularly if they contained even a hint of Jack's or Bobby's flirtation with Monroe. Using the Freedom of Information Act and the private archives of Robert Slatzer, whose collection now numbers more than a million documents, we were able to read more than five hundred pages of this collection, which FBI director J. Edgar Hoover kept in a special filing cabinet in a locked 'safe room' – hidden behind a bookshelf.

Ostensibly, this unsavoury task gave Hoover great joy: phone logs at both the White House and the Justice Department show that he called frequently to discuss one gossip column or another.

Every time a reporter got too close, Hoover dispatched agents to look into the background of the author. In the late sixties, when Robert Slatzer was preparing to publish his study of Monroe's last six months and her strange revelations about the First Family, Hoover gleefully assembled details of Slatzer's background and quotes he had made over the years about the way Monroe died and filed them away. He never even questioned Slatzer.

Somehow Hoover got a copy of Slatzer's book, *The Strange*

Life and Curious Death of Marilyn Monroe, even before it was mailed to the nation's book reviewers.

Even after Monroe, JFK and RFK were dead, Hoover held onto his files, only turning them over to the press, one by one, in answer to Freedom of Information requests.

The book and magazine analyses by the Hoover agents even included an investigation of sources.

Dorothy Kilgallen eventually thought she knew enough about the liaison between Bobby and Monroe to publish. Yet, mysteriously, she never did; nor did Walter Winchell or Earl Wilson. Over the years, major articles on Monroe and the Kennedys were killed, in succession, by *Time*, *Esquire*, *Life* and *Modern Screen*.

In the late fall of 1962, Hoover decided to warn the Attorney General when he heard that *Photoplay* was ready to publish a lengthy article which FBI agents noted 'all but named Bobby Kennedy as Marilyn Monroe's lover'.

Even worse, said agent John de Loach, 'the writer implies that Bobby, whose name was not mentioned, was the last person to talk to Monroe before she died.' Indeed, the *Photoplay* article painted a remarkably accurate picture of the affair, using the old 'blind item' trick. 'The man who was involved with Marilyn had reached career heights which he never expected; and there were better things in store for him. And what better for his success than to have the world's most desirable sex symbol fall in love with him?'

Photoplay portrayed the mystery man as one who was 'free from scandal'. It continued, 'He also never before had been anything but totally devoted to his wife.'

The FBI analysts were most alarmed by a section in the article that said, 'Marilyn called this man the night before she died. The man said he could not leave his wife and could not see Miss Monroe any longer.'

Despite the advance warning, Bobby Kennedy told Hoover to back off. To kill the piece at that point would only attract unwanted attention to it. Columnist Sydney Skolsky learned of the story from a source in the FBI and shared it with Louella Parsons.

From that moment on, the FBI's 'Monroe containment squad' became even more vigilant, perusing radio bulletins, television specials, and the storm of books that eventually became a blizzard, starting in 1966 with Fred Lawrence Guiles's breakthrough biography, *Norma Jean*. Some of the FBI reports on these movie-star biographies went so deeply into their contents that they resembled Reader's Digest Condensed Books.

Hoover's concern about Robert Kennedy's reputation may well have been justified. Fourteen days after Monroe's death, FBI wiretaps picked up an underworld conference call, during which three mobsters threatened to release evidence about Monroe and the Attorney General. The three wiseguys were looking for a way to stop the feds from prosecuting them. The wiretaps recorded their proposed blackmail scheme.

'Would he like to see a headline about Marilyn Monroe?' asked one of the mobsters. 'He's been to Marilyn's house plenty of times, so this is obviously a major affair.'

If carried out, this blackmail scheme would have derailed Bobby Kennedy's political future. But shortly after the FBI wiretaps picked up the conversation among the mobsters, they were arrested on charges of racketeering – unrelated to the blackmail scheme – and hauled off to prison.

These threats and the flurry of 'blind item' magazine articles were little more than thorns in Bobby Kennedy's side.

A far more disturbing document was in the works.

A year after John Kennedy's assassination, when the Attorney General was seeking the Democratic nomination for vice president, a small book with a blood-red cover appeared across the country and was soon an underground best-seller with the movers and shakers of the Republican party. Titled *The Strange Death of Marilyn Monroe* and published by right-wing journalist Frank Capell, a dedicated foe of RFK, the book claimed that

Bobby was secretly a member of the Communist party. At first it was sold via mail order through a series of ads in conservative publications. Then Capell began making it available, in bulk, to political groups of any persuasion. Radio ads in ultraconservative Orange County, California, Phoenix and Indianapolis warned: 'Before you consider voting for Bobby Kennedy, learn the truth about him.'

Hoover obtained twenty-five copies of the book, which he turned over to his book reviewers. Even before the full reports were made, Hoover warned the Attorney General, 'This book will make reference to your alleged friendship with Miss Monroe and will state that you spoke with her last.'

The book was – and still is – remarkable for the amount of inside data Capell was able to uncover. Secret results from the Los Angeles Suicide Investigation Team's investigation of Monroe's death fill page after page. There are hotel bills proving that Bobby Kennedy was in town the week Monroe was hurried off to Lake Tahoe, bills from Dr. Ralph Greenson and Dr. Hyman Engleberg detailing all her visits, and an inventory of the drugs she ingested during the final weeks of her life.

This little red book circulated widely among journalists in both Hollywood and Washington. Earl Wilson and Hedda Hopper both had copies, as did powerful editors at the *Los Angeles Herald Examiner* and the *Los Angeles Times*. Despite the fact that Capell revealed most of the ingredients in the Monroe scandal – the same facts and figures which would later make Anthony Summers's *Goddess* a best-seller – no major reporter of the period wrote about it.

'You just did not report those sorts of things about an American President,' said Harriet Parsons. 'Mother just filed it away.'

When Ted Landreth polled the Washington press corps for the 1985 BBC documentary, he found that the political press operated on a self-imposed gag order as well. 'Everyone knew about the affairs, but nobody was willing to write about it,' Landreth said.

There was another explanation: Monroe's death was shrouded by one of the slickest media coverups in Hollywood history.

– Chapter 39 –

Conclusion

Early on the morning of August 5, 1962, two uniformed security guards from Twentieth Century-Fox stationed themselves at the front and back entrances to Monroe's house. An hour later, another studio guard took up a post at the enormous gates at the front of the estate.

Their faces were impassive, but their fingers lingered on their service revolvers, reminding everyone that serious Hollywood business was transpiring behind the thick adobe walls.

The press was kept at bay while Frank Neill, Arthur Jacobs, Eunice Murray and, at one point, Peter Lawford rifled through the disarray left behind by the world's most enigmatic film star.

Publicists, studio policemen and members of Monroe's personal staff, particularly Murray and Monroe's business manager, Inez Melson, poured thousands of prescription drugs down the toilet, removed the star's contracts and memos, and carted off armloads of personal belongings.

Clues that pointed to foul play vanished, probably carried away in the briefcases of lawyers and studio executives. Once cleaned up, the death scene indicated suicide. All Monroe's bed linen and personal laundry had already been washed, dried and put carefully into hall cupboards.

By sealing the crime scene, Fox was merely adhering to tradition. The studio's policy of sanitising real-life Hollywood murder scenes, unimaginable now, had been supported by City Hall since the era of the silent movie. In 1922, when director William Desmond Taylor was murdered in a swanky Hollywood bungalow, executives from Paramount Pictures swept the scene clear of love letters, drugs and even the pink step-ins left behind by Taylor's lover, Mary Miles Minter, a Paramount star. At first the executives tried to have Taylor's death classified as a suicide – even though the handsome director had been shot in the back. When they learned that the murderer was probably Minter's mother, Paramount pulled strings at police headquarters, making sure that the case was classified as an unsolved murder – which it is to this day.

In 1935, when Thelma Todd, the 'ice-cream blonde', was murdered by gang boss Lucky Luciano, employees of Paramount and the Santa Monica Homicide Squad carted away all the evidence. Todd's death was soon ruled 'accidental suicide' despite the evidence that a brutal beating had occurred.

Few believed the suicide theory. Since Todd supposedly died of carbon-monoxide poisoning in her garage – with one of the doors open, no less – the police should have been surprised that the ignition key was turned off. Several recent books, notably *Hot Toddy* by Andrea Edmonds, have proved that Luciano had Todd beaten to death, then locked in her garage. But the suicide ruling stands.

When Paul Bern, Jean Harlow's husband, was murdered by a former wife, MGM publicists told reporters his death was a suicide – in part to protect Harlow. They also created an alibi for the actress, who may or may not have been in the house at the time.

The murder of Marilyn Monroe had the best stage manager of all – Los Angeles Police Chief William Parker, the single most powerful man in the city.

From the very first, Parker classified Monroe's death as a

suicide, plain and simple. He told his force to investigate it as a suicide, and gave the coroner similar guidelines.

To make sure the point was made, he turned the case over to the new 'Suicide Investigation Team', which he knew by its definition could only determine *why* Monroe had killed herself. The team was not allowed to investigate *how* she had died.

It was a brilliant move. By giving the team a burst of publicity, Parker headed off an official inquest or a grand-jury hearing – which the case urgently demanded. An inquest would have forced Lawford, Newcomb, Murray and even Attorney General Robert Kennedy to testify under oath. Not only was Parker a friend of Bobby Kennedy, but they had worked together on the Attorney General's battle against organised crime. Some speculated that Parker would succeed J. Edgar Hoover as head of the FBI.

At the Justice Department Christmas party in 1961, Ethel Kennedy dropped a note into the department's suggestion box. It said, 'Chief Parker of Los Angeles for Director, signed Mrs. Robert F. Kennedy.' Hoover himself was obsessively focused on Bobby Kennedy and was always looking for dirt on the family. He even deployed agents to shadow the Attorney General during the last weekend of Monroe's life.

Parker was actively seeking the FBI job when Monroe was murdered. Perhaps to curry favour, he shut down the investigation into her death just five days later, officially ruling it a suicide.

The chief was fortunate that Twentieth Century-Fox was on his side. Without the elaborate studio conspiracy against Monroe – and its attendant publicity – his job would have been infinitely harder.

As it was, Fox had already labelled its errant star 'mentally ill' and 'suicidal' in a thousand newspaper articles. In the hundreds of accounts of Monroe's death, many reporters dutifully printed Harry Brand's fictional version of her firing from *Something's Got to Give*. Cukor's mean-spirited description of her supposed 'madness' was recycled dozens of times. Indeed, he restated it many times after her death.

When Peter Lawford embarked on his whistle-stop media tour – in which he was hell-bent on proving that Monroe had 'accidentally' swallowed too many pills – he seized again and again upon the circumstances surrounding *Something's Got to Give*.

In hindsight, it is clear that Monroe was the victim of two conspiracies during the last fourteen weeks of her life. In the first, a great film corporation made her the scapegoat for its multimillion-dollar maladies. To serve the studio's purposes, she had to be portrayed as an emotional wreck drifting towards madness.

And this conspiracy led directly to the second conspiracy – the coverup of *all* the circumstances surrounding her death.

After Fox publicists so successfully 'leaked' word of Monroe's so-called suicide attempt during the first week of filming, they found it that much easier to disguise the foul play leading to her death as 'self-inflicted'.

To this day, many of the old-timers at Fox deny that such a conspiracy existed. Some of them actually believe what they say.

But the nature of the plot was outlined in actor Dean Martin's countersuit filed in June 1962 in response to Fox's suit against him for $2.8 million. In part, Martin's suit stated that 'certain of the persons presently managing the affairs of Fox determined that they would circulate and publish to the national press, and the trade press of the entertainment industry, false, fraudulent and misleading statements concerning defendant Martin's position and that of Monroe, as well.'

The star's suit further claimed that Fox circulated those statements so that the studio 'could duck criticism from private stockholders over film investments'.

Martin contended that Monroe's dismissal from *Something's*

Got to Give had been political, and that she had been capable of completing the film. In mid-June 1962, his position was validated by a special investigative committee of the Screen Actors Guild. After the actor appeared before the session, SAG released this statement: 'In the opinion of the Guild Committee, Mr. Martin is being unduly criticised for a situation not of his making.'

Monroe's reinstatement in late July negated both lawsuits.

Publicity surrounding the countersuit did little to combat Fox's portrayal of Monroe as 'a suicide waiting to happen'.

Actually, the physiological framework on which the suicide ruling rested was false. And the coroner's office knew it at the time.

The chemistry just wasn't right. Monroe's blood contained 4.5 per cent barbiturates – namely, Nembutal. Toxicologist Raymond Abernathy found a lethal dose of Nembutal and an equally fatal dose of chloral hydrate in her system – enough drugs, Deputy Coroner Thomas Noguchi said, 'to kill three persons'.

Monroe couldn't have taken these massive doses orally. In the first place, she didn't have enough pills.

On August 3, the day before her death, Dr. Hyman Engleberg prescribed twenty-five 1.5-grain Nembutal capsules. According to Eunice Murray, Monroe took three of these capsules that same night. That left twenty-two. She had also been given a maintenance dose of Nembutal by Dr. Lee Siegel a week earlier. However, she had consumed most of those during her disastrous trip to Lake Tahoe.

Chief Parker noted that Monroe 'might have been secretly hoarding pills'. But Murray had searched the house a week earlier and found no stash of barbiturates. And Monroe had borrowed two Nembutals from her friend Jeanne Carmen shortly before she died. The police were so concerned about the source of the drugs in her system that they falsified Engleberg's prescription, doubling it, in a report to the coroner. Los Angeles detectives insisted the vial of Nembutal had contained fifty pills; instead, there were twenty-five.

These erroneous reports of a 'secret stash of narcotics' had their origins in the rumour that Monroe had imported a 'suitcase full of pills' from Mexico in February. However, all those capsules – and all the bottles Monroe had brought from New York – were confiscated by a UCLA psychiatrist who treated the actress when Ralph Greenson was in Europe. Monroe was left without a single sleeping pill.

When we asked a spokeswoman at Abbott Laboratories, the manufacturer of Nembutal, about the high percentage of drugs in Monroe's system, she at first said, 'That's just not possible.'

But if it was possible, we asked, how many capsules would she have had to take to reach that level?

The Abbott spokeswoman estimated that it might have taken seventy-five to ninety capsules. Two Abbott chemists told Robert Slatzer, 'It might have taken far more than ninety!'

Even the members of the district attorney's team which reinvestigated Marilyn Monroe's death in 1982 admitted, 'In an attempt to reconstruct the source of her pills, the various conflicting reports could not be resolved.'

Monroe's business manager, Inez Melson, who arrived at 5 A.M., found that 'dozens of pills', including Nembutal, were scattered across the night table. 'There were sleeping pills and sedatives of all kinds. Whoever had been there before us didn't take them, so we threw them all down the toilet.'

This crucial bit of evidence, ignored by the police and unknown to Deputy Coroner Thomas Noguchi, all but proves that the fatal dose was administered by injection or, as Noguchi suspects, by enema or suppository.

Of course, Inez Melson unwittingly destroyed the very evidence that would have proved the murder. Monroe would have needed each one of those pills found by Melson to achieve the level of barbiturates found in her system.

When the 'pill question' was first raised in 1962, detectives rushed to recover Monroe's medicine bottles, only to find they had been destroyed. 'It was technically against the law to dispose of that evidence,' said former Police Chief Thomas Reddin. Inexplicably, detectives found ten capsules left from a bottle of fifty chloral hydrate capsules – supposedly prescribed on July 31. If Monroe had been intent on killing herself, why would she leave ten capsules in the bottle? Besides, since she sometimes took four to six mild chloral hydrate capsules each night to conquer her insomnia, she had only a dozen chloral hydrates left. This number could not have accounted for the levels of the drug in her bloodstream.

The Los Angeles coroner's chemists estimated it would have taken fifty to seventy chloral hydrate capsules to achieve the toxic level in her bloodstream at the time of her death.

But counting pills is an academic exercise. Monroe died from the effects of one, maybe two, massive injections.

'A cursory examination of Monroe's kidneys found them to be clear of drugs,' said Deputy District Attorney John Miner, who investigated her death. 'This should have indicated that the stomach may have been bypassed. And the only way that could have happened was by injection.'

Realising the seriousness of this implication, Noguchi ordered the microscopic analysis of tissue taken from the small intestine – which could have settled the question. But the tissue sample had vanished – along with the pill bottles.

In addition, if Monroe had ingested a large number of pills, a clear residue should have remained in her stomach.

In 1964, one of the world's foremost forensic scientists, Dr. Keith Simpson of London University, reviewed the entire autopsy for biographer Anthony Summers. His conclusion: the barbiturate levels in her blood and liver should have produced a moderate amount of residue. Yet nothing was found.

Through the decades, Noguchi's findings have been misunderstood and misrepresented. In fact, he never said – or wrote – that Monroe died after 'taking fatal doses of sleeping pills'. From the first, he was sceptical. 'Marilyn Monroe would had to have gulped an enormous number of pills to have killed herself,' he was quoted as saying in the *Los Angeles Times*.

In boldface type on the preliminary report he cautioned, 'The liver, kidneys, stomach and its contents are saved for *further toxicological study.*'

Five days later, he complained to the the *Los Angeles Herald Examiner*, 'The lab technicians have not tested the organs I sent them – and this is disturbing since *the routine tests were not profound*,' meaning conclusive.

When he received no definitive answer, Noguchi called toxicologist Raymond Abernathy to ask where the organs were stored.

'I'm sorry, Tom. I disposed of them because we have closed the case.'

'We should have done those tests,' Noguchi concluded.

Since Monroe would have had to gulp down more than seventy capsules in less than ten minutes, death by an oral overdose seems unlikely. Further, the actress had a terrible time taking pills. Often she broke open the capsules and poured the powder into champagne. Peculiarly, detectives found no drinking glass in her locked bedroom.

The most likely argument against suicide or accidental death came from the Suicide Investigation Team. 'Marilyn would have had to gulp down those pills, all of them, within a matter of minutes – a very few minutes,' said Robert Litman, the UCLA psychiatrist who headed the team. 'If she had taken those pills a few at a time, she would have been unconscious before she could ingest the amount needed to achieve that degree of barbiturates in her bloodstream.'

Overdose by injection was always the most likely cause of death. The police considered this possibility, but ruled it out on August 7, when Noguchi announced that he had made an exhaustive search for needle marks on Monroe's body and found none.

Yet she had had an injection on Thursday evening in her bedroom, and a second in Dr. Engleberg's office late Friday. Both of these should have shown up in the 'exhaustive study'.

When District Attorney Mike Carroll learned of these shots, his mouth flew open. 'I wasn't aware of that,' he said. 'And yes, the needle marks should have shown up.'

Sergeant Jack Clemmons believes that 'Marilyn was given chloral hydrate, a colourless, odourless liquid, in her champagne. It would have worked on her like a Mickey Finn. Then, after she drifted off, the fatal injection of Nembutal was administered.'

Monroe may have received a third shot early on the afternoon of her death – when Bobby Kennedy visited her for the first time. Sources in the Los Angeles Police Department who caught glimpses of the original 723-page report on Monroe's death compiled by homicide detectives say that Kennedy came to her house with an unidentified physician. A shot was given to 'calm her down', according to the police source. Despite many filings under the Freedom of Information Act, in 1991 the department said all detailed reports had been destroyed.

Robert Slatzer also stumbled upon a source who provided him with portions of a secret statement the Attorney General had given Parker concerning his involvement in Monroe's death. 'Bobby admitted that he went to Marilyn's house when she became too distraught to handle,' said Slatzer's source. 'He admitted to bringing a doctor, who in turn gave her a mild sedative.'

Ralph G. Martin, who wrote a book about John and Bobby Kennedy called *A Hero for Our Time*, also disclosed this confession in his book, citing well-placed sources for its origin. Tony Sciacca, a New York investigative reporter, also admits that he was given key portions of Robert Kennedy's statement.

According to Sciacca in *Who Killed Marilyn Monroe?*, 'Bobby told the guys handling the investigation that Marilyn was annoying Jack Kennedy, chasing him and making lots of phone calls to him. He was upset because Jackie Kennedy was bitching and talking about getting a divorce.' The account goes on to say that Bobby brought a physician to the house with 'an injection to calm Marilyn down'.

But only thirty inconsequential pages of the huge report titled 'Investigations into the Death of Marilyn Monroe' still exist. 'When I saw the report, it was so fragmentary that I said, "This can't be the Police Department's complete file," ' said former Police Chief Tom Reddin. 'When they said, "It's all there is," I thought, so there is no source . . . no valid source to help us find out what happened to Marilyn Monroe.'

The intelligence division of the Los Angeles Police Department has always denied that such a report ever existed. But five years ago, parts of it were found in the estate papers of homicide detective Thad Brown. Included were photocopies of Monroe's phone records – which Parker had always denied receiving.

It seems certain that Bobby Kennedy's statement will eventually turn up in someone's long-lost files.

Those involved in covering up Monroe's death must have held their breaths in the beginning, hoping the public and the Hollywood power structure would accept their claims that the actress had died of an accidental overdose.

Her psychiatrist, Ralph Greenson, dismissed the suicide theory immediately. He angrily told the investigation team, 'Suicide is not an option in this case.'

In his discussions with Deputy District Attorney John Miner, Greenson was vehement. 'My patient did not commit suicide.'

'I had more than six hours of interviews with Dr. Greenson,' Miner recalled. 'I was requested to do this by the chief medical examiner, and I came away convinced that the actress could not have killed herself deliberately. And I wrote a report saying just that.'

In part, the memorandum read, 'From the information I have obtained as an Assistant District Attorney, I can only conclude that Marilyn Monroe did not commit suicide.'

The 'Miner Report' disappeared – probably taken by detectives from the Los Angeles Police Department's intelligence squad. Of course, Monroe's friends never believed the official ruling.

Fox production chief Peter Levathes, one of the last people to talk with her, pointed out that 'she never sounded better. She knew we were going to finish the picture and that it would start in a matter of weeks.

'You know, they all went around saying that she was despondent at her treatment by the studio, and because she had been fired,' Levathes said. 'That was all nonsense. We had hired her back at a salary of half a million dollars. And she was ecstatic.'

Greenson told associates at the time, 'Marilyn was finally making spectacular headway in therapy. She was on her way to achieving a degree of security for the first time in her life. She was really getting better. She knew it, and I knew it.'

To prove it, the analyst played tapes to John Miner 'of Marilyn saying certain things. I was sold,' Miner said. 'And I included all of this in the Miner Report, which vanished so quickly.'

Almost everyone studying the crime scene missed the most compelling physical evidence of all – the arrangement of Monroe's room and the condition of her body. When Eunice Murray and Ralph Greenson told police that 'nothing was out of the ordinary,' they were lying and they knew it.

Everything was out of the ordinary. Monroe *never* went to sleep in the nude – with all the lights on and the curtains open. She had an elaborate bedtime ritual – an unvarying routine that she observed even if she had further phone calls to make.

The thick blackout curtains were tacked shut each evening before Murray brought her a glass of milk. Then Monroe would slip on a fresh brassiere – from a supply she kept in her bureau – to keep her breasts from sagging. After that, she'd take her chloral hydrate with the milk. Additionally, the ritual included an eye mask and earplugs.

Monroe did none of these things on her last night. Her having fallen asleep nude in a room ablaze with light should have alerted Murray to foul play – unless, of course, Murray was fully aware of what happened.

Thus the evidence leads right back to Bobby Kennedy, who by August 4 knew that public exposure of his illicit affair could destroy his family's hold on the American power structure.

'High political stakes were riding on her life – and even more were riding on her death,' said Norman Mailer in an interview promoting his 1973 biography of Monroe.

In 1975, investigative reporter Anthony Scaduto was one of the first to charge that Monroe may have been killed by men protecting Attorney General Robert Kennedy.

This scenario was not so different from the veiled suggestions that novelist Mailer concocted. 'Which wing of the FBI seized the phone records?' Mailer asked. 'And were they protecting Bobby Kennedy or trying to amass evidence against him?'

Perhaps the most interesting analysis of the death came from Tass, the news agency of what was then the Soviet Union. On the 25th anniversary of Monroe's death, Tass published a remarkably insightful series of articles that accused 'highly influential people in Hollywood' with covering up the true circumstances of the star's death.

The investigative team that produced the five-part study had access to detailed information from the KGB. 'Marilyn was killed by the CIA because she planned to expose a U.S. plot to murder Cuban dictator Fidel Castro,' claimed Tass.

In an article on Monroe's relationship with both Kennedy brothers, the writers claimed to have absolute proof of these affairs. 'We could not rule out the fact that operatives protecting the Kennedys had Marilyn killed,' the article said.

The theory is not far-fetched.

In July 1962, Monroe sat on the rocks above Malibu and told a startled Robert Slatzer about the CIA's intention to murder Castro with the help of the Mafia. Slatzer warned her that 'this sort of information could get you killed'.

She had also made notations about the CIA, about the Mafia, and about the Kennedy administration's views of Fidel Castro, including hints that the CIA and the Mob may have conspired to assassinate the Cuban dictator.

Eyewitnesses have placed Bobby Kennedy at Monroe's house at least once – and probably twice – on the evening of her death. After ruthless grilling by BBC producer Ted Landreth, Eunice Murray finally admitted that he was there. She also admitted that the hours had slipped by before the police were informed so that Peter Lawford and the Secret Service could spirit Bobby Kennedy out of town.

Writer Ray Strait spoke of a violent argument between Monroe and Kennedy, which finally ended with the Attorney General storming out and heading for the Lawford beach house.

By this time, Kennedy must have been deeply alarmed at the depths of Monroe's rage. Apparently she also repeated her threat to hold a press conference.

Bobby Kennedy was not the type to keep these fears to himself.

It seems entirely plausible that agents from the Secret Service or even the FBI made sure that Monroe received just one more shot – thereby pushing her over the edge to death.

A top executive at Twentieth Century-Fox, who insisted on anonymity, asked a later U.S. Attorney General, under a Republican administration, if such a murder could possibly have been engineered by government agents.

'You're naïve,' this Attorney General said. 'All the President or Attorney General has to do is insinuate his displeasure with somebody, and then somebody else picks it up and does it. The political world is built around that sort of thing. That's the kind of power that really, truly exists.' The Fox executive looked up at his host with a shocked expression. The man smiled. 'Well, *you're* the one who asked.'

'I haven't felt completely safe since that time,' said the executive.

Former Police Chief Reddin said, 'If you've been intimate with the President and the Attorney General of the United States, as Monroe was, and if you have overheard high-level, sometimes top-secret, conversations – learning things you shouldn't know – what else do you need to be perceived as a threat?'

Reddin was asked whether Monroe could have been in worse danger because of the stenographer's notebooks she kept on JFK's and RFK's conversations.

'Absolutely,' Reddin said. 'She absolutely could have been in terrible danger.'

From Hazel Washington's description of the 'evidence' being incinerated in Monroe's fireplace at noon on Sunday, it's clear that the star's complete collection of notepads – key souvenirs from her affairs with the Kennedy brothers – were reduced to ashes.

It was Bobby Kennedy's own fault that Monroe kept these small steno pads handy. He had berated her at one party for her failure to remember things he had told her. 'How can we carry on a conversation about current events if you can't remember the details?' he asked, according to Peter Lawford.

So Monroe began taking notes on their conversations on the small pads which she stored next to her bed.

Evelyn Moriarity often saw her writing in them on the set.

After the Secret Service, the Los Angeles Police Department and the publicity department of Twentieth Century-Fox were through at Monroe's house, not a scrap of paper remained. Even the five drawers of Twentieth Century-Fox contracts had disappeared.

Some of Monroe's papers found their way to Bobby Kennedy. About a week after her death, the Attorney General was having his hair styled at the White House when he said to Mickey Song, 'I want to thank you, buddy, for always thinking of the family; for always protecting the family from danger.'

Song was puzzled. 'What do you mean?'

'Remember the night Marilyn called you over and pumped you for information about us?'

'Yes,' Mickey said quietly, horrified that Kennedy knew about the visit.

'I'm sure you didn't know it, but Marilyn taped you and then later took notes on what you said.'

Song took a breath and said, 'My God.'

'Don't worry about it,' Kennedy said. 'I just want you to know that the whole family thanks you.'

Other reel-to-reel tapes were burned in Monroe's fireplace by the two well-dressed men who broke into the filing cabinet in the guest house.

The Kennedys were equally grateful to Pat Newcomb, who kept not only Monroe's secrets but the Kennedy secrets as well. Later Newcomb got a job with the United States Information Agency on the recommendation of Peter and Pat Kennedy Lawford.

Evidence shows that much of the document-burning and political tidying up was a collaboration between Lawford and Twentieth Century-Fox.

'Lawford was involved with the studio on this project after Marilyn died,' said Assistant District Attorney Mike Carroll.

'Of course, that kind of stuff had gone on in Hollywood for decades.'

The presidential brother-in-law's major contribution was to throw up a smokescreen so that Bobby Kennedy could get back to San Francisco before Monroe's body was reported to the police.

The 1985 BBC documentary *Say Goodbye to the President* summed up the nature of this smokescreen. 'For hours, news of Marilyn's death was withheld from the police.'

The third of Lawford's four ex-wives, Deborah Gould, added, 'They needed every minute of that time to get the Attorney General out safely.'

For a decade, police and Kennedy supporters, including Ed Guthman and attorney John Bates, have scoffed at claims that Monroe was murdered. Writers have been accused by the Los Angeles district attorney of spinning exploitative fantasies. The closer any reporter got to the true story, the more likely he was to be called a bloodsucking muckraker by the Kennedy family and its lawyers.

The Kennedy lawyers told journalists they were crazy to believe that Monroe's phone records had been seized by police and government agencies. It never happened, Bobby Kennedy's supporters said. And then a photocopy of those exact records turned up in a homicide investigator's garage.

JFK aide Kenneth O'Donnell said it was disgusting to believe that Marilyn Monroe had had an affair with President John F. Kennedy. And then Judith Campbell Exner told Congress of her affair with JFK, adding that it ran concurrently with Marilyn Monroe's.

Lawford, O'Donnell and other aides had always told reporters that Bobby Kennedy hadn't ordered a coverup at Monroe's house. Today, Mickey Song has broken a vow of silence and offers valuable evidence that Kennedy had tapes taken from Monroe's personal recorder.

As we followed the tangled story of Monroe's last film,

we soon realised that her death was caught up in the story of *Something's Got to Give.*

We expected to uncover an accidental death and instead found a murder. Here is the true story as we see it:

The misadventures and dangerous conditions that led to Monroe's murder began Friday morning, August 3. After the Attorney General's aides relayed the alarming messages Monroe had left at the St. Francis Hotel, Bobby Kennedy must have realised that she was ready to publicly reveal her ties with his family. Because he now shunned her calls, Monroe revealed a vindictive spirit that caught the Attorney General off guard. In calls to Pat Lawford, Earl Wilson and others, she exhibited an angry new determination.

Shaken by the ease with which she reached him in San Francisco, Kennedy probably promised to fly to Los Angeles early Saturday. We also believe that Monroe threatened to hold a press conference about both her affairs, and that she might have been willing to publicise excerpts from the notebooks she had filled with details of the romances, which provided a record of sorts of everything her political lovers had told her over the previous year or so. As she told Robert Slatzer, 'I'm going to blow the lid off this thing.'

Along with trusted members of the Secret Service, Bobby Kennedy dashed to the Lawford mansion for a strategy session. We believe he made another call to Monroe, who by then was hysterical and told him to get out of her life.

It also seems clear that the Attorney General's contingent of Secret Service agents moved into action and may have brought CIA operatives into the situation as well. Because of Monroe's loose words on the plot to kill Fidel Castro, the CIA had a strong stake in her demise.

As a last resort, Kennedy collected a family doctor in Beverly Hills and travelled to Brentwood about 6:30 P.M. The doctor gave Monroe a strong sedative.

But when Kennedy returned to the Lawford mansion at

7 P.M., Monroe was already on the phone, raging about her mistreatment by the Kennedys. She was laughing, crying, semihysterical, much as she had been the previous year in her rages against Arthur Miller.

Kennedy was stunned. His problems with Monroe were getting worse, not better. He called the President in Washington and his mother in Hyannis Port.

Some time between 6:30 and 9 P.M., someone entered Monroe's house and administered a potent shot of Nembutal in her rectum or under her armpit. An injection in either of these places would not be detected during an autopsy that missed evidence of the shots she had received in the preceding two days.

Thomas Noguchi, then deputy coroner, has belatedly admitted that he did discover clues that pointed to foul play. 'I did find evidence which indicated violence. There were bruises on her lower back area – a very fresh bruise – and bruises on the arms.'

In 1982, in an interview on Los Angeles television station KABC, Noguchi said that 'murder might have been involved'. He also called for a new 'scientific inquiry into the death'. His challenge was never accepted.

Eunice Murray's coy denials and lapses of memory when confronted by the press endured until 1985, when BBC producer Ted Landreth persuaded her to admit that 'the cops were called hours after the death because they needed time to get Bobby out of town.'

Monroe died at approximately 10 P.M., and one of the most complicated coverups in Hollywood history was set in motion. Publicist Arthur Jacobs rushed from his box at the Hollywood Bowl just before 10:30 P.M. – on the way to the Brentwood house to sweep the site clear of all incriminating documents (perhaps destroying a note Monroe had written about her involvement with the First Family). At the same time a chopper landed on the beach next to the Lawford mansion and collected Bobby Kennedy who, according to one witness, was wearing chino pants and a sweat shirt.

Dr. Ralph Greenson was called to the house just before 11 P.M. Arriving next was the delegation from Twentieth Century-Fox: Frank Neill and John Campbell.

According to Fred Otash, Milo Speriglio and judging from the 1982 District Attorney's Reinvestigation of the Death, Lawford was on hand for hours – probably directing the sweep. We do know that Lawford reported back to his brother-in-law, JFK, early in the morning with a progress report.

In early 1992, record of Lawford's oral report was found in formerly suppressed telephone logs kept by the White House switchboard. The very first entry in the presidential log of August 5, 1962 shows that Lawford talked to Kennedy for twenty minutes, beginning at 9:05 (6:05 Pacific time).

Operators listed the caller as Peter Lawford and the origin as a house on 'Pacific Coast Highway' in Santa Monica, Ca. To be more precise, the telephone of origin was GL-1-1800 – identified by private detective Fred Otash as one of the numbers of the Lawford beach house. According to Otash, there was a bug on the phone at the time.

Some reporters noted that the record of the telephone call might finally be 'the smoking gun' – the tie between Monroe's death and the administration of a sitting president. It also fingers Lawford as the architect of the coverup.

'This is a dramatic and telling incident,' noted Anthony Summers, who worked nine years to get the phone log declassified. 'The link between President Kennedy and Lawford was significant, coming as it did only two hours after Marilyn's death was reported.' Summers continued: 'The conversation between Lawford and JFK could have been about nothing other than the death of Marilyn Monroe.'

Hazel Washington heard that Lawford had made an even earlier call from the phone in Monroe's bedroom, but a White

House log from those hours does not exist. It would surely have shown up on Monroe's phone bill – but it has vanished from the files of the phone company.

The deserted street was yet another indication that a well-organised coverup had been completed. It was 4:34 A.M. when Clemmons turned into the small cul-de-sac.

But the block-long lane had been teeming with activity at 1 A.M. At that moment a Los Angeles financier named Arthur Landau, who lived next door to Monroe, turned onto Fifth Helena and found it crammed with vehicles. He saw a Mercedes, a station wagon, a small foreign convertible, and two plain sedans which had the appearance of official unmarked police cars.

After Landau squeezed into his own driveway, he tried to question one of several men guarding the gates to the Monroe compound. 'Don't worry about it,' he was told.

'Of course, we all knew when we turned the radio on the next morning,' he said later.

'The guys who killed her are the guys who got the phone records,' said Sergeant Jack Clemmons. 'Who else would have known?'

Ralph Greenson may have been privy to this unexpected 'hit' by federal agents. 'God knows, it wasn't ordered by Bobby,' he said. And Greenson learned much too late to stop it.

When Clemmons asked the analyst what went on during the hours before the cops were called, Greenson answered:

'I cannot explain myself without revealing things I don't want to reveal. You can't draw a line in the sand and say, "I'll tell you this, but I won't tell you that." It's terrible to have to say, "I can't talk about it, because I can't tell you the whole story." '

'Listen,' Greenson said conspiratorially. 'Talk to Bobby Kennedy.'

PART FIVE
Aftermath

– Chapter 40 –

Cast of Characters

Monroe was to be buried within the cinder-block walls of Westwood Memorial Park, a down-on-its-luck establishment with ill-tended grounds and a smudgy pink mausoleum. It was half in shadow from the sterile concrete towers that surrounded it, and was always blighted by the commercial roar of Los Angeles's mighty west side.

Westwood had none of the silver-screen splendours of lofty Forest Lawn, where most of the Hollywood idols were laid to rest. Nor did it have the bronze-and-onyx patina of Hollywood Gardens, with its lush shrines to Rudolph Valentino and Wallace Reid.

The movieland glitterati, locked out of the funeral, were mutely represented by hundreds of outré bouquets bedecked with pink carnations and tuberoses.

With dignified firmness and old-world courtesy, Joe DiMaggio brushed aside the industry that had served Monroe so cruelly in her last months. Unable to protect her from Hollywood politics during her life, he was determined to do so now.

After spending the night on his knees next to the bier, DiMaggio, in a flawlessly tailored suit, slowly preceded the simple bronze casket into the unrelenting August sun.

He explained this spartanism in a brief statement: 'This will be a small funeral so she can go to her final resting place in the quiet she always sought.'

As the walk to the mausoleum began, spirals of heat spread upward from the asphalt roadway and whirled around the legs of the pallbearers.

Preceded by a single battered hearse, the procession was a symbolic march of strangers – most of them paid functionaries who were barely polite to one another.

Attorneys Milton Rudin and Martin Gang, Lee and Paula Strasberg, Pat Newcomb and Arthur Jacobs, the Greensons and Eunice Murray walked through the stultifying heat to a small chapel that was little more than an overgrown mobile home.

There a Lutheran minister, a stranger to Monroe and the mourners, conducted a short service punctuated by heartfelt sobs from Joan Greenson and Pat Newcomb.

Outside the chain-link fence, three hundred photographers drowned out the scratchy recorded music with the noise of their shutters and motor drives.

Lee Strasberg, who had dodged Monroe for months during her career troubles, raised his thin voice in eulogy.

'In her own lifetime, Marilyn Monroe created the myth of what a poor girl from a depressed background can obtain,' he said. 'For the entire world she became a symbol of the eternal feminine. But I have no words to describe the myth and the legend. I did not know this Marilyn Monroe.'

As the coffin was borne to the small mausoleum, Frank Sinatra, in an eight-hundred-dollar black suit, came to pay his respects. Guards, who had specific orders to bar his entrance, turned him away at the main gate. Also excluded were the Dean Martins, Rupert Allan, Patricia Kennedy Lawford and Robert Slatzer.

Ironically, many of those outside the gates had offered the

star more comfort during those last months than those whose names were on the arbitrary guest list. 'When Joe took over the funeral, he crossed name after name from the preliminary list,' said publicist John Springer. 'He looked it over and said, "So-and-so can't come, and so-and-so can't come." There were a lot of hurt feelings.'

Also standing outside with Slatzer was New York gossip columnist Walter Winchell, who was trying to make sense of the strange ceremony unfolding behind the gates.

'Who are all those people?' Winchell asked.

'Strangers,' answered Slatzer. 'Strangers who worked for her.'

The black-suited men and women, memorialised in newspapers and on newsreels, rarely crossed paths again – except to appear in print in the landslide of books on Monroe. Many of them, though not all, cashed in on their brief brush with fame.

Lee Strasberg emerged into the sympathetic glow that followed Monroe's death, appearing in a clutch of documentaries. Trading on the growing cult status of Monroe and other Method-acting heroes, he built his acting school into a booming concern with campuses on both coasts.

Monroe's bequest to Strasberg – a pittance at the time of her death – grew into a multimillion-dollar industry as the estate cashed in on the star's name and likeness with tacky 'Marilyn dresses', cheap editions of 'Marilyn Monroe Toilet Water' and even 'Marilyn Wine', a concoction with a taste of vinegar. It's estimated that the licensing agreements bring in at least $1 million per year in America alone.

The two women closest to Monroe during the last fourteen weeks of her life – housekeeper Eunice Murray and publicist Pat Newcomb – found their lives permanently entwined with the fate of their doomed employer.

Just before her death, Monroe had learned that Murray was a psychiatric nurse and that Ralph Greenson had placed her in the actress's home as a combination spy and caretaker. 'Marilyn caught on just before she died and felt very betrayed,' recalled Ralph Roberts. 'Plans to fire [Murray] were already in the works.'

In the hours after Monroe died, Murray had a hand in what she referred to as 'tidying up the house'. After the murder, the housekeeper not only washed all the linens in the Brentwood house, but disposed of all food and alcohol and, according to police reports, 'threw away a mountain of trash long before officers were on the scene'.

Some believe that Murray was 'paid off' by the Kennedy family for 'services rendered'. Although she had few assets at the time of Monroe's death, the housekeeper took three tours of Europe in the sixties. 'I believe there *was* a payoff,' said Sergeant Jack Clemmons. 'We had information to that effect.'

For whatever reason, Murray kept her silence concerning those final hours. She steered clear of the Kennedys and all hints of foul play in her own book, *Marilyn: The Last Months*.

Since 1985, the former psychiatric nurse has retreated into her 'vow of silence', telling one reporter, 'I'm sorry I talked to the BBC.'

Pat Newcomb, now one of Hollywood's most successful independent public relations consultants, has turned down more than a score of 'six-figure book contracts' during the past thirty years.

Since she left the Brentwood house in tears, Newcomb's life was dramatically affected by her years as Monroe's image-shaper. After she flew to the Kennedy compound in Hyannis Port the weekend following Monroe's funeral, she worked for the Kennedys on a variety of special projects. At one point, when she held a key governmental position, her office was just down the hall from Attorney General Robert Kennedy's office. Later, Newcomb also aided Bobby Kennedy's successful campaign for the Senate and did a stint with the United States Information Agency.

During the past decade, Newcomb has worked for such luminaries as Jane Fonda, Robert Redford and Barbra Streisand. She has no plans to write her version of the Marilyn Monroe saga.

Newcomb's boss Arthur Jacobs was richly rewarded by Twentieth Century-Fox for his role in the coverup. Just weeks after Monroe's death, he was launched as a Fox producer specialising in such extravagances as *What a Way to Go* which was originally planned as a Monroe blockbuster, and *Goodbye, Mr. Chips*. His chief claim to fame was the *Planet of the Apes* series of blockbuster films.

Like Newcomb, Jacobs never discussed the events of August 4 and 5, 1962.

Perhaps the saddest figure in the saga of Monroe's last months was Ralph Greenson, whose controversial treatment of her was ridiculed throughout the psychoanalytical profession.

'He was never the same guy after she died,' said Lucy Freeman, the *New York Times* journalist who interviewed him several times in the decades that followed. 'The death profoundly affected him; he blamed himself even though it was hardly his fault.'

Greenson's textbook, *The Technique and Practice of Psychoanalysis*, is used in two hundred universities throughout the world.

Chapter 41

Cleopatra II

During the hot Roman summer of 1962, a sleek white ambulance appeared on the edge of the *Cleopatra* set – insurance in case Elizabeth Taylor tried suicide again.

At first it was hidden behind a monstrous plaster sphinx in the hope that the increasingly distraught Taylor wouldn't see it. As June passed without incident, the attendants started parking it in the open, with the handsome young doctor and the starch-capped nurse mingling with the exotically dressed extras.

The 'suicide mobile', as the crew called it, soon led to company jokes. Stories about the ambulance's most crucial feature, a gleaming stomach pump, enlivened the afternoon coffee breaks.

But Taylor's stability was no laughing matter to producer Walter Wanger. 'As soon as Elizabeth finished filming in June, her affair with Richard began to collapse,' Wanger wrote to Darryl Zanuck. 'She was scared to death that he would return to his wife, Sybil.'

Fox had reluctantly shelled out another $200,000 so that Taylor could film through June 21. Then the studio's executives expected her to pack her 156 suitcases and flee Rome, leaving Burton, and 'the scandal', behind.

Taylor didn't dare leave. Burton had already tried to run back to Sybil. Three times Taylor held onto him – through histrionics, through a king's ransom in gifts and through the sheer force of her personality. Through it all, Burton remained free and uncommitted. Tom Mankiewicz remembered that he 'eluded her for a bit; marriage seemed unlikely'.

Film critic Hollis Alpert visited the set and was shocked to see the ambulance. 'Everyone felt the breakup could come at any minute, and everyone feared she would take it badly.'

Finally the enforced separation came. When the company moved to Egypt, Taylor, who had ostentatiously converted to Judaism several years earlier, was left behind. The Egyptians refused to give her an entry visa because of her religion.

Mankiewicz and Burton set sail for the Nile delta. There, with the help of three hundred Roman extras, they finished principal photography on *Cleopatra* just before sundown on July 28. Leaning on an ivory cane, with white gloves protecting hands that were bleeding from constant nail-biting, Mankiewicz congratulated Burton.

'I've just completed the hardest three films of my career,' he said.

Burton pulled a bottle of French brandy from beneath his tunic and guzzled. He winked at the director, saying, 'Luv, I have a feeling it isn't over yet.'

Through a series of explosive battle scenes and sandstorms, through the wettest winter in recorded history and through the most publicised adultery in recent times, *Cleopatra* had filmed for 225 days, exposing a mountain of film. The first rough cut was eight hours long.

Working around the clock in three editing labs, Mankiewicz whittled it down to six hours and then to five – which he nervously screened for new Fox president Darryl Zanuck on October 13.

Zanuck, who had been Mankiewicz's biggest supporter

during the director's fourteen years at Fox, emerged from the screening room in a panic. He had just seen five hours of chaos, overwrought dialogue, and semi-neurotic performances. It was 'hours too long'.

'Think of it,' he said to fellow Fox board member Arnold Grant. 'Forty-two million dollars down the drain and we still don't have a presentable film. If we don't get this into the theatres soon, the company could collapse.' Zanuck presided over the editing of the film to ready it for release.

Finally, on June 12, 1963, *Cleopatra*, the film Spyros Skouras had promised would be 'the greatest in Fox history', opened to universally dismal reviews. 'A monumental mouse', declared the *New York Herald Tribune*, setting the stage for the world-wide derision that greeted the film.

The worst notices were reserved for the Queen of Egypt herself. Taylor, who had promised friends another Oscar nomination – at least – was crushed by the weight of the scorn unleashed by the critics. 'How could they do this?' she wailed to Peter Lawford. 'This is the best work I've ever done.'

Reviewers acted as if the film, and the lurid headlines it generated, had insulted their intelligence. 'Miss Taylor is overweight, overbosomed, overpaid and undertalented,' wrote David Susskind. 'She has set the acting profession back a decade.'

The *New Republic* was even less sympathetic: 'Miss Taylor is monotony in a slit skirt. There is no depth of emotion in her kohl-laden eyes and no modulation in a voice that too often rises to fishwife levels.'

'When she portrays "Cleopatra" as a political animal, she screeches like a ward healer's wife at a block party,' wrote *Time* magazine.

With her lover filming *Becket*, Taylor barricaded herself in the penthouse of the Dorchester Hotel in London and collapsed in tears.

'When she read the reviews for the first time, she had an attack of the vapours and took to her bed,' recalled *Becket* producer Hal Wallis.

Burton was devastated for Taylor. During their long debauchery, he had never seen her like this – defeated, crushed like a flower. Not even a twelve-carat-diamond bracelet cheered her up. He was overcome with chivalry and, with tears in his eyes, knelt to beg for her hand in marriage. Thus ended the chase, a shameless pursuit by Taylor that had ranged over four continents.

'Gallantry decided the matter,' said Melvyn Bragg, the British television producer who wrote the definitive biography of Burton. 'After the reviews, he said he would marry her; no ifs; no buts.'

There were still divorces to obtain – Burton's from his enormously likeable wife, Sybil, and Taylor's from the scrappy Eddie Fisher. 'But, luv, I've got to make an honest woman of her,' Burton told Peter O'Toole.

The better-late-than-never wedding came too late for militant churchgoers, who flooded Washington with letters and petitions asking that 'the Hollywood Jezebel and her Welsh gigolo' be denied admission to the United States. The National Council of Churches even launched a vituperative campaign against the embattled lovers, causing a blizzard of protest letters to descend on Hollywood columnists. At one point Hedda Hopper was receiving forty 'anti-Taylor' letters a day.

Darryl F. Zanuck was besieged by angry stockholders, most of them demanding some form of redress from Taylor and Burton. Two weeks after *Cleopatra* opened, Zanuck capitulated and sued the lovers for $50 million, claiming damages from 'the deplorable and amoral conduct of Richard Burton and Elizabeth Taylor'. It looked as if the morals clause would come in handy after all.

This was too much for Richard Burton. He had himself

fitted for a pin-striped suit, hired a stiff-backed barrister and flew to Manhattan for a face-to-face confrontation with Darryl Zanuck.

Over coffee and out of hearing of the lawyers, Burton reminded Zanuck about the data he had assembled on Fox's mismanagement of *Cleopatra*. He whispered to Zanuck, 'I'll make all that sludge public. And my lawyers will look into *all of your* business, all of Skouras's business, and every bit of dirty laundry in this corporation!'

Zanuck was shocked. Given Burton's threat – and the depth of his knowledge – the mogul saw that the scandal could come crashing down on him with the stroke of a lawsuit. He quickly agreed to settle out of court, paying Burton and Taylor $2 million, submitting a public apology, and offering Taylor a $1-million role of her choosing. She finally accepted *The Only Game in Town* opposite Warren Beat.y.

As *Cleopatra* played to half-empty houses across America, Burton flew back to London to begin the ten-year drunken rout of a marriage he shared with Taylor.* Their love affair, to some the most poignantly romantic in screen history, was to be the most enduring legacy of the foolish sun-and-sandals epic. At last, in the rainy spring of 1964, a blushing Taylor, in a yellow chiffon gown, wedded a brandy-soaked Burton in Toronto, where the groom was performing in *Hamlet*.

The couple earned $50 million for their movie work alone. Shortly after they took home $1.8 million for *The Sandpiper*, Burton joked, 'It's a shame, isn't it, luv? But for money, we will dance.'

They traipsed the world in the manner of a royal couple, legendary for their mountains of suitcases, four children, three male secretaries, pair of governesses, two hairdressers, four dogs and two Siamese cats with diamond-studded collars.

---

*Cleopatra would not earn back its cost until it was sold to television networks in the U.S. and Europe.

But much of the desperation nurtured on the set of *Cleopatra* lingered beneath the foundation of their marriage. The drugs and drinking continued, as did the midnight brawls and the physical abuse. Through it all, Taylor was the pursuer and Burton the romantic quarry, always just beyond her reach.

On June 13, 1973, a world-weary Burton bolted free of the marriage, resignedly telling journalists, 'When Liz loves you, she isn't happy until she owns your soul. But, now, to save myself, I must go my own way.'

Within weeks, they made a lame attempt at reconciliation. Again Burton fled. He pleaded for understanding. 'If two people are sick of each other, then they should divorce as quickly as possible.'

The world's Cleopatra and her Mark Antony were romantically bankrupt. Still Taylor sought Burton's love. In 1975, they held a heartbreaking remarriage ceremony on a river bank in Africa. The reunion lasted only twenty-one days. Nevertheless, Taylor hovered around Burton until the day of his death in 1984.

When she was forbidden to attend his funeral, she came to his fresh grave after dark, kissing a single white rose and setting it atop the small mound. Then she climbed into the Rolls-Royce they had shared during the golden years and drove off. Twenty-two years had passed since they had their first kiss – on the steps of the Roman forum.

Chapter 42

The Studio

Four days after Monroe's death, fans from the Netherlands walked through the heat to the marble crypt where the star was entombed. Two of them were weighted down with a large floral arrangement in the shape of a heart. Tucked into a bed of baby-pink roses was a legend on gilded paper.

'Marilyn,' it said, 'this story's not over; our love protects you.' The two girls knelt and then each touched the slab of marble covering the vault.

They were right. The story was just beginning.

In her life-and-death conflict with the Kennedys, and in her battles with Twentieth Century-Fox, Monroe had been bolstered by the fierce loyalty of her fans. Hollywood had never been on her side, but the rest of the world had.

Less than a week after her death, the demand for her films became insatiable. Theatre chains across the globe launched Marilyn Monroe specials at such a rate that, by late 1963, Fox had almost every print of every Monroe film in release.

A special team of producers, on orders from Darryl Zanuck, Jr., was editing the best of Monroe's scenes into a documentary called *Marilyn* – which became the first documentary ever to be listed among the top-twenty box-office champions.

Within four years, five other documentaries were produced for network television – none of which presented a single revealing fact about Monroe's life and death, or a whisper about foul play, or murder, or sex scandals.

At the studio, the Monroe version of *Something's Got to Give* was consigned to the film graveyard, and those who were involved with it scattered.

Director George Cukor moved to Warner Brothers to direct *My Fair Lady*, which finally won him an Oscar as Best Director.

Like others involved in the Monroe story, Cukor told author Peter Harry Brown that he felt increasingly guilty as time went by. 'At the time I didn't realise how many emotional troubles she had, and how the Kennedys were ruining her,' he told Brown in 1979. 'If I had known, I could have helped.' Cukor expressed great anger when asked about the Kennedy scandal. 'Power and money killed her,' he said. 'It was Marilyn against too much power and too much money. She was just too innocent and it destroyed her.'

Two days after Monroe died, Twentieth Century-Fox drastically reorganised as well, as a result of the executive mismanagement that had been slowly destroying it for years. The big, bustling Hollywood studio Monroe had known was gone forever – having outlasted her by a mere forty-eight hours.

At 9 A.M. on Monday, August 6, more than eight hundred employees received pink slips, along with a notice announcing that the Fox lot was to be vacated in ten days.

Workers stood around in shocked groups. 'It was like losing my family,' remembered David Bretherton, who was still editing scenes from *Something's Got to Give* when he got his pink slip. 'I had grown up here. I considered it home.'

In New York, Darryl Zanuck bowed to the inevitable. 'We could see that the Levathes administration had ruined the place,' said his son Richard Zanuck. 'It was completely fucked up. It was amazing that we could save it at all.'

Darryl Zanuck's first decision as president was to shut down the studio and cancel all film and television production, including the unfinished *Cleopatra*. He said he needed to screen the *Cleopatra* footage so that he could determine what to do with it.

But when Zanuck had wrested control of Fox from financiers Milton Gould and John Loeb, he had had no idea how to run the business end of this megacorporation.

'Zanuck called me and said, "What do we do now?" ' recalled Louis Nizer, who represented Zanuck in the takeover.

Nizer took Zanuck to his villa in the south of France and conducted a crash course on how to run a big corporation. 'He was particularly weak when it came to economics,' said Nizer. This tutorial allowed Zanuck and his son Richard to revive the corporation – although on a much smaller scale. The New York office was to be closed and the payroll cut in half. By 1965, money was again pouring in. In that year, *The Sound of Music*, a film conceived by Peter Levathes and produced at a cost of $8 million, earned $110 million at the box office. Fox's other hits that year included *Those Magnificent Men in Their Flying Machines*, *Von Ryan's Express*, *Zorba the Greek* and *The Agony and the Ecstasy*. Domestic rentals of all the films totalled $115 million (excluding *The Sound of Music*).

Before long, however, the *Cleopatra* pattern of extravagance again reared its ugly head. Emboldened by the bonanza of cash from *The Sound of Music*, the Zanucks embarked on a series of films with bloated budgets and bloated expectations. *Dr. Dolittle* cost $17 million and earned back $6.2 million; *Star*, a Julie Andrews vehicle, devoured $14.5 million and brought in slightly more than $4 million; and *The Only Game in Town*, with Elizabeth Taylor and Warren Beatty, cost $10 million and earned $1.5 million.

By 1970, the corporation was in big trouble again, with an annual loss of $77 million. Stockholders revolted and kicked Darryl Zanuck upstairs, crowning him with the honorary title of chairman emeritus. Decades of upheaval followed as Fox was sold five times in twenty years, finally becoming part of Rupert Murdoch's far-flung media empire in the late eighties.

Chapter 43

The Media

On July 8 1964, a young FBI agent marched down the halls of the U.S. Justice Department on a high-priority mission for his boss, J. Edgar Hoover. Under his arm was a dark blue envelope bearing the department's fancy gold crest.

'Don't give this to a secretary or an assistant,' Hoover had cautioned. 'If you can't hand it directly to Robert Kennedy, bring it back to me.'

The Attorney General must have flinched as the agent handed him yet another 'secret communiqué' from the meddling, secretive director of the FBI. Since Marilyn Monroe's death, Hoover had forced an avalanche of intelligence data about the actress on Bobby Kennedy.

The deluge of data amounted to a subtle form of blackmail – a paper trail that insinuated that Hoover was well aware of what had transpired behind the walls of the Brentwood estate.

This nasty standoff between Hoover and his boss began on August 20, 1962, with a ten-page report detailing 'rumours of an affair between Mr. Kennedy and film actress Marilyn Monroe'.

Unaware that he was opening Pandora's box, Kennedy replied to Hoover, 'I'm aware that there have been several allegations concerning my involvement with Marilyn Monroe. Naturally, I've met her; she was a good friend of my sister, Pat Lawford. These allegations have a way of growing beyond any semblance of truth.'

'It was in Hoover's best interests for these rumours to remain hidden,' said one of his righthand men, William C. Sullivan, head of the bureau's domestic division. 'But within the FBI, the gossip spread like wildfire. And J. Edgar Hoover was right there, gleefully fanning the flames.'

Once again, Bobby Kennedy was saved by the unprofessional lethargy of the American press.

'Bobby once again escaped disastrous revelations,' said writer Anthony Summers in an interview. 'He was already beholden to the FBI director and had been from the midnight Marilyn died – when he seized Marilyn's telephone records and rescued them from exposure. That obligation was deeply humiliating, to say the least, and Hoover, with his utter dislike for the Attorney General, was not about to let Kennedy forget it.'

Year by year, as the gossip grew in intensity and Hollywood tongues began to loosen, certain members of the American press attempted to break through the coverup. The Kennedys consistently resisted all queries. For instance, when Joe Hyams called Bobby Kennedy's office for reaction to the charge that he was the last person who had talked to Monroe, a high-level aide returned the call. 'The Attorney General would appreciate it if that story was killed.'

'It was incredible,' said Ted Landreth, who produced the 1986 BBC exposé *Say Goodbye to the President*. 'Here was the biggest story in Hollywood history, and it was completely suppressed.'

The first article of any consequence appeared in 1975 in *Oui* magazine. Written by investigative reporter Anthony Scaduto, the essay ran under a blunt subheading: 'Marilyn did not commit suicide. She was murdered. And the evidence of the murder was suppressed to protect John and Robert Kennedy.'

Scaduto theorised about the identity of the killers: 'She may have been killed by those protecting Bobby, JFK and the future Kennedy presidential dynasty from scandal.'

Oui was also the first to declare that the Brentwood house had been bugged and that the surveillance produced sensational audiotapes of Kennedy and Monroe fighting on the last afternoon of her life.

Also in the early seventies, Norman Mailer, in his lavishly illustrated book *Marilyn*, threw out a literary hand grenade by suggesting that the CIA, perhaps in league with high-ranking Secret Service agents, might have assassinated the film star.

These allegations made no cracks in the tough skin of the masterful conspiracy – and the establishment press remained silent on the subject.

Another decade drifted by – a decade in which JFK and his fallen brother became icons and their administration was remembered as a long-lost Camelot, an idyll of lovers and heroes.

As the flint-hard eighties dawned, two men appeared on the Hollywood scene, determined to unlock the enduring mystery. Ted Landreth, a former CBS News producer, and Anthony Summers, a London *Times* journalist who was writing a Monroe biography, teamed up to produce a ninety-minute special for the BBC.

When Landreth and his team of camera operators, researchers and assistants started work in 1984, they expected to conduct interviews for several weeks on both U.S. coasts and then spend several months editing the documentary for its debut in Britain.

But their project became a two-year journey of discovery during which they interviewed five hundred people and did principal research in ten cities. They uncovered a trail of police corruption, in which Los Angeles detectives purposely destroyed evidence; broke down Eunice Murray's story until, bit by bit, she admitted her knowledge of Monroe's relationships with the Kennedys; and discovered compelling evidence of extensive wiretaps at the Lawford beach mansion.

So many credible witnesses depicted Monroe's sexual relationships with John and Robert Kennedy that they should have laid to rest all questions.

'The White House press corps all knew of the affairs at the time,' said Landreth. 'But the story was too hot to print.'

Landreth and Summers also found 'that many high-ranking LAPD detectives had always believed that Marilyn Monroe was murdered'.

Say Goodbye to the President debuted on the BBC in 1986, creating a European sensation.

The reception was different in the United States.

As explosive and well-researched as the special was, no major American network would touch it. 'The power remaining to the Kennedy family kept it from getting widespread exposure,' said a journalist who worked on the documentary. 'Network after network turned it down.'

An NBC executive called the BBC project 'extremely dangerous'.

Landreth suspected that 'powerful political pressure was brought to bear on all three networks.'

Finally the show was syndicated to a moderately large audience and began attracting headlines.

Perhaps the most dramatic example of the nefarious influence that the Kennedys have on the media establishment came when *20/20*, the prestigious ABC news anthology, tried to air a segment on Monroe and the Kennedys in 1986.

Prepared by a crack journalistic team with Sylvia Chase as anchorwoman, the segment fully documented the affair between Bobby and Monroe, and proved beyond a shadow of a doubt the love affair between JFK and the screen goddess.

But at the last minute, Roone Arledge, director of ABC News – and a close friend of Ethel Kennedy – pulled the segment, saying that it was polluted with gossip. An indignant Geraldo Rivera resigned from *20/20* over the dispute.

'My longtime friendship with Ethel Kennedy had no part in that decision,' Arledge told the Associated Press. 'I withdrew the story because it wasn't ready and because it needed a larger context than simply whether the Kennedy brothers engaged in separate, illicit affairs with Marilyn Monroe.'

But one highly placed ABC executive theorised that the *20/20* segment was cancelled because there'd never been anything like it on television – talking about the Kennedys in terms that linked them with illicit affairs and, perhaps, murder.

Obviously, stalwart supporters of the Kennedys are still determined to protect them from the spreading Monroe scandal.

Maybe it's because of the close calls Bobby Kennedy experienced when he was alive. When his presidential campaign picked up speed in 1968, a cabal of conservatives offered a $75,000 reward to anyone who could produce the tapes of his affair with Monroe.

An unnamed Los Angeles police officer answered the ad and met secretly with a representative of the cabal. That representative found the tapes 'impressive'. An exchange was set up.

The day the officer and the political operative were to meet was the day after the California primary. Naturally, Bobby Kennedy's assassination ended the negotiation.

The tapes vanished.

– Chapter 44 –

Peter Lawford

In the entire Monroe saga, Peter Lawford was perhaps the saddest figure. After the Kennedy assassinations, he was left behind to keep the terrible secrets of his brothers-in-law and to guard their legend.

In an ingenious bit of subterfuge, Lawford told the same story over and over again. A depressed Marilyn Monroe had committed suicide. The Kennedys must have considered him the ideal Eagle Scout.

Towards the end of his life, in 1982, Lawford summoned the *Los Angeles Times* for a deathbed interview. His face was white, his hands were shaking and his voice quaky. But he denied that Bobby had had any involvement with Monroe and that Kennedy had been anywhere near the scene of her death.

Reporters noted that he seemed dreadfully sincere.

But he added a chilling codicil: 'But if any of this were true, I would never, never admit it.' One of the reporters noted that he had raised himself up and was no longer shaking. 'I would not, and could not, tell you anything about this.'

The years of protecting the First Family finally destroyed Peter Lawford. After Monroe's death, his British vivacity –

for which he was so famous – disappeared and was replaced by cocaine, scotch whisky and mountains of prescription drugs, such as Percodan and Valium.

Once, in Las Vegas, Lawford secured the services of a $1,000-a-night call girl – a former showgirl who was also an acquaintance of publicist Rupert Allan. 'Lawford brought her to a penthouse suite,' said Allan. 'This lady told me that all he wanted to do was hold her in his arms and cry for hours over what had happened to Marilyn Monroe.'

The woman asked Lawford if he wanted to talk about it. 'It's too terrible to talk about,' he said. 'And believe me, you wouldn't want to know.'

Then he grabbed the call girl again and collapsed in tears. 'She told me he cried the night away, downing glass after glass of scotch, and stumbling around the room like Oedipus after he was blinded,' Allan recalled.

Allan was on hand for one of the Lawford tragedies – a glittering appearance by the Sinatra Rat Pack in Vegas. 'Everyone was up on the stage,' recalled Allan, 'but Peter wasn't in on the act. He came – out of loyalty – and sat at a front-row table. This was shortly after Marilyn's death. Frank caught sight of Lawford and stalked over to him as if he were going to walk right through him. Peter had to jump out of the way,' said Allan. 'It was like a Sicilian vendetta. In a way, Frank blamed Lawford for Marilyn's death.'

Eventually Lawford ended up in the Betty Ford Center to purge himself of his addictions. While there in 1984, he wrote a letter to President John F. Kennedy in heaven. In part the letter said, 'I know you're having a good time up there, you always do. Are you the president of anything yet? How are Bobby and Marilyn? Please give them my love. See you soon, your buddy, Peter Lawford.'

– Chapter 45 –

In Search of Marilyn Monroe

Milton Rudin, one of the most powerful entertainment lawyers in the world, sat on the terrace of his Bel Air home and talked of the haunted, almost paranoid Marilyn Monroe he had known during the last three weeks of her life.

The flatlands of Beverly Hills stretched out into the distance. Rudin's face assumed a look of sadness as he told of holding back changes the movie star wished to make in her will. 'I couldn't,' he said, turning his head away. 'I could not legally confirm that she was of sound mind.'

Across Los Angeles in a 'new wave' café in Beverly Hills, former Fox production chief Peter G. Levathes mused about the savvy, scintillating Monroe who shared witticisms and champagne with him eleven days before her death.

In a little-known restaurant practically in the shadow of the vast MGM studio, Fox executive secretary Lee Hanna whispered about a pitiful, beaten creature – a Monroe on the skids – who had covered the walls of her dressing room with cries for help and had sat staring into the mirror for hours.

To Ralph Greenson, Monroe was a waif doomed to wander through the tunnel of loneliness for the rest of her life; to Rupert Allan, she was a star about to come out from under a gloomy cloud and dazzle Broadway; to Evelyn Moriarity, she was a sweet girl so generous that her heart was always on her sleeve; to Robert Slatzer, she was an angry superstar about to blow the whistle on America's First Family; to Sheilah Graham, she was a lost soul with unwashed hair and dirty underwear who would have died early in any case; to writer Fred Lawrence Guiles, she was a wounded, suicidal lady who finally got her death wish.

Marilyn Monroe was all of these things – a mercurial actress who loved to play dramatic roles, both on and off the screen. She loved mystery; she loved intrigue. Ironically, the controversy surrounding her death helped make her a legend – which was what she wanted to be.

Her last months, as portrayed in this book, can be viewed as a microcosm of her whole life: an enduring riddle which may never be solved.

Unless those who knew her best finally tell what they know, and unless the police and FBI files on her are declassified, we may never be able to understand the three-dimensional person called Marilyn Monroe.

For now, she remains the most enduring enigma in Hollywood history.

– *Source Notes* –

This story began to emerge when Peter Harry Brown was in the midst of twenty-two preliminary interviews for the Fox Entertainment News documentary *Something's Got to Give*. These audiotaped interviews became the basis for this book when they were augmented by 310 interviews and a cache of 500 studio documents obtained from a confidential source. The Fox documentary written and directed by journalist Henry Schipper, was an excellent basic source, since it provided a wealth of details from the studio's legal archives. It also offered an 'official' version of the *Something's Got to Give* and *Cleopatra* debacles – a version which was checked by corporate lawyers for accuracy.

All of the principals in the documentary were reinterviewed at greater length for this book, along with more than 200 others.

Another valuable research tool was the unedited film from *Something's Got to Give*. Videos of the six hours were screened by the authors four times and compared with hundreds of documents. The Twentieth Century-Fox documents, including memos, letters, production logs, script rewrites and telephone notes, offered a paper trail of the Fox conspiracy against Monroe. These are discussed in some detail in the 'Sources' section which follows.

The precise details of Monroe's illnesses came from Fox medical logs and memos from Dr. Lee Siegel and Dr. Philip Rubin to Spyros Skouras, Otto Koegel and Milton Gould in the New York offices of the corporation. The only copies of these logs were found in Special Collections at Stanford University, among the Darryl F.

Zanuck papers. Some of Siegel's and Rubin's rulings on Monroe's illnesses were briefly discussed in the daily and weekly production logs compiled by *Something's Got to Give* assistant director Buck Hall.

Prologue

The 'lost film' found by Henry Schipper in the Fox storage facility was traced through routing numbers in the Fox archives and through a series of telephone calls to the men who have charge of the vast Fox film library. The evolution of the Fox Entertainment News documentary was traced through interviews with Schipper, William K. Knoedelseder and Shawn Griggs, who was associate producer of the documentary.

Details on the film sources for this book are in the 'Sources' section which follows.

Our account of the special fans' screening in August 1988 involved interviews with Monroe's foster sister, Bebe Goddard, columnist May Mann, hairdresser Mickey Song, and archivist Sabin Gray, at whose Hollywood office the event was held. Additional data came from Monroe's friend Robert Slatzer.

Chapter 1

The material on Monroe's reluctant return to Fox and the state of her personal life in the spring of 1962 came from multiple interviews with Rupert Allan, Henry Weinstein, Whitey Snyder, Robert Slatzer and George Cukor (who granted a series of interviews to author Brown in 1979 and 1980 for a *Los Angeles Times* Calendar story).

Eunice Murray's book, *Marilyn: The Last Months*, provided a rich portrait of life at Monroe's new home in Brentwood, as did Patte Barham's interview with Murray, which was conducted by phone in 1986 when *Goddess* was published. *Goddess*, by former London *Times* journalist Anthony Summers, which remains the breakthrough account of Monroe's last years, was helpful throughout the preparation of this book, as was a brief interview with Summers by Brown which was completed when the Fox Entertainment News documentary was being produced.

The account of Monroe's years at Fox came from dozens of documents in the Fox archives, the Hedda Hopper Collection, the Louella Parsons Collection, the Spyros Skouras Collection, the Darryl F. Zanuck Collection in Sources and the clipping files of the Film and Television Library of the University of Southern California. Interviews for this section included multiple discussions with Whitey Snyder, William Travilla, Lee Hanna and Susan Strasberg.

The account of the decline and fall of Twentieth Century-Fox was assembled from data contained in the corporation's annual reports for the years 1958, 1959, 1960 and 1961. Especially helpful was a candid and top-secret report made by Fox production chief Peter Levathes to the board of directors in May 1962 – just as the corporation was collapsing. Levathes's 'special report' outlined corporate excesses and offered a plan for the salvation of the once-powerful studio. It included salary data, line-item costs and a profit-and-loss statement. The accounts of Monroe's affair with Fox president Spyros P. Skouras came from Nico Minardos, Rupert Allan and Hazel Washington. The star's fear of the old moguls Skouras and Zanuck was described by Peter Levathes in January 1990.

Chapter 2

Information on Monroe's makeup and dressing ritual was assembled from interviews with Whitey Snyder and his wife, Marjorie Plecher, along with an account by Monroe's fellow Fox star Sheree North. The startling disclosure that Cukor refused to direct Monroe's costume tests was all but wiped out of the official production documents. It only shows up in the notes for a Cukor memo written on June 8 and sent to *Something's Got to Give* producer Henry Weinstein. There is also a notation on the costume test reel which reads 'April 10: Weinstein/Franz Planer', indicating that Weinstein was the director and Planer the cinematographer. This information was discovered by Henry Schipper when the Fox documentary was being assembled. Cukor also discussed his decision at some length with actor Thomas Tryon. The decision was also described by producer Weinstein in a series of interviews. Descriptions of Monroe's new look came from designer Jean Louis, Whitey Snyder, Marjorie

Plecher, Evelyn Moriarity, William Travilla and Sheree North.

The scandal on the set of *Let's Make Love*, which turned Cukor against Monroe, was documented in the film's production logs, memos and weekly reports. Further evidence was found in the Hedda Hopper Collection. Moriarity, editor David Bretherton, Tryon and Rupert Allan offered additional data. Travilla discussed Cukor's attraction to Montand.

The description of the *Something's Got to Give* costume and hairstyling tests came from Weinstein, Bretherton and Snyder and from our viewing of 27 minutes of film which survived only in a private archive. Monroe's attorney, Milton Rudin, talked of Monroe's need to go back to work.

Chapter 3

A record of Monroe's overdose the morning after the costume tests was discovered on a microfilm reel of Fox insurance memorandums. Included were the unofficial minutes of a meeting between 'Ferguson, Brand, Feldman, Weinstein, McLean concerning Monroe and *Something's Got to Give* completion bonds'. Weinstein also discussed the overdose in detail during interviews in June and October 1990. Schipper also found evidence of it when he was writing the script for the Fox Entertainment News special on the unfinished film. Some background for the incident came from Dr. Ralph Greenson's wife, Hildi, and daughter, Joan Greenson Aibe. David Brown, Richard Zanuck, David Bretherton and Walter Bernstein offered powerful testimony on the appointment of Henry Weinstein and the dismissal of Brown. Monroe's attorney, Milton Rudin (in his first interview ever on the subject of Monroe), described the reasoning behind Weinstein's selection and Greenson's rationale in making the unusual deal. Greenson was Rudin's best friend and brother-in-law. Greenson's incredible influence over Monroe was described by Ralph Roberts, Whitey Snyder, Fred Lawrence Guiles and Eunice Murray (in *Marilyn: The Last Months*). Monroe's emotional state was depicted by Milton Rudin in a February 1992 interview.

Chapter 4

The profile of George Cukor and his problems grew out of an early interview with one of Monroe's biographers, Carl Rollyson, Jr. (*Marilyn Monroe: A Life of the Actress*). Rollyson recommended that we take a hard look at Cukor to find out whether *Something's Got to Give* was sabotaged. The profile of the peculiar set and descriptions of Cukor's house came from a cache of 100 photos of the set and the Cukor house in the Fox photo archives. Also helpful was a personal tour of the mansion and photographs in *Architectural Digest* and *The Los Angeles Times*. The documents threatening Cukor with legal action unless he agreed to direct *Something's Got to Give* were found in the Spyros Skouras Collection. The telegrams from Cukor to Zanuck during the production of *Let's Make Love* were described by Fox secretary Lee Hanna, to whom Cukor dictated the messages.

The bleak description of Cukor's years at MGM came from interviews with Howard Strickling, head of the studio's publicity department from the twenties through the sixties. Patrick McGilligan's biography of Cukor, published in December 1991, provided valuable details on Cukor's homosexuality. Tryon, Gene Allen, David Brown, Dorris Johnson (Nunnally's widow), Nora Johnson (Nunnally's daughter) and Milton Rudin provided a three-dimensional portrait of the director.

Our descriptions of the relationship between Johnson and Monroe was derived from interviews with Dorris Johnson and Fox story editor Theodore Strauss and from the collected Johnson letters and Tom Stempel's profile of the screenwriter. Interviews with Bernstein and Gene Allen dealt with Cukor's frustration over the Johnson screenplay, and Bernstein's reminiscences in *Esquire* magazine established that writer's difficulties with Monroe. A study of the ten versions of the *Something's Got to Give* screenplay, particularly the vastly changed Johnson screenplay, testified to the last-minute rewrites, and rewrites of rewrites, which caused the star such obvious grief.

Accounts of Monroe's complicated relationships with Method acting guru Lee Strasberg came from interviews with Cindy Adams, Ralph Roberts and Gene Allen. Adams's book *Lee Strasberg: The Imperfect Genius of the Actors Studio* and Carl Rollyson's account of Monroe's career were also very helpful.

Chapter 5

Monroe's tangled, disastrous affairs with President John F. Kennedy and Attorney General Robert Kennedy were established in interviews with Ralph Roberts, former Los Angeles mayor Sam Yorty, Peter Lawford biographer James Spada, biographer Anthony Summers, Los Angeles deputy district attorney Mike Carroll, Hazel Washington, Gene Allen, Natalie Jacobs, Rupert Allan, Pat Newcomb, Dorris Johnson, Dorothy Manners, Ed Guthman (who testified to Bobby's first meetings with Monroe), Robert Slatzer, Terry Moore and journalist James Bacon.

In addition, the unaired special report by ABC News (for a proposed 1986 segment of *20/20*) was obtained from a private source: it included interviews with more than 25 political and show business figures. Most important of these were Fred Otash, Terry Moore, Eunice Murray (who finally admitted to ABC news reporter Sylvia Chase that 'there was a romantic relationship between Monroe and Bobby Kennedy'), and Monroe's confidante Jeanne Carmen.

A wide-ranging interview with former CBS News producer Ted Landreth – who also produced the 1986 BBC documentary, *Say Goodbye to the President – Marilyn Monroe and the Kennedys* – further nailed down sexual and romantic relationships between the film star and the two most powerful men in America.

A surprising source was the collection of Hollywood gossip queen Hedda Hopper, which contained letters from readers remarking about the secret link between Monroe and the First Family. Though the letters offered powerful clues to the affairs, Hopper never wrote a line about them.

The so-called tabloid shows *Geraldo*, *Sally Jesse Raphael*, *Donahue* and *Hard Copy* have all produced segments on the affair and provided further evidence of what is now a historically accepted fact – that Monroe had tempestuous affairs with both brothers. On February 15, 1992, Hugh Downs, the dean of ABC broadcast journalists, said on the Arts and Entertainment Channel's exhaustive *Class of the Twentieth Century* that 'history has proven the relationship'.

JFK's tryst with Monroe in late April (just before her illness began) was first documented in James Spada's 1991 biography of Peter Lawford, *The Man Who Kept the Secrets*, but interviews with Ralph Roberts, Robert Slatzer, Hazel Washington (who accompanied Monroe on the trip to New York) and Rupert Allan (who talked to Monroe from the Royal Palace at Monaco when the star was in Manhattan for the Kennedy tryst) confirmed it. Milt Ebbins, Lawford's manager, discussed the weekend in great detail with Spada. The calls between Monroe, in her Fox dressing room, and the President (in the White House and at Hyannis Port) were verified by Fox choreographer Stephen Papich and two studio switchboard operators, speaking off the record. The rendezvous in Palm Springs just before filming began on *Something's Got to Give* was documented by Landreth and the BBC, by *20/20*, by *Hard Copy* and by Robert Slatzer. C. David Heymann further documented the affair in *A Woman Named Jackie*. In a pair of interviews, Ralph Roberts provided the glimpses of Monroe on Air Force One in disguise. Costume designer Travilla repeated gossip on the affairs which circulated during *Something's Got to Give*.

Other helpful sources were Patricia Seaton Lawford's book, *The Peter Lawford Story*; psychological writer Lucy Freeman's upcoming work, *Why Norma Jean Killed Marilyn Monroe*; *Time* magazine's 'JFK's Women' (December 25, 1975); the 1982 report of the Los Angeles district attorney on 'The Reinvestigation of Marilyn Monroe's Death'; the *New York Post* 1986 exposé 'The Bobby Kennedy Connection'; Justice Department memorandum of August 20, 1962, which quotes Bobby Kennedy on his connection with Monroe; an account of 'The Bobby–Marilyn Affair' in the August 19, 1988, issue of *National Review*; an Arthur Schlesinger interview in the *Boston Globe* on October 18, 1978; Monroe's spring 1962 letter to Ralph Greenson about a new 'mystery man' in her life; Paula Strasberg's interview with James Haspiel, as reported by Anthony Summers in *Goddess*; an account of 'The Kennedys in California' from the *Los Angeles Times*, March 23 to 28, 1962; Sydney Skolsky's book, *Don't Get Me Wrong – I Love Hollywood*; FBI Document 77-51387-310 of August 20, 1962, recounting Bobby Kennedy's admission of rumours regarding his relationship with Monroe; Chapter 22 of Heymann's *A Woman Called Jackie*; and Chapter 27 of Spada's Lawford biography.

Chapter 6

The information on the beginnings of Monroe's illness come from documents and logs compiled originally by the Twentieth Century-Fox physicians, Philip Rubin and Lee Siegel. The only references to the medical data were found in the lawsuit which Fox later filed against Monroe. But Henry Schipper found references to Siegel's claims that Monroe 'was very ill' on microfilm in the studio's legal archives. Fortunately, memos to Spyros Skouras from Siegel survive among the mogul's papers. In addition, Siegel's widow, Noreen, provided dozens of details concerning the star's sinus infection and virus, which kept her in bed for three weeks. Weinstein, Gene Allen, Whitey Snyder, Jean Louis and Ralph Roberts discussed Monroe's health in a series of interviews. The details of Monroe's temperatures and the messages she sent to Cukor and Buck Hall are contained in the production logs and the Skouras memos. Noreen Siegel recalled her husband's discussions about the seriousness of Monroe's sinusitis. Walter Bernstein attested to Hall's prediction that Monroe would be out for weeks.

The administration of amphetamine shots to both Monroe and Cukor throughout the history of *Something's Got to Give* was documented by eyewitness testimony (from Bretherton, Moriarity, Travilla, Bernstein and Slatzer) and by Monroe's fellow star Sheree North, who discussed the long-term practice. Thomas Tryon also recalled conversations between himself and Cukor on the director's amphetamine use. Patrick McGilligan also wrote briefly about Cukor's use of diet pills. Lee Siegel, in his last interview, also discussed the practice with Anthony Summers and BBC interviewers. The drug discussions between Monroe and JFK came from Spada's book *The Man Who Kept the Secrets*, and Peter Levathes recalled Monroe's descriptions of her 'bedtime cocktails'.

Chapter 7

In the depiction of the excesses and scandals of *Cleopatra*, Brad Geagley's unpublished study of the film, 'Cleopatra, The Last Movie', was very helpful. Compiled from hundreds of interviews over a five-year period, the book provides a sweeping portrait of the

$42-million disaster. Also helpful were Walter Wanger's *My Life with Cleopatra*, *The Cleopatra Papers* by Jack Brodsky and Nathan Weiss, and the official 1963 premiere programme for the film. In understanding the personal problems and professional decline of Joseph Mankiewicz, Kenneth Geist's *Pictures Will Talk* (Charles Scribner's Sons, 1978) was an invaluable guide. Aubrey Solomon's *A Corporate History of Fox* contained other pertinent facts. Peter Levathes, who inherited the debacle from departing production chief Robert Goldstein, provided a broad narrative during three days of interviews in January 1961, as did Mankiewicz's sons Chris and Tom, who both worked on the film in a variety of positions. Christina Levathes's remembrances of life with her husband during those troubled days were also revealing. Milton Gould provided both facts and comments about the Taylor-Burton disaster. Monroe's resentment of the money pouring into the Roman production was described by Ralph Roberts, Whitey Snyder, Rupert Allan, Robert Slatzer and Stephen Papich. Her desire to portray the doomed Egyptian queen was described in a chronological history of the film written by Skouras and his assistants. Also, Monroe talked at some length of this desire to both Evelyn Moriarity and Wally Cox on the set of *Something's Got to Give*. Monroe's affair with Skouras was described in great detail by Nico Minardos. Details of Taylor's million-dollar contract came from the Fox archives. Debbie Reynolds graphically described the way Taylor stole Eddie Fisher from her in a series of interviews, which were augmented by an interview with Fisher in San Francisco in April 1991. Taylor's temperament and her costly habits on the *Cleopatra* set came from Kitty Kelley's *The Last Star*, Joan Joseph's *For the Love of Liz* (Manor Books, 1976) *Who's Afraid of Elizabeth Taylor* by Brenda Maddox and Bragg's biography of Burton. Harsh words about the decline of Mankiewicz also came from Levathes and both Mankiewicz sons.

The exorbitant costs of the film were set out in a series of Twentieth Century-Fox documents, including a June 1962 report of Taylor's absences; a Western Union telegram from Skouras to Fox executive Buddy Adler detailing Taylor's demands; the full transcript of an interview between David Slavitt of *Newsweek* magazine and Spyros Skouras; a legal history of *Cleopatra* compiled by Fox attorneys when the studio sued Richard Burton and Elizabeth Taylor, and the 1961 budget estimates for *Cleopatra*, written in pencil. Further details on these documents appear in 'Sources'.

Chapter 8

The profile of Monroe's illness and her premature return to the studio came from interviews with Ralph Roberts, Eunice Murray, Hazel Washington and Noreen Siegel. Her illnesses on the set are fully documented in the Fox production logs of April 22 to May 16. Details of her work with child actors Christopher Morley and Alexandra Heilweil came from interviews with both actors and with Eva Wolas Heilweil, Whitey Snyder, Marjorie Plecher, Henry Weinstein, Evelyn Moriarity, Robert Slatzer, Fox story editor Theodore Strauss, *Something's Got to Give* editor David Bretherton, Henry Schipper and Buck Hall. George Cukor's mistreatment of Monroe during the scene with the dog was described by Susan Strasberg, Eva Wolas Heilweil, Stephen Papich, Ralph Roberts and Moriarity. Much of the dialogue between Cukor and Monroe came from the raw film itself, since the camera was allowed to run many seconds after the scenes were completed. Cukor's insistence on rewriting the script the night before was described by both Eunice Murray and Pat Newcomb and is evident in the many versions of the screenplay in the Special Collections of the University of Southern California. The script rewrites are also documented in Murray's *Marilyn: The Last Months* and in Tom Stempel's book *Screenwriter: The Life and Times of Nunnally Johnson*. The claim that Monroe's absences should have been listed officially as 'excused by illness' came from the production logs, from Lee Siegel's widow, Noreen, and from the rule book of the Screen Actors Guild.

Chapter 9

The story of Monroe's sudden return to the set was assembled from Fox security logs and an interview with Thomas Tryon. The account of Cukor's misrepresentations to Phil Feldman comes from Feldman's own notes on telephone conversations in the Skouras papers. Moriarity, Gene Allen, Bretherton, Snyder and

Susan Strasberg provided relevant details. Walter Bernstein recalled Monroe's near-paranoia over Cyd Charisse and over the platinum-blonde starlet, as did Snyder. Weinstein recreated his frantic telephone conversations with Monroe. Both Summers, in *Goddess*, and Fred Lawrence Guiles, in *Legend*, touch on these incidents, as does Bernstein's July 1973 article in *Esquire*. Henry Weinstein's memo to Fox casting executive Owen McLean about 'blonde extras' also was helpful. Timothy Leary's bizarre meetings with Monroe came from Leary's own book, *Flashbacks*, from an interview with Leary in May 1991 and from *Goddess*.

Chapter 10

The affair between Elizabeth Taylor and Richard Burton was documented by those who watched it happen: Tom and Chris Mankiewicz, Peter Levathes, Cesare Danova, Eddie Fisher, Dorothy Manners and Milton Gould. Its effect on Twentieth Century-Fox was documented by a series of studio papers which include a business letter from Spyros Skouras to Joseph Mankiewicz dated April 6, 1962; a confidential letter from Skouras to *Cleopatra* producer Walter Wanger dated April 14; Wanger's reply to Skouras, dated April 26; and a mid-1967 letter from Skouras to Darryl F. Zanuck which recapped Taylor's suicide attempts and the brutal beating she received from Burton just before Easter 1962. Details on these documents appear in the 'Sources'.

Kelley's *The Last Star*, Bragg's *Burton*, Wanger's *My Life with Cleopatra* and Brodsky's and Weiss's *The Cleopatra Papers* helped provide a backdrop for the affair and subsequent scandal. Stephen Papich and William Travilla documented Monroe's reaction to the troubles in Rome.

Ferguson's warning letter to Monroe and Milton Rudin was found in the Zanuck papers. It was dated May 16, three days before the Kennedy birthday gala.

Chapter 11

Monroe's departure for New York was described by gossip columnist Dorothy Manners, Parsons's writer-researcher, who was on the Fox lot that afternoon, by Fox executive secretary Lee Hanna, who observed the helicopter landing, and by Walter Bernstein, Gene Allen and Pat Newcomb. Bobby Kennedy's intercession with Fox executive committee chairman Milton S. Gould was described in detail by Gould and by Rupert Allan, who learned of Kennedy's language from Fox marketing director E. Charles Einfeld. Anthony Summers found a reference to the phone call when he was researching *Goddess* in the early 1980s. Weinstein described Monroe's determination to attend the gala.

Chapter 12

Interviews with Jean Louis, Marjorie Plecher, Richard Adler, Mickey Song, Dorothy Manners and Hazel Washington all focused on Monroe's incredible $12,000 dress for the Kennedy gala. The star's rehearsals and preparations were described by Joan Greenson Aibe and Evelyn Moriarity. Adler, the Tony-winning composer of *Damn Yankees* and *The Pajama Game*, described the organisation of the gala and the rehearsals in New York. Adler's book, *You Gotta Have Heart*, also offered insights into Monroe's state of mind at the time.

Chapter 13

Richard Adler also described his premature decision to fire Monroe and replace her with Shirley MacLaine, and his confrontation with the star at the run-through on Saturday morning, May 19.

Jean Louis recounted Monroe's call from President Kennedy while Louis was doing final fittings of the gown, a story which had been relayed to Patte Barham during an interview in late 1972. Mickey Song, the Kennedy family hairstylist, described Monroe's preparations for the gala in the Madison Square Garden dressing rooms. Hazel Washington, who carried Monroe's dress to New York, discussed Monroe's reactions to the event and her relationship with the President at that time.

The description of Monroe's highly personal serenade to JFK came from a full-length film clip of the event in David L. Wolper's *The Legend of Marilyn Monroe*, produced in 1967 for ABC. A transcription of that programme was viewed in the Fox film library. Ralph Roberts, Pat Newcomb and Song, who all observed the event, discussed their impressions. The comments made by the President and Robert Kennedy came from Ted Landreth's BBC documentary, which first aired in 1986. Kitty Kelley in *The Last Star* and Anthony Summers in *Goddess* offered other details.

The final rendezvous between Monroe and JFK (at the Carlyle Hotel) was described by Song, Washington and Dorothy Manners during a series of interviews in early 1991. That final fling was also touched upon by C. David Heymann in *A Woman Called Jackie*, by James Spada in *The Man Who Kept the Secrets*, and by Earl Wilson in *Show Business Laid Bare*.

The most detailed coverage of the gala came from the *New York Times* on May 19 and 20, 1962, but clips from the *Washington Post*, the *Boston Globe* and the *Los Angeles Herald Examiner* were also useful

The suspicious action by the Secret Service to protect Robert Kennedy was described by Richard Adler in an interview. Papich, Slatzer and Washington attested to Monroe's disappointment with JFK's sexual performance.

Ralph Roberts also remembered Monroe's comments and appearance after the gala, which were also described by James Haspiel, one of Monroe's closest New York confidants.

Chapter 15

Monroe's envy of Elizabeth Taylor's professional and economic clout was discussed by Ralph Roberts, Hazel Washington and Eunice Murray (in Barham's telephone interview in the 1970s).

Dean Martin's virus, Monroe's reactions to it and Cukor's fury over the situation were all graphically documented in production logs, weekly reports and *Something's Got to Give* memos. Studio doctor Siegel's support for Monroe's decision came from memos in the Skouras Collection which are undated but were presumably written in June 1962.

The memo from Monroe, apparently written to Arthur Jacobs or one of the star's secretaries, is referred to in a Skouras letter to Darryl Zanuck and came from a private source. The apparent 'slowdown' by Cukor shows up when the production logs are compared with the completed film.

The nude swimming scene was recreated through interviews with photographer Lawrence Schiller, Whitey Snyder, Marjorie Plecher, David Bretherton, Henry Weinstein, Pat Newcomb, Walter Bernstein, Gene Allen, Thomas Tryon, journalist James Bacon, Ralph Greenson, Peter Levathes, Evelyn Moriarity, Stephen Papich, Rupert Allan and Robert Slatzer.

New coverage of the event was also helpful, including stories in the *New York Herald Tribune* of May 25 to 27, 1962; the *Los Angeles Herald Examiner*, May 26, 1962; *Time*, June 7, 1962 and *Life*, June 22, 1962.

Chapter 16

The excitement within the Fox executive corps when the rushes from *Something's Got to Give* were screened was expressed in the chronological history of *Something's Got to Give* prepared by the studio's legal affairs division. (Full details of the document appear in 'Sources'.)

Monroe's emotional troubles on the set were described by Thomas Tryon in a pair of interviews in December 1990. Monroe's search for Frank Sinatra was depicted by Lee Hanna, Hazel Washington and Stephen Papich. Henry Weinstein provided graphic details of Monroe's mental state at the time of the 'lost weekend'.

Sinatra's fall from grace with the JFK administration came from Kitty Kelley's *His Way* and James Spada's *The Man Who Kept the Secrets*. Dorothy Manners was also helpful. The singer's position was also described in *The Kennedys* by David Horowitz and Peter Collier and by C. David Heymann in *A Woman Called Jackie*. Eunice Murray recalled a long-distance call from 'someone in the Kennedy family', in BBC interviews and in her discussion with a crew from ABC's *20/20*.

Monroe's danger to the First Family was described by Anthony Summers, Ted Landreth, Robert Slatzer and former Los Angeles mayor Sam Yorty in interviews. In addition, one of Lawford's former wives, Deborah Gould, discussed it at some length in the BBC documentary *Say Goodbye to the President – Marilyn Monroe and the*

Kennedys. Another wife, Patricia Seaton Lawford, gave her version in her book, *The Peter Lawford Story*. Terry Moore's interview contained the revelation that 'it got too hot for Jack so she was passed to Bobby'.

Dr. Ralph Greenson's warnings to stay away from the Kennedys were discussed in the 'psychological autopsy' which was prepared after the star's death.

Chapter 17

Monroe's despair over the ravages of time was reported in Eunice Murray's *Marilyn: The Last Months* and in interviews by Fox Entertainment News with Whitey Snyder, Sidney Guilaroff, Jean Louis and Joan Greenson.

The production logs show that Monroe worked most of the days between May 21 and June 1.

The thirty-sixth birthday party was described by Evelyn Moriarity, Lawrence Schiller, Ralph Greenson, Snyder, Gene Allen and Hazel Washington.

Information on Elizabeth Taylor's birthday fetes came from receipts, telegrams and actual bills from the Fox archives. The bills also showed up in an audit of *Cleopatra* expenses ordered by Zanuck in 1964.

Chapter 18

See notes for Chapter 10 on the Taylor–Burton affair.

The decision to fire Elizabeth Taylor as of June 9 was described by Peter Levathes and Tom and Chris Mankiewicz. The dismissal was also announced in a letter from Spyros Skouras to Joseph Mankiewicz written on May 31, 1962, and delivered by a courier from New York. It was also depicted by Jack Brodsky and Nathan Weiss in *The Cleopatra Papers* and by Walter Wanger in *My Life with Cleopatra*.

The beating Burton gave Taylor was uncovered in the 1967 letter from Skouras to Zanuck and was verified by Eddie Fisher. Monroe's suicide attempts were also discussed in the Skouras letter and verified by Lee Hanna, who became production secretary for *Cleopatra* after *Something's Got to Give* was cancelled. Tom and Chris Mankiewicz also discussed the overdoses in interviews.

The report of the actual negotiations between Levathes and the *Cleopatra* team came from three interviews with Levathes in 1991. Mankiewicz's use of drugs was noted in Kenneth Geist's *Pictures Will Talk*, which quoted Mankiewicz directly, and was verified by the Mankiewicz brothers. Taylor's drug problems were discussed by Eddie Fisher in a 1991 interview and touched on by Kitty Kelley in *The Last Star* and by Fisher in *My Life, My Loves*.

Philip Feldman's reports to Levathes were part of a nine-page, single-spaced document which proved to be a blow-by-blow description of Monroe's dismissal. This document was in the form of a telephone log and included an analysis of Feldman's dealings with Milton Rudin, Ralph Greenson, Dean Martin, Martin's agent, Herman Citron, and George Cukor. It provided a basic source for the following chapters on the firing and the disastrous 'anti-Marilyn campaign' mounted by the Fox publicity department. These developments were verified by Levathes, Rudin, Milton Gould, Hildi Greenson, Joan Greenson, Henry Weinstein and Rupert Allan. Other crucial interviews were with Noreen Siegel, Gene Allen, Ralph Roberts, writer Lucy Freeman, a psychological writer who knew Ralph Greenson, and Robert Slatzer. Allen, Weinstein, Newcomb, Noreen Siegel, Roberts, Joan Greenson and Hildi Greenson all testified that Monroe was physically ill (with aggravated sinusitis) on June 1.

Chapter 19

The events of June 1 through 9 were described by Eunice Murray in *Marilyn: The Last Months*, and by Joan Greenson, Gene Allen, Milton Gould and Milton Rudin. Again, the Philip Feldman document was an important source. Both Allen and Walter Bernstein attested to Cukor's refusal to believe Lee Siegel's assertion that Monroe's sinusitis had flared up again. 'None of us believed him,' said Allen in a December 1990 interview.

The demeaning set of conditions drafted for Monroe to sign was found in the Fox legal archives and obtained from a private source.

Chapter 20

Cukor's view of *Something's Got to Give* and his opinion that Monroe's career was over were discovered in a series of typed notes which Hedda Hopper preserved, now in the collection of the Academy of Motion Picture Arts and Sciences. Gene Allen verified Cukor's opinions in an interview and also discussed the director's running joke involving the sentence 'It's what's up on the screen that counts.' Cukor's appearance before Fox executives was recorded in the telephone conference notes drafted by Feldman. Thomas Tryon talked of Cukor's attitude in a telephone interview in February 1991.

In a June 1990 interview, comedy writer Hal Kanter described Fox's insistence that he fashion a script which would allow the studio to release *Something's Got to Give* using Monroe's completed film. Kanter also said he had found a way to do it.

Ralph Greenson's frustration with the studio was discussed by Milton Rudin and Joan Greenson during a series of interviews.

Fox's conditions for Monroe's reinstatement were contained in the Feldman telephone logs. Henry Weinstein talked of the political motivation behind the dismissal in three interviews in October 1990.

Monroe's reactions were defined by Ralph Roberts, Weinstein, Robert Slatzer, Joan Greenson, Whitey Snyder, Pat Newcomb, Rupert Allan, Sidney Guilaroff, Dorris Johnson and Susan Strasberg in 1990 interviews.

Chapter 22

The publicity campaign mounted by Fox to destroy Monroe's professional credibility was described by Joan Greenson, Ralph Roberts and Milton Rudin. Rudin's anger – even thirty years later – over the 'dirty tricks' played by Fox's chief publicist, Harry Brand, his deputy Perry Lieber and director of marketing E. Charles Einfeld was demonstrated in an interview on February 9, 1992. Cukor's cooperation with Brand and his crew was demonstrated by documents in the Hedda Hopper Collection of the Academy of Motion Picture Arts and Sciences.

Press releases from Perry Lieber, Frank Neill and John Campbell were found in the library of the *Los Angeles Herald Examiner*. Earl Wilson's columns of June 7 and June 8 – as quoted in his *Show Business Laid Bare* – testified to the columnist's 'scoop' in the race to report Monroe's imminent dismissal. Henry Weinstein and Peter Levathes both testified that there was no press conference – despite Brand's release of a packet of quotations by Levathes, Cukor and Weinstein. Lee Remick, in a December 4, 1990, interview, said she made no comments to the press after she was asked to take over Monroe's role in *Something's Got to Give*. Though Remick never talked to a reporter – or a publicist – Brand released a series of statements in Remick's name slamming Monroe. The release, accompanied by a photo of Remick and Cukor reading the *Something's Got to Give* screenplay, was located in the *Los Angeles Herald Examiner*'s library.

Extensive files – literally hundreds of clippings – from the Margaret Herrick Library of the Academy of Motion Picture Arts and Sciences were used to trace the careers of Brand, Einfeld, Lieber, Neill and Campbell. Sybil Brand talked of her husband's distaste for the 'anti-Monroe' campaign. She also told of Brand's marketing plan, which helped make Monroe a superstar.

Lieber's malicious involvement in the release of Monroe's nude calendar photo was described by Louella Parsons's secretary Dorothy Treloar in a 1983 *Los Angeles Times* Calendar story called 'Gossip,' by Peter Harry Brown.

The 'leaks' to Hedda Hopper are indicated in the columnist's papers.

On June 10, 1962, an unidentified publicist was credited by Murray Schumach of the *New York Times* with spreading the rumour that Monroe was going insane and that her instability was evident in the unedited film from *Something's Got to Give*. Sheilah Graham's involvement in the spreading scandal was described by that reporter in an interview on New York's WOR television in 1982.

The bulletins announcing Monroe's dismissal were carried on both the Associated Press and United Press International 'radio wires' and were broadcast over hundreds of radio stations on

Friday, June 8, at 2 P.M. – two hours before the studio informed Milton Rudin that his client was indeed fired from *Something's Got to Give*.

Joan Crawford's blistering diatribe on Monroe's conduct was printed in the *Hollywood Reporter*, *Daily Variety*, the *Hollywood Citizen-News* and the *Los Angeles Herald Examiner* on Monday, June 11.

The effect of the campaign on Monroe's emotional health was described by Joan Greenson, Ralph Roberts, Whitey Snyder, Evelyn Moriarity and writer Lucy Freeman in interviews. Freeman's account was supported by statements from Fred Lawrence Guiles, author of both *Norma Jean* and *Legend*. The description of Monroe's mental problems and her family's history of such troubles came from *Legend* and Freeman's book.

Maurice Zolotow described Monroe's trouble with line readings on the sets of *Some Like It Hot*, *The Misfits*, *How to Marry a Millionaire* and *Let's Make Love* during an August 1990 interview. Zolotow's 1961 Bantam book, *Marilyn Monroe*, provided another excellent source for our account of the star's perception problems. And it was Zolotow who first suggested that Monroe must have had a learning disability. Robert Slatzer concurred.

Monroe's crucial call to Darryl F. Zanuck in Paris after her dismissal was recalled by Whitey Snyder, who was in Monroe's living room when she placed the call.

Chapter 23

The mood on the set after Monroe's firing was recreated through interviews with Whitey Snyder, Evelyn Moriarity, Henry Weinstein, Lee Remick, Gene Allen and Peter Levathes.

The bulletin stating that Dean Martin refused to work without Monroe was sent over the United Press International Wire at 6:12 P.M. on Friday, June 8. It was located in the files of the *Los Angeles Herald Examiner*. Since Snyder was with Martin when it was announced that Remick would take over the role, his version is definitive.

Philip Feldman's deal with Remick was confirmed by the actress in a December 1990 interview.

The *New York Daily News* and the *New York Times* headlines ran on Saturday, June 9.

Remick's indignant reaction to the publicity releases in her name came in the same December 1990 interview.

Feldman's frantic attempts to coerce Martin into accepting Remick were described in the nine-page telephone notes written by that executive and discovered in the Fox archives (from a private source).

Details from the lawsuits against both Monroe and Martin came from the suits themselves. Monroe's was filed in Santa Monica Superior Court on June 8 (the day she was fired); Martin's much more comprehensive action was filed on June 19 in the same court. Monroe's attorney, Milton Rudin, confirmed Martin's sensitivity to Monroe's troubles in a February 1992 interview.

Lee Hanna described the nastiness directed at Martin in an October 1990 interview.

Hedda Hopper's column on the probable retaliation against Martin ran in the *Los Angeles Times* on June 12, 1962.

Chapter 24

Monroe's fight to be reinstated was described by Pat Newcomb, Whitey Snyder, Ralph Roberts, Rupert Allan and Joan Greenson.

The telegrams to all members of the cast and crew were noted in the bills to Monroe's estate filed in September 1962 and provided to the authors by Robert Slatzer. The note to Robert and Ethel Kennedy from Monroe was found in the John F. Kennedy Presidential Library. Monroe's calls to Spyros Skouras are documented in three interviews the mogul gave to Hedda Hopper, Sheilah Graham and Murray Schumach, which exist in note form among the Skouras papers.

Some evidence exists that Robert Kennedy moved to help Monroe save *Something's Got to Give* even before the actress contacted him. U.S. Justice Department files show that Monroe did not call him on the government line until June 12. But the Attorney General telephoned Fox board chairman Samuel Rosenman on Monday, June 11 – after the disastrous PR campaign against Monroe broke into print in the Washington newspapers. Rosenman told Skouras to find a way to help Monroe, according to lengthy Skouras memoirs in the Spyros Skouras Collection at Stanford University. Peter

Levathes verified that the 'powers in New York' told him to open negotiations with Monroe ten days or so after the star was fired.

Nunnally Johnson later told Rupert Allan that the 'Kennedys were involved in getting Monroe reinstated'. Allan recalled the conversation in a telephone interview on January 15, 1991.

Nunnally Johnson's communications with Zanuck over 'the Monroe dilemma' were included in the screenwriter's letters to his daughter Nora and in interviews with Johnson's biographer, Tom Stempel. Zanuck's displeasure over Monroe's dismissal was verified through interviews with Zanuck's son, Richard, and with his daughter, Darrilyn, both in late 1990. An interview with Johnson's widow, Dorris, confirmed his low opinion of Cukor's part in the plot against Monroe. Rudin's anger over the 'dirty tricks' perpetrated by Perry Lieber was recounted in the nine-page Feldman report, 'The Dismissal of Marilyn Monroe,' and by Rudin himself in a February 1992 interview.

Chapter 25

For basic source information on Monroe and the Kennedy brothers, see the notes for Chapter 5.

RFK's visit to Monroe's Brentwood house was described in Eunice Murray's *Marilyn: The Last Months* and by the housekeeper in a wide-ranging interview with Sylvia Chase of ABC's *20/20* in 1986. The Attorney General's career advice was described by Murray to Robert Slatzer, and by Slatzer in an interview. Monroe also recounted the conversation to Peter Lawford, who repeated it to a reporter for the *San Francisco Chronicle* on August 14, 1962.

Monroe's desperate calls to the President through the White House switchboard were unearthed by author James Spada in *The Man Who Kept the Secrets*. Anthony Summers had found indications of these dangerous calls when researching *Goddess*.

The beginnings of Monroe's affair with the Attorney General were described by James Bacon, Robert Slatzer and Monroe's fellow Twentieth Century-Fox star Terry Moore in interviews. Backup sources included Deborah Gould Lawford's video interview with the BBC, Patricia Seaton Lawford's appearance on *Sally*

Jesse Raphael and Ralph Greenson's 1973 interview with the *Chicago Tribune*.

Verification came in interviews with Dr. Robert Litman, who heard of the 'friendship-romance' between RFK and Monroe from Ralph Greenson when the latter testified before the Suicide Prevention Team convened to investigate Monroe's death.

Monroe's frequent calls to the Attorney General were discussed by his press aide, Ed Guthman, during a March 1991 interview, and by Hazel Washington.

The glittering Lawford party which threw Monroe and RFK together for the first time was discussed in interviews with Whitey Snyder, Guthman, Murray, Washington and Slatzer.

Backup information came from *Goddess*, in which Lawford neighbours Lynn Sherman and Peter Dye talked of watching the romance grow in the early summer of 1962.

Snyder, who gave Monroe a ride to the party, discussed the stir her arrival caused.

Washington, who became unusually close to Monroe during the last seven weeks of her life, characterised RFK as the 'last great love of Monroe's life'. She also said in the same February 1991 interview that 'JFK was just another man passin' through'.

The romantic bond between RFK and Monroe, which still causes controversy among Kennedy confidants, was, in the words of ABC newscaster Hugh Downs, 'a historical fact'. Downs made that statement in the Arts and Entertainment Channel documentary *Class of the Twentieth Century* which aired on February 15, 1992. As the anchorman of *20/20* Downs had access to the twenty-five hours of interviews conducted for the show's segment on Monroe and the Kennedy brothers, which was pulled from the programme less than thirty hours before it was to air.

The love affair was first documented by crusading conservative journalist Frank A. Capell in his 1964 book, *The Strange Death of Marilyn Monroe*. It was discussed more fully in Robert Slatzer's 1974 book, *The Curious Death of Marilyn Monroe*. More recently, James Spada and Anthony Summers offered convincing evidence of the clandestine affair, and Milton Rudin commented tersely that 'the Kennedys misused her terribly'.

Bobby Kennedy's role as a messenger from JFK to Monroe was described by Terry Moore, Gould, Patricia Seaton Lawford and Slatzer in a variety of interviews with Summers, Spada, BBC journalists and reporters from *20/20*.

Summers discussed Monroe's increasing danger to the First Family in *Goddess* and in the BBC documentary. Eunice Murray told ABC in 1985 that JFK was warned of the peril of continued association with Monroe.

Chapter 26

Dr. Michael Gurdin described his treatment of a battered Monroe in a 1992 interview, and Robert Slatzer theorised in an October 1991 discussion that 'someone beat her up'.

Press releases about Fox's lawsuit against its former star came from the Monroe collection of the *Los Angeles Herald Examiner*.

Monroe's flirtation with Fox production chief Peter Levathes was described by Levathes, Eunice Murray and Pat Newcomb, who hid in Monroe's bedroom taking notes during one of the meetings. Cukor's dismissal from *Something's Got to Give* was confirmed by director Jean Negulesco, who was hired by Levathes to direct the star in the resurrection of the film.

The demeaning document of public apology which E. Charles Einfeld wanted to force on Monroe was first discussed by *Cleopatra* publicist Jack Brodsky, who wrote part of the document. Several paragraphs of this apology were described by Spyros Skouras in a 1967 letter to Darryl F. Zanuck.

Chapter 27

Documentation of Bobby Kennedy's affair with Monroe can be found in the source notes for Chapters 5 and 25.

Robert Kennedy's role as the family's sexual policeman was described by Kitty Kelley in *Jackie Oh!*, by James Spada in *The Man Who Kept the Secrets*, by C. David Heymann in *A Woman Called Jackie* and by Peter Collier and David Horowitz in *The Kennedys*.

Monroe's habit of writing down conversations with her lovers (in secretarial notebooks) was described by Evelyn Moriarity and Hazel

Washington. Ed Guthman described RFK's telephone relationships with both Monroe and Judy Garland in a 1991 interview.

RFK's presence on the Fox lot during preproduction of *The Enemy Within* is described in a series of memos in the Skouras and Zanuck papers and by screenwriter Budd Schulberg in his autobiography, *Moving Pictures*.

Details of the Lawford beach house and the sexual and social doings there came from the following articles: 'Presidential Brother-in-Law' by Stephen Birmingham, *Cosmopolitan*, October 1961; 'The Lawfords', by Helen Markel, *Good Housekeeping*, February 1962; the obituary of Lady May Lawford in the *Los Angeles Times*, January 24, 1972; and 'The Lawford House', the *Los Angeles Times*, April 15, 1978.

The exchange between Elizabeth Courtney and Hazel Washington was described by Washington in a January 1991 interview. Monroe's reports on the sexual performance of both JFK and RFK came from interviews with James Bacon, Ralph Roberts, Robert Slatzer, Stephen Papich, Washington and Jeanne Carmen, the last in interview with BBC journalists. Additional sexual details were found in Ralph G. Martin's *A Hero for Our Time*, Tony Sciacca's *Kennedy and His Women* and *The Intimate Sex Lives of Famous People* by Irving Wallace, Amy Wallace et al.

Deputy Los Angeles district attorney Mike Carroll talked of finding 'plenty of evidence' about Monroe's relationships with the Kennedys. Dr. Robert Litman heard similar stories – some of them directly from Dr. Ralph Greenson – during Monroe's 'psychological autopsy'.

In several interviews, the BBC's Ted Landreth talked of finding a consensus among Washington political journalists that affairs took place between Monroe and both Kennedy brothers.

Fox choreographer Stephen Papich was in Monroe's *Something's Got to Give* bungalow when the star made her brazen call to JFK in the Oval Office. Chuck Pick's run-in with the Secret Service was recounted in Spada's *The Man Who Kept the Secrets*. Lynn Sherman's vignette about Pat Lawford came from Anthony Summers's *Goddess*.

The strange note signed by Jean Kennedy Smith which bears the address of the Kennedy Palm Beach mansion came from Monroe's estate papers and was also discovered by Anthony Summers.

The hints of Monroe's 'destructive relationships' were included in the 'psychological autopsy'.

Chapter 28

The accounts of Monroe's failure to reach Bobby Kennedy and her forced estrangement from both JFK and RFK was described fully in both Spada's and Summers's accounts of the star's last weeks. Additional information came from *Legend* by Fred Lawrence Guiles. Monroe discussed her betrayal in long conversations with Arthur James (who spoke of it to Ted Landreth and the BBC journalists), Robert Slatzer and Hazel Washington. The latter two discussed it in interviews in March 1991.

Details of the threat Monroe posed to the Kennedy presidency came from the following accounts: *JFK – The Presidency of John F. Kennedy*, a 1967 book by Herbert Parmet; *A Thousand Days* by Arthur Schlesinger, 1965; *Bay of Pigs* by Peter Wyden, 1979; *Portrait of a President* by William Manchester; and *Kennedy Justice* by Victor Navasky, 1981.

Details of Ted Kennedy's campaign for the Senate came from the *Boston Globe* in stories which ran from July through November 7, 1962.

Chapter 29

Monroe's meetings with Peter Levathes were described by the former Fox executive in January 1991 interviews, with verification from Pat Newcomb via telephone in February 1991.

Details of Monroe's photo sessions came from Eunice Murray's *The Last Months* and Anthony Summers's *Goddess*.

The account of Darryl F. Zanuck's drive to save Twentieth Century-Fox came from *Zanuck* by Roy Mosely and *Don't Say Yes Until I Finish Talking* by Mel Gussow. More than fifty clippings on the Zanuck revolution came from *Daily Variety*, the *Hollywood Reporter* and the *Wall Street Journal* from May 14, 1962, through August 4, 1962. Also helpful were the minutes of the Fox executive committee from May 18, 1962; June 9, 1962; July 26, 1962, and July 28, 1962, which were obtained from a private source, and interviews with Milton Gould, Levathes and Richard Zanuck (in June 1990). Darrilyn Zanuck was helpful by describing her father's fear that *Cleopatra* would ruin the corporation. Zanuck's attorney, Louis Nizer, described his client's drive to reclaim the presidency of Fox in telephone interviews during December 1990.

Chapter 30

The details of Monroe's home were gathered by touring of the house and studying a series of photos in the files of the *Los Angeles Herald Examiner*.

The star's flirtation with anorexia surfaced in interviews with Eunice Murray, Robert Slatzer and in Murray's *The Last Months*. Dr. Lee Siegel's warnings came from his memos to Spyros Skouras.

Monroe's battles with insomnia were reported in interviews with Whitey Snyder, Rupert Allan, Joan Greenson, Lucy Freeman, Ralph Roberts, Pat Newcomb and Hazel Washington. Also helpful were *Goddess, Legend, The Last Months* and the 1982 report of the Los Angeles district attorney by Mike Carroll.

Information on Monroe's doctor bills came from Monroe's estate papers, from Slatzer's *The Curious Death of Marilyn Monroe* and from *Legend*.

Chapter 31

Peter Lawford's responsibility for containing the 'Monroe disaster' was discussed at length by James Spada and in the Lawford segments of *Donahue* and *Sally Jesse Raphael* (see the 'Sources').

The threats to Ted Kennedy's senatorial campaign were described in the *Boston Globe* in a series of articles in August 1962 and in a Tass wire story in August 1987, translated from the Russian by Yuri Gogol, a UCLA student. Private detective Fred Otash admitted to the BBC in 1985 that a disgruntled employee had warned Bobby Kennedy that there were wiretaps at Monroe's house.

Monroe's conversations with Robert Slatzer were described in an August 1990 interview with the authors.

The editorial cartoons which appeared in the summer of 1962 were found in *The Education of Edward Kennedy*.

Susan Strasberg discussed Monroe's persona in a January 1991 interview.

Rumours that Monroe aborted Robert Kennedy's baby came from an interview with Otash (by Ted Landreth for the BBC) and in February 1991 interviews by the author with Hazel Washington, Robert Slatzer and Michael Selsman. Anthony Summers discussed the calls to Dr. Krohn in *Goddess*, as did Natalie Jacobs in a March 1991 interview with the authors.

The traumatic trip to the Cal-Neva Lodge was discussed at some length in *Goddess*, *Legend*, *The Man Who Kept the Secrets* and John Austin's *Hollywood's Unsolved Mysteries*, 1987.

Additional verification came from interviews by the authors with Ralph Roberts, Landreth, Washington, Evelyn Moriarty and Eunice Murray. Paul D'Amato's strange confession was made to Summers. Deborah Gould Lawford and Patricia Seaton Lawford also discussed the trip on various talk shows in 1987 and 1988.

Lucy Freeman, who was an acquaintance of Greenson's, also depicts the weekend and the abortion (which Freeman presents as a fact) in her upcoming book, *Why Norma Jean Murdered Marilyn Monroe*. Since Freeman had access to Dr. Ralph Greenson's papers and conducted exhaustive interviews with Hildi and Joan Greenson, this may be as close to proof as we will ever come.

The 'ancient resentment of the Kennedy family' is described by Arthur Schlesinger in his book on RFK.

Ralph Roberts's recollection of Monroe's question, 'Have you heard about Bobby and me?' came in a pair of interviews in early 1991.

Chapter 32

Details of Yves Montand's brutal treatment of Monroe came from Rupert Allan, who represented both Monroe and Montand at the time. The authors conducted four interviews with Allan in November and December 1990 and February 1991.

Arthur Miller's conduct on *The Misfits* and during the divorce came from interviews with Allan, Jean Louis and Hazel Washington.

Monroe's calls to Bobby Kennedy were found in Justice Department telephone logs, and they also appeared on her telephone bills for July, which were discovered by Anthony Summers and Ted Landreth in 1986. Eunice Murray's version of Monroe's torment came from *The Last Months*.

Mickey Song told of his last meeting with Monroe and of the 'secret audiotapes' during interviews in December 1990, March 1991 and June 1991.

Monroe's fabulous million-dollar deal with Fox was discussed by Peter Levathes in January 1991 interviews and by Lee Hanna in an October 1990 interview.

The special screening of the J. Lee Thompson films shows up on the Twentieth Century-Fox screening room logs in the Spyros Skouras papers.

Levathes talked of banishing the Monroe retainers Pat Newcomb and Paula Strasberg and probably Dr. Ralph Greenson as well.

Paula Strasberg's influence on Monroe and Strasberg's conduct on the set were depicted in interviews with Thomas Tryon, Whitey Snyder, David Bretherton, Walter Bernstein, Robert Slatzer and Evelyn Moriarity. In addition, these books were helpful: John Huston's *An Open Book*, Maurice Zolotow's *Marilyn*, and Laurence Olivier's *Confessions of an Actor*.

Slatzer documented Monroe's decision to fire Strasberg.

Jean Negulesco chronicled Cukor's dismissal from the film in *Things I Did, and Things I Think I Did*.

Monroe's celebration with Snyder and Marjorie Plecher was recalled in interviews in December 1990. Monroe's last conversation with Fox production chief Levathes was reconstructed by Hazel Washington, who was in the Brentwood house at the time. Levathes also mentioned the call in January 1990 interviews.

Chapter 33

Dorothy Kilgallen's veiled warning to the Kennedy family was documented in Lee Israel's *Kilgallen* and in Anthony Summers's *Goddess*.

Monroe's desperate attempts to find Bobby Kennedy the day before her death were described by Robert Slatzer, Summers, James

Spada and Jack Clemmons. Terry Moore also talked of it in a series of interviews with journalists from ABC and from the tabloid show *Hard Copy*.

Florabel Muir's attempts to find the Attorney General in San Francisco were discussed by Jack Clemmons, the Los Angeles police sergeant who was Muir's close friend. Anthony Summers got similar verification from Elizabeth Fauncher, Muir's secretary.

Rupert Allan confirmed Monroe's Friday call, as did the star's friend Jeanne Carmen.

In a telephone interview in February 1991, Jean Louis talked of Monroe's rush order for an 'afternoon dress' and a 'formal evening gown'. Monroe's discussion of her tapes with Peter Lawford was described by Mickey Song, who heard of the conversation in the winter of 1962 when he was styling the Attorney General's hair.

The depiction of Bobby Kennedy in 1962 came from Thomas C. Reeves's 1991 book, *A Question of Character*. The 'dirty tricks' during Ted Kennedy's senatorial campaign were detailed in *The Education of Edward Kennedy*.

Chapter 34

The helicopter landing on the Fox lot was discussed by Robert Slatzer and by Lee Hanna, who heard of it from publicist Frank Neill.

RFK's popularity among teenagers was described in Arthur Schlesinger's biography of the Attorney General. RFK's visit to calm Monroe, and perhaps to avoid a nasty public incident, was verified by the authors in interviews with Anthony Summers, former Los Angeles mayor Sam Yorty and Dorothy Manners and by Eunice Murray in an interview by Landreth. In addition, former Los Angeles police chief Tom Reddin talked of a long conversation between him and former chief William Parker. 'He *was* here,' said Reddin. 'Parker would not have lied to me.'

Monroe's discussion with Jule Styne was found in *Goddess*.

The exact movements of the star's last day (Saturday, August 4) were recalled in interviews with Murray, Slatzer, Lawrence Schiller, Ralph Roberts and Hazel Washington. Jeanne Carmen told *20/20* about the midnight call warning Monroe to 'stay away from Bobby Kennedy'.

Ray Strait, Fred Otash's co-author on a forthcoming book, provided the entire 'bugging scenario' as it is related in this chapter.

Additionally, Dr. Norman Tabachnick of the Los Angeles Suicide Investigation Team told Anthony Summers that he heard from Dr. Ralph Greenson that Monroe was disappointed when 'a VIP' failed to see her at all during July. And Milton Greene told Summers that 'Bobby was in town on Saturday afternoon'. Reporters for *Hard Copy* were so certain that Kennedy was in the Brentwood house 'fighting with Monroe' that they reenacted the scene with actors in their February 1992 special *Marilyn – The Last Word*. Other details came from FBI File 77-51387.

Accounts of the Mafia bugging of Monroe's home came from FBI File 67–B (1962).

Chapter 35

Accounts of Monroe's death and the beginning of the coverup came from interviews with Eunice Murray, James Spada, Ralph Roberts, Sergeant Jack Clemmons, Deputy District Attorney Mike Carroll, Natalie Jacobs, Rupert Allan, Ted Landreth, Robert Slatzer, Tom Reddin, Sam Yorty and Deputy District Attorney John Miner.

The 'missing telephone records' were described by Clemmons and Slatzer, and by Anthony Summers in *Goddess*.

Also helpful were the report from 'The 1982 Reinvestigation of the Death of Marilyn Monroe', by Mike Carroll; FBI File 66-1700-39; the BBC's 1986 special *Say Goodbye to the President*; Dr. Ralph Greenson's interview with photographer William Woodfield in which Greenson said 'Ask Bobby Kennedy what happened'; the illustrated telephone logs in *Goddess*; the August 6 stories of the death in the *New York Herald Examiner*, the *Los Angeles Times* and *Santa Monica Evening Outlook* and the *Chicago Tribune*; and Florabel Muir's interview about the 'missing telephone bills' in the *Long Beach Press Telegram*, undated but believed to have run in 1968.

Jack Clemmons's arrival at the Brentwood house was described in three interviews with the former police sergeant in January and February 1961. The presence of Fox publicists was verified by James Bacon, Slatzer, Clemmons, Hazel Washington, Natalie Jacobs, Fred

Otash (*20/20*) and Peter Levathes, who remembered sending security guards to the death site.

Chapter 36

Descriptions of Southern Californians stunned by news of Monroe's death came from personal recollections by author Brown, who lived in Santa Monica at the time, and by Barham, who covered the death for the *Los Angeles Herald Examiner*.

Barham learned of Lady Lawford's claims during an interview in 1970.

The 'official version' came from *Goddess, Legend, The Man Who Kept the Secrets*, Patricia Seaton Lawford's *The Peter Lawford Story* and C. David Heymann's *A Woman Called Jackie*.

Whitey Snyder described his own actions on August 5, 1962, in November and December 1990 interviews with the authors.

Other interviews for this section included sessions with Robert Slatzer, Jack Clemmons, Hazel Washington, James Bacon, Evelyn Moriarity, Dorothy Manners, Theodore Strauss, David Bretherton, James Spada, Anthony Summers (a brief telephone interview), Natalie Jacobs, Rupert Allan and Michael Selsman.

Chapter 37

The 'official version' came from interviews with James Spada, Hazel Washington, James Bacon, Dorothy Manners, Robert Slatzer, Jack Clemmons and Natalie Jacobs.

The news sources on Monroe's death and aftermath were the same as those listed in the notes for Chapters 34 through 36.

Descriptions of the funeral came from articles in the *Los Angeles Times* and the *Los Angeles Herald Examiner* on Wednesday, August 8.

Chapter 38

Details of the coverup were convincingly reported by Jack

Clemmons, Ted Landreth, James Spada, Tom Reddin, Sam Yorty, John Miner, Dorothy Manners, Robert Slatzer, Anthony Summers and Eunice Murray in 1990 interviews.

Hints of murder were found in the Hedda Hopper Collection, along with letters from readers informing the gossip queen of the affairs between Monroe and the Kennedy brothers.

Deputy District Attorney Mike Carroll said that his investigators found 'evidence that Lawford and representatives of Fox' were at the house in Brentwood during the early morning.

Ezra Goodman's suppressed article was to have run in the January 9, 1963, issue of *Newsweek*.

J. Edgar Hoover's protection of Robert Kennedy and suppression of rumours about Monroe was made clear in FBI documents through the years and by Summers in *Goddess*.

Chapter 39

A wide variety of sources was consulted for our conclusion. Here are the most important:

– An August 10 bill from Dr. Hyman Engleberg which showed that he gave Monroe two injections on Friday. Dr. Thomas Noguchi's autopsy missed these needle marks.

– An interview with gossip columnist Dorothy Manners and Parsons assistant, who quoted Louella Parsons as saying, 'We knew that Bobby rushed up there on Saturday, August 4.'

– A Los Angeles Police Department document containing follow-up interviews with Eunice Murray and Milton Rudin; document number 62-509-403.

– An FBI report from 'DeLoach' to M. A. Jones on July 9, 1963, discussing allegations against the Attorney General in an upcoming *Photoplay* article. The report was later found in FBI director J. Edgar Hoover's private files.

– A *Confidential* magazine story in December 1962 which speculated that Frank Sinatra was the last person to speak with Monroe. The story hinted that Sinatra knew of Monroe's betrayal by the Kennedy brothers.

– An October 5, 1985, story by John Carmody in the *Boston Globe* alluding to revelations in the *20/20* special and discussing

the controversial order by ABC, which pulled it the day before it was to run.
– Fred Otash's descriptions in February 1962 interviews on *Hard Copy* of the massive bugging operations at both the Lawford and Monroe houses.
– The report of the 'Suicide Squad' as reported by Stan Leppard in the August 19, 1962, edition of *The Los Angeles Times*.
– A discussion of the telephone bills for Monroe's Brentwood house in *Goddess* and *The Man Who Kept the Secrets*.
– The evidence assembled by crusading journalist Frank Capell in *The Strange Death of Marilyn Monroe* on Monroe's drug consumption on her last night.
– Patricia Seaton Lawford's interview on *Geraldo*, December 7, 1988, about the effect of Monroe's death on Peter Lawford.
– Peter Lawford's statement to the Los Angeles Police Department – his first real interview on Monroe's death – in 1982, in which he discussed her alleged overdose at Cal-Neva Lodge the last weekend in August. Despite claims that she had tried suicide, Lawford told detectives that it was an accidental overdose, and that she had been revived 'without professional medical assistance'.
– Lady May Lawford's statements about her son's involvement in the coverup from her own autobiography, *'Bitch!'*
– Statements by Jack Clemmons on *Geraldo* on November 10, 1988, in which he described 'Greenson's guilty reaction' when Clemmons was shown onto the death scene.
– The FBI report from F. Miller to T. J. Smith on the contents of the upcoming Norman Mailer book, which warned Smith and J. Edgar Hoover that Mailer was suggesting 'that Bobby Kennedy might have been involved in Monroe's death'. The report was filed on July 23, 1973.
– The August 5, 1962, Associated Press story by Bob Thomas reporting that 'empty bottles of pills' were found on Monroe's dressing table.

Interviews for the conclusion were conducted with Robert Slatzer, John Miner, Thomas Noguchi, Ted Landreth, Jack Clemmons, Eunice Murray, Whitey Snyder, Jean Louis, Ed Guthman, Mike Carroll, Dorothy Manners, Joan Greenson, Pat Newcomb, Anthony Summers, Fred Lawrence Guiles, James Spada, Hazel Washington, Evelyn Moriarity, Rupert Allan and Peter Levathes.

– The *Tass* reports (five in all) accusing 'highly influential people in Hollywood and Washington, D.C., of covering up the true circumstances of the star's death'. The reporters – unnamed – were given access to the KGB file on 'The Kennedys and the Death of Marilyn Monroe'. The articles, which ran in drastically reduced form in the *Boston Globe*, hinted that anticommunist forces in the American government killed Monroe. It was hinted that the CIA did the job. Translated for the authors by Yuri Gogol, a UCLA language student. They ran in 1988.

Chapter 40

'The aftermath' was based on interviews with Eunice Murray, Robert Slatzer, Ed Guthman, Susan Strasberg, Joan Greenson, Hildi Greenson, Lucy Freeman, Milton Rudin, Pat Newcomb, Evelyn Moriarity, Chris and Tom Mankiewicz, Peter Levathes, Richard Zanuck, Natalie Jacobs, Rupert Allan, Tom Reddin, Sam Yorty, Cesare Danova, Milton Gould and Larry Schiller.

Additional sources included Bragg's *Burton*, Kitty Kelley's *The Last Star*, James Spada's *The Man Who Kept the Secrets*, Patricia Seaton Lawford's book *The Peter Lawford Story*, the '1982 Report on the Reinvestigation of Marilyn Monroe's Death' and Lucy Freeman's *Why Norma Jean Killed Marilyn Monroe*.

– *Sources* –

Film

All eight hours of the remaining film from *Something's Got to Give*, which includes foggy prints of the shoe store scene, the complete nude scene, and some of the lost segments of the fantasy sequence involving Monroe, Thomas Tryon and Dean Martin. From a variety of sources – including three private collections of film and video, and the six hours pieced together by producer-director Henry Schipper for Fox Entertainment News.

Video

20/20 ABC News Special 'Marilyn Monroe and the Kennedys', featuring Sylvia Chase – a thirty-seven-minute news programme which was pulled from *20/20* the day before it was to have aired. Includes interviews with Terry Moore, Jeanne Carmen, Anthony Summers, Ralph Roberts, Senator George Smathers, Robert Slatzer and private detective Fred Otash. 1986.

'Marilyn Monroe – What Really Happened?' episode of *Geraldo*, with Jack Clemmons, Robert Slatzer and others. This programme features some in-depth research by Geraldo Rivera and a team of investigative reporters. Aired November 10, 1988.

'Peter Lawford, the Kennedys and Marilyn Monroe' segment of *Sally Jesse Raphael*, featuring Patricia Seaton Lawford and others. Aired November 23, 1988.

'The Dark Side of Camelot – the Peter Lawford Story' segment of *Geraldo*, featuring Patricia Seaton Lawford and others, detailing the relationship between Monroe and President John F. Kennedy. Aired December 7, 1988.

Something's Got to Give, a forty-seven-minute television special about Monroe's last film, written, produced and directed by Henry Schipper of Fox Entertainment News. This special contains a survey of all the documents and studio decisions which led to Monroe's dismissal from the uncompleted film. Executive produced by William K. Knoedelseder, director of Fox Entertainment News. 1990.

Twenty-two interviews of most *Something's Got to Give* principals by Peter Harry Brown for Fox Entertainment News. 1990.

Say Goodbye to the President – Marilyn Monroe and the Kennedys, a ninety-two-minute television documentary produced by Ted Landreth and the British Broadcasting Corporation, obtained from the BBC archives in London. (This documentary included the participation of biographer Anthony Summers; it proves that President John F. Kennedy and Attorney General Robert Kennedy had affairs with Monroe and hints that she may have been murdered.) 1986.

'Marilyn Monroe and Her Secrets – What She Knew', a special episode of *Donahue*, including in-depth interviews with Monroe biographers Anthony Summers and Gloria Steinem. Aired July 1990.

'Marilyn Monroe and the Kennedys' segment of *Geraldo*, featuring interviews with Milo Speriglio, Maurice Zolotow and others. Aired July 20, 1990.

Studio Documents

These papers, letters, telegrams, logs and telephone notes came from a variety of sources, including the Twentieth Century-Fox archives; the Spyros Skouras Collection at Stanford University; the Darryl F. Zanuck Collection at American Film Institute; the Hedda Hopper Collection at the Academy of Motion Picture Arts and Sciences; the Louella Parsons Collection; the library files of the *Los Angeles Herald Examiner* and the *Los Angeles Times*; the Film and Television Library of the University of Southern California, Special Collections; the University of California at Los Angeles; the special screenplay collections of the Academy of Motion Picture Arts and Sciences; the script collection of the University of Southern California; and the University of Texas library. Additional documents came from Stanford University and the New York Public Library.

Although the legal affairs department of Twentieth Century-Fox did not reply to five requests to view documents related to *Cleopatra* and *Something's Got to Give*, more than five hundred of these documents were obtained from a private source. Press releases regarding Monroe's dismissal from *Something's Got to Give* were found in the library of the *Los Angeles Herald Examiner*, the Hedda Hopper Collection, and the collection of Patte Barham, who covered *Something's Got to Give* for the *Los Angeles Herald Examiner*.

'Something's Got to Give'

Scripts
The original screenplay for *My Favourite Wife*, the 1939 film on which *Something's Got to Give* was based. The RKO Collection; additional pages from the Howard Hughes archives.

Irving Shulman's original screenplay for *Something's Got to Give*, written for Joan Collins and Jayne Mansfield. Script collection, University of Southern California. March 1959.

Three drafts of the Nunnally Johnson screenplay, including the final version with approval by Monroe. University of Southern California and the collection of Mrs. Dorris Johnson. December 1961, January 1962 and February 1962.

Two plot outlines by *Something's Got to Give* associate producer and art director Gene Allen to serve as the basis for a rewrite of the Johnson screenplay. 1962.

The 110 pages of changes and additions by writer Walter Bernstein, inserted into the Johnson script to form a rainbow of changes – yellow, blue and cream-coloured pages. George Cukor Collection, University of Southern California. March to June 1962.

Other Documents

Marilyn Monroe's original Fox contract, 1946; a draft from the Fox archives, October 1946; her forty-six page contract draft, 1955; and the final version of her sixty-page contract, 1956. Fox archives.

Letter from Frank Ferguson to George Cukor threatening him with legal action unless he reports for *Something's Got to Give* in December 1961, following postproduction work on *The Chapman Report*. Private source. September 1961.

Brief corporate memo from Spyros Skouras to Peter G. Levathes, which states that 'we have Cukor over a barrel – he will report for "Something's Got to Give" any time and any place we tell him.' Skouras papers. September 1961.

Letter from Frank Ferguson to Monroe threatening her with suspension and legal action unless she makes herself available to start *Something's Got to Give* by February 1962. Fox legal archives. October 1961.

Memo from Henry Weinstein to Fox casting executive Owen McLean, warning against casting 'blonde extras' in the crowd scenes of *Something's Got to Give*. Private source. February 19, 1962.

Memo from George Cukor cancelling his participation in the costume tests for Monroe. Spyros Skouras Collection. April 10, 1962. Note form only.

Daily editing record listing Franz Planer as the director of the costume tests. Private collection. April 10, 1962.

Something's Got to Give daily production logs running from the day of the costume tests through the film's shutdown after Monroe's dismissal. Compiled by *Something's Got to Give* assistant director Buck Hall, with additions by George Cukor and production secretary Lee Hanna. More than thirty-two pages. This is a record of great detail which includes the number of shots made each date; the number of script pages completed; Monroe's entrance and exit times from the studio; the condition of her health on a given day;

and the amount of film footage exposed. Private source. April 10 to June 11, 1962.

Something's Got to Give weekly reports, Nos. 1 through 6. A blow-by-blow account of Monroe's absences and appearances. Eleven pages. Private source. April 10 to June 11, 1962.

Dr. Lee Siegel's and Dr. Philip Rubin's medical records for *Something's Got to Give*, cataloguing symptoms of Monroe's virus and sinusitis; this formed the basis for Buck Hall's notation in the daily production logs. Private source. April 20 to June 8, 1962. Handwritten on memo pads.

Something's Got to Give week-by-week diary prepared by John Campbell of the Fox Publicity Department; includes notes, partial production reports and a list of publicity releases. Private source. May 1962. Microfilm.

Something's Got to Give publicity releases and news bulletins, from various collections. Included are:

Peter Levathes's statement on Monroe's firing, with Perry Lieber listed as the contact. June 8, 1962.

Bulletin announcing that Lee Remick would take over the role from Monroe, read to Peter Harry Brown by Lee Remick in December 1990.

Hedda Hopper's notes on releases from Fox, and on a personal interview with Cukor in which the director discussed Monroe's failure to complete *Something's Got to Give*. Cukor also discussed the end of Monroe's career and her mental state. Library of *The Los Angeles Times*. June 8, 1962.

Dictation to Louella Parsons's secretary, Dorothy Treloar, from Perry Lieber to Louella Parsons on Monroe's mental problems. Louella Parsons file at the *Los Angeles Herald Examiner*. June 9, 1962. Typed.

'The Firing of Marilyn Monroe' document depicting Twentieth Century-Fox's step-by-step executive plan to fire Monroe and to publicise her personal and professional troubles. Written and annotated by Fox vice-president Phil Feldman; includes re-creations of conversations between Feldman and Levathes; between Martin and Feldman; between Cukor and Levathes; between Feldman and

Milton Rudin. Fox legal archives. June 12, 1962. Nine-page, single-spaced typewritten document.

Chronological history of *Something's Got to Give*, compiled by Fox counsel Frank Ferguson for the million-dollar lawsuit against Monroe. Private source. July 1962. Notes only.

Something's Got to Give contract and noncontract salary sheets, which offer data on everyone involved with the production. Fox archives. 1962.

Undated 'apology and special conditions' for Monroe to sign in the event that she was reinstated and allowed to continue *Something's Got to Give*. Written by Phil Feldman, the document rescinded all of the artistic gains made by Monroe in her 1956 contract. It also banished acting coach Paula Strasberg and publicist Pat Newcomb from the set. [July 10, 1962.]

'Warning letter' from Fox counsel Frank Ferguson to Monroe, the Music Corporation of America and Milton Rudin, warning Monroe against appearing at the gala birthday party for President Kennedy at Madison Square Gardens. July 16, 1962. From the Fox archives.

Parts of a 'public apology' – of which Fox publicist Jack Brodsky was apparently an author – to be released if Monroe was reinstated. Fox archives. July 22, 1962. Microfilm.

'Cleopatra'

Original casting notes – made by Spyros Skouras to himself – on the back of a piece of 'Prudential Grace Lines' stationery. They list, in order, Elizabeth Taylor, Gina Lollobrigida, Joanne Woodward, Susan Hayward and Juliet Prowse. Private source. Summer 1959.

Western Union telegram from studio head Buddy Adler to Skouras on the 'increasing interference by Elizabeth Taylor'. Skouras papers. June 10, 1960.

Western Union telegram from Skouras to Adler on Elizabeth Taylor's demands for higher salary and cast changes. Fox archives. June 24, 1960.

Budget estimates for *Cleopatra*, which include wild guesses for filming in Spain and Egypt. Believed to have been written by Fox attorney Otto Koegel. Fox archives. 1961. A single legal-sized page.

RCA Radiogram from Skouras in New York, firing *Cleopatra*'s first director, Rouben Mamoulian, who was in London. Fox archives. January 24, 1961.

Minutes of an executive meeting called to see if *Cleopatra* was going out of control. Private source. November 19, 1961.

Telegram from Peter G. Levathes to Spyros Skouras on the troubles Fox was having with Joseph L. Mankiewicz, director of *Cleopatra*. Fox archives. [January 30, 1962.] A 'draft copy'.

Peter G. Levathes letter which delineates the debacle. Skouras papers. January 30, 1962.

Business letter from Skouras to Mankiewicz lamenting the publicity over the Taylor–Burton affair. April 6, 1962. Two pages, typed on Fox letterhead. The Fox Archives.

'Confidential letter' from Skouras to producer Walter Wanger on the Taylor–Burton affair, April 14, 1962; and Wanger's reply from Rome, April 26, 1962. Fox archives.

List, writer unknown, which indicates that Elizabeth Taylor was unable to work from April 19 to May 7, 1962, due to personal troubles. Fox archives. 1962. Handwritten on the back of a spiral notebook.

'Personal and confidential' memo from Skouras to Wanger, expressing great alarm at the Taylor–Burton affair, Fox archives. April 22, 1962. Wanger's reply, private source. April 30, 1962.

Letter from Skouras to Mankiewicz, written at the behest of Fox attorney Milton Gould and the Fox Executive Committee, informing the director that 'Elizabeth Taylor is to be terminated no later than June 9'. Private source; also believed to be in Skouras Collection, Stanford University. May 31, 1962.

Attendance report, 'Elizabeth Taylor in Italy'. Includes a summary of Taylor's tardiness and sick days. Spyros Skouras papers. June 1962. Typed.

Corporate letter from Darryl F. Zanuck to director George Sidney on the ego of Joseph L. Mankiewicz and the extravagances of *Cleopatra*. Fox archives. November 7, 1962. Ten pages typed on Fox letterhead.

Chronological history of *Cleopatra*, a nineteen-page blow-by-blow description of the filming in Hollywood, London, Rome and Egypt. Prepared by a team of studio lawyers as a defence document when Walter Wanger sued Twentieth Century-Fox in 1963. Much of the paranoia about the Monroe film was detailed here as well. Private source. November 1962.

Full transcript of an interview with Spyros Skouras by David Slavitt of *Newsweek*. Interview was conducted in New York and dealt with most of the issues involved in the *Cleopatra* debacle. Nineteen pages. Skouras papers. March 11, 1963.

Letter from Spyros Skouras to Darryl F. Zanuck which recapped Elizabeth Taylor's excesses in Rome – including 'two suicide attempts' and the beating she received from Burton. Private source. [mid-1967.]

Books and Articles

Adams, Cindy. *Lee Strasberg: The Imperfect Genius of the Actors Studio*. New York: Doubleday, 1980.

——. *My Friend the Dictator*. New York: Bobbs-Merrill, 1967.

Adler, Bill. *Sinatra, the Man and the Myth*. New York: New American Library, 1987.

Agan, Patrick. *The Decline and Fall of the Love Goddesses*. Los Angeles: Pinnacle, 1979. Photographs. Filmography.

Allan, Rupert. 'Marilyn Monroe: A Serious Blonde Who Can Act.' *Look*, Oct. 23, 1951.

Allen, Maury. *Where Have You Gone, Joe DiMaggio: The Story of America's Last Hero*. New York: Dutton, 1975.

Alvarez, A. *The Savage God: A Study of Suicide*. New York: Bantam, 1973.

Anderson, Janice. *Marilyn Monroe*. New York: Hamlyn, 1983. Photographs.

Barcon, Hallis Alpert. *Burton*. New York: G. P. Putnam's Sons, 1986.

Bernstein, Walter. 'Monroe's Last Picture Show.' *Esquire*, July 1973.

Blair, Clay, Jr., and Joan Blair. *The Search for J.F.K.* New York: Putnam, 1976.

Brashler, William. *The Don: The Life and Death of Sam Giancana*. New York: Ballantine, 1977.

Broeske, Pat H. 'The Misfits,' *Magill's Survey of Cinema, English Language Films*, Vol. 3. Englewood Cliffs, NJ: Salem Press, 1980.

——. 'Some Like it Hot,' *Magill's Survey of Cinema, English Language Films*, Vol. 4. Englewood Cliffs, NJ: Salem Press, 1980.

Brown, Gene. *The Kennedys: A New York Times Profile*. New York: Arno Press, 1980.

Bryant, Traphes, and Frances Spatz Leighton. *Dog Days at the White House*. New York: MacMillan, 1975.

Buck, Pearl S. *The Kennedy Women*. New York: Cowles, 1970.

Butler, Paul F., Jr. *Presidential Wives*. Oxford: Oxford University Press, 1988.

Capell, Frank A. *The Strange Death of Marilyn Monroe*. Indianapolis: Herald of Freedom, 1964.

Capote, Truman. *The Dogs Bark: Public People and Private Lives*. New York: Random House, 1973.

——. *Music for Chameleons*. New York: Random House, 1980.

Carey, Gary. *Cukor & Co.: The Films of George Cukor and His Collaborators*. New York: Museum of Modern Art, 1971.

Carpozi, George. *Marilyn Monroe – Her Own Story*. London: World Distributors, 1961.

—— *The Agony of Marilyn Monroe*. London: World Distributors, 1962.

Carroll, Ronald H. (Assistant District Attorney), and Alan B. Tomich (Investigator). 'The Death of Marilyn Monroe,' report to the District Attorney. Dec. 1982.

Churcher, Sharon. *New York Confidential*. New York: Crown, 1986.

Clarens, Carlos. *George Cukor*. London: Secker and Warburg, 1976.

Cleopatra Program. For the film's Hollywood premier: National Publishers, Inc., 1963.

Clinch, Nancy Gager. *The Kennedy Neurosis*. New York: Grosset & Dunlap, 1973.

Collier, Peter, and David Horowitz. *The Kennedys*. New York: Summit, 1984.

Conover, David. *Finding Marilyn*. New York: Grosset and Dunlap, 1981. Photographs.

Conway, Michael, and Mark Ricci. *The Films of Marilyn Monroe*. New Jersey: Citadel, 1964. Photographs.

David, Lester, and Irene David. *Bobby Kennedy, the Making of a Folk Hero*. New York: Dodd, Mead & Company, 1986.

Davis, John H. *The Kennedys: Dynasty and Disaster*. New York: McGraw-Hill, 1984.

Davis, William, and Christina Tree. *The Kennedy Library*. Philadelphia, Pennsylvania: Schiffer, 1980.

DeToledano, Ralph. *R.F.K.: The Man Who Would Be President*. New York: Putnam, 1967.

Dunleavy, Stephen, and Peter Brennan. *Those Wild, Wild Kennedy Boys!* New York: Pinnacle, 1976.

Easty, Dwight. *On Method Acting*. Tampa, Florida: House of Collectibles, 1980.

Exner, Judith, as told to Ovid Demaris. *My Story*. New York: Grove Press, 1977.

Fisher, Eddie. *Eddie: My Life, My Loves*. New York: Berkeley, 1981.

'The Fortunes of Cleopatra.' *Newsweek*, March 25, 1963.

Gallagher, Mary Barelli. *My Life with Jacqueline Kennedy*. New York: David McKay, 1969.

Giancana, Antoinette, and Thomas C. Renner. *Mafia Princess: Growing Up in Sam Giancana's Family*. New York: Morrow, 1984.

Graham, Sheilah. *Confessions of a Hollywood Columnist*. New York: Morrow, 1969.

——. *My Hollywood*. London: Michael Joseph, 1984.

Greenson, Ralph. *Explorations in Psychoanalysis*. New York: International University Press, 1978.

'The Growing Cult of Marilyn.' *Life*, Jan. 25, 1963. Paintings and poems.

Guiles, Fred Lawrence. *Legend: The Life and Death of Marilyn Monroe*. New York: Stein and Day, 1984. Photographs.

——. 'Marilyn Monroe.' *This Week*, March 1, 1969.

——. *Norma Jean: The Life of Marilyn Monroe*. New York: Bantam, 1970. Photographs.

Gussow, Mel. *Darryl F. Zanuck: Don't Say Yes Until I've Finished Talking*. New York: Dacapo, 1971.

Hecht, Ben. *Marilyn Monroe: My Story*. New York: Stein and Day, 1974.

Heymann, C. David. *A Woman Called Jackie*. New York: Lyle Stuart, 1989.

Hopper, Hedda. 'Marilyn Tells the Truth to Hedda Hopper.' *Photoplay*, Jan. 1953.

Hoyt, Edwin P. *Marilyn: The Tragic Venus*. London: Robert Hale, 1967. Photographs.

Hudson, James A. *The Mysterious Death of Marilyn Monroe*. New

York: Volitant, 1968.

Hunt, Irma. *The Presidents' Mistresses*. New York: McGraw-Hill, 1978.

Huston, John. *An Open Book*. New York: Ballantine, 1982.

Israel, Lee. *Kilgallen*. New York: Dell, 1979.

Johnson, Dorris, and Ellen Levanthal. *The Letters of Nunnally Johnson*. New York: Knopf, 1981.

Kaminsky, Stuart. *John Huston: Maker of Magic*. Boston: Houghton Mifflin, 1978.

Kanin, Garson. *Hollywood*. New York: Viking, 1974.

Kennedy, Robert F. *The Enemy Within*. New York: Harper & Row, 1960.

——. *In His Own Words: The Unpublished Recollections of the Kennedy Years*. Eds. Edwin O. Guthman and Jeffrey Schulman. New York: Bantam, 1988.

——. *Thirteen Days: A Memoir of the Cuban Missile Crisis*. New York: Norton, 1969.

——. *To Seek a New World*. Garden City, NY: Doubleday, 1967.

Kobal, John, and David Robinson. *Marilyn Monroe: A Life on Film*. New York: Hamlyn, 1974.

Kramer, Frieda. *Jackie: A Truly Intimate Biography*. New York: Grosset & Dunlap, 1979.

Lambert, Gavin. *On Cukor*. New York: Putnam's, 1972.

Lamparski, Richard. *Hidden Hollywood, Where the Stars Lived*. New York: Crown Books, 1985.

Lawford, Lady Mary (May) Sommerville, as told to Buddy Galon. *'Bitch!': The Autobiography of Lady Lawford*. Brookline, MA: Brandon, 1986.

Leary, Timothy. *Flashbacks: An Autobiography*. Los Angeles: Tarcher, 1984.

Lowe, Jacques. *Kennedy, a Time Remembered*. London: Quartet Books, 1983.

Luce, Clare Boothe. 'The "Love Goddess" Who Never Found Any Love.' *Life*, Aug. 7, 1964, pp. 70–76.

Lytess, Natasha. *My Years with Marilyn*. Maurice Zolotow collection, Humanities Research, University of Texas at Austin. 28-page manuscript.

MacPherson, Myra. *The Power Lovers: An Intimate Look at Politics and Marriage*. New York: Putnam, 1975.

Mailer, Norman. *Marilyn: A Biography*. New York: Grosset and Dunlap, 1973.

Manchester, William. *Controversy and Other Essays in Journalism, 1950–1975*. Boston: Little, Brown, 1976.

——. *The Death of a President: November 20–November 25, 1963*. New York: Harper & Row, 1967.

——. *One Brief Shining Moment: Remembering Kennedy*. Boston: Little, Brown, 1963.

——. *Portrait of a President: John F. Kennedy in Profile*. Boston: Little, Brown, 1962.

Marilyn Monroe: Rare Recordings, 1948–1962. Sandy Hook Records, 1979.

Martin, Pete. *Will Acting Spoil Marilyn Monroe?* Garden City, NY: Doubleday, 1956. Photographs.

Martin, Ralph G. *A Hero for Our Time*. New York: MacMillan, 1983.

McGilligan, Patrick. *George Cukor: a Double Life*. New York: St. Martin's Press, 1991.

McGuiness, Richard. 'On the River of No Return.' *Film Comment*, Sept. 1972.

McIntyre, Alice T. 'Waiting for Monroe or Notes from Olympus.' *Esquire*, March 1961.

Mellen, Joan. *Marilyn Monroe*. New York: Pyramid, 1973. Photographs. Filmography. Bibliography.

Meryman, Richard. 'Behind the Myth of Norma Jean.' *Life*, Nov. 4, 1966.

——. 'Fame May Go By: An Interview.' *Life*,' Aug. 3, 1962.

Messick, Hank. *The Mob in Show Business*. New York: Pyramid, 1973.

'Monroe Magic.' *After Dark*, Aug./Sept. 1981. Photographs.

Moseley, Roy. *Rex Harrison, a Biography*. New York: St. Martin's Press, 1987.

Muir, Florabel. *Headline Happy*. New York: Holt, 1950.

——. 'Reporting.' *The Hollywood Mirror*, Feb. 10, 1953.

Murray, Eunice. *Marilyn: The Last Months*. New York: Pyramid, 1975.

Negulesco, Jean. *Things I Did and Things I Think I Did: A Hollywood Memoir*. New York: Linden, 1984. Photographs and drawings.

Oppenheimer, Joel. *Marilyn Lives!* New York: Delilah, 1981. Photographs.

Otash, Fred. *Investigation Hollywood*. Chicago: Regnery, 1976.

Parish, James Robert. *The Fox Girls*. New York: Arlington House, 1971.

Parks, Lillian Rogers, with Frances Spatz Leighton. *My Thirty Years Backstairs at the White House*. New York: Avon, 1961.

Parmet, Herbert S. *Jack, the Struggles of John F. Kennedy*. New York: Dial, 1980.

——. *JFK, the Presidency of John F. Kennedy*. New York: Dial, 1983.

Parsons, Louella. *Tell It to Louella*. New York: Putnam's, 1961.

Patrick, Bob, ed. *Marilyn*. New York: O'Quinn Studios, 1980. Photographs.

Pepitone, Lena, and William Stadiem. *Marilyn Monroe Confidential*. New York: Pocket Books, 1980. Photographs.

Phillips, Gene D. *George Cukor*. Boston: Twayne, 1982.

Rachlin, Harvey. *The Kennedys: A Chronological History, 1823–Present*. New York: World Almanac, 1986.

'Reminiscences of Monroe.' *The Best of Playboy*, No. 4. Chicago: Playboy Press, 1970.

Rollyson, Carl. *Marilyn Monroe: A Life of the Actress*. London: New English Library, 1986.

Roman, Robert C. 'Marilyn Monroe: Her Tragedy Was Allowing Herself to Be Misled Intellectually.' *Films in Review*, Oct. 1962, pp. 449–468. Filmography.

Rosten, Norman. *Marilyn: An Untold Story*. New York: Signet Books, 1973. Photographs. Documents.

——. *Selected Poems*. New York: George Braziller, 1979.

Rosten, Patricia. 'Patricia Rosten on Marilyn Monroe.' In *Closeups*. Ed. Danny Peary. New York: Workman, 1978.

Roud, Richard. *Cinema: A Critical Dictionary*. Vols. 1 and 2. Norwich, England: Secker and Warburg, 1980.

Scheim, David E. *Contract on America: The Mafia Murders of John and Robert Kennedy*. Silver Spring, MD: Argyle, 1983.

Schjeldahl, Peter. 'Marilyn: Still Being Exploited?' *New York Times*. Dec. 17, 1967, p. 40D.

Schlesinger, Arthur M., Jr. *A Thousand Days, John F. Kennedy in the White House*. Boston: Houghton Mifflin, 1965.

——. *Robert Kennedy and His Times*. Boston: Houghton Mifflin, 1978.

Sciacca, Tony. *Kennedy and His Women*. New York: Manor, 1976.

——. *Sinatra*. New York: Pinnacle, 1976.

——. *Who Killed Marilyn?* New York: Manor, 1976.

Segreve, Kerry. *Sex and Politicians: Affairs of States.* Boston: Branden Books, 1990.

Signoret, Simone. *Nostalgia Isn't What It Used to Be.* New York: Penguin, 1979.

Skolsky, Sydney. *Don't Get Me Wrong – I Love Hollywood.* New York: Putnam's, 1975.

——. *Marilyn.* New York: Dell, 1954. Photographs. Documents. Filmography.

Slatzer, Robert. *The Curious Death of Marilyn Monroe.* New York: Pinnacle, 1974. Photographs. Documents. Filmography.

Smith, Malcolm E. *John F. Kennedy's 13 Great Mistakes in the White House.* New York: Suffolk House, 1980.

Smith, Milburn. *Marilyn.* New York: Barven, 1971.

Smith, Ronnie, and Bob Webster. 'Dead Man's Papers Shed Light on Marilyn Mystery.' *Riverside Press Enterprise*, Feb. 22, 1981, p. B5.

Spada, James, and George Zeno. *Monroe: Her Life in Pictures.* New York: Doubleday, 1982.

Spada, James. *Peter Lawford. The Man Who Kept the Secrets.* Bantam, July 1991.

Speriglio, Milo. *Marilyn Monroe: Murder Coverup.* Van Nuys, CA: Seville Publishing, 1982.

Steinem, Gloria. 'Growing Up with Marilyn.' *MS.*, Aug. 1972. New York: New American Library, 1986.

Stempel, Tom. *Screenwriter: The Life and Times of Nunnally Johnson.* San Diego: A. S. Barnes, 1980.

Stern, Bert. Untitled photographic layout. *Eros*, Autumn 1962.

——. *The Last Sitting.* New York: William Morrow, 1982.

Strasberg, Susan. *Bittersweet.* New York: Putnam's, 1980.

Strean, Dr. Herbert S., and Lucy Freeman. *The Severed Soul.* New York: St. Martin's Press, 1990.

Summers, Anthony. *Goddess: The Secret Lives of Marilyn Monroe.* New York: MacMillan, 1985.

Taylor, Robert. *Marilyn Monroe in Her Own Words.* New York: Delilah, 1983.

Thimmesch, Nick, and William Johnson. *Robert Kennedy at 40.* New York: W. W. Norton, 1965.

Thomas, Bob. *Winchell.* New York: Doubleday, 1971.

Thompson, Nelson. *The Dark Side of Camelot.* Chicago: Playboy Press, 1976.

Todd, Mabel Elsworth. *The Thinking Body: A Study of the Balancing Force of Dynamic Man.* New York: Paul B. Hoeber, 1937.

Trent, Paul, and Richard Lawton. *The Image Makers: Sixty Years of Hollywood Glamour.* New York: Crescent, 1972. Photographs.

Twentieth Century-Fox Memorabilia Catalogue. Los Angeles: Sotheby Parke Bernet, 1971.

Wagenknecht, Edward, et al. *Marilyn Monroe: A Composite View.* Philadelphia: Chilton, 1969. Photographs. (Contains Monroe's last two interviews; memories by Hollis Alpert, Flora Rheta Schreiber, Edith Sitwell, several photographers, Adele Whitely Fletcher, and Norman Rosten; reflections by Cecil Beaton, Lee Strasberg, Lincoln Kirstein, Diana Trilling, David Robinson, Alexander Walker and Wagenknecht.

Wallace, Irving, et al. *The Intimate Sex Lives of Famous People.* New York: Dell, 1982.

Wanger, Walter. *You Must Remember This.* New York: Putnam's, 1968.

Warren, Doug. *Betty Grable: The Reluctant Movie Queen.* New York: St. Martin's Press, 1974.

Waters, Harry. 'Taking a New Look at MM.' *Newsweek*, Oct. 16, 1972.

Weatherby, W. J. *Conversations with Marilyn.* New York: Mason Charter, 1976.

Whitcomb, John. 'Marilyn Monroe – the Sex Symbol Versus the Good Wife.' *Cosmopolitan*, Dec. 1960.

Wills, Gary. *The Kennedy Imprisonment.* Boston: Little, Brown, 1982.

Wilson, Earl. *The Show Business Nobody Knows.* New York: Bantam, 1971.

——. *Show Business Laid Bare.* New York: Putnam, 1975.

——. *Sinatra: An Unauthorized Biography.* New York: MacMillan, 1976.

——. *Hot Times: True Tales of Hollywood and Broadway.* New York: Contemporary Books, 1984.

——. 'The Things She Said to Me!' *Photoplay*, May 1956.

Zolotow, Maurice. 'Joe & Marilyn: The Ultimate L.A. Love Story.' *Los Angeles*, Feb. 1979, pp. 138, 140, 238–247.

——. *Marilyn Monroe*. New York: Bantam, 1961. Photographs.
——. 'Marilyn Monroe's Psychiatrist: Trying to Untarnish Her Memory.' *Chicago Tribune*, Sept. 16, 1973, Sect. 5.

Index

Marilyn's films are found under her name and subheading: films. Other films are under their titles.

A Selected List of Non-Fiction Titles Available from Mandarin

While every effort is made to keep prices low, it is sometimes necessary to increase prices at short notice. Mandarin Paperbacks reserves the right to show new retail prices on covers which may differ from those previously advertised in the text or elsewhere.

The prices shown below were correct at the time of going to press.

☐ 7493 0961 X	**Stick it up Your Punter**	Chippendale & Horrie	£4.99
☐ 7493 0988 1	**Desert Island Discussions**	Sue Lawley	£4.99
☐ 7493 0938 5	**The Courage to Heal**	Ellen Bass and Laura Davis	£7.99
☐ 7493 0637 8	**The Hollywood Story**	Joel Finler	£9.99
☐ 7493 1032 4	**How to Meet Interesting Men**	Gizelle Howard	£5.99
☐ 7493 0586 X	**The New Small Garden**	C. E. Lucas-Phillips	£5.99
☐ 7493 1172 X	**You'll Never Eat Lunch in This Town Again**	Julia Phillips	£5.99

All these books are available at your bookshop or newsagent, or can be ordered direct from the publisher. Just tick the titles you want and fill in the form below.

Mandarin Paperbacks, Cash Sales Department, PO Box 11, Falmouth, Cornwall TR10 9EN.

Please send cheque or postal order, no currency, for purchase price quoted and allow the following for postage and packing:

UK including BFPO £1.00 for the first book, 50p for the second and 30p for each additional book ordered to a maximum charge of £3.00.

Overseas including Eire £2 for the first book, £1.00 for the second and 50p for each additional book thereafter.

NAME (Block letters) ....

ADDRESS...

....

☐ I enclose my remittance for ....

☐ I wish to pay by Access/Visa Card Number ☐☐☐☐☐☐☐☐☐☐☐☐☐☐☐☐

Expiry Date ☐☐☐☐